The Digital Personal Data Protection Act

Implementing India's DPDP Act across cloud, SaaS, and enterprise systems

Updated as per DPDP Rules, 2025

Ashish Kumar

Nisha Narasimhan

Amit Sachdev

bpb

www.bpbonline.com

First Edition 2026

Copyright © BPB Publications, India

ISBN: 978-93-65890-372

To View Complete
BPB Publications Catalogue
Scan the QR Code:

Dedicated to

My Mom,
Salochana Kumar, your learnings are forever !

– Ashish Kumar

To my mom, my first influencer and lifelong inspiration.

– Nisha Narasimhan

To my late father, D S Sachdev, whose strength, wisdom,
and quiet support made this book and many other achievements possible.

– Amit Sachdev

Foreword 1

In today's digital world, data is not just information; it is identity, trust, and power. As India accelerates its journey towards a digitally empowered society and economy, the need to protect personal data and uphold the fundamental right to privacy has never been more critical. The Digital Personal Data Protection Act (DPDPA) is India's bold and timely response to this need, ushering in a new era of responsible data governance.

This book serves as a thoughtful and thorough exploration of the DPDPA, starting with a clear and structured overview of the Act, its objectives, principles, and the roles of key stakeholders. It helps demystify the legal language and brings the Act to life through real-world relevance.

What truly sets this book apart is its focus on the role of tools and technologies in enabling compliance. From automating consent management to deploying privacy-enhancing technologies, the author explores how modern solutions can be leveraged to bridge the gap between legal expectations and operational realities. This is especially valuable for organizations seeking to embed Privacy by Design and by default.

Equally important is the book's coverage of regulatory requirements, including the responsibilities of data fiduciaries and processors, Data Principal rights, and enforcement mechanisms through the Data Protection Board. These sections are presented with clarity and structure, offering readers a solid foundation to navigate the compliance landscape confidently.

What enhances the practical value of this book is its use of real-life examples to explain complex concepts. These relatable scenarios help readers, from legal teams and compliance officers to IT professionals and business leaders, grasp the implications of the DPDPA in day-to-day operations and strategic decision-making.

Every organization, regardless of its size or sector, will face unique challenges in interpreting and implementing the DPDPA. This book does not shy away from these difficulties—it addresses them head-on. Whether it's legacy infrastructure, lack of awareness, or resource constraints, the author outlines how technology can be a powerful ally in overcoming these barriers and achieving scalable, sustainable compliance.

While the DPDPA is in its nascent stages, its long-term vision is profound. It promises to reshape the digital fabric of India, empowering individuals, fostering transparency, and building trust. The Act lays the groundwork for a more ethical and resilient digital economy, one where privacy is not an afterthought, but a fundamental design principle.

Ashish, Amit, and Nisha draw on decades of combined experience in this book. Their integration of legal, operational, and technological insights makes it a valuable guide for professionals and organizations focused on privacy.

This book is not just a guide; it is a call to action for stakeholders across sectors to understand, adopt, and embrace the DPDPA with foresight and responsibility. It is a timely contribution to the ongoing dialogue on data protection and will prove invaluable for anyone invested in building a privacy-first future for India.

Lalit Kalra
Partner and Data Privacy Leader, EY India

Foreword 2

The significance of the DPDP Act 2023

India's Digital Personal Data Protection Act, 2023 (DPDP Act) marks a pivotal turning point in our nation's digital journey. It reshapes how organizations handle personal data with transparency, accountability, and security as guiding principles. As technology leaders and citizens alike grapple with new responsibilities under this law, the timely arrival of this book is truly a boon. It is a privilege for me to pen this foreword at such a crucial moment. The DPDP Act isn't just another regulation; it represents a broader commitment to safeguarding privacy as a fundamental right and building trust in the digital ecosystem. In this context, the comprehensive guidance offered by this book is invaluable. The authors have created more than a summary of the law; they have provided us with a roadmap to navigate and embrace this change.

Acknowledging the authors and key themes

First and foremost, I want to thank and commend the authors – Ashish, Nisha, and Amit – for undertaking the monumental task of distilling the DPDP Act and its rules into an accessible, practical guide. They bring decades of combined experience in technology, regulatory frameworks, and enterprise risk management to the table, which shines through in every chapter. Their thought leadership and deep understanding of data protection challenges have been instrumental in shaping this book's substance and structure. The result is a practical and comprehensive resource that translates complex legal obligations into measurable enterprise actions and solutions.

Throughout the book, several **key themes** emerge consistently:

- **Bridging policy and practice:** The content aligns the DPDP Act's requirements with real-world tools, processes, and best practices. Abstract principles like consent or data minimization are brought to life with concrete examples and solutions, from setting up consent dashboards to implementing data classification frameworks. This approach ensures that readers not only understand the law but also know *how to Act on it* within their organizations.

- **Transparency and accountability:** A unifying thread across all chapters is the sanctity of trust between individuals and those handling their data. The book reinforces that compliance is not about ticking boxes, but about fundamentally upholding transparency to data principles and accountability in data handling. Whether it's drafting clear privacy notices or establishing audit trails, the message is that trust is the cornerstone of effective data protection – a message that the DPDP Act itself embodies and which the authors emphasize richly.

- **End-to-end data protection:** The scope of topics covered is truly end-to-end. The book lays the foundations by explaining why this Act is necessary and how it fits into the global data protection landscape. It then guides the reader through every major facet of compliance: defining personal data and its importance, instituting consent mechanisms, strengthening data security controls, enabling individuals' rights, preparing for breach response, navigating cross-border data transfers, documenting compliance efforts, undergoing audits, and even building a privacy-first culture within the organization. By the final chapter, the reader has a 360-degree view – from high-level principles down to specific operational checklists – of what it takes to comply with the DPDP Act. This holistic treatment is one of the book's great strengths.

Trust, the foundation of data protection

One theme that resonated deeply with me is trust – the foundation of all data protection efforts. In Chapter 1, Getting Started with DPDP Act and Draft Rules the authors illustrate this vividly, opening with a cautionary real-life story of a young student unwittingly exposing his personal information through a "free" app. The incident escalates from nuisance spam to a frightening privacy breach, even revealing the individual's home address to strangers. This example brings home a simple truth: in the digital bazaar, sometimes *"free" comes with a hidden and dangerous price tag*. It underscores exactly why legislation like the DPDP Act is so essential for India today.

The story and the discussion that follows highlight what is at stake when we talk about personal data. Personal data is not just a collection of bytes, but a tapestry of our lives; a digital portrait of our choices, habits, relationships, and dreams. Misuse of this data can lead to consequences ranging from minor inconveniences to life-altering crises. Thus, protecting personal data is protecting people. The authors eloquently note that whether you are an individual or a large enterprise, both paths converge on a singular imperative: to uphold the sanctity of trust. Individuals need to trust that their data will be handled with care and respect. Organizations, in turn, must earn that trust by acting responsibly and transparently.

This emphasis on trust is not just philosophical; it is threaded through actionable guidance. Chapter 1 Getting Started with DPDP Act and Draft Rules lays out core principles of data protection – purpose limitation, data minimization, consent, accuracy, security, storage limitation, and user rights – all of which ultimately serve to build trust with data subjects.

The authors delve into each principle with relatable scenarios. For instance, they describe how being transparent and obtaining informed consent isn't merely legal compliance, but an opportunity to respect the individual's autonomy and choice, thereby strengthening trust. Similarly, they show that practices like limiting data collection and promptly deleting data when no longer needed demonstrate respect for privacy and can foster goodwill and confidence among customers. By going deep into these principles early on, the book sets a tone that compliance is fundamentally about respecting people – a perspective that elevates the entire discussion beyond just legal checkbox ticking.

Personally, as someone who has worked closely with technology and data governance, I find this focus on trust both apt and inspiring. It reminds us that privacy is not an abstract legal requirement but a human value. The DPDP Act has effectively codified what should be our ethical stance: to treat personal data with the utmost care. The authors have done a wonderful job bringing this to life and preparing the reader to instill these values in their organizational policies and day-to-day processes.

An optimistic outlook for compliance

What truly sets this book apart is its optimistic, forward-looking outlook on the future of compliance. Often, discussions about new regulations can be mired in compliance challenges and fear of penalties. However, the concluding chapter here flips that narrative, encouraging a growth mindset: it paints compliance as an area of innovation and continuous improvement, rather than a burden. After walking the reader through the how-to of complying with today's requirements, the authors invite us to imagine the near future where compliance is "ongoing, intelligent, and embedded," aka Agentic, into business operations.

The vision they share is exciting. Compliance in the future will be autonomous and always-on, driven by advancements in AI and automation. Organizations are expected to move from periodic manual audits to continuous monitoring and enforcement of data protection controls. The book describes a world where intelligent agents work in the background: monitoring access logs, flagging unusual data activities, and even interacting with each other to verify compliance in real time. For example, a "Consent Validator" agent might continuously ensure that every piece of personal data being used aligns with a valid consent on record, while a "Data Lineage" agent could trace how data flows through systems and who accesses it. These autonomous compliance agents can collaborate (machine-to-machine) to resolve issues instantly or escalate to humans when necessary. It's a glimpse into a self-correcting compliance ecosystem that seemed like science fiction just a few years ago.

Crucially, the authors balance this tech-driven future with the reaffirmation that human judgment remains irreplaceable in governance. In their vision, tomorrow's Data Protection

Officer (DPO) or compliance lead becomes a strategic orchestrator of these intelligent systems. Rather than combing through logs, the DPO will set risk thresholds, handle exceptional cases, and ensure that the AI agents are aligned with ethical considerations and the organization's values. Humans will still define the "north star" of compliance – interpreting the spirit of laws and upholding fairness – while intelligent tools handle the heavy lifting of enforcement. This harmonious interplay between human oversight and AI-powered automation is presented as the ideal model going forward, combining the best of both worlds.

Another inspiring aspect of the conclusion is how it foresees empowering individuals in unprecedented ways. The DPDP Act strengthens Data Principal Rights, and the book imagines technology taking this further: individuals could soon have real-time, interactive visibility into how their data is used. Instead of just receiving a static report when they ask for their data, one might log into a portal and see a live map of where their personal data lives, which teams or services have used it, and for what purpose. Envision the level of trust this transparency could build – when, as a customer, I can literally see that, for example, my mobile phone provider accessed my location data to improve network coverage and *nothing more*, it reinforces my confidence that the company is handling my data responsibly. Such innovations will make compliance a front-facing benefit and a market differentiator, not just an internal obligation.

This optimistic narrative turns compliance into a competitive advantage rather than a constraint. It suggests that companies that invest in good compliance practices (and technologies) will earn greater trust from users, face fewer incidents, and be more agile in adapting to new regulations. In fact, the authors suggest that compliance itself may evolve into a service-oriented industry, much like cybersecurity, with "Compliance-as-a-Service" platforms and solutions becoming common. Indian enterprises, especially startups and tech firms, should view this as an opportunity to innovate. By embedding privacy and security into product design and by leveraging automation for compliance, they can both meet regulatory requirements and deliver superior value to customers. The mindset advocated here is one of *embracing the DPDP Act as a catalyst for positive change*, spurring better data management practices, adoption of advanced tools, and ultimately building a more trustworthy digital business environment.

Reading this conclusion filled me with optimism. It aligns well with the broader vision of Digital India: to create a digitally empowered society and economy where technology and trust go hand in hand. The DPDP Act provides the legal backbone for privacy and trust, and this book shows that with the right approach, compliance can drive innovation rather than hinder it. The future outlined – where compliance is real-time, automated, and user-centric – is one that will benefit businesses, consumers, and regulators alike. It's a future where India can be a leader in ethical, intelligent data governance, fostering both security and growth.

Embracing the journey ahead

In closing, I wholeheartedly endorse this book to every organization, professional, and student looking to understand and implement the DPDP Act. It is rare to find a text that covers policy, process, and technology with such clarity and cohesiveness. Whether you are a chief privacy officer formulating your company's compliance strategy, an IT manager tasked with implementing data protection measures, or an informed citizen curious about your data rights, this book will speak to you. The combination of legal insight, practical steps (including references to tools and frameworks), and forward-looking perspective makes it a definitive guide about personal data protection in India.

I congratulate Ashish, Nisha, and Amit for this noteworthy contribution. Their work will undoubtedly help many organizations not only comply with the law but do so in a way that strengthens their ethical core and relationship with customers. After reading these chapters, I am personally inspired to approach compliance with a renewed mindset – one that sees regulatory adherence as part of a broader mission of building digital trust.

As you dive into the book, I encourage you to absorb its lessons and consider how you can apply them in your context. The journey to compliance is not always easy, but with the guidance provided here, it becomes an opportunity to innovate, educate your teams, and put data protection at the heart of your operations. The authors have illuminated the path; it is now up to us to walk it with commitment. By doing so, we not only respect the letter of the law but also uphold the spirit of dignity and privacy that everyone in this digital age deserves.

Thank you for picking up this book — an investment toward a more secure and trustworthy digital future. I am confident that it will serve you well. Now, let us embark on this journey together, towards excellence in data protection and compliance.

Nishan DeSilva
Partner Group Product Manager, Microsoft

About the Authors

- **Ashish Kumar** is a seasoned technology leader with over 28 years of cross-disciplinary experience in engineering, consulting, technology sales, and product development. Currently serving as principal PM manager at Microsoft, he leads strategic initiatives that bridge business goals with cutting-edge technology solutions. Ashish's global experience—spanning roles at Microsoft, HCL, TCS, Star TV, and ICI—has shaped his ability to drive transformation at scale, deliver product innovation, and enable customer success across diverse industries and geographies.

  His engineering and consulting background has empowered enterprises to adopt digital transformation strategies with confidence, while his product leadership ensures scalable, secure, and market-aligned solutions. With a keen understanding of both technology and business, Ashish has played a critical role in shaping compliance-ready solutions in the evolving regulatory landscape.

  Ashish is also the co-author of Managing Risks in Digital Transformation (2023), a practical guide for technology leaders dealing with digital threats in the post-pandemic world, including insider risks and cyberwarfare. Back in 2020, while writing the book, he also explored the idea of chatbots and digital humans taking on roles as digital managers and AI assistants—a vision that is now fast becoming reality.

  His commitment to responsible innovation extends beyond the enterprise. Ashish actively contributes to the development of sustainability frameworks, including the EU CSRD template in Microsoft Purview, and is a vocal advocate for the One Earth initiative—promoting ecological harmony through responsible digital development.

  Ashish continues to focus on empowering organizations to embrace data protection, cybersecurity, and sustainability as core pillars of digital leadership, with a vision for a more secure and sustainable digital future.

- **Nisha Narasimhan** is a principal product manager at Microsoft, where she leads compliance and security innovation in Microsoft Purview. She leads the modernization of eDiscovery, enabling organizations to conduct investigations with greater efficiency, scalability, and security. Her work focuses on bridging regulatory requirements with product innovation, reducing operational risk, and empowering enterprises to strengthen their compliance posture in a rapidly evolving landscape.

- **Amit Sachdev** is a visionary technologist and serial entrepreneur with a relentless drive to transform industries through cutting-edge AI solutions, ERP innovation, and secure and scalable digital architectures. With a career spanning leadership roles at Microsoft, Oracle, Sage, and Start-ups, as well as founding and advising high-growth tech ventures, he has mastered the art of turning complex challenges into disruptive opportunities.

  As a CTO and chief architect, Amit has designed and deployed enterprise-grade solutions that optimize operations, enhance decision-making, and future-proof businesses at companies like Microsoft. Oracle and Sage, he has led complex AI-driven ERP modernization projects, empowering Fortune 500 companies with intelligent automation.

  Beyond corporate leadership, Amit is a published author, advisor to various start-ups and incubation companies through Xerox Research Centre of Canada (XRCC), a guide mentor at Schulich School of Business, York University, and an active member of various media and art clubs.

  A sought-after speaker and thought leader, Amit is passionate about the ethical future of AI, modern and secure data solutions, scaling tech without losing agility, and "next-generation intelligent and autonomous ERP ecosystems".

Acknowledgements

We would like to express our sincere gratitude to all those who contributed to the successful completion of this book.

First and foremost, we extend our heartfelt thanks to our family and close friends for their consistent encouragement and understanding throughout this rigorous journey. Their support provided the foundation that allowed us to stay focused and committed to delivering a technically sound and practically useful resource.

We thank the Government of India for introducing the Digital Personal Data Protection Act, 2023—a pivotal step in building a secure digital foundation for Digital India and the broader Viksit Bharat vision. This book is a contribution toward helping organizations align with that national mission.

We are especially grateful to our co-authors, *Nisha* and *Amit*, for their thought leadership, domain expertise, and dedication. Their collaborative spirit and deep understanding of regulatory frameworks and enterprise risk practices were instrumental in shaping the structure and substance of this book.

We are also indebted to our knowledge partner, K&S Digiprotect Services Pvt Limited, for their precise guidance on compliance interpretation and regulatory design. Their review significantly strengthened the legal underpinnings of this work.

We also extend our appreciation to our reviewers—*Mehul* and *Akash*—for their critical feedback and careful attention to detail. Their insights ensured the technical accuracy and clarity needed for a practitioner-focused guide.

Special thanks to *Ishaan*, our Technical Writer, for shaping this book—aligning Microsoft technologies with DPDP Act mapping, coordinating reviewers and publishers, and driving its successful completion.

Finally, we express our gratitude to our industry mentors from the Big Four, whose insights into implementation challenges and enterprise controls were invaluable in grounding the book in real-world relevance.

To BPB Publications, thank you for your support and expertise in bringing this project to life. And to our readers—thank you for your trust and engagement. This book is for you.

Preface

The Digital Personal Data Protection (DPDP) Act, 2023, marks a critical turning point in India's digital governance journey, shaping how organizations handle personal data with transparency, accountability, and security. This book was created to serve as a practical and comprehensive resource for professionals responsible for translating legal obligations into measurable enterprise action. Designed for IT, compliance, legal, and GRC teams, it aligns regulatory requirements with real-world tools, processes, and enterprise practices.

The links to the DPDP acts is provided as follows:

https://www.meity.gov.in/static/uploads/2024/06/2bf1f0e9f04e6fb4f8fef35e82c42aa5.pdf

https://static.mygov.in/innovateindia/2025/01/03/mygov-999999999568142946.pdf

Chapter 1 lays the foundation by introducing the DPDP Act's key terms, objectives, and structure. It explains why this regulation is timely for India and how it fits into the broader global data protection landscape. Readers will walk away with a strong understanding of the Act's intent and practical relevance.

Chapter 2 examines the changing nature of enterprise data—how it is generated, stored, and classified. It provides clear methods for categorizing sensitive information, reviewing IT assets, and implementing AI-based data classification frameworks to ensure compliance-readiness.

Chapter 3 demystifies the legal and operational nuances of consent. From lawful processing to real-time consent dashboards, it equips organizations with the ability to operationalize privacy with tools like OneTrust, TrustArc, GoTrust and Microsoft Priva which meet notice and opt-out requirements efficiently.

Chapter 4 looks into securing data assets by establishing strong access control, authentication, and alert triage processes. It introduces techniques for proactive breach prevention, including policy design, employee training, and SLA-based audits.

Chapter 5 offers a deep dive into the rights of Data Principals—India's equivalent to global data subjects. It provides practical guidance on how to recognize, validate, and fulfill rights requests while managing technical and legal complexities in large organizations.

Chapter 6 is focused on data breach management and response readiness. It introduces structured plans, notification templates, and regulatory timelines, and highlights tools like Microsoft Purview DSPM to continuously monitor and manage breach risks.

Chapter 7 explains cross-border data transfers and the rise of cloud-first ecosystems. It guides readers through data residency considerations, audit logs, and compliance strategies when dealing with hyperscalers or regional SaaS vendors.

Chapter 8 emphasizes the critical role of documentation and accountability. It introduces DPIA frameworks, ediscovery tools, and structured record-keeping practices to help organizations demonstrate compliance and reduce regulatory exposure.

Chapter 9 equips readers with audit frameworks—comparing point-in-time versus continuous compliance models. It helps teams develop internal review processes and assess third-party readiness across vendors and Data Processors.

Chapter 10 explores how to interface with the Data Protection Board of India, including roles of the DPO, incident reporting, and maintaining regulatory audit trails. It ensures readers are prepared for both inquiry and engagement phases.

Chapter 11 focuses on building a culture of data protection across the organization. It outlines how leadership, HR, and finance functions can collaborate to embed privacy awareness, tone-at-the-top accountability, and policy alignment into daily workflows.

Chapter 12 addresses business-critical applications like CRM, HRMS, and ERP systems, outlining best practices for securing personal data within operational systems. It introduces controls for SaaS and ISV solutions tailored to India's DPDP requirements.

Throughout this book, the ideas, structure, and insights were conceived and led by the authors. AI technologies, particularly Microsoft Copilot, were used to accelerate writing, formatting, and reviewing tasks—enhancing clarity without replacing original thinking. We thank the developers of such tools for making compliance communication more accessible and productive.

Coloured Images

Please follow the link to download the
Coloured Images of the book:

https://rebrand.ly/d62fc6

We have code bundles from our rich catalogue of books and videos available at https://github.com/bpbpublications. Check them out!

Errata

We take immense pride in our work at BPB Publications and follow best practices to ensure the accuracy of our content to provide an indulging reading experience to our subscribers. Our readers are our mirrors, and we use their inputs to reflect and improve upon human errors, if any, that may have occurred during the publishing processes involved. To let us maintain the quality and help us reach out to any readers who might be having difficulties due to any unforeseen errors, please write to us at :

errata@bpbonline.com

Your support, suggestions and feedback are highly appreciated by the BPB Publications' Family.

At www.bpbonline.com, you can also read a collection of free technical articles, sign up for a range of free newsletters, and receive exclusive discounts and offers on BPB books and eBooks. You can check our social media handles below:

Instagram

Facebook

Linkedin

YouTube

Get in touch with us at: business@bpbonline.com for more details.

Piracy

If you come across any illegal copies of our works in any form on the internet, we would be grateful if you would provide us with the location address or website name. Please contact us at business@bpbonline.com with a link to the material.

If you are interested in becoming an author

If there is a topic that you have expertise in, and you are interested in either writing or contributing to a book, please visit www.bpbonline.com. We have worked with thousands of developers and tech professionals, just like you, to help them share their insights with the global tech community. You can make a general application, apply for a specific hot topic that we are recruiting an author for, or submit your own idea.

Reviews

Please leave a review. Once you have read and used this book, why not leave a review on the site that you purchased it from? Potential readers can then see and use your unbiased opinion to make purchase decisions. We at BPB can understand what you think about our products, and our authors can see your feedback on their book. Thank you!

For more information about BPB, please visit www.bpbonline.com.

Join our Discord space

Join our Discord workspace for latest updates, offers, tech happenings around the world, new releases, and sessions with the authors:

https://discord.bpbonline.com

Table of Contents

CHAPTER 1

Getting Started with DPDP Act and Draft Rules

Introduction

The **Digital Personal Data Protection (DPDP) Act,** 2023, marks a significant milestone in India's regulatory landscape, addressing the urgent need for personal data protection in our digital era. As technology advances, safeguarding personal data has become essential for individuals and organizations alike. This Act provides a comprehensive framework for data management, including collection, processing, storage, and sharing, while ensuring transparency, purpose limitation, and data minimization. It grants individuals robust rights over their data, such as access, correction, and erasure. The Act empowers the Data Protection Board of India to enforce compliance and violations upon reference as mentioned in the Act, and impose penalties, emphasizing the importance of data protection responsibilities. This book offers an in-depth exploration of the DPDP Act, mapping its requirements to technological capabilities and practical implementations. Readers will gain insights into aligning their operations with the new regulation, configuring compliance tools, and integrating data protection solutions. With practical examples and step-by-step instructions, this book equips Data Protection Officers, IT managers, and compliance professionals with the knowledge and tools necessary to meet the DPDP Act's stringent requirements and maintain robust data security.

The recent addition of Draft DPDP Rules, 2025, further strengthens and provides more clarity to the applicability of the Act.

Structure

This chapter will cover the following topics:

- Need for Personal Data Protection Act in India
- Defining personal data
- Key principles of data protection
- Scope and applicability of the Data Protection Act, 2023
- DPDPA journey
- Draft Digital Personal Data Protection Rules, 2025
- Introducing compliance manager as regulatory governance tool

Objectives

This chapter aims to provide a comprehensive foundation for understanding the DPDP Act, 2023. By the end of this chapter, readers will gain a clear and precise understanding of what constitutes personal data under the DPDP Act, bringing clarity on personal data. It is noteworthy herein that the DPDPA, unlike other privacy laws and regulations like GDPR, does not differentiate between personal data and sensitive personal data affording equal protection to both. We will explore the fundamental principles that underpin data protection, including transparency, purpose limitation, data minimization, and confidentiality. Additionally, readers will identify the entities and activities covered by the DPDP Act, including the geographical scope and the conditions under which the Act applies to both domestic and international organizations.

Furthermore, this chapter will help readers understand how the DPDP Act fits within the broader legal framework of India's Information Technology Act, 2000, and Companies Act, 2013, examining the interplay between these laws and their collective impact on data protection practices. Through these objectives, readers will establish a solid foundation for navigating the complexities of data protection legislation in India, setting the stage for more detailed discussions in subsequent chapters.

Need for Personal Data Protection Act in India

To understand the relevance of India's DPDP Act, it is important to first look at the risks associated with unregulated personal data usage. The following scenario illustrates how everyday digital interactions can lead to serious privacy concerns when adequate data protection measures are not in place.

Ravi, a college student in Bengaluru, had always been enthusiastic about trying out new apps. One day, while browsing the Play Store, he came across the Photo Magic app, an app promising high-quality photo filters. The best part is it was free! Without a second thought, he downloaded it. Soon, Ravi started receiving odd promotional texts and calls, everything from property deals in Mumbai to discounts on jewelry in Jaipur. Initially dismissing them as random spam, he noticed something alarming one evening: a message containing his exact home address, offering house-cleaning services.

Panicking, he reached out to his tech-savvy friend Meera. She decided to inspect his phone and came across the Photo Magic app. Looking into the app's permissions, they discovered it had access not just to photos but also to contacts, messages, and even location.

Curious, Meera further investigated and found that the app's developer was based in a dubious location, notorious for fraud and digital fraud. Connecting the dots, they realized that the Photo Magic app was not just a photo filter app. It was designed to silently harvest Ravi's private data and sell it to the highest bidder.

Ravi and Meera decided to alert others. They started an online campaign, warning users about the dangers of such innocent-seeming apps. Their story quickly gained traction, and national news channels picked it up. The incident reminded many of a comparable situation some years back when a popular flashlight app had been found secretly collecting user data.

In the ensuing outcry, the Photo Magic app was pulled from the store, and a public advisory was issued about app permissions. However, the incident left an impression on millions of Indians. They realized that in the digital bazaar, sometimes *free* came with a hidden and potentially dangerous price tag.

In the tale of Ravi and Photo Magic, the paramount importance of data protection is simply illuminated. As consumers navigate the digital realm, simple choices, like downloading a free app, can expose them to alarming vulnerabilities.

Data, once compromised, can lead to breaches of personal security, financial risks, and deep invasions of privacy. Such incidents erode trust in digital platforms, hinder technological adoption, and emphasize the ethical responsibility of developers and companies alike. The story stands as a stark reminder that in our modern digital age, safeguarding personal data is not just a technical necessity but a fundamental right and a cornerstone of individual autonomy and safety.

In the digital age, the importance of data protection cannot be undermined, whether you are an individual consumer or a sprawling enterprise.

For consumers, navigating the digital world is akin to traversing a vast landscape filled with both wonders and pitfalls. It is crucial to understand one's digital footprint; the trace we leave with every click, download, or share. Being discerning about which apps to trust, what permissions to grant, and how to secure personal data with strong, unique passwords becomes second nature. Every email opened, every link clicked, requires a moment of pause, a split second to verify its authenticity. It is about reclaiming control and ensuring that personal details remain just that, personal.

The following figure highlights the pervasive role of data in both our personal and professional lives, underscoring the need for robust data protection as outlined in the DPDP Act, 2023:

Figure 1.1: *Data across our consumer and corporate lives*

Enterprises, on the other hand, face a labyrinth of complexities. These are responsible for safeguarding their proprietary company data, but also the vast amounts of customer information they manage. It begins with a thorough risk assessment, understanding where vulnerabilities might lie. Employee training is not a one-off; it is a continual process to ensure everyone is abreast of the latest in cybersecurity threats and best practices. Compliance is not just a box to tick but an ongoing commitment, ensuring that the business aligns with local and international data protection standards.

Both paths, though distinct, converge on a singular truth: *the sanctity of trust.*

Trust that personal data, once shared, will be guarded with the utmost care. Trust that businesses will Act in the best interests of their customers. As we progress through this book, we will look further into these realms, unraveling strategies, challenges, and solutions, all with the aim of fortifying this digital trust.

Defining personal data

Living in the digital universe, we would want to protect our personal data. Even the government wants to protect our personal data.

Our personal data reflects our identity, encompassing our thoughts and actions. It includes traces of our online activities and private queries made to search engines. Every shared photograph, liked post, and completed online form collectively represents a detailed portrait of our presence in the digital realm. Our personal data becomes our silent avatar, narrating tales of our choices, desires, and dreams, making each of us a singular star in the vast digital night sky.

Moreover, enterprises function as the powerful guardians of the digital world. They face a crucial question: What exactly are they protecting by their strong firewalls and encrypted vaults? Is it the same asset, personal data, but on a much larger scale?

For enterprises, personal data is not just about numbers or records. It is the lifeblood that cruises through their systems, bringing them closer to their customers. It is the golden key to understanding markets, predicting trends, and crafting bespoke experiences. However, with great power comes great responsibility. This data signifies a critical trust relationship between the organization and its customers, who have entrusted their personal information for specific, authorized purposes. What is the challenge? To uphold this trust, to ensure that every bit remains untouched, unviolated.

As we stand at this crossroads, one thing becomes clear: Whether consumer or enterprise, the quest to understand, protect, and respect personal data is a journey both profound and pivotal.

What exactly is personal data, and why are so many governments and regulations focused on protecting it? Understanding the benefits of effectively safeguarding personal data is crucial for individuals, companies, and governments alike. Effective protection offers security and privacy, while the risks of inadequate protection can lead to significant harm and breaches.

Let us first define and check what personal data is. The formal definition of *personal data* can vary depending on jurisdiction and specific data protection regulations. However, a widely accepted definition, as provided by the **General Data Protection Regulation (GDPR)** of the European Union, states:

Personal data means any information relating to an identified or identifiable natural person ('Data Principal); an identifiable natural person is one who can be identified, directly or indirectly, in particular by reference to an identifier such as a name, an identification number, location data, an online identifier or to one or more factors specific to the physical, physiological, genetic, mental, economic, cultural or social identity of that natural person.

DPDP Act, 2023 defines personal data in *Chapter I, section,2(t)* as:

Personal data means any data about an individual who is identifiable by or in relation to such data.

It also states the definition of what data is as in *Chapter I, preliminary section,2(h)*

Data means a representation of information, facts, concepts, opinions, or instructions in a manner suitable for communication, interpretation, or processing by human beings or by automated means."

As we stand on the cusp of the digital revolution, we are continually sharing, knowingly or unknowingly, fragments of ourselves with the virtual world. A name, an email address, a birth date, each a tiny piece of the larger puzzle. As each such information can identify an individual or is identifiable, i.e. has the potential to relate to an individual, it will be considered as personal data. This is not just a sterile definition from a legislative document. As illustrated through everyday examples, this *personal data* encapsulates the essence of our digital identity. It is the sum of our behaviors, preferences, relationships, and even our vulnerabilities. To understand the importance of protecting this personal data is to recognize the intrinsic value of our individuality in the digital cosmos.

Imagine that you are walking through a busy marketplace. Each stall you visit, each vendor you interact with, records a piece of information about you: the color of your shoes, your preference for spicy food, the songs you hum under your breath, and so on. Imagine if all these small, harmless pieces of information were combined to create a detailed picture of who you are, including your habits, preferences, and even your deepest fears. Consider something as routine as visiting a doctor, and the potential risks involved with your health records being exposed. This is the reason the protection of personal data is of utmost significance.

Additional categories of personal data

Here are some documents/information that can be considered as personal data:

- **Health records**: Think about your last visit to the doctor. The diagnosis, prescriptions, personal health history, and information that you would wish to remain confidential. If unprotected, this could lead to discrimination, higher insurance premiums, or even extortion.

    o **Example**: Consider Raj, a senior executive in a multinational company. After a routine check-up, his medical data revealed a genetic predisposition to a particular illness. This information, leaked to an insurance firm, resulted in his health coverage premium skyrocketing, placing unexpected financial burdens on his family.

- **Financial information**: Every time you swipe your card or make an online transaction, a trail of your financial habits is left behind. In the wrong hands, this could lead to fraud, theft, or misuse, affecting your credit score and financial stability.

    o **Example**: Meena, an avid online shopper, once clicked on a suspicious link that promised an unbeatable sale. The next thing she knew, large sums of money had vanished from her bank account, all because her transaction data was compromised and misused by cybercriminals. This is also a common headline nowadays in the leading newspapers.

- **Online behavior**: Your search histories, the videos you watch, the articles you read— each action creates a digital fingerprint. Companies could use this to manipulate your choices, push targeted ads, or even influence your opinions.

    o **Example**: Arjun, a college student, had been researching a paper on a controversial topic. His search data, accessed by a biased organization, resulted in him being bombarded with misleading information and skewed articles, influencing his perspective.

- **Personal contacts and communications**: The calls you make and the messages you send contain snippets of your personal and professional life. A breach could mean broken relationships, loss of trust, or even professional setbacks.

- o **Example**: Pooja, an up-and-coming journalist, had her communication data intercepted. A story she was working on, meant to be exclusive, was prematurely leaked, costing her professional credibility and trust among her sources.

- **Location data:** With smartphones and wearable tech, your every movement can be tracked. This could lead to stalking, unauthorized surveillance, or threats to personal safety.

  - o **Example**: Karan, an activist, always felt the need for privacy. Yet, with compromised location data from his smartphone, he found himself under constant surveillance, leading to threats and endangering his safety and the causes he fought for.

The following figure highlights various categories of personal data, including health records, financial information, behavioral patterns, communication data, location details, and digital identity. It emphasizes how interconnected systems collect and process this information, reinforcing the importance of robust data protection mechanisms.

Figure 1.2: Illustration of personal data types and privacy risks

The gravity of these examples underscores a profound truth: personal data is not just a collection of bytes but a tapestry of our lives. Its misuse can lead to consequences ranging from mere inconveniences to life-altering events.

In recognizing the immense weight of responsibility that comes with handling personal data, governments worldwide have felt the imperative to step in. This has led to the formulation of stringent data protection regulations, aiming to provide a robust shield against the unwarranted invasion of our digital selves. These laws are not just statutory mandates but reflections of a global commitment to preserve the sanctity of individual privacy in the digital age.

The Government of India introduced the **Digital Personal Data Protection Act (DPDPA)** 2023 in response to the rapidly evolving digital landscape and the growing concerns over the safety and privacy of personal data of its citizens. With an increasing number of businesses and services moving online and the rise of digital transactions, there was a pressing need to establish a comprehensive legal framework to protect individuals against unauthorized data collection, storage, and misuse.

DPDP Act 2023 aims to empower individuals by giving them control over their personal data, holding organizations accountable for personal data breaches, and ensuring that data processing is transparent, fair, and respects the rights of the Data Principal. The introduction of this Act signifies the government's commitment to safeguarding the digital rights and privacy of its citizens in the modern age.

Key principles of data protection

The key principles of data protection serve as foundational guidelines to ensure the privacy and security of individuals' personal data. While these principles might vary slightly based on different jurisdictions and specific data protection laws, the core concepts remain consistent. Here are some of the widely accepted key principles:

- **Transparency, fairness, and lawfulness**: Personal data must be processed lawfully, fairly, and transparently. It is essential to ensure that individuals are fully informed about how and why their personal data is being used.

    - **Example**: Suppose a bank is collecting income details for processing a loan. It should provide a clear rationale, i.e. purpose, through a consent notice before collecting such personal data, explaining the necessity of such data for the loan approval process.

- **Use data for its intended purpose (purpose limitation):** Personal data should be used exclusively for the reason it was collected. Avoid the temptation to repurpose personal data without clear consent.

    - **Example**: Imagine a customer signing up for a product's warranty and providing an email for correspondence. Using that email for promotional campaigns, without their direct consent, deviates from the original purpose.

- **Only collect what you need (data minimization)**: In the age of data overload, it is tempting to amass as much data as possible. However, collecting only pertinent personal data reduces risk and builds trust.

- o **Example**: If someone is registering for a store's loyalty program, just acquiring the essential contact details, rather than an exhaustive personal history, highlights a respect for customer privacy.

- **Keep data accurate (data accuracy):** Ensuring that the information you have is current and correct is crucial. It reduces errors and potential misunderstandings.

  - o **Example**: For institutions like health clubs where member details can directly affect services like customized training, it is imperative to routinely verify and update the health and contact information of members and ensure that if an individual has requested to correct his/her personal data, the same is adhered.

- **Do not store data forever (Storage Limitation):** Implement a structured data retention policy. Once data has served its purpose and is no longer needed, it should be securely disposed of.

  - o **Example**: Even after a user ends a subscription with a digital service, personal data may continue to be retained beyond its original purpose if required by applicable laws or regulations. While immediate deletion may not always be feasible due to system constraints like backup cycles, it is essential to ensure that such data is securely deleted once the legally mandated retention period has expired.

- **Secure the data (security):** With increasing cyber threats, the importance of robust data security measures cannot be overstated. Implement both technical and organizational safeguards.

  - o **Example**: E-commerce platforms, entrusted with financial data of a personal nature, should employ state-of-the-art encryption and continually update their cybersecurity protocols.

- **Be accountable (accountability):** The core of accountability lies in the ability to clearly demonstrate compliance with applicable obligations. It goes beyond mere adherence to rules, fostering a culture of responsibility supported by documented evidence of compliance when required.

  - o **Example**: A forward-thinking business could engage in periodic third-party audits, ensuring they are not just meeting but exceeding data handling standards.

DPDP Act, 2023 of India, underscores the paramount importance of consent in the digital landscape, recognizing it as the bedrock of ethical personal data practices. Central to this legislation is the emphasis on clear, informed, and specific consent, ensuring that companies do not merely collect data but are granted explicit consent by individuals to process their personal data.

An integral facet of this consent framework in the DPDP Act 2023 is the consideration given to the protection of children's data. The Act mandates a heightened level of care, stipulating that in cases involving minors, verifiable consent must be obtained from their parents or lawful guardians. This ensures that the vulnerability of the younger population is adequately addressed, and their data remains shielded from potential misuse.

Apart from these consent mechanisms, the Act directs companies to operate with full transparency, adhere to data minimization principles, ensure data accuracy, and establish stringent security measures. It further bolsters individual rights, allowing them to access, correct, or erase their data.

On the global front, the DPDP Act 2023 also sets clear guidelines for international data transfers, ensuring the same rigorous standards are applied, even beyond India's borders. Together, these provisions and the foundational emphasis on consent make the DPDP Act 2023 a beacon for safeguarding personal data in India's evolving digital epoch.

In the subsequent sections, we will look into the intricacies of this law, to understand its broader implications for both individuals and businesses. We will also discuss its real-world impact, and most crucially, we will explore the tools and best practices that companies can employ to remain compliant with the DPDP Act 2023. It is not just about understanding the regulations but also about effectively implementing them.

Scope and applicability of the DPDP Act, 2023

Before we read the scope of the Act, let us define some terms and taxonomy that are commonly used in the Act:

- **Data Fiduciary:** Any person who alone or in conjunction with other persons determines the purpose and means of processing of personal data. (Ch I, sec 2, (i))

- **Significant Data Fiduciary**: The entities, as notified by the Central government to be such, on the basis of such relevant factors as the Central Government may determine including volume and sensitivity of personal data, risk to the rights of Data Principals, security of the state, public order, etc. It is expected that entities like e-commerce platforms, social media intermediaries, etc. will fall under this category. (Ch I, sec 2, (z))

- **Data Processor**: Any person who processes personal data on behalf of a Data Fiduciary. Processing activity, in relation to personal data, means any fully or partly automated activity or set of activities done on digital personal data. This includes actions like collecting, recording, organizing, storing, changing, retrieving, using, combining, indexing, sharing, transmitting, publishing, limiting access, deleting, or destroying the data. (Ch I, sec 2, (k))

- **Data Principal:** The individual to whom personal data relates. They have rights over their data and can control its use and disclosure. DPDP Act further differentiates personal Data Principals as either Child based on age, or person with a disability. In both these cases of Data Principal, the expectation is laid out by legal guardians or parents, as applicable. (Ch I, sec 2, (j))

- **Data Protection Board:** Read it as Data Protection Board of India, established by Central Government of India. Its regulatory authority was established to oversee and enforce the DPDP Act. It manages grievances and ensures compliance with DPDPA. (Ch I, sec 2, (c))

- **Data Protection Officer:** A designated officer within an organization responsible for ensuring compliance with data protection laws. As per the current Act, only Significant Data Fiduciaries are mandated to have this role in their organization. (Ch I, sec 2 (l))

- **Consent manager:** A person registered with the Data Protection Board who acts as a single point of contact to help Data Principals give, manage, review, and withdraw consent through digital tools or platforms. (Ch I, sec 2, (g))

- **Processing:** In relation to personal data, means a wholly or partly automated operation or set of operations performed on digital personal data, and includes operations such as collection, recording, organization, structuring, storage, adaptation, retrieval, use, alignment or combination, indexing, sharing, disclosure by transmission, dissemination or otherwise making available, restriction, erasure or destruction (Ch I, sec 2, (x))

- **Legitimate use of data:** Data processing activities that are conducted for lawful purposes, under legal grounds as specified in Chapter II, Section 7 of the Act. It is important to note that certain provisions under this section allow processing of personal data if the Data Principal has voluntarily provided the data and has not explicitly objected to its use.

- **Notice and consent**: Notice involves informing Data Principals about data processing activities, whereas consent requires explicit permission from the Data Principal to process their personal data. Both are essential for transparency and accountability. Consent can be obtained by way of a Consent Notice.

Now that we understand the terminology of this legislation, let us look at the applicability or scope of this law.

The scope and applicability of India's *DPDP Act 2023* are broad, aiming to ensure the protection of personal data in an increasingly digitized world. The following highlights its primary areas of applicability:

- **Geographical scope:** The *DPDP Act 2023* applies to the processing of personal data within the territory of India, where personal data is collected in digital form or in non-digitized form and digitized subsequently. This implies that irrespective of where the entity is situated, if the processing of personal data is conducted within the territory of India, the DPDP Act will be applicable to such processing.

  o This law is equally applicable if the processing of digital personal data occurs outside the geographical boundary of India, if such processing is in connection with any activity related to the offering of goods or services to Data Principals within the territory of India.

- **Types of data covered:** The Act focuses on the protection of digital *personal data.* Personal data refers to any data relating to a natural person, which can directly or indirectly identify the individual. This means if the data is in physical format, it is not covered in the scope of this law. If we click a photograph and scan the physical format into a digital copy, then it is covered by this law. (Ch I, sec 3, (a)(ii))

- **Data Fiduciaries and Data Processors**: DPDP Act 2023 applies to both *data Fiduciaries and Data Processors.* (Ch I, sec 2, (i)(k))

- **Rights of Data Principals:** The Act fortifies the rights of Data Principals (individuals whose data is being processed). These rights include access, correction, deletion, nomination, among others. (Ch III, sec 11-15)

- **Cross-border data transfer**: The DPDP Act 2023 states that the Central Government may by notification, restrict the transfer of personal data for processing to such country or territory outside India as may be so notified. This implies that as long as the personal data is transferred to a country or a territory not so notified by the Central Government, personal data may be so transferred. Details regarding how such transfer of personal data will be effectuated are yet to be notified by the Central Government in terms of Rules/guidelines, etc. in the coming future. (Ch IV, sec 16)

- **Exceptions**: Certain categories of data processing are exempted from the provisions of the Act. These can include processing for personal or domestic purposes or by the State for certain specified functions. (Ch I, sec 3(c)), (Ch IV, sec 17)

- **Child consent**: The Act also has special provisions related to the collection and processing of children's data. It mandates verifiable consent from their parents or a lawful guardian before processing such data. (Ch II, sec 9)

Given its expansive nature, the *DPDPA 2023* has significant implications for various sectors, be it technology companies, healthcare institutions, financial firms, or even non-profit organizations. The intention behind the Act is to ensure that personal data is treated with the utmost care and respect, safeguarding the rights and interests of Data Principals in the digital age.

DPDPA journey

The DPDP Bill, 2022, having secured endorsements from both chambers of the parliament and having received the President's assent, has been formalized as the DPDP Act, 2023. This law, now operational, administers the treatment of digital personal data in India, including data that might have initially been non-digitized but was later digitized. While the Act primarily promotes data protection for entities like digital platforms, apps, and businesses handling citizen data, it also provides exemptions for certain state bodies. Notably, the DPDP Act aligns with international standards, thereby influencing India's global trade dialogues.

The journey of the DPDP Bill, 2022, was noteworthy. Endorsed by the Union Cabinet on July 5, 2023, it made its way to the Monsoon Session of Parliament, beginning August 3, 2023. With swift legislative maneuvering, it gained the Lok Sabha's approval on August 7, 2023, followed by the Rajya Sabha's on August 9, 2023. Upon the President's assent on August 11, 2023, it was formally notified in the Gazette of India as the DPDP Act, 2023.

Further solidifying its framework, the **Ministry of Electronics and Information Technology (MeitY)** published the DPDPA draft rules on January 3, 2025. This draft rule details additional guidelines and procedural measures for implementing the Act, ensuring that the operational aspects of DPDP are clear for both consumers and businesses. It also opens the floor for public feedback, allowing stakeholders to contribute to refining data protection practices in India. The public consultation is over now and numerous feedback have been submitted to MeitY.

For those wanting to look further into India's proactive approach towards DPDP, the government has provided a comprehensive document detailing the nuances and provisions of the law. To access the full text of the Act, along with the DPDPA draft rules and other related guidelines, please refer to the official link provided by MeitY.

DPDP Act, 2023, Official Document:

(**https://www.meity.gov.in/documents/Act-and-policies?**)

Draft DPDP Rules,2025:

(**https://www.meity.gov.in/documents/Act-and-policies/rules-2025**)

In an era where data is the new oil, the DPDP Act 2023 emerges as a pivotal legislative framework. This Act aims to safeguard individuals' personal data while balancing the interests of businesses and innovators. It outlines clear obligations for data fiduciaries and robust rights for Data Principals, ensuring transparency, accountability, and security in the digital ecosystem. Most organizations and individuals will be going through the bare Act. For the purpose of this book, let us quickly look at how to read the Act and what chapters and sections are covered in the bare Act. A short synopsis for each chapter will also be shared, so that once you are familiar with a higher level, it is easy to read the Act. Further chapters will cover relevant chapters and sections from the Act, explaining what it means, what software to choose to stay compliant, and the steps needed in the software to stay compliant.

Let us first have a quick look at what the law covers. The bare Act is divided into nine chapters, and let us review the synopsis of each one of them:

- **Chapter I:** Preliminary:
  - Addresses the scope, objectives, and definitions related to the Act, providing a foundational understanding of key terms and the legislation's intent.

- **Chapter II:** Obligations of the Data Fiduciary:
  - Outlines the duties and responsibilities of data fiduciaries, emphasizing the importance of consent, data accuracy, and measures to safeguard personal data.

- **Chapter III:** Rights and duties of Data Principal:
  - Describes the rights of individuals (Data principals) regarding their personal data, such as access to personal data, knowledge about data sharing, and related information.

- **Chapter IV:** Special provisions:
  - Highlight specific scenarios and conditions under which data processing and sharing regulations might be adjusted or exempted, ensuring flexibility in unique circumstances.

- **Chapter V:** Data Protection Board of India:
  - Establishes the creation and functions of the Data Protection Board of India, emphasizing its role in overseeing and ensuring adherence to the Act's provisions. (This board, at the writing of this book, was still in the making).

- **Chapter VI:** Powers, functions, and procedure to be followed by the board:
  - Details the powers and functions of the board, particularly in addressing breaches and complaints, and ensuring compliance with the Act's provisions. The board does provide, in case of disagreement ways to appeal, which is covered in the next chapter.

- **Chapter VII:** Appeal and alternate dispute resolution:
  - Describes the process for appealing against the board's decisions and emphasizes the digital nature of the Appellate Tribunal's proceedings.

- **Chapter VIII:** Penalties and adjudication:
  - Elaborate on the penalties for significant breaches of the Act, detailing the factors the Board considers when determining the extent of monetary penalties. We do have separate chapters, where we look at the penalties in detail. What is critical to keep in mind is that penalties for non-compliance are non-trivial and in the range up to INR 250 Crores (Schedule – I).

For the scope of this book, we are leaving chapter IX, which is titled Miscellaneous and most importantly focuses on the power of the central government, amendments, and adjustments over acts like the IT Act 2000.

The legislation offers a comprehensive framework for data protection in India, beginning with foundational definitions and objectives. It emphasizes the obligations of entities managing data and delineates the rights of individuals regarding their personal data. Special provisions ensure flexibility in unique circumstances, while the establishment of the Data Protection Board of India signifies a dedicated body for oversight and enforcement. The Act provides mechanisms for addressing breaches and lodging appeals and ensures a fair system of penalties, underlining a balanced and comprehensive approach to data protection.

Draft Digital Personal Data Protection Rules, 2025

The Draft **Digital Personal Data Protection Rules 2025** (Draft **DPDP Rules, 2025**) provide the granular framework for enforcing the DPDP Act, 2023. These draft rules define legal obligations, compliance measures, and enforcement mechanisms that organizations must follow when processing personal data in India.

Key features of the Draft DPDP Rules, 2025

The rules include 22 regulatory provisions, detailing compliance requirements for **data fiduciaries (DFs)**, **Significant Data Fiduciaries (SDFs)**, Consent Managers, and Data Processors. This section highlights only the most significant and operationally impactful rules that directly influence compliance obligations and governance practices. These rules provide critical insights into the core responsibilities of entities under the Act.

- **Notice and Consent (Rule 3):** Data fiduciaries must provide a clear, independent notice explaining what data is collected, the purpose of processing, and how consent can be withdrawn.

- **Consent Managers (Rule 4):** A regulatory framework for Consent Managers ensures secure handling of consent between users and data fiduciaries.

- **Security Safeguards (Rule 6):** Data Fiduciaries must implement encryption, access control, and logging to prevent unauthorized data breaches.

- **Personal Data Breach Notification (Rule 7):** Any breach must be reported within 72 hours to the Data Protection Board of India.

- **Data Retention and Erasure (Rule 8):** Data fiduciaries must erase personal data after a specific period unless legally required to retain it. Users must receive a 48-hour notice before data deletion.

- **Protection of Child Data (Rule 10 and Rule 11):** Processing of children's data requires verifiable parental consent, with exceptions for education, healthcare, and child safety.

- **Rights of the Data Principal (Rule 13):** This rule outlines how individuals can exercise their rights under the Act, such as the right to access, correction, erasure, and grievance redressal. Data fiduciaries must enable secure, user-friendly mechanisms (such as portals or dashboards) for Data Principals to submit and track their requests, and ensure timely, documented responses.

- **Cross-Border Data Transfers (Rule 14):** Personal data can be transferred outside India only under government-approved conditions.

- **Exemptions for Research and Archiving (Rule 15):** Certain data processing activities related to research and statistical analysis are exempt from some obligations under the DPDP Act.

The two key schedules for compliance are:

- **Second Schedule (Linked to Rules 5 and 15):** Establishes security and governance standards for state agencies processing personal data for public services like subsidies, permits, and benefits.
- **Third Schedule (Linked to Rule 8):** Specifies data retention periods for different industries, including e-commerce, gaming, and social media, ensuring user data is erased after three years of inactivity.

The Draft DPDP Rules, 2025, create a privacy-first legal framework that ensures data security, transparency, and user control. By aligning with global privacy standards while incorporating India-specific mandates, these rules play a crucial role in shaping digital governance and corporate compliance. These rules are not final and are subject to change by MeitY

Introducing compliance manager as regulatory governance tool

Once you embark on your compliance journey, you will need a reliable tool to navigate and govern your progress, just like having a GPS or a map to guide you on a road trip. It ensures you stay on the right path, avoid detours, and reach your destination smoothly and efficiently.

The utilization of tools or SaaS services, such as Microsoft Purview Compliance Manager, plays an instrumental role in ensuring adherence to regulations like *DPDPA 2023*. These tools offer a streamlined approach to regulatory compliance, automating compliance checks and providing real-time monitoring, thereby significantly reducing the chances of oversight and enabling swift corrective actions across IT and compliance teams.

Moreover, as regulations often undergo amendments, compliance manager SaaS services remain updated with the latest regulatory changes, ensuring businesses stay informed without continuously revisiting legal documents.

Another distinct advantage of Microsoft Purview Compliance Manager is its ability to centralize documentation and central evidence collection, making it easier during audits or when highlighting evidence of adherence.

Compliance managers also let you integrate with other enterprise systems like Salesforce, Zoom, or multi-cloud assets across Azure, Google, or AWS, providing you with a unified approach to compliance management across various IT assets.

With the ability to conduct risk assessments, generate detailed reports, and guide remediation in the event of discrepancies, compliance tools have become indispensable for businesses striving to maintain a robust data protection posture in today's stringent regulatory landscape.

Purview Microsoft Compliance Manager

Purview Compliance Manager is a feature in Microsoft 365 that serves to help organizations meet complex compliance obligations like GDPR, ISO 27001, India DPDP Act 2023, and many others. It provides a comprehensive solution for managing an organization's compliance posture by offering assessments mapped to common regulations and standards.

You can access Purview Compliance Manager by visiting (**https://purview.microsoft.com**)

Here is a summary of its key terminology and functionalities:

- **Assessment templates**: Purview Compliance Manager offers pre-built templates for common regulations and standards, which can be used to assess an organization's compliance status. *Figure 1.3* shows the dashboard interface of Compliance Manager, illustrating key metrics such as the overall compliance score, improvement actions, and regulatory assessment progress:

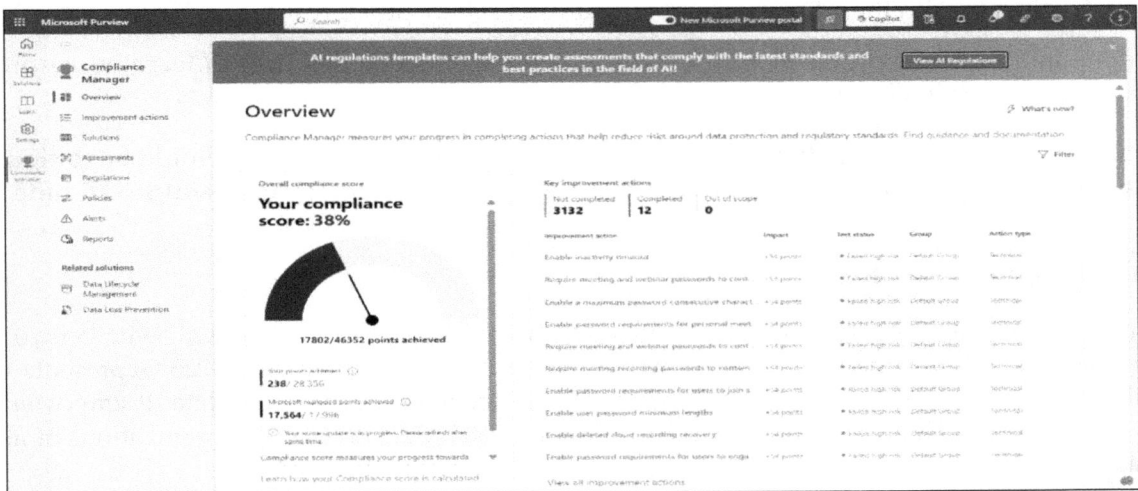

Figure 1.3: Using tools like Microsoft Purview Compliance Manager to track your compliances

- **Compliance score**: Organizations get a compliance score that provides a quantifiable measure of their compliance posture. actions that help mitigate compliance risks will improve this score, giving a clear indication of the organization's progression toward meeting compliance goals.

- **actionable insights:** The tool provides recommended actions to enhance the organization's compliance posture. Each recommendation comes with action items, implementation details, and the impact it has on the compliance score.

- **Integrated solution**: Compliance Manager is deeply integrated with Microsoft 365 services. This means data from these services can be automatically analyzed, and insights can be provided without requiring manual data input.

- **Custom assessments**: While there are pre-defined templates for many regulations, organizations can also create custom assessments based on their unique needs.

Microsoft Compliance Manager is a tool to simplify, manage, and track an organization's compliance activities, offering both pre-built solutions for common standards and flexibility for bespoke needs.

Testing or trying out Microsoft Compliance Manager typically involves leveraging the trial or demo versions provided by Microsoft. Here are the steps to evaluate or trial the Microsoft Compliance Manager for customers who have subscribed to Microsoft 365 E3 or E5 trial:

1. Navigate to the Microsoft 365 trial page and sign up for the Microsoft 365 trial.
2. Access the Microsoft 365 Compliance Center.
3. Once your E5 trial is active, go to the Microsoft 365 Compliance Center by navigating to **https://purview.microsoft.com.**
4. Sign in with the admin account of your trial subscription.

More information is provided with Microsoft Learn documentation (**https://learn.microsoft. com/en-us/purview/purview**)

Note: **For those not already subscribed to Microsoft 365 E5, the first step would be to sign up for a trial version. Microsoft Compliance Manager is a part of the Microsoft 365 E5 suite.**

Conclusion

In the digital age, the importance of data protection cannot be understated, whether you are an individual consumer or a sprawling enterprise. The DPDP Act, 2023, represents a significant step forward in India's commitment to safeguarding personal data. It empowers individuals with robust rights over their digital personal data and holds organizations of all sizes accountable for personal data breaches.

As we navigate the complexities of data protection legislation in India, the DPDP Act is not just a legal mandate but a reflection of the ethical responsibility we all share. Let us embrace this journey together, fortifying digital trust and ensuring that our personal data remains secure in the vast digital landscape of our country.

The next chapter explores how the evolving data landscape within enterprises affects compliance efforts under the DPDP Act. It looks into the importance of understanding various data types, identifying data sources, and maintaining a comprehensive IT asset inventory. Readers will also be introduced to tools for compliance tracking, methods for data classification, including AI-based techniques, and practical strategies for safeguarding both structured and unstructured data. By addressing these areas, the chapter lays the foundation for building robust data governance frameworks and aligning organizational practices with legal and regulatory obligations.

CHAPTER 2

Evolving Data Landscape in Enterprises

Introduction

In the context of India's **Digital Personal Data Protection (DPDP)** Act 2023, data mapping and inventory are critical processes for data fiduciaries. These processes involve identifying, classifying, and documenting all data assets within an organization. Effective data mapping ensures that organizations can maintain transparency, adhere to regulatory requirements, and enhance data governance. By clearly understanding what data is held, where it resides, and how it flows, data fiduciaries can better protect personal data, manage risks, and ensure compliance with the DPDP Act. However, while data mapping provides numerous benefits, including improved data quality and streamlined operations, it also presents challenges such as resource allocation and ongoing maintenance. Leveraging the right tools and adhering to best practices can help data fiduciaries create and maintain accurate data maps, fostering a culture of data accountability and protection.

Structure

In this chapter, we will cover the following topics:

- Navigating the data maze
- Types of data
- Identifying data sources

- Organization IT asset view
- Compliance tracking tool
- Categorizing and classification of data
- Mapping the India DPDP Act, 2023
- AI-based classification
- Safeguard application data
- Classification across structured data
- Data protection steps

Objectives

This chapter aims to equip data fiduciaries with a practical understanding of how to discover, classify, and protect data across a modern enterprise's complex digital environment in alignment with the DPDP Act, 2023. With personal data scattered across on-premises systems, cloud platforms, and third-party services, this chapter outlines key steps for gaining visibility and control over structured, unstructured, and semi-structured data. It introduces critical processes such as data discovery, IT asset mapping, data classification, and the use of tools like Microsoft Purview and Compliance Manager to meet regulatory obligations. The chapter emphasizes the importance of knowing where data resides, how it flows, and how it can be effectively protected, highlighting that without visibility, protection is impossible. It also introduces AI-driven classification methods, EDM safeguards, and consent-aware governance, providing readers with foundational knowledge to build a privacy-first, compliant data management strategy under the DPDP Act and its rules.

Navigating the data maze

In large organizations, the vastness and diversity of operations often lead to data being stored and managed across a multitude of locations and systems. For example, employee information might be stored in **Human Resource Management Systems** (**HRMS**), while customer data could reside in **customer relationship management** (**CRM**) platforms. Financial data may be kept in separate accounting software, and project-specific data might be housed in dedicated project management tools. Additionally, some data might be stored on premises servers, while other datasets are kept in cloud storage solutions. This scattered data landscape reflects the multifaceted nature of large organizations, where different departments and functions have specific data storage and management needs.

If you do not know where your data is, protecting it becomes a significant challenge.

This statement underscores a critical issue in the realm of information protection. In today's digital landscape, data sprawls across various platforms and systems, from cloud storage and mobile devices to IoT gadgets and remote servers. Losing track of where your data resides is akin to having unguarded treasures scattered in unknown locations.

Without a comprehensive understanding of your data's whereabouts, implementing effective protection strategies becomes a complex, if not impossible, task. It is essential for organizations to employ robust data discovery and classification tools to gain visibility into their data ecosystem. Only then can they apply the right security measures, comply with data protection regulations, and safeguard their most valuable digital assets against breaches and unauthorized access. In the journey of information protection, knowing your data's location is the first, crucial step towards ensuring its security. Let us explore what kind of data we will uncover as we explore across the digital estate and how to manage distinct categories of data.

Understanding the location and classification of your data is fundamental to effective data management. The following figure illustrates the essential steps to know your data, govern it efficiently, and ensure its protection, aligning with best practices and regulatory requirements:

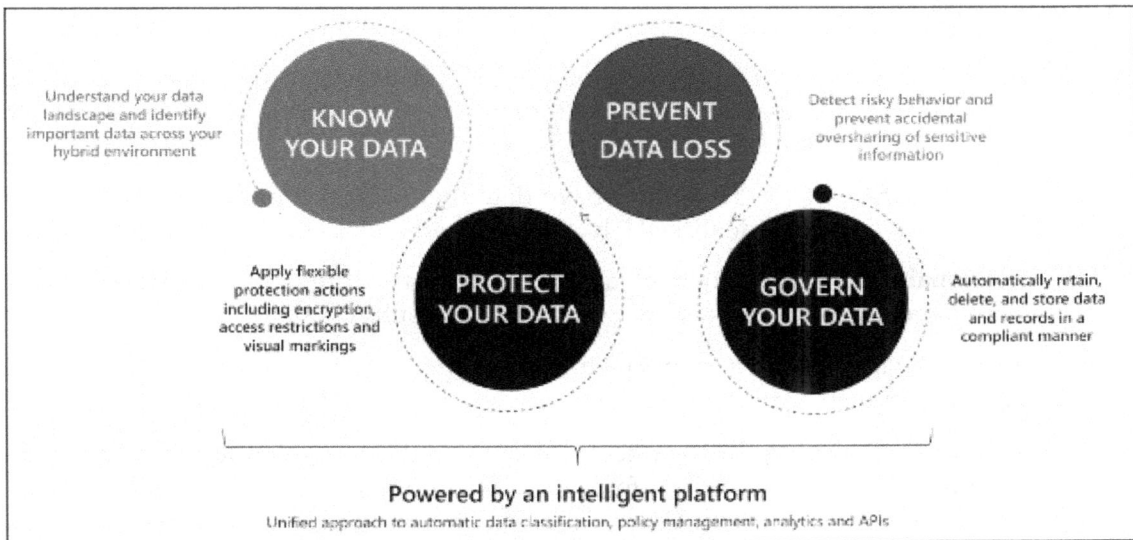

Figure 2.1: Data lifecycle

For any organization to get a view into its data, it is important to first understand the types of data in the organization. Let us look at distinct types of data that are spread across organization data estates.

Types of data

Data comes in various forms and can be broadly categorized into structured, unstructured, and semi-structured types. Each of these types has distinct characteristics and is used in diverse ways across various industries. The following are each type with examples:

- **Structured data**: Structured data is highly organized and formatted in a way that makes it easily searchable and understandable by data processing systems. Its examples are as follows:

- o **Databases**: Information stored in a SQL database, like a customer database with fields for name, address, phone number, and transaction history.

- o **Spreadsheets**: Data in Excel files where each column represents a specific category, like sales data with columns for date, product, quantity, and price.

- **Unstructured data:** Unstructured data lacks a predefined format or structure, making it more complex to process and analyze using conventional data tools. Its examples are as follows:

  - o **Text files**: Documents, emails, and articles that contain text without a structured format.

  - o **Multimedia content**: Images, audio files, and videos. For example, customer service call recordings, photos uploaded on social media, or video content.

- **Semi-structured data**: Semi-structured data is not as organized as structured data but contains some elements that make it easier to process than unstructured data. Its examples are as follows:

  - o **XML/JSON files**: These files have data that is tagged or marked up, making certain elements identifiable, like configuration files or data from web services.

  - o **Email**: While the body of an email is unstructured, it contains structured elements like the sender, recipient, date, and subject line.

In the context of the DPDP Act, recognizing and managing diverse types of data, structured, unstructured, and semi-structured, is crucial for compliance and effective data protection.

Enterprise Resource Planning (ERP) systems integrate and manage core business processes in real-time, providing a centralized platform for efficient operations. Leading ERP software includes SAP, Oracle, and Microsoft Dynamics, each offering robust solutions to streamline and optimize organizational workflows.

Also, **Line of Business (LOB)** refers to a specific business unit or department within an organization that focuses on a particular set of related products or services. Examples include the Human Resources department managing employee-related functions and the Finance department overseeing financial activities.

Let us look at structured data that will be mostly found in organization ERP systems. Usual suspects will be financial records like invoices, purchase orders stored in SAP or other ERP systems, inventory management systems, records of inventory, or customer sensitive data in CRM systems or custom LOB applications running all sorts of databases from Oracle, SQL servers, NoSQL, or MongoDB. Structured data gets created or consumed as part of a business process and is critical to any organization's functioning. Organizations need to be careful while managing compliance, especially since structured data sets will have vast amounts of **Personal Data**. Properly securing this data and ensuring its use adheres to the Act's provisions are essential.

Gaining a comprehensive view of your organization's data landscape under the DPDP Act can be challenging, with unstructured data posing one of the most daunting tasks. A vast amount of unstructured data is stored across device endpoints and cloud environments, often embedded in marketing materials, customer feedback, and creative content. Ensuring DPDPA compliance is particularly complex, as this data is dispersed across various formats such as PowerPoint presentations, PDFs, Word documents, and images, making governance and protection more intricate. To make things complex, this data sits across your digital estate on SharePoint servers, in Amazon S3 buckets, in OneDrive accounts, across Microsoft Teams and team sites, and in Zoom or Azure cloud storage services. This data, often qualitative and less organized, requires sophisticated tools for identification and processing. Moreover, organization emails will have lots of unstructured data that has been built over the last few decades, running into terabytes of sensitive, critical data that needs to be protected. Organizations must ensure that data embedded in an unstructured format is protected and used in accordance with the DPDP Act. Often, an organization spends fewer calories on discovering semi-structured data, and it needs equal attention when looked at from DPDPA compliance. Semi-structured data can be found across web development and data interchange. Semi-structured data combines elements of both structured and unstructured data, like CSV files used in data exchange, XML interchange, or API exchange formats. Semi-structured data often calls for a hybrid approach. Effective management of these data types is key to not only adhering to the DPDP Act's requirements but also maintaining the trust and confidence of customers and stakeholders in how their personal data is managed.

Identifying data sources

The imperative of data discovery within the enterprise domain cannot be understated, particularly in an era where data sprawls across multiple digital estates, from traditional databases and collaborative platforms like *SharePoint*, *OneDrive*, and *Teams*, to third-party services such as *Salesforce*. The vast distribution of data across these varied repositories presents a significant challenge for organizations striving to secure personal information, comply with regulations, and leverage data for strategic decisions. This complexity underscores the necessity for sophisticated data discovery tools and practices. Data discovery is part of "know your data," which refers to the processes and technologies employed to identify, classify, and manage data across an organization. It is the foundation upon which data security, compliance, and value realization are built. Without a thorough understanding of what data exists, where it is stored, and its relevance to the business, organizations are at a disadvantage, unable to protect against breaches, ensure regulatory compliance, or harness data for insights.

Given the dispersion of data across various platforms, each with its unique structure and purpose, the need for comprehensive data discovery tools becomes evident (as we discussed earlier on structured, unstructured, and semi-structured data). These tools must be capable of scanning environments as diverse as cloud-based storage, such as OneDrive and SharePoint, collaborative suites like Microsoft Teams, databases that form the backbone of organizational operations, and external SaaS platforms like Salesforce, *Zoho, Zoom,* and others. The goal is not just to locate data but to understand its context, sensitivity level, and compliance requirements.

One of the primary challenges in data discovery is the sheer volume and variety of data. Organizations generate and store data on an unprecedented scale, and much of this data is unstructured (e.g., emails, documents, multimedia files). Additionally, the dynamic nature of digital environments, where data is constantly created, modified, and deleted, adds to the complexity.

Data discovery tools address these challenges by using sophisticated algorithms, machine learning techniques, and pattern recognition to automate the identification and classification of data. These tools can discern personal information, such as personal data or financial details, across different data types and platforms. By doing so, they enable organizations to apply appropriate security measures, manage access controls, and implement data protection policies effectively.

For more information, visit **https://learn.microsoft.com/en-us/purview/data-map**.

The benefits of effective data discovery are manifold. Firstly, it enhances data security by ensuring that sensitive data is accurately identified and adequately protected. Secondly, it supports compliance efforts by providing a clear view of data assets in relation to regulatory requirements, such as those mandated by the India DPDP Act and others like GDPR and CCPA. Thirdly, it empowers organizations to make informed decisions based on accurate, accessible data, thereby driving innovation and strategic initiatives.

Organization IT asset view

As a CISO or DPO embarking on the data protection journey, creating a bird's-eye view of your digital estate becomes the starting point. It offers a comprehensive overview of the organization's digital estate, vendor, and size of data estate, enabling precise targeting in data classification and protection efforts. By understanding the landscape of digital assets, including their owners and the types of data they contain, your team can prioritize resources and strategies effectively. This preparatory step ensures that data protection measures are aligned with the sensitivity of the data and compliance requirements, laying a solid foundation for a robust data security framework. Let us look at a sample organization's IT assets:

Asset type	Location/URL	Data protection asset ID	Owner/ Department	Data Type(s)	Sensitivity Level	Compliance Requirements	Notes
Share-Point Sites	http:// sharepoint. company.com/ site1	D1	HR Department	Employee records	High	DPDP Act, GDPR	Contains PII and HR records
Team Sites	http://teams. company.com/ projectX	D2	Project X Team	Project documents	Medium	Internal Policy	Collaboration space for Project X
One-Drive Locations	http://onedrive. company.com/ user1	D3	User 1	Personal work documents	Low	N/A	User 1 personal work area

Asset type	Location/URL	Data protection asset ID	Owner/ Department	Data Type(s)	Sensitivity Level	Compliance Requirements	Notes
File Servers	\companyserver\shared	D4	IT Department	Software licenses, IT docs	Medium	Internal Policy	IT documentation and software licenses
SaaS Services	Salesforce	D5	Sales Department	Customer data	High	DPDP Act, GDPR	Sales leads and customer interactions
SaaS Services	Zoom	D6	All Departments	Meeting recordings	Medium	DPDP Act	Recorded meetings and webinars
SaaS Services	D365	D7	Finance Department	Financial records	High	DPDP Act, Financial Regs	Financial transactions and reports

Table 2.1: IT asset view table

Once you have compiled a table of IT assets, uniquely identifying each asset becomes crucial for crafting effective data protection and compliance tracking policies. This unique identification (above data protection asset ID) allows for the precise application of security measures tailored to the specific needs and risks associated with each asset. Furthermore, it facilitates accurate monitoring and reporting, enabling organizations to demonstrate compliance with regulatory requirements systematically. By uniquely tagging assets, you can ensure that data protection efforts are both comprehensive and nuanced, aligning with the strategic goals of your organization's data governance framework.

The landscape of IT digital assets within an organization is dynamic, with assets continually evolving, some being retired while new ones are introduced. This constant flux underscores the necessity of maintaining a *live* inventory, regularly updated to reflect these changes. Such vigilance ensures that data protection and compliance policies remain relevant and effective, covering all active assets while removing or archiving policies related to obsolete ones. Keeping the inventory current is essential for safeguarding against emerging threats and ensuring ongoing compliance with applicable data protection regulations.

Compliance tracking tool

Let us pick our conversation on the primary compliance tool to help your organization with your India DPDPA compliance journey, Purview Compliance Manager. We looked at various templates in the first chapter. If we look closely at the services list in the **Regulations** tab in **Compliance Manager**, we will find *Universal* names across various templates, as shown in the following figure:

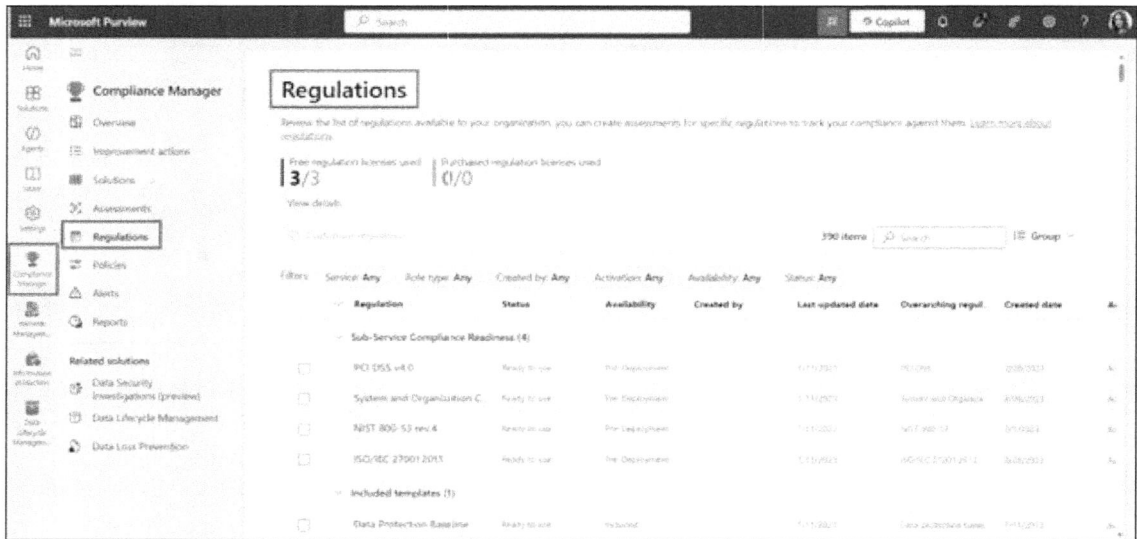

Figure 2.2: Compliance manager as DPDPA assessment tool

Universal Templates in Purview compliance managers offer a versatile and robust approach.

To manage compliance across an organization's digital landscape. These templates are foundational tools that enable organizations to streamline their compliance processes, making them indispensable for several reasons, such as:

- **Extensive coverage for diverse digital services**: Universal templates are designed to extend compliance management capabilities beyond Microsoft services, covering a wide range of digital services and platforms. Whether it is a mobile app, an ERP system like SAP, or any other non-Microsoft service, universal templates allow organizations to apply consistent compliance assessments across their entire digital estate. This ensures that all aspects of an organization's operations, regardless of the technology or platform used, are compliant with relevant regulations.

- **Customization of unique regulatory requirements**: Not all regulatory requirements or industry standards are directly available in Compliance Manager. Universal templates address this gap by allowing organizations to create custom assessments for regulations that are not pre-included. Whether it is a specific industry guideline or a newly enacted Act, custom templates enable organizations to rapidly adapt their compliance posture to meet these unique requirements, ensuring they remain ahead in compliance management.

- **Establishing organizational gold standards**: Organizations often aim to achieve a compliance level that goes beyond the minimum requirements of any single regulation. Universal templates empower them to create their own *gold standard* of compliance by combining elements from multiple regulations available within compliance managers. Most of the time, organizations are just looking to add a few controls that are prescribed by their board or consulting partners to create the organization's own complete interpretation of any regulation, standard, or posture definition. This amalgamation enables organizations to set higher benchmarks for their compliance efforts, fostering a culture of excellence and robust data protection practices.

Universal templates in Microsoft Compliance Manager are not just tools for compliance; they are strategic assets that enable organizations to navigate the complexities of regulatory adherence. By providing flexibility to cover a wide range of digital services, the capability to customize for unique regulatory landscapes, and the option to create an organizational gold standard, universal templates are pivotal in ensuring comprehensive and effective compliance management across an organization's digital environment. We covered how to create an assessment in Compliance Manager in the previous chapter. Let us say that in your organization, you have M365 services, an LOB mobile app, and Azure infrastructure; you should be creating three assessments of the DPDP Act, one for each digital asset, as shown in the following figure:

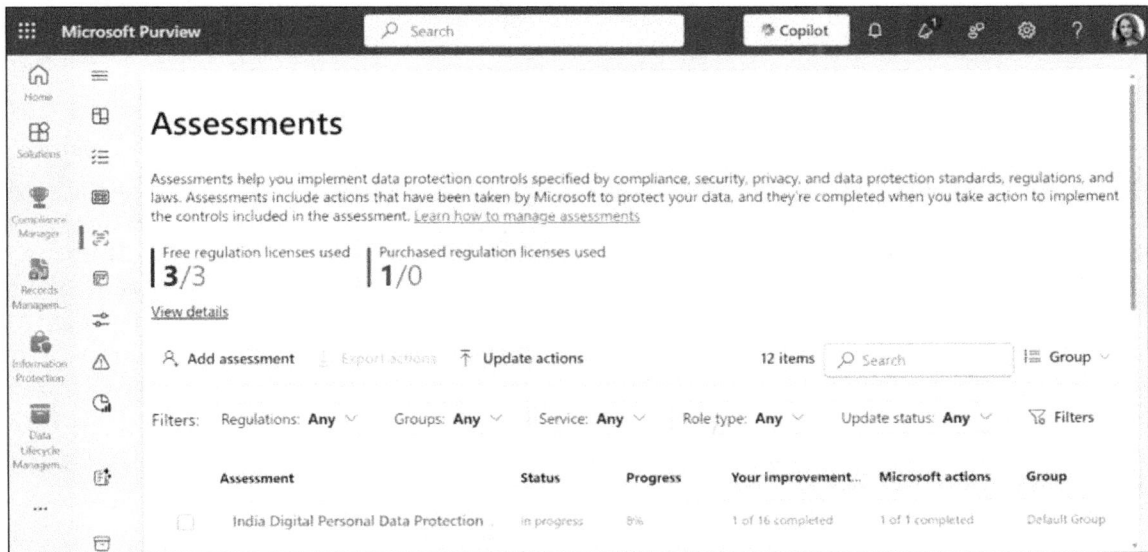

Figure 2.3: Choosing the India DPDPA template

Categorizing and classification of data

Once assessments have been created in Microsoft Compliance Manager for the various digital services and data estate within an organization, the next critical step is to identify and protect personal information as mandated by the India DPDP Act. This Act, like many global data protection regulations, requires organizations to take specific measures to ensure the privacy and security of personal data. Identifying personal information within an organization's digital estate, both structured and unstructured, across various digital estates, is pivotal to complying with these requirements.

The next step is to find personal information across your digital services and assets. The process begins with the data discovery phase, where organizations must use data discovery tools to scan through their digital environments, be it cloud services, on-premises data stores, or third-party applications like SAP, Salesforce, or custom-built mobile apps. The goal here is to locate Personal data, financial details, health records, or any other data types considered sensitive under the DPDP Act.

Embarking on a treasure hunt for personal information within your organization might look like searching for a needle in a digital haystack, except this needle is made of passport numbers, credit card details, employment letters, and supplier contracts. Begin by donning your digital archaeologist hat and meticulously digging through every nook and cranny of your data estate. Remember, every piece of data, no matter how seemingly trivial, from Aunt Stefanie's pickle recipe shared over email to that top-secret supplier contract, could be the map leading to the treasure trove of personal information you need to protect. So, grab your digital shovel and start the expedition.

Data classification

Imagine piloting data classification, organization needs like flying an airplane in the vast skies of your organization's digital landscape. In this high-flying analogy, Microsoft's purview Content Explorer acts as a powerful tool providing visibility into the content across your digital assets. On the other hand, the data map tool in the purview of Microsoft ensures you have a comprehensive understanding and inventory of your data, no matter where it resides. At the heart of this aircraft, the compliance manager serves as the cockpit, offering you the controls and instruments needed to navigate through the complex airspace of regulations and compliance requirements. Classifying data significantly enhances visibility, much like the following figure, which shares distinct islands from above and reveals their unique characteristics and relationships. This improved perspective allows for better data management and decision-making.

Figure 2.4: Visibility with classification

As you fly over various data asset islands, each representing different repositories like SharePoint sites, team sites, OneDrive locations, file servers, and SaaS platforms like Salesforce, you are fueled by a common, essential resource: the classification service. This service acts as jet fuel, powering your journey by consistently identifying, classifying, and tagging data according to its sensitivity and compliance needs.

However, to ensure a smooth flight and avoid any turbulence, it is crucial to define your classification service in detail. This involves setting up sensitivity labels, trainable classifiers, and other elements of classification that we will cover below in detail. By doing so, you ensure that every piece of data, no matter how hidden or scattered across your data asset islands, is appropriately classified and labeled for the right policies and implement safeguards like retention, encryption, and **data loss prevention** (DLP) throughout your compliance journey.

In this aviation adventure, your goal is to achieve a state where data is not only secure and compliant but also easily accessible and productively utilized within your organization. With Content Explorer in **Microsoft Information Protection** (MIP) and Data Catalog in Purview Governance serving as your engines, Compliance Manager as your cockpit, and a well-defined classification strategy as your flight plan, you are set to navigate the complexities of data governance with precision. Now, let us look into the details of classification and explore how these tools can be leveraged effectively.

Elements of classification services

Exploring the elements of classification services in Microsoft Purview Information Protection is akin to assembling a sophisticated puzzle, where each piece plays a crucial role in the bigger picture of data protection and compliance.

Starting with **Sensitive Information Types** (SIT) and **Regular Expressions** (Reg-Ex), we lay the foundation for identifying predefined and custom patterns within data. Custom SITs allow organizations to tailor classification to their unique data elements, while **Exact Data Match** (EDM) takes precision to the next level by matching data to a secure repository of personal information. Lastly, trainable classifiers employ machine learning to recognize data types that are too complex for simple pattern matching, evolving with your data to ensure comprehensive protection.

Once you visit **purview.microsoft.com** and click on data classification, it gives you a view of data across your organization's digital estate and the type of personal information. Let us start exploring them more. When you can visualize the types of documents, such as sensitive data, across your data estate in a graphical view, it dramatically enhances your ability to manage and protect your information assets effectively, as depicted in the following figure:

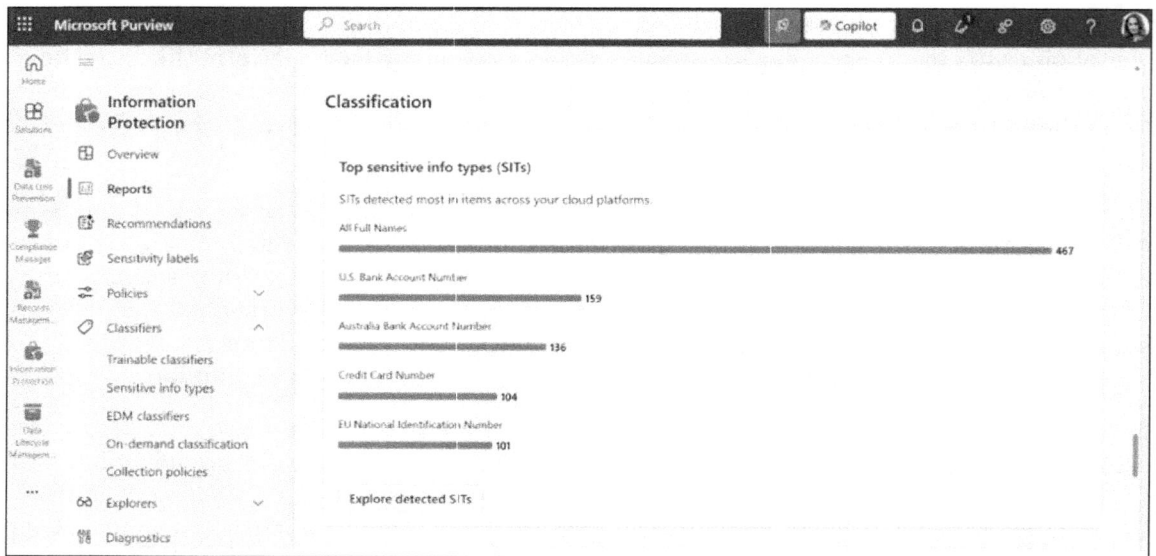

Figure 2.5: *Visualization of sensitive data across your data estate*

Selecting the necessary sensitive information types for your organization is crucial in safeguarding critical data. The following figure illustrates this process, highlighting the importance of tailored DPDPA compliance as per your business and vertical needs:

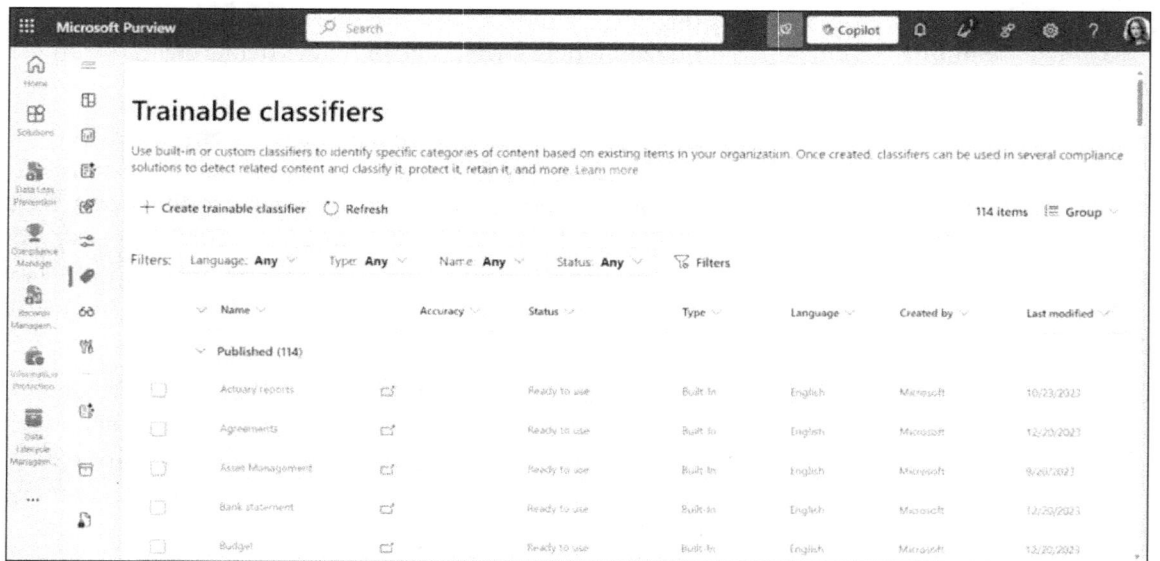

Figure 2.6: *Choosing which sensitive information types are relevant*

Sensitive information types

A SIT is a label used in data protection services to identify and categorize data based on its level of sensitivity. Think of it as a digital sticky note that says, *Hey, this information is private!* Like an Aadhar number, credit card details, or personal address. By tagging data with SITs, organizations can apply specific rules and protections to ensure that personal information is managed safely and in compliance with privacy regulations.

Within MIP services, administrators have the powerful capability to meticulously evaluate, tag, and manage content across their organization (as shown in the preceding figures). This process is crucial for ensuring that personal information is controlled, protected, and managed in alignment with organizational policies and requirements. By utilizing sensitivity labels, retention labels, and classifying content based on SITs, administrators can effectively oversee the lifecycle and security of organizational data.

Identifying SITs is crucial for compliance as it directs focus on protecting data that is most at risk. For example, pinpointing customer personal information, such as email addresses, phone numbers, credit card details, and other personal information, can be activated quickly by searching for India in the **Sensitive info types** tab. Choosing sensitive information types relevant to India is essential for compliance and data protection. The following figure demonstrates how to select these specific data categories to ensure your organization meets local regulatory requirements:

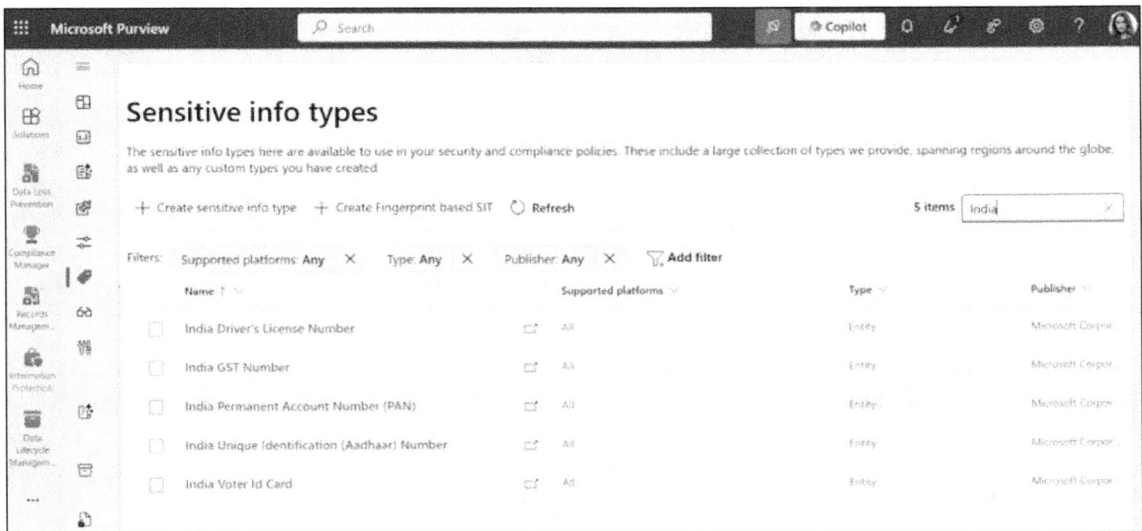

Figure 2.7: India-specific sensitive info types

In addition to selecting list a of SITs that will be relevant for India, it is also important to select SITs, like a credit card, credentials or user identity as shown in the following figure:

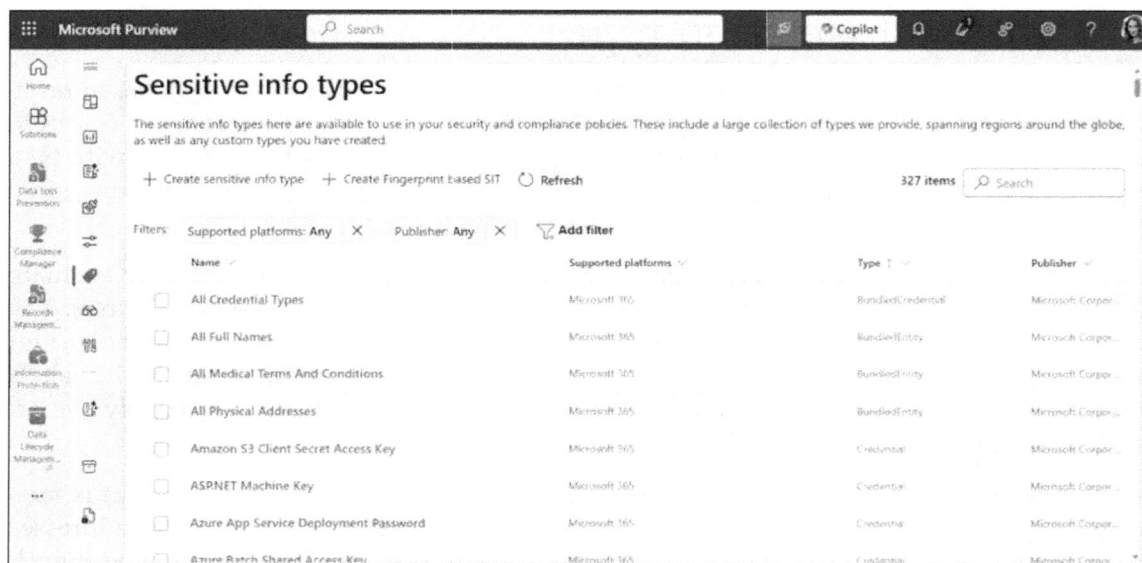

Figure 2.8: Sensitive information type exhaustive list

The data classification overview in MIP services provides a comprehensive snapshot of this labeling ecosystem. The out-of-the-box sensitivity labels are of the following two types:

- **Un-bundled**: These are more specific and might focus on just one country or a particular type of information. They are great when you want to be specific in finding certain details, like making sure you are only looking at addresses from India.

- **Bundled**: These labels are more general. For instance, one might find all types of physical addresses, no matter the country. Use these when you want to cast a wide net and catch all similar types of information in one go. As you see in *Figure 2.8,* the administrator has control over which out-of-the-box sensitivity labels to select. In addition, it is very normal for organizations to have their own customs sensitivity labels.

As you look at the list of built-in SITs, you will see a lot with type credentials. The *all-credentials* label is a kind of bundled-entity label designed to find login details across a wide range of platforms and services. This includes big names like *Amazon, Azure, GitHub, Google,* and *Microsoft,* among others. It is a one-stop label that covers credentials from all supported environments, making sure nothing slips through the cracks.

If the standard sensitive information types provided do not fit what you are looking for, there is flexibility to tailor them to your specific requirements. For instance, you might need a custom sensitive information type for Indian bank account numbers that are not covered by the default settings. You can either start from scratch to define these custom types according to your needs or tweak an existing one to better suit your criteria. This customization ensures that your data protection measures are precisely aligned with the unique data privacy challenges faced by your organization in the context of complying with the India DPDP Act. Once such a custom SIT is created, you can deploy it across your structured, semi-structured, or unstructured data across the data estate. The following figure gives you a view into the quick steps that can be taken to create your own SIT to meet DPDP Act requirements:

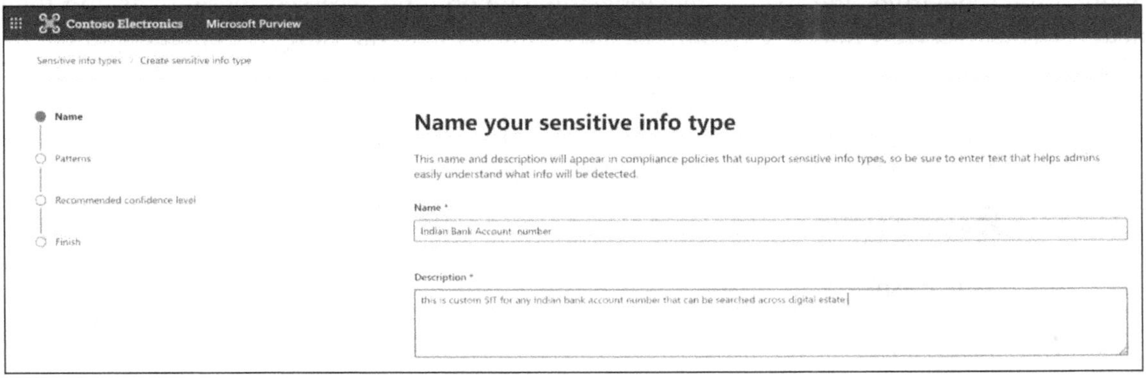

Figure 2.9: Creating custom SIT

Configuring confidence levels and other metadata when creating custom SIT in Microsoft MIP enhances data accuracy and relevance. This ensures precise data classification, improving the effectiveness of your data protection policies, as shown in the following figure:

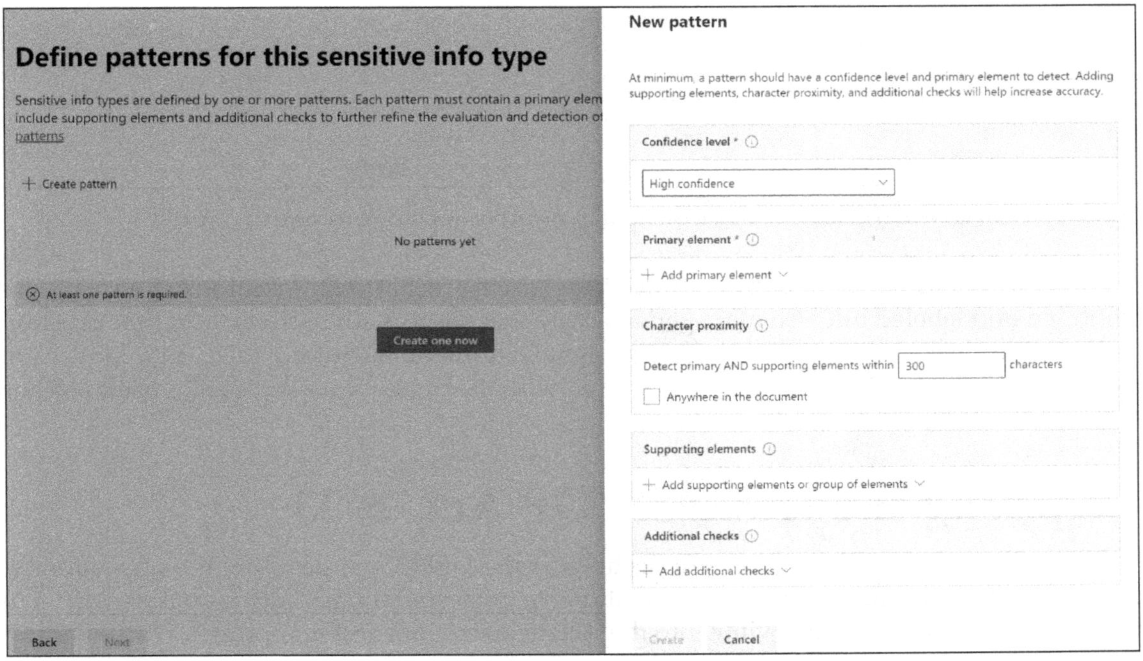

Figure 2.10: Setting confidence level and metadata for accuracy

Once SITs are defined in MIP, the Content Explorer transforms into an invaluable dashboard for overseeing your organization's sensitive data. It enables a comprehensive view of labeled content, organizing it by the specific SITs identified, from personal identifiers to financial details. You gain insights into the exact locations of sensitive items across platforms like SharePoint, OneDrive, and Exchange, alongside data on who accessed these items and their actions. This overview not only aids in risk assessment by highlighting the spread and nature of sensitive data but also facilitates direct management actions such as re-labeling, encryption, or deletion, right from the interface. MIP's Content Explorer, post-SIT definition, provides a detailed, actionable perspective on data protection and compliance posture within the digital environment, as shown in the following figure:

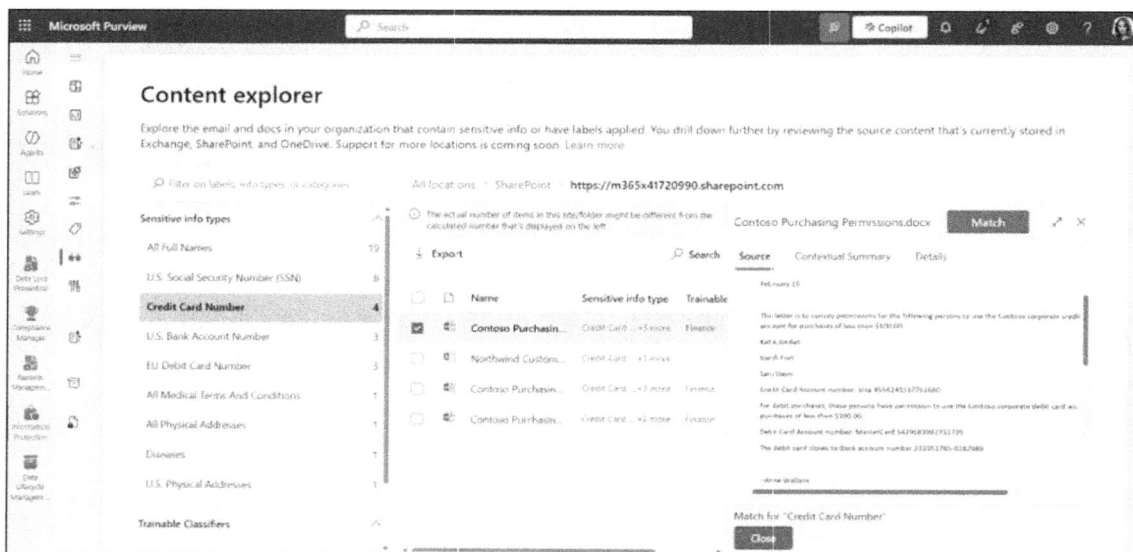

Figure 2.11: Data Estate view with Optics around India DPDPA relevant information

This level of visibility is pivotal for administrators to ensure that personal information is not just identified and labeled but also managed in a way that aligns with both security best practices and regulatory compliance. It empowers organizations to safeguard their data landscape, ensuring that personal information is managed with the utmost care across Microsoft 365 and Azure environments.

Mapping the India DPDP Act, 2023

In this section, we will outline specific sections of the DPDP Act, detailing the obligations of data fiduciaries and mapping these obligations to corresponding solutions within MIP. The following table shows a quick view into the Act, its narration, and mapping:

Chapter	Section	Definition name	Narration	Solution mapping
2	8	General Obligations of Data Fiduciary	A Data Fiduciary may engage, appoint, use, or otherwise involve a Data Processor to process personal data on its behalf for any activity related to offering of goods or services to Data Principals only under a valid contract.	Need to have agreements in place, recognized and possible visible with Trainable Classifiers.
2	8	General Obligations of Data Fiduciary	Where personal data processed by a Data Fiduciary is likely to be.	Need to have agreements in place, recognized and possible visible with Trainable Classifiers.
2	8	General Obligations of Data Fiduciary	Used to make a decision that affects the Data Principal.	Need to have SIT pre-identified with Data lineage tracking.
2	8	General Obligations of Data Fiduciary	Disclosed to another Data Fiduciary.	Need to have agreements in place, recognized and possible visible with Trainable Classifiers.
2	8	General Obligations of Data Fiduciary	The Data Fiduciary processing such personal data shall ensure its completeness, accuracy, and consistency.	Need to have agreements in place, recognized and possible visible within Data Explorer to maintain the accuracy and consistency of data.
2	8	General Obligations of Data Fiduciary	A Data Fiduciary shall implement appropriate technical and organizational measures to ensure effective observance of the provisions of this Act and the rules made thereunder.	Need to have agreements in place and Security tools like MIP, DLP, IRM implemented within the Organisation.
2	8	General Obligations of Data Fiduciary	A Data Fiduciary shall protect personal data in its possession or under its control, including in respect of any processing undertaken by it or on its behalf by a Data Processor, by taking reasonable security safeguards to prevent personal data breach.	Need the Data Fiduciary implement SIT, extend SITs to include relevant personal information and have right policies like encryption, DLP offering reasonable security safeguards.

Chapter	Section	Definition name	Narration	Solution mapping
2	11	Right to access information about personal data	A summary of personal data which is being processed by such Data Fiduciary and the processing activities undertaken by that Data Fiduciary with respect to such personal data.	Need for tools like activity Explorer, Content Explorer, and Data Catalog.

Table 2.2: Quick view into DPDP Act chapters and sections

Section 8 of the DPDP Act requires data fiduciaries to manage personal data with care. They must have valid contracts for processing personal data, ensure data used for decision-making is complete, accurate, and consistent, and protect personal data against breaches. The Act also mandates effective technical and organizational measures for compliance.

The MIP solution mapping suggests the use of trainable classifiers to recognize and classify agreements. For ensuring data accuracy and consistency, SITs with data lineage tracking are recommended. To protect personal data, MIP's capabilities like encryption, DLP, and extending SITs to include various personal information is advised.

For the rights to access information about personal data, tools like activity Explorer, Content Explorer, and Data Catalog are suggested to provide visibility and control over how personal data is processed and to maintain a summary of these processing activities.

This mapping demonstrates how MIP can be strategically utilized to address the requirements of the DPDP Act by providing the necessary tools for data classification, protection, and compliance management.

Further, we will look into the term "reasonable security safeguards" called out in chapter II, section 8 (5) of the Act for the general obligations of data fiduciaries.

The Draft DPDP Rules, 2025, under Rule 6, provide a clear definition and expectation for reasonable security safeguards that organizations must implement to protect personal data. These safeguards ensure that data breaches, unauthorized access, and data manipulation are prevented, maintaining the confidentiality, integrity, and availability of personal data.

The following table outlines key sub-sections under Rule 6 as per the Draft DPDP Rules, summarizing each definition, its practical interpretation, and recommended solution mappings that organizations can adopt to meet compliance requirements:

Rule	Sub Rule	Definition name	Narration	Solution mapping
6	a	Data Protection Measures	Personal data must be protected through encryption, obfuscation, masking, or virtual tokenization to prevent unauthorized access.	Implement AES-256 encryption, use tokenization for sensitive identifiers, and apply data masking techniques to protect user data at rest and in transit.
6	b	Access Control Mechanisms	Organizations must implement **role-based access control (RBAC)** to restrict access to personal data only to authorized individuals.	Deploy **identity and access management (IAM)** solutions such as Microsoft Entra ID or Okta, enforce **multi-factor authentication (MFA)**, and conduct regular access audits.
6	c	Logging and Monitoring	Organizations must track access logs, conduct continuous monitoring, and review logs to detect unauthorized access.	Use SIEM tools like Microsoft Sentinel, Splunk, or IBM QRadar for real-time monitoring, implement automated anomaly detection, and retain audit logs for at least one year.
6	d	Data Backup and Recovery	Ensure data availability through backup mechanisms and maintain continuity plans in case of data corruption, deletion, or compromise.	Implement cloud-based backup solutions (AWS Backup, Azure Backup, Google Vault), run disaster recovery simulations, and store redundant backups in separate geographical locations.
6	e	Retention of Logs and Data	Logs and personal data should be retained for at least one year, unless required otherwise by Act.	Use Log Management Systems (e.g., Elastic Stack, Graylog) with retention policies aligned with compliance requirements.
6	f	Security Provisions in Contracts	If a Data Processor is involved, contractual agreements must ensure that it also follows security safeguards.	Establish **Data Processing Agreements (DPAs)** enforcing ISO 27001 compliance and security obligations in third-party contracts.
6	g	Technical and Organizational Measures	Implement both technical (firewalls, encryption, endpoint protection) and organizational (security policies, employee training) measures	Use DLP tools, conduct security awareness training, and enforce Zero Trust architecture.

Table 2.3: *Key sub-sections under Rule 6*

AI-based classification

Everyone aims to meticulously analyze their documents, uncovering the details hidden within contracts, agreements, bank statements, and budget files. Enter the world of trainable classifiers, advanced tools in data protection. These intelligent, ever-learning systems ensure the confidentiality of sensitive content, providing clarity and organization to your digital files. *Trainable classifiers* in MIP represent a sophisticated approach to content categorization, especially useful for types of data that are complex and cannot be accurately captured through simple pattern recognition or manual examination. These classifiers leverage machine learning, gaining understanding from a broad set of examples to accurately identify and categorize content by its intrinsic characteristics. For instance, a trainable classifier can be taught to recognize GST invoices by analyzing numerous instances and understanding the subtleties that make up the format and content of an invoice, beyond just numbers or keywords. This capability allows organizations to efficiently automate the classification and management of specific documents like GST invoices, which are crucial for financial reporting and compliance, ensuring that personal information is consistently and accurately managed across the board. A list of some out-of-the-box trainable classifiers is shown in the following figure:

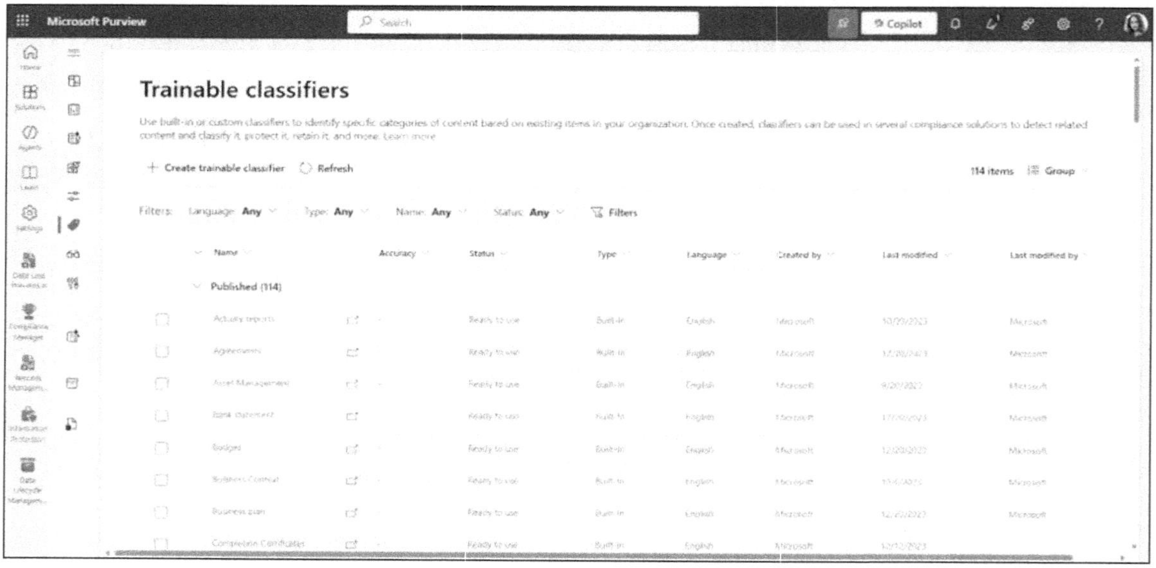

Figure 2.12: Select AI-based pre-build trainable classifier

It comes with 100+ inbuild trainable classifiers, let us pick up a few to understand what they can do:

- **Agreements classifier:** This classifier is designed to detect legal documents such as nondisclosure agreements, statements of work, and various other contractual agreements. It works across a range of file types, including Word documents, PDFs, and emails, primarily in English, with capabilities for contextual summary and keyword highlighting.

- **Bank statement classifier**: Capable of identifying financial documents that detail banking transactions, this classifier recognizes content like deposits, withdrawals, account balances, and bank charges within .docx, .pdf, .txt, and other document formats.

- **Budget classifier:** This classifier is adept at spotting budget-related documents, including forecasts and statements that encompass an organization's income and expenses. It operates across a wide array of file types, from text documents to spreadsheets and presentations, again in English and with summary and keyword highlighting features.

These built-in classifiers are part of MIP's arsenal for protecting personal information, providing organizations with a powerful way to automatically detect and manage critical data embedded in documents.

Safeguarding application data

Let us say there is a concern about an insider at a hospital who might be siphoning off patient data. EDM technology can be the superhero swooping in to save the day.

With EDM, the hospital can create an index of sensitive patient information, including details like Patient ID, Name, and Date of Birth, and securely store this index in the MIP system. When someone tries to send out an email containing this personal information, EDM compares the content of the email against the indexed data. If there is a match, the system flags it, preventing unauthorized sharing of sensitive data. This way, EDM acts as a vigilant watchdog, ensuring that patient data within the hospital's digital environment is not being misused or stolen, keeping the organization in line with the data protection standards set by the DPDP Act. Let us understand this with an example.

In a bustling city hospital, among endless files of patient records, lies sensitive data that must be shielded from thieves. Here, we will understand how MIP's EDM technology becomes useful in guarding personal details.

Picture a diligent IT specialist at the hospital configuring EDM. They meticulously index sensitive data, patient IDs, names, and birthdates, transforming them into a hashed code that is as indecipherable as an ancient language. This index becomes a secret map, a guide to what needs protection, as shown in the following figure:

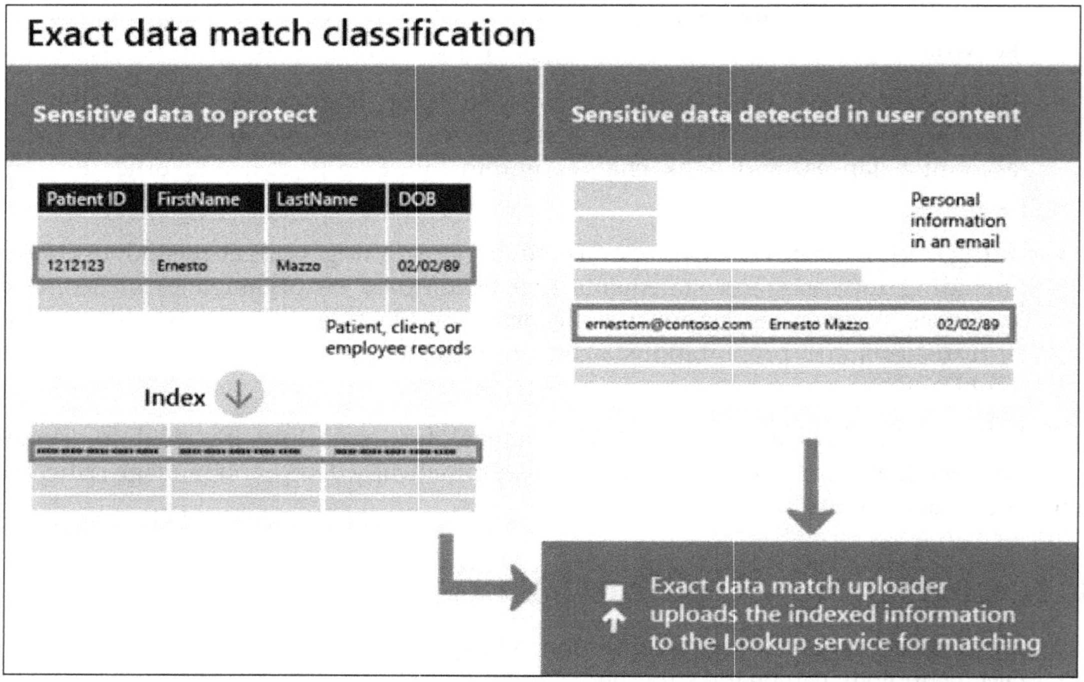

Exact data match classification

Sensitive data to protect	Sensitive data detected in user content

Patient ID	FirstName	LastName	DOB
1212123	Ernesto	Mazzo	02/02/89

Patient, client, or employee records

Personal information in an email

ernestom@contoso.com   Ernesto Mazzo   02/02/89

Index ↓

Exact data match uploader uploads the indexed information to the Lookup service for matching

Figure 2.13: Using EDM to protect application data

Assume an employee with ill intent attempts to send out an email with a patient's confidential information. As they hit send, EDM springs into action, comparing the email's content with the indexed data.

The system finds a match, and immediately, the email is stopped in its tracks, an alarm bell in the digital ether. Alerts are sent, and the potential personal data breach is thwarted, ensuring the patient's privacy remains intact. The hospital remains a trusted custodian of personal data, and EDM, the quiet hero, continues its vigilant watch. This is the new reality in the world of data protection, a narrative where advanced technology meets compliance, and where personal stories are kept safe, as they rightly should be.

You can start configuring your organization's EDM journey by visiting the EDM classifier tab on the same data classification service where you find SIT and trainable classifiers. The following figure showcases the steps you need to take, including identifying the structure database that has sensitive content, which needs to be protected:

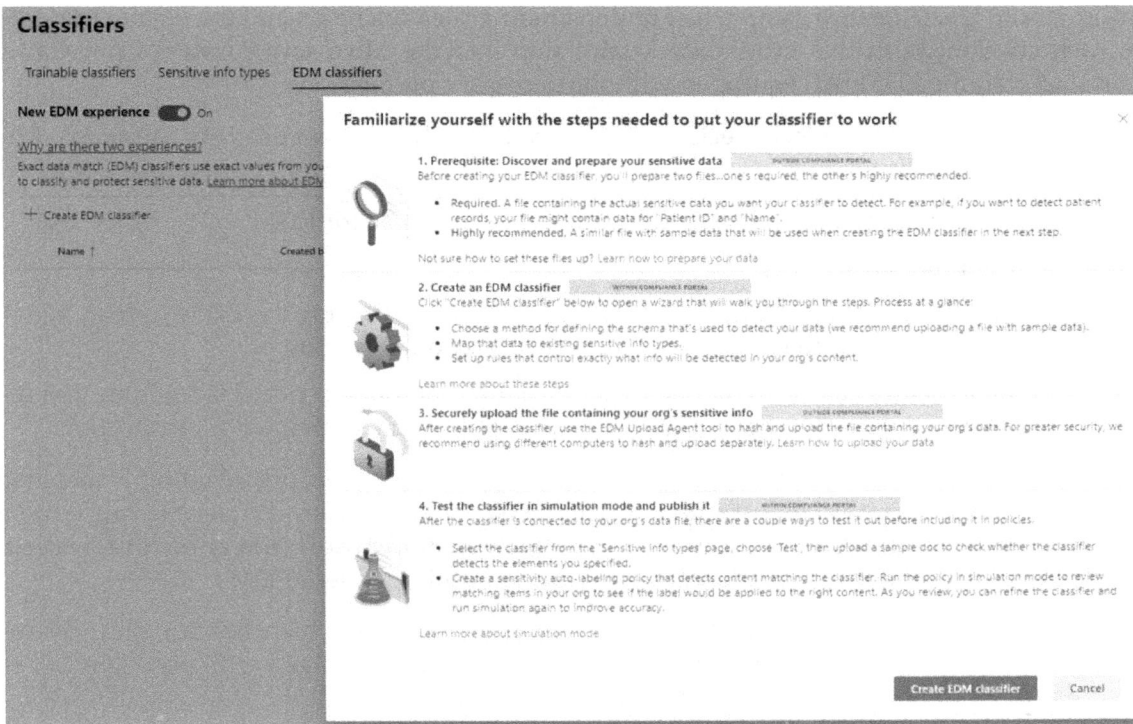

Figure 2.14: Use of EDM as a data classifier

The magic of EDM extends far beyond its prowess in DLP. This multi-phase marvel begins with the creation and deployment of an EDM-based SIT. Once brought to life, it serves as a chameleon in the vast ecosystem of Microsoft Purview, blending seamlessly into various roles.

In DLP, EDM is the vigilant guardian, watching over the flow of digital communication to ensure personal information remains within the safety of the organization's walls. However, its utility stretches further, lending its keen eye to the nuanced world of eDiscovery, where it aids in sifting through mountains of data to unearth the crucial pieces needed for legal investigations which again become critical when you exercise consent management tracking of the DPDP Act and when it comes to content governance, EDM shows its flexible nature, helping enforce retention policies that keep an organization's data lifecycle in check again very critical for DPDP Act in context of what personal information can you retain of Data Principal. It is not just about preventing data from slipping away. It is also about knowing when to hold on and when to let go, in compliance with regulatory mandates and organizational policies agreed upon in the compliance journey to the India DPDP Act.

Implementing EDM and looking into structured databases requires experience and is not a simple click configuration. To utilize EDM effectively, one embarks on a five-phase journey. First, export the source data you wish to match, ensuring you have read access to this personal information. Next, create a sample file, understanding the data fields and the format required in each column. With this groundwork laid, step into the Microsoft Purview Compliance portal to craft the EDM SIT, equipped with the necessary permissions.

In the fourth phase, technical precision is integrated with stringent security measures. The steps involved are as follows:

1. Hash and upload the personal information source table for EDM.

2. Form a custom security group if necessary.

3. Ensure local administrative access to a secure computer for the EDM upload agent, guaranteeing that the information is hashed without exposure.

4. Test the EDM SIT within the Microsoft Purview Compliance portal to validate that the EDM functions as intended and that your sensitive data is primed for protection.

This structured process ensures that the sensitive data within your organization is matched precisely, safeguarding it against unauthorized access and breaches. While one can write a complete book on EDM, the best is to visit **https://learn.microsoft.com/en-us/purview/sit-create-edm-sit-unified-ux-workflow** to learn how to best implement EDMs.

Thus, EDM emerges as a versatile tool, one that not only prevents breaches but also governs the lifespan of information, ensuring that data is retained and managed with precision and in accordance with the intricate dance of governance requirements.

Classification across structured data

As you navigate the world of structured data with classification services, you are stepping into the broader domain of Microsoft Purview, the compass of the data governance universe. Traditionally, they have had to weave a complex tapestry of solutions to shield their data estate, often encountering the steep costs of integrating disparate systems. Most customers have one vendor system for unstructured data and multiple other vendor systems for structured data and LOB applications. However, in the wise words of the digital age: *You cannot protect what you cannot see.* Microsoft Purview steps up as the beacon of visibility, offering a unified platform that simplifies the oversight of your data across a myriad of sources, including Microsoft Fabric, Azure, AWS, and beyond. We have already seen in the classification section how purview classification services as part of MIP can help you visualize your data estate and personal information present across the data estate across SharePoint, OneDrive, emails, and other collaboration locations.

This seamless experience extends beyond office experiences, enables connections to various data sources, and employs a single scanning and classification engine that ensures consistent labeling and access control policies are applied, regardless of where your data calls home. By scanning and classifying data, Microsoft Purview equips you with critical insights, empowering you to fortify your data security strategy with informed decisions.

Imagine having an eagle's eye view that not only spans the breadth of your data estate but also dives into the granular details of each file. That is the transformative capability Microsoft Purview brings to the table.

Yet, a common hurdle that organizations leap over is the disparity in how structured and unstructured data are protected. As our digital universe widens, this challenge magnifies, often due to differing enforcement policies such as data transitions from one system to another or morphs to fit new environments. Microsoft 365's sensitivity labels, once confined to documents and emails, are now set to extend their reach into the realm of structured data. Azure SQL, Azure Data Lake Storage, and Amazon S3 buckets are prepared to be enveloped in these comprehensive protection policies, as shown in the following figure:

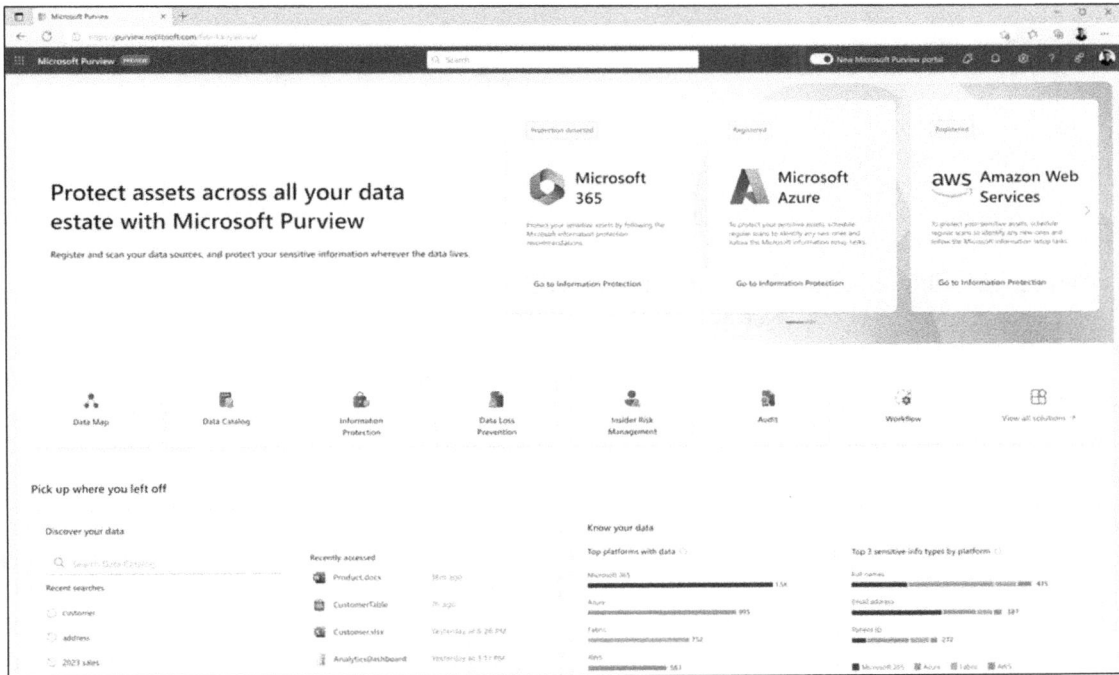

Figure 2.15: Singular view into your complete data estate

For instance, tailored label-based protection policies allow you to dictate the scope of data sources, databases, or storage buckets, and specify who gets to peek inside the data labeled with a certain degree of sensitivity. Microsoft Purview automatically swings into action, denying unauthorized eyes from gazing upon sensitive data, irrespective of the data's shape or dwelling place. It is a game of access: if someone outside the privileged circle attempts to access a table or file marked *Confidential,* they find their path blocked.

For more information, you can visit: **https://techcommunity.microsoft.com/t5/security-compliance-and-identity/protect-your-entire-data-estate-with-microsoft-purview/ba-p/3978758.**

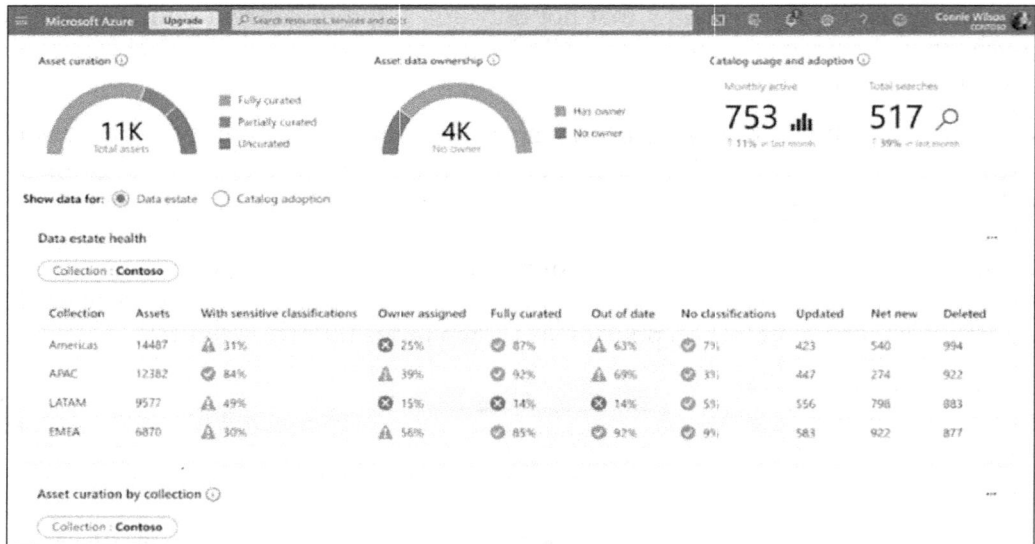

Figure 2.16: Single pane view across cloud assets

A single pane view, as shown in the figure above, across your structured database, gives you a perspective of your sensitive data. It is like being in the control tower, overseeing the entire landscape of your data management operations.

From this vantage point, you can monitor the vital signs of your hybrid data estate, keeping an eye on the pulse of your data's health metrics. Visualize the entirety of your data realm, appreciating its vastness as you categorize assets by their source, classification, and size.

Stay updated with the latest on your data scanning operations, celebrate the successes, investigate the failures, and note the cancellations. These insights are not just about numbers; they guide you in refining your data glossary, enhancing search efficiency, and ensuring that your sensitive data does not just exist but thrives under your vigilant gaze. As we stretch the canvas of access controls, you are assured that your data wears a shield of security, transitioning seamlessly and safely from system to system, crafting an end-to-end protection narrative that is in line with the DPDP Act's vision for a secure data ecosystem.

Data protection steps

As organizations begin to map and classify their data using tools like Microsoft Purview, a critical inflection point is reached: data protection through consent management. Under Section 6 of the Digital Personal Data Protection Act, 2023, a Data Fiduciary must obtain free, specific, informed, and unambiguous consent from the Data Principal before processing personal data, unless the processing falls under legitimate uses defined in Section 7. Consent must be based on a clear notice (as detailed in Rule 3 of the Draft Rules) and must be as easy to withdraw as it is to give, ensuring fairness and autonomy.

This underscores that consent is not just a regulatory obligation, but the foundation of trust and lawful processing. Once data is classified, especially as personal or sensitive personal data, data fiduciaries must implement policies that ensure processing aligns strictly with the purpose for which consent was obtained, in accordance with Chapter II Section 8(2) of the Act and Rule 13 of the Draft Rules.

Furthermore, Consent Managers, defined in Chapter II Section 7(5) and governed under Rule 4 of the Draft Rules, should provide an interoperable platform through which individuals can manage their consent across services for Data Fiduciary, enabling transparency, auditability, and control.

As organizations scale their data protection programs, it becomes essential to integrate consent status into access controls, retention, and sharing policies, ensuring data is processed only when the legal basis is valid and user rights are respected. Every byte of personal data must be treated under the vigilant eye of the Data Principal, embodying the DPDP Act's principles of purpose limitation, data minimization, and user empowerment.

Conclusion

In this chapter, we looked into the crucial processes of data mapping and inventory for data fiduciaries under India's DPDP Act. Understanding the location and classification of data assets within an organization is fundamental to maintaining transparency, enhancing data governance, and ensuring compliance with regulatory requirements. Through effective data mapping, organizations can accurately identify, classify, and document their data, leading to improved data management, enhanced security, and better risk management.

Although this process offers significant benefits, it also presents challenges such as resource allocation and continuous maintenance. Employing advanced tools (EDM, Trainable classifiers, single-view services) and adhering to best practices can help data fiduciaries overcome these challenges and maintain an accurate, up-to-date data map. This fosters a culture of data accountability and protection, safeguarding personal data and ensuring adherence to the DPDP Act.

In the next chapter, we will look further into critical aspects of data protection, focusing on lawful data processing and consent management within the framework of the India DPDP Act. The discussion will begin with an examination of the lawful basis for data processing, helping organizations understand the specific legal grounds that justify the collection, use, and retention of personal data. This ensures that every data handling activity is grounded in legitimacy and aligned with regulatory expectations. We will also explore practical strategies for obtaining and managing consent from Data Principals, emphasizing the importance of clear, informed, and purpose-specific consent across the data lifecycle. These topics form the foundation of a strong data protection framework, one that not only meets legal requirements but also upholds the rights and autonomy of individuals. By understanding these obligations, organizations can manage data responsibly and ensure ongoing compliance with the Digital Personal Data Protection Act, 2023.

Join our Discord space

Join our Discord workspace for latest updates, offers, tech happenings around the world, new releases, and sessions with the authors:

CHAPTER 3

Data Collection, Processing, and Consent

Introduction

Data is the cornerstone of modern business, driving everything from personalized customer experiences to targeted marketing strategies. It is collected through various interactions, whether online or offline, and processed to extract valuable insights.

This process of data collection and processing enables businesses to understand customer behavior, optimize operations, and stay competitive. However, the use of personal data comes with the responsibility to respect individual privacy, which is where consent plays a crucial role.

Consent ensures that individuals have control over how their personal data is used, allowing them to decide whether and how their data is processed. This balance between data utility and privacy is vital for maintaining trust in the digital economy.

As we explore these concepts further, we will look into the rights individuals have over their data, the legal frameworks governing data processing, and the tools that help ensure compliance and data protection, such as Microsoft Purview, Priva, and Consent Manager.

Structure

In this chapter, we will cover the following topics:

- Data, data collection, and role of consent
- Lawful basis for data processing
- Obtaining and managing consent
- DPDP law and its consent sections
- Procedures and obligations for Notice of Consent Violation
- Getting to know OneTrust
- TrustArc at a glance
- GoTrust simplified

Objectives

This chapter aims to equip readers with a comprehensive understanding of how personal data must be lawfully collected, processed, and managed in compliance with the Digital Personal Data Protection Act, 2023, and the Draft Rules, 2025. It explores the foundational role of consent in data processing, emphasizing its legal definition, types, and lifecycle under Section 6 of the Act and Rule 3 of the Draft Rules. The chapter also examines lawful bases for processing (Section 4), legitimate uses (Section 7), and special obligations when handling children's data (Section 9). Readers will learn how to operationalize these requirements using modern tools like Microsoft Purview, Priva, and leading consent Manager tools like Onetrust, Trustarc, Gotrust, enabling transparency, accountability, and automation in consent handling. By the end of the chapter, readers will be able to design compliant consent strategies, manage consent withdrawal, and honor Data Principal Rights, laying the groundwork for secure, ethical, and regulation-aligned data practices.

Data, data collection, and role of consent

In a small town, there was a bakery owned by Mr. Sharma, who carefully noted his customers' preferences, such as their favorite pastries or special occasions, ensuring personalized service and building trust. Can Mr. Sharma collect and process customer data to offer personalized preferences to his customers?

Consider another example of "ContosoGadgets," an online electronics store. ContosoGadgets collects browsing history and purchase data from customers like Amit, who frequently searches for the latest smartphones. By analyzing this data, ContosoGadgets can send Amit personalized offers and recommendations. Can ContosoGadgets send a personalized offer to Amit?

There was no such clarity until the government of India introduced the DPDP Act and its subsequent Draft Rules, which stated that it was mandatory for the business to obtain user consent. Under the DPDP Act, data processing must be conducted lawfully and transparently. Explicit consent from the Data Principal is required, as outlined in Chapter II Section (6) of the Act, and further elaborated in the notice given by Data Fiduciary to Data in Rule 3 of the Draft Rules, 2025. Consent must be clear, explicit, informed, freely given, and capable of easy withdrawal.

Before we look further into consent, let us look forward to some important concepts related to the DPDP Act and consent as a topic:

- **Data collection:** The gathering of personal data from individuals, explicitly disclosed in simple and clear terms.

    o **Example**: ContosoGadgets collects Amit's browsing data and purchase history.

- **Processing:** Any action performed on collected data, such as analysis, storage, or communication, is clearly defined under Section 2(x) of the DPDP Act.

    o **Example:** ContosoGadgets' analysis of data to be delivered for personalized marketing messages and improve customer service.

- **Consent:** Explicit permission given by individuals (Data Principals), clearly informed about the use of their data, including the purpose, the type of data collected, and the means of consent withdrawal (Section 5 and 6, DPDP Act, and Rule 3 of Draft Rules 2025).

    o **Example:** ContosoGadgets, before processing, must have explicitly obtained Amit's consent, clearly specifying the data collected (i.e., personalized marketing messages), its intended use, and how Amit can withdraw the consent if desired, complying fully with the DPDP Act and its Draft Rules.

Strategic data collection and processing enable businesses, especially in dynamic markets like India, to deliver tailored services effectively. Customer mishandling data can severely impact customer trust and business reputation, highlighting the critical importance of compliance with laws such as the DPDP Act, ensuring responsible data management, and maintaining consumer trust.

Organizations can leverage tools like Microsoft Purview, Priva, and Consent Managers, which assist in maintaining compliance with the DPDP Act by enabling transparency, facilitating clear consent management, and providing robust data protection frameworks.

Lawful basis for data processing

In data protection, the concept of a lawful basis for data processing involves having a legitimate, legally approved reason to process someone's personal data. It provides the legal justification necessary for organizations to process personal data under regulations such as India's Digital Personal Data Protection Act, 2023 (DPDP Act, 2023).

Let us understand this with a case study: The Case of Ananya and CONTOSO Bank.

In the city of Mumbai, Ananya visits "CONTOSO Bank" to open a new bank account. During the process, Mr. Sharma, the bank manager, requests specific personal data, including Ananya's name, address, PAN number, and phone number.

Ananya inquires, "Why do you need all this information?"

Mr. Sharma explains, "Our operations comply with strict privacy regulations under the DPDP Act. Section 4 of the Act mandates explicit, lawful reasons for processing personal data. Your address helps us verify your identity, complying with **know your customer (KYC)** norms. Your PAN number is crucial for accurate financial records and compliance with tax regulations, and your phone number is needed for secure communication regarding account activities and transaction verification. Mr Sharma also shared that some data is mandatory for a bank to even open an account, like an Aadhar number for identity verification and PAN as per **Reserve Bank of India (RBI)** KYC norms. Personal data like mobile number is also mandatory to enable the transactions and the consent to send her an offer over her mobile number."

Understanding the clearly defined purposes, Ananya confidently provides her consent, reassured by Mr. Sharma's transparent explanation.

Alignment with DPDP Act, 2023: This practical scenario aligns clearly with Chapter II (Sections 4, 5, and 6) of the DPDP Act, 2023. The bank explicitly communicated lawful and specific reasons for collecting Ananya's data, reflecting the principles of transparency, legality, and accountability emphasized by the Act.

Additionally, CONTOSO Bank's practices comply with the Draft Rules, 2025, specifically Rule 3, mandating clear, detailed, and independent consent notices about the data collected, its intended purposes, mechanisms for consent withdrawal, and providing contact details of the **Data Protection Officer (DPO)**.

Sample consent form

In alignment with the requirements of the Digital Personal Data Protection Act, 2023, organizations must present clear and accessible consent forms to inform individuals, referred to as Data Principals, about the collection, use, and processing of their personal data. These forms serve as a foundational element of consent management, enabling transparency and empowering individuals to make informed choices. The following example illustrates how such a consent form may be designed and presented in a user-facing digital environment.

This form is intended to inform you, the Data Principals, about the collection and use of your personal data by [Organization Name] in compliance with the Digital Personal Data Protection Act, 2023. Your privacy is important to us, and we are committed to ensuring transparency, fairness, and accountability in how your data is handled.

The following figures showcase sample consent interfaces in multiple languages and formats, illustrating how organizations can present cookie and data usage options in compliance with the DPDP Act, 2023. These examples reflect best practices in user interface design, enabling Data Principals to exercise meaningful control over their personal data through clear, accessible, and customizable consent preferences.

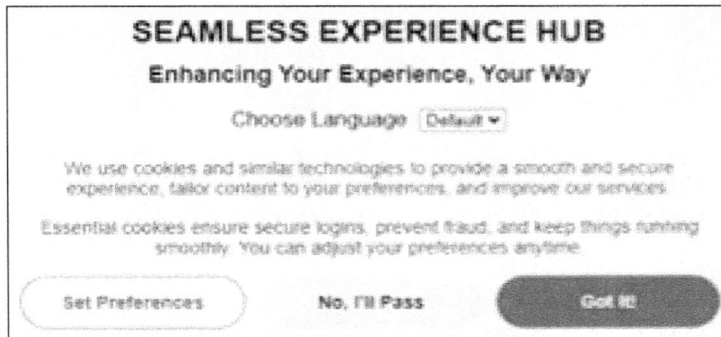

Figure 3.1: *Initial consent prompt with basic options*

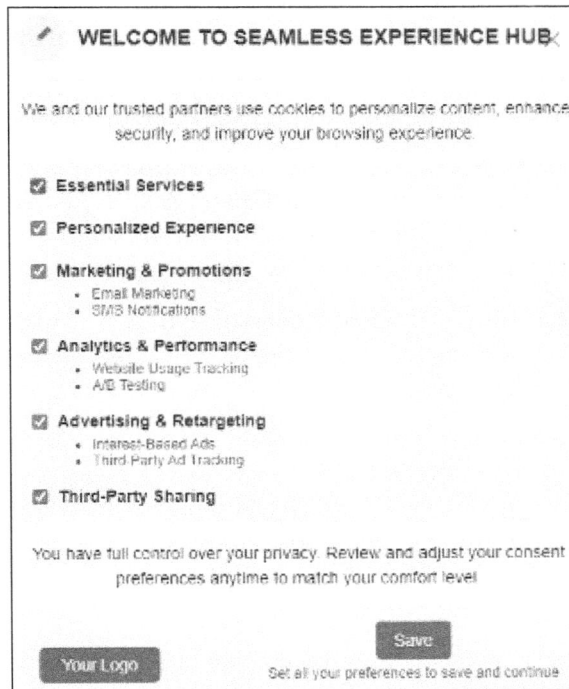

Figure 3.2: *Sample consent form in English*

The key takeaways are as follows:

- **Lawful processing:** Explicit lawful reasons must justify data processing, clearly communicated and documented in compliance with Chapter II, Section 4 of the DPDP Act, 2023.

- **Consent:** Explicit, informed consent is required under Chapter II, Section 6 of the DPDP Act, ensuring transparency in communicating the specific use and purpose of data collection.

- **Transparency and accountability:** Organizations must clearly and transparently communicate the purposes of data collection and processing, aligning fully with DPDP Act provisions.

To summarize, this case of Ananya illustrates the practical applications of the principles outlined in Chapter II, Section 4 of the DPDP Act, 2023, highlighting the importance of lawful data processing in everyday interactions between consumers and businesses in India. Now that we understand the role of consent to process data, let us take a deeper look into the consent world.

Obtaining and managing consent

Obtaining and managing consent involves clearly requesting, receiving, and documenting an individual's explicit permission to collect, use, or share their personal data. According to Section 6 of India's DPDP Act, 2003, this process must be clear, explicit, informed, freely given, and capable of easy withdrawal.

Let us explore different types of consent and then associate them with the DPDP Act:

- **Explicit consent**: Let us say that your healthcare app is explicitly requesting permission to access medical records. Under the DPDP Act, explicit consent is required for processing personal data, clearly communicated through affirmative actions such as clicking a checkbox or agreeing explicitly.

- **Implied consent:** Consent inferred from the user's actions or behavior, such as continued website use after cookie notification. Suitable for lower-risk data processing activities like processing your airline tickets on the travel portal.

- **Withdraw of consent**: Users must be able to withdraw consent easily at any time, just as easily as it was provided. For example, a clear unsubscribe link in emails complies with Section 6 of the DPDP Act. As the Act clearly calls out to companies to provide each type of digital consent to ensure clear communication about what data is collected, how it will be used, and how consent can be withdrawn, companies must comply with the DPDP Act.

Broadly, as per the DPDP Act, organizations must ensure the consent process is straightforward, transparent, and compliant by:

- Clearly communicating what data is being collected and how it will be used.

- Using simple language across multiple Indian languages to ensure user understanding.

- Maintaining clear, detailed consent records, including the method and time of consent.

- Ensuring mechanisms are in place for easy consent withdrawal, aligning with DPDP Act requirements.

Effective management of consent is fundamental for compliance with data protection laws, protecting user rights, and maintaining trust between businesses and Data Principals. We will look into each part of consent in the context of the Act.

Types of consents

In the digital world, consent takes on various forms to address the unique challenges and contexts of online interactions, data collection, and privacy concerns. Here are several notable types of digital consent:

- **Cookie consent**: Specifically relates to the use of cookies on websites. Users must consent to their personal data being tracked and stored.

- **Terms and conditions consent**: When users sign up for digital services or products, they often agree to the service's terms and conditions. This form of consent is usually required to use the service.

- **Data processing consent**: In contexts where personal data is collected and processed, users must give consent for how their data is used. This is especially important under regulations like the India DPDP Act 2023. Explicitly required under Section 6 of the DPDP Act, clearly stating the purpose of data usage.

- **App permissions consent**: When installing or using apps, users are often asked to give consent for the app to access certain features or data on their device, such as contacts, cameras, or location services.

- **Age verification consent:** Certain websites require users to verify their age before accessing content. This is particularly common for content that is not suitable for minors.

- **Subscription consent**: For email newsletters and other subscription-based services, users must consent to receive ongoing communications.

- **Biometric consent**: For technologies that use biometric data (like facial recognition or fingerprint scanning), consent is needed to collect and use such sensitive information.

- **Research consent:** In online research involving human subjects, digital consent is obtained to ensure participants are informed about the nature of the research and agree to participate.

Each of these types of digital consent has evolved to address the specific needs and challenges of the digital environment, ensuring that users' rights and privacy are protected while enabling the functionality and benefits of digital services.

In the *banking sector*, digital consent takes on specific forms tailored to the needs of financial services, security requirements, and regulatory compliance. Here are some key types of digital consent relevant to banks:

- **Online account opening consent**: When customers open accounts online, they provide consent to the bank's terms and conditions, privacy policy, credit checks, and identity verification processes.

- **Transaction consent**: For online banking transactions, such as transfers or payments, customers must give explicit consent for each transaction, often verified through secure methods like **one-time passwords (OTP)** or biometric verification.

- **Data sharing consent**: Banks may request consent to share a customer's financial data with third parties for purposes like credit scoring, fraud prevention, or offering personalized financial products.

- **E-statement and E-document consent**: Customers often consent to receive electronic statements and documents instead of paper versions. This can include account statements, tax documents, and notifications.

- **Mobile banking app consent**: When using mobile banking apps, customers consent to various permissions like access to device features (camera for check deposit, GPS for branch locations) and agree to the app's terms of use.

- **Marketing and communication consent**: Banks ask for consent to send marketing materials or communications about new products, services, or changes to existing ones.

- **Biometric transaction consent**: For banks using biometric authentication (like fingerprints or facial recognition), explicit consent is needed for collecting and using such sensitive data. Most banks today are using biometrics to open banking applications on mobile; at times, they are reusing phone OEM/device biometric consent or taking explicit consent. It is advisable to obtain explicit consent to sufficiently comply with privacy regulations.

These types of consent are integral to maintaining the customer's trust, ensuring compliance with financial regulations, and protecting both the bank and its customers from fraud and personal data breaches. Digital consent in banking is also continually evolving with advancements in technology and changes in regulatory landscapes.

DPDP law and its consent sections

As we advance further into our exploration, we will examine the pivotal elements explicitly outlined in Chapter II of the DPDP Act, 2023, Obligations of Data Fiduciary.

Our discussion will include an in-depth analysis of Chapter II, Section 4 of the DPDP Act, which covers the lawful grounds for processing personal data, examining foundational legal justifications that permit data processing under specific conditions. We will further explore Section 6, which emphasizes the critical aspects of notices and explicit consent, ensuring that Data Principals are transparently informed and willingly consent to data processing activities.

Additionally, we will explore Chapter II, Section 7, regarding certain legitimate uses, highlighting scenarios where data processing aligns explicitly with legal and ethical standards without explicit consent in specified situations. A thorough examination of the general obligations under Chapter II, Section 8 will detail the responsibilities that data fiduciaries must fulfill, ensuring accountability and compliance with the DPDP Act.

We will also cover Chapter II Section 9, addressing the specific obligations and care required when processing personal data relating to children, reflecting the heightened sensitivity in such scenarios. Lastly, Chapter III Section 11, outlining the right to access information, will provide clarity on Data Principals' entitlements concerning their personal data.

Through these structured discussions, we aim to offer a comprehensive understanding of the DPDP Act's legal framework, enhancing clarity and supporting effective compliance with data protection obligations.

Grounds for processing personal data

In data protection, understanding the lawful basis for data processing is crucial, as mandated by the DPDP Act, 2023. The Act requires organizations to have explicit, legally justified reasons for collecting, processing, and managing personal data.

To illustrate, let us revisit the case of Ananya and CONTOSO Bank:

When Ananya visited CONTOSO Bank to open an account, the bank explicitly requested her consent to process her personal data. This explicit consent was especially crucial if the bank intended to offer additional services such as credit cards or insurance products, clearly mandated under Section 6 of the DPDP Act.

The DPDP Act, specifically under Chapter II of the Act, which requires CONTOSO Bank to transparently inform Ananya about the exact purposes her personal data, such as email, phone number, birth year, and address, would serve. This might include internal analytics or data sharing across the bank's various divisions, such as credit cards, insurance, and wealth management. Importantly, consent must also clearly extend to data management by any subcontractors the bank employs, holding them equally responsible for preventing unauthorized access, leakage, or loss of data.

Additionally, as per the Act, Chapter II, Section 5, sub-section (3): *The Data Fiduciary shall give the Data Principals the option to access the contents of the notice referred to in sub-sections (1) and (2) in English or any language specified in the Eighth Schedule to the Constitution.*

Thus, the narrative constructed around consent in the DPDP Act is clear, responsible, and emphasizes stringent protection, laying a strong foundation for the next discussion on Data Security Measures.

Act mapping

The following table provides a clear overview of the specific chapters and articles within the India DPDP Act 2023 that govern consent management. This will help understanding these provisions is crucial for ensuring compliance with the legal requirements surrounding the obtaining, managing, and withdrawing of consent in data processing activities. These sections form the legal backbone for how organizations must lawfully manage consent, highlighting both the obligations placed on data fiduciaries and the rights granted to Data Principals.

Chapter	Section	Definition Name	Narration of DPDP Act 2023	Solution Mapping	Draft Rules Mapping, 2025
2	4	Obligations of Data Fiduciary	For which the Data Principals has given her consent	So, Ananya needs to open Bank account, so bank needs the details. As a data principle for her to be able to open a bank account open, she will have to give her consent. Should the bank take consent for selling her credit card, insurance is what this Act focuses on for explicit consent, the Act also expects banks to spell out how will they use Ananya PII data (email, phone, birth year, where she lives) to derive what type of analytics if any.	Rule 3 - Clear and detailed consent notices.
2	4	Obligations of Data Fiduciary	For certain legitimate uses	This aspect is important, where in the consent solution should not just take consent but also share with the Data Principal, how the Data Fiduciary plans to use the data. This includes any AI service getting trained on data, including sharing data with other business units like credit cards, insurance, and wealth management division. The consents given should also be maintained by any sub-contractor of bank including need to protect the data from unauthorized access, data leakages, data loss or unauthorized data exfiltration from the bank or its sub-contractors.	Rule 6 - Reasonable security safeguards.
2	4	Obligations of Data Fiduciary	For the purposes of this section, the expression "lawful purpose" means any purpose which is not expressly forbidden by law.		Rule 9 - Publishing Data Protection Officer contact details clearly for queries.

Table 3.1: Quick view into DPDP Act 2023 and Draft Rules,2025

Procedures and obligations for Notice of Consent Violation

Let us now take our journey to what happens after the consent is taken. Let us look again into the case of Ananya, where she recently opened an account with the CONTOSO Bank, giving her consent.

The bank, acting as the Data Fiduciary, must provide notices explicitly outlining data usage, withdrawal mechanisms, and grievance redressal channels, as stipulated in Section 5 of the DPDP Act and Rule 3 of the Draft Rules, 2025. These notices must be issued to Ananya from time to time, especially when there is a change in processing purposes, data sharing practices, or cross-border data transfers.

These notices are not merely formalities; they are an essential part of the data processing ecosystem. They create a transparent communication pathway between the Data Fiduciary and the Data Principals, giving the latter clarity and control over how their personal data is being handled. The law mandates that the Data Principals be kept fully informed throughout the lifecycle of data processing, not just at the time of consent.

One of the key aspects under the DPDP framework is that continued processing of data, especially when consent was obtained before the Act came into force, is subject to a new standard of accountability. The Act allows such processing to continue only until the Data Principals, like Ananya, decide to withdraw their consent. This safeguards individual autonomy and ensures that legacy consents are not misused indefinitely under the guise of compliance.

Furthermore, linguistic accessibility is a cornerstone of this obligation. Notices must be provided not just in English, but also in any of the languages listed in the Eighth Schedule of the Indian Constitution. This ensures that individuals can read and understand their rights and obligations in a language they are comfortable with, reinforcing inclusivity in digital governance. Whether the notice is served via physical forms, digital platforms, banking apps, or email communications, the intent must be clarity and comprehension.

In digital settings, notice mechanisms must be embedded into the user interface, such as prompts, checkboxes, dropdowns for preferred languages, or pop-ups that explain policy updates. For instance, if CONTOSO Bank changes its data sharing policy with third-party financial service providers, Ananya should receive a real-time notice through the app or email, and the interface should allow her to accept, decline, or modify her preferences.

The consequences of failing to provide proper notice are not trivial. Under the DPDP Act, such violations may trigger penalties, especially if the Data Fiduciary continues data processing without renewed consent after policy changes. It is considered a Consent Violation if data is processed without appropriately informing the Data Principals or without enabling an opportunity to withdraw consent after changes to processing conditions.

Moreover, the **Data Protection Board of India (DPBI)** may initiate an inquiry upon receipt of a grievance or on its own, where procedural lapses in issuing or recording notices are found. As a result, organizations are encouraged to maintain detailed records of notices served, consent withdrawal logs, and delivery acknowledgements, all of which support defensibility during audits and investigations.

In sum, notice mechanisms are not a one-time compliance checkbox. They are ongoing obligations that reflect an organization's commitment to transparency, user empowerment, and lawful processing. For individuals like Ananya, this means not only being in control of their data decisions but also having access to clear channels to revoke or modify those decisions over time. For organizations, it demands robust notice management systems, multilingual accessibility, and audit-ready documentation, ensuring that consent is not just taken once but respected throughout the data lifecycle.

Consent clarification according to rules 2025

The DPDP Act mandates clear and accessible consent management. Personal data requests must be communicated simply and clearly in the Data Principal's preferred language, aligning with the Eighth Schedule of the Constitution. Consent notices must include DPO contact details as mandated by Draft Rule 9 (2025) for Significant Data Fiduciary.

The Digital Personal Data Protection Rules, 2025, consist of 22 rules that further clarify the Digital Personal Data Protection Act. These rules outline the responsibilities of Data Fiduciaries and detail the procedures for obtaining consent, including using a registered consent provider known as a Consent Manager.

Rule 3: Consent through Clear Notice:

Consent obtained from a Data Principal is considered valid only when the Data Fiduciary provides a clear, specific, and separate notice. This notice must:

- Clearly specify each type of personal data being collected.
- Explicitly describe the purpose for processing each data type and explain the goods or services that will be provided as a result.
- Offer an accessible communication link or method for the Data Principals to:
  - Easily withdraw consent, matching the simplicity of giving consent.
  - Exercise their rights related to personal data.
  - Lodge complaints with the Data Protection Board.

Rule 9: Facilitating Consent-Related Queries:

Data Fiduciaries must prominently display contact information for the DPO or another designated responsible person on their website as applicable. This ensures that Data Principals can conveniently:

- Ask questions about their given consent, the purposes for data processing, or other aspects of data handling.

- Clarify doubts or easily modify or withdraw their consent.

Rule 10: Verifiable Consent for Sensitive Groups (Children and Persons with Disabilities):

Special consent guidelines are mandated for processing the personal data of sensitive groups, specifically:

- Children (individuals under 18 years).
- A person with disabilities who has a legally appointed guardian.

Data Fiduciaries must adopt rigorous technical and organizational procedures to verify that consent is genuinely given by a parent or lawful guardian. This verification process includes:

- Confirming identity and age through:
  - o Official government-issued identity documents.
  - o Digital Locker services or government-authorized virtual tokens.

The Act explicitly grants the right to withdraw consent to be as straightforward as its provision. Upon consent withdrawal, banks must promptly cease data processing unless legally required otherwise. A Consent Manager, responsible for transparent consent handling and duly registered with the board (Rule 4 of Draft Rules, 2025), is available to manage consent on behalf of Data Principals.

Furthermore, customers have the option to manage their consent via a Consent Manager role that carries the weight of accountability and action on their behalf as defined by the Act. This Consent Manager must not only operate transparently but also be registered with the board, meeting stringent operational and financial criteria.

The Act weaves a safety net around customer data, giving them the reins to their personal data while ensuring that the bank and its processors respect their choices, providing a benchmark for consent management that aligns with the highest standards of data protection.

Act mapping

The DPDP Act mandates explicit and clearly communicated consent, requiring notices to be accessible in the Data Principal's preferred language per the Eighth Schedule. Consent withdrawal must be as straightforward as the consent provision, with banks obligated to immediately halt processing upon withdrawal. A registered Consent Manager, operating transparently under stringent criteria, is essential. Compliance includes detailing DPO contact (as applicable) information (Draft Rule 9, 2025), ensuring transparency and accountability. These provisions establish robust standards for managing consent under the DPDP Act and its Draft Rules.

The following table outlines the key consent-related provisions under Section 6 of *Chapter 2, Evolving Data Landscape in Enterprises* of the DPDP Act. It provides a comprehensive view of the legal requirements, corresponding technical or procedural solutions, and the specific rules from the Draft DPDP Rules that map to these consent obligations.

Chapter	Section	Definition Name	Narration of DPDP Act 2023	Solution Mapping	Draft Rules Mapping, 2025
2	6	Consent	Data principals have the right to explicit and informed consent and straightforward withdrawal mechanisms. Consent requests must be clear, simple, and accessible in the Data Principal's preferred language as per the Eighth Schedule of the Constitution. Withdrawal of consent must be as easy as giving consent, and processing must cease immediately upon withdrawal unless otherwise legally required.	Provide clear, specific, and easily accessible consent requests. Offer simple withdrawal procedures and enable management through registered Consent Managers. Consent notices must include details of the DPO for queries and concerns. Consent Managers must be transparently registered and meet defined operational and financial criteria.	Rule 3 – Consent through Clear Notice; Rule 4 – Registration and Obligations of Consent Managers; Rule 9 – Facilitating Consent-Related Queries; Rule 10 – Verifiable Consent for Sensitive Groups (Children and Persons with Disabilities).

Table 3.2: Quick view into DPDP Act 2023 and Draft Rules,2025

Certain legitimate uses

The DPDP Act delineates *certain legitimate uses* for which, upon providing their personal data to a Data Fiduciary, like a bank, for opening an account, a user or Data Principal inherently consents to the use of data for clearly specified purposes. This legitimate use covers routine yet crucial operations such as the issuance of service-related documents or compliance with legal and regulatory requirements.

A customer's data could also be legitimately used by state agencies to facilitate government subsidies or services they are entitled to, ensuring their data serves them without unnecessary barriers. The Act ensures that if a customer's data needs to be disclosed to any state instrumentality, it will be done in strict adherence to the prevailing legal provisions on data disclosure. Furthermore, customers' data may be used in circumstances that necessitate legal compliance, such as court orders or judgments, both within and outside India, provided they pertain to contractual or civil matters. Importantly, the Act carves out provisions for emergencies, allowing their data to be used in life-threatening situations or to manage public health crises like epidemics, ensuring that their well-being, along with that of the public, is prioritized.

These provisions collectively uphold a balanced approach where their consent, the state's duty to provide services, and the imperative of public health and legal compliance coexist within the framework of the DPDP Act, fostering an ecosystem where personal data is not only protected but also effectively utilized for legitimate and potentially lifesaving purposes.

Exemptions under Rule 11 and the Fourth Schedule (Rules, 2025)

According to the Digital Personal Data Protection Rules, 2025, Rule 11 provides specific exemptions from standard consent procedures as detailed in the Fourth Schedule. The Fourth Schedule specifies certain conditions and classes of Data Fiduciaries exempted from standard consent requirements, particularly focusing on the personal data of children.

Fourth Schedule Summary (Rule 11 Exemptions):

The Fourth Schedule outlines exemptions for specific classes of Data Fiduciaries, including:

- **Clinical establishments, mental health establishments, healthcare professionals:** Data processing restricted to necessary healthcare services.

- **Allied healthcare professionals:** Data processing limited to healthcare treatment and referral plans.

- **Educational institutions:** Data processing confined to educational activities or ensuring children's safety.

- **Child day-care providers:** Data processing restricted to safety and monitoring of children.

- **Transportation providers contracted by educational institutions:** Data processing limited to tracking child safety during transportation.

Examples:

- A school may track student attendance and behavioral data for educational or safety reasons without obtaining explicit consent for each activity.

- A healthcare provider may process patient data for delivering essential medical treatment without needing repeated explicit consent for routine care.

Act mapping

The DPDP Act recognizes implicit consent for specific legitimate purposes, such as service provision, regulatory compliance, and facilitating state-provided benefits. It ensures data disclosure to state entities or compliance with legal orders (including international judicial processes) and adheres strictly to lawful standards. Additionally, it permits data processing during emergencies like public health crises, safeguarding individual and public welfare. Draft Rules (Rule 6, 2025) reinforce these uses through mandated security safeguards. Collectively, these provisions balance data utility with stringent privacy protections.

The following table summarizes provisions under Section 7 of the DPDP Act, highlighting scenarios where data can be processed without explicit consent for legitimate purposes. It also maps the corresponding safeguards and exemptions outlined in the Draft Rules.

Chapter	Section	Definition Name	Narration of DPDP Act, 2023	Solution Mapping	Draft Rules Mapping, 2025
2	7	Certain Legitimate Uses	The DPDP Act allows implicit consent for specific legitimate purposes, including service provision, regulatory compliance, state-provided benefits, and emergency scenarios. It mandates strict adherence to legal standards when disclosing data to state entities or complying with court orders, including international judicial processes.	Clearly outline and justify data processing under lawful, regulatory, or emergency situations, ensuring compliance and individual/public welfare protection.	Rule 6 – Reasonable Security Safeguards; Rule 11 – Exemptions under Fourth Schedule

Table 3.3: Quick view into DPDP Act 2023 and Draft Rules,2025

General obligation of Data Fiduciary

Under the DPDP Act, the Data Fiduciary holds a position of great responsibility to open a new account. The bank must implement robust security measures to safeguard its personal data against any breach. This protective umbrella extends over all activities, including those executed by Data Processors on behalf of the Data Fiduciary.

The Act enshrines the customer's right to retract their consent and mandates the prompt erasure of their personal data when they do so, or if it is inferred that the original purpose for which the data was collected is no longer pertinent. Additionally, should the Data Fiduciary have engaged third parties for processing Ananya's data, it is incumbent upon them to ensure these entities also expeditiously delete her data in the event of her withdrawal of consent.

Particularly sensitive is the handling of data pertaining to children or individuals with disabilities. Here, the Data Fiduciary, our bank in this scenario, must obtain verifiable consent from a parent or lawful guardian before processing any of their personal data, navigating this process with utmost care and in accordance with prescribed methods. Such meticulous provisions aim to empower individuals like Ananya with control over their personal data while imposing on Data Fiduciaries the duty to respect and protect the Data Principals' autonomy and privacy.

Act mapping

In the field of consent management, the obligations of the Data Fiduciary are paramount. These responsibilities encompass ensuring that consent is obtained transparently, managed effectively, and can be easily withdrawn by the Data Principal. The following table looks into the specific duties imposed on Data Fiduciaries, emphasizing the need for rigorous compliance to maintain trust and adhere to legal standards:

Chapter	Section	Definition Name	Narration of DPDP Act,2023	Solution Mapping	Draft Rules Mapping, 2025
2	8	General Obligations of Data Fiduciary	A Data Fiduciary shall protect personal data in its possession or under its control, including in respect of any processing undertaken by it or on its behalf by a Data Processor, by taking reasonable security safeguards to prevent personal data breach.	Need the Data fiduciary implement SIT, extend SITs to include relevant sensitive information and have right policies like encryption, DLP offering reasonable security safeguards.	Rule 6 – Reasonable Security Safeguards
2	8	General Obligations of Data Fiduciary	Erase personal data, upon the Data Principals withdrawing her consent or as soon as it is reasonable to assume that the specified purpose is no longer being served, whichever is earlier.	If Ananya comes back to the bank after opening an account and withdraws her consent, then the bank must at a reasonable time delete all our personal data that is not required. The bank must also stop processing her data, including any sharing with any other division for which consent was obtained. If Bank has any vendor, who received the data from the bank for processing including calling Ananya, bank must also ensure that the vendor or sub processor has also deleted the data and will not process it.	
2	8	General Obligations of Data Fiduciary	Cause its Data Processor to erase any personal data that was made available by the Data Fiduciary for processing to such Data Processor.		

Table 3.4: Quick view into DPDP Act 2023 and Draft Rules,2025

Children's data and consent

Under the DPDP Act, the careful protection of children's personal data is a matter of utmost priority. Suppose Ananya visits the bank not for herself, but to open an account for her young son, Roshan. In this case, the bank, as the Data Fiduciary, is mandated to obtain verifiable consent from Ananya, the lawful guardian, before any of Roshan's personal data is processed. This consent must be acquired in a manner that is clear, understandable, and officially prescribed, safeguarding the child's best interests.

The Act goes further to proscribe any processing of Roshan's data that might negatively impact his wellbeing, placing his safety and privacy at the forefront of the bank's data handling responsibilities. Moreover, stringent restrictions are placed against tracking or behaviorally monitoring Roshan's online activities or subjecting him to targeted advertising. These stipulations reflect the Act's proactive stance on nurturing a safe digital environment for children like Roshan, ensuring that their data is used responsibly, without exploiting their vulnerability or infringing upon their rights.

Act mapping

When it comes to vulnerable groups such as children and especially abled individuals, the Act imposes heightened obligations on Data Fiduciaries to ensure their consent is informed, voluntary, and adequately protected. The following table outlines these special provisions, emphasizing the additional safeguards required to uphold their rights:

Chapter	Section	Definition name	Narration of DPDP Act,2023	Solution mapping	Draft Rules Mapping, 2025
2	9	Processing of personal Data of Children	The Data Fiduciary shall, before processing any personal data of a child or a person with a disability who has a lawful guardian obtain verifiable consent of the parent of such child or the lawful guardian in such manner as may be prescribed.	In this case, if bank is opening an account for minor child. Then it is critical that it has this meta data that the Data Principal is child, and consent must be taken from lawful guardian. Also, the law expects that processing of any data that is detrimental to the wellbeing of child cannot be done regardless of consent. law calls out behavior monitoring for target advertising as an example of such processing.	Rule 10 – Verification of Parental Consent
2	9	Processing of personal Data of Children	A Data Fiduciary shall not undertake such processing of personal data that is likely to cause any detrimental effect on the well-being of a child.		
2	9	Processing of personal Data of Children	A Data Fiduciary shall not undertake tracking or behavioral monitoring of children or targeted advertising directed at children.		

Table 3.5: Quick view into DPDP Act 2023 and Draft Rules,2025

Right to access information about personal data

In accordance with the DPDP Act, Ananya, after providing her consent for her personal data to be processed by her bank, retains the right to access information about how her data is being used. She can request details about all other entities, Data Fiduciaries, or Data Processors, with whom her bank has shared her personal data, ensuring transparency in the handling of her data. This includes a detailed description of what specific personal data has been shared, serving as a protective measure against unauthorized use. Furthermore, the Act empowers Ananya with the ability to appoint a nominee who can manage her rights over her personal data in case she becomes unable to do so herself due to any form of incapacity. This safeguard provides Ananya with peace of mind, knowing that her rights to her personal data will be upheld, even if she is not able to personally oversee this due to health reasons or other incapacities. It is a commitment to the continuity of data protection, irrespective of life's uncertainties.

The rule references are:

- **Rule 3(c):** Provision of an easy-access link to manage consent, including changes or withdrawal.
- **Rule 9**: Clear and prominent display of contact information for the DPO or designated responsible person.

Act mapping

Data principals are empowered with the right to review and manage their consent at any time. The Act ensures that individuals can easily access a record of the consents they have granted, providing them with control over their personal data. The following table explains these provisions, highlighting how Data Principals can stay informed about and manage the consent they have given, reinforcing their autonomy in the data processing relationship:

Chapter	Section	Definition name	Narration of DPDP Act ,2023	Solution mapping	Draft Rules Mapping, 2025
3	11	Right to access information about personal data	The Data Principals shall have the right to obtain from the Data Fiduciary to whom she has previously given consent, including consent as referred to in clause (a) of section 7 (hereinafter referred to as the said Data Fiduciary), for processing of personal data, upon making to it a request in such manner as may be prescribed.	Bank, while using Ananya personal data for processing, is also expected to share with her what data was shared or processes.	
3	11	Right to access information about personal data	The identities of all other Data Fiduciaries and Data Processors with whom the personal data has been shared by such Data Fiduciary, along with a description of the personal data so shared.		Rule 3(c) – Easy-access link to manage consent; Rule 9 – Clear contact information

Chapter	Section	Definition name	Narration of DPDP Act ,2023	Solution mapping	Draft Rules Mapping, 2025
3	14	Right to nominate	A Data Principals shall have the right to nominate, in such manner as may be prescribed, any other individual, who shall, in the event of death or incapacity of the Data Principals, exercise the rights of the Data Principals in accordance with the provisions of this Act and the rules made thereunder.	Need to have SIT pre-identified with Data lineage tracking.	Rule 7 – Nomination Procedure
3	-	Duties of Data Principal	For the purposes of this section, the expression "incapacity" means inability to exercise the rights of the Data Principals under the provisions of this Act or the rules made thereunder due to unsoundness of mind or infirmity of body.	Need to have agreements in place, recognized and possible visible with Trainable Classifiers.	

Table 3.6: Quick view into DPDP Act chapters and sections

Drawing from the provisions of the DPDP Act, Ananya's journey to open a bank account illustrates the nuanced requirements of consent and data processing. From the need for explicit consent to the right to withdraw consent, and from the obligation of banks to clarify the use of personal data to the protection of children's data, these scenarios underscore the comprehensive nature of the DPDP Act. It highlights the importance of transparent notices, the ease of managing consents, and the protective measures in place for the well-being of data principles, especially for the young and vulnerable.

Now, transitioning from these scenarios, we explore the capabilities of the Microsoft Purview Priva tool, designed to streamline and manage these very consent processes effectively. Priva offers an integrated solution to navigate the intricacies of consent management as mandated by the DPDP Act, ensuring organizations can maintain compliance with ease and reliability.

Consent management tools

As we have seen from the sections and rules above, the **consent manager** plays a key role in enabling Data Principals to give, manage, and withdraw consent in a standardized, transparent, and interoperable manner. These platforms ensure that consent is freely given, specific, informed, and capable of being withdrawn at any time, in line with DPDP's requirements.

Many consent management tools are available globally, with leading solutions like OneTrust, TrustArc, and GoTrust. Given the Make in India focus, indigenous solutions such as GoTrust are emerging as competitive alternatives.

Across these platforms, common DPDP-aligned capabilities include:

- **Centralized consent dashboards** for individuals to review and modify their consents.
- **Granular consent capture** tied to specific purposes of processing.
- **Audit trails** to document consent history for regulatory readiness.
- **Interoperability** to integrate with multiple data fiduciaries and service providers.
- **Real-time withdrawal mechanisms** ensure processing stops promptly when consent is revoked.

Let us look at some of the leading consent management platforms and uncover what they truly bring to the table, how they capture, manage, and transform the way organizations handle user choices and privacy.

Getting to know OneTrust

OneTrust is a leading privacy and consent management solution that helps organizations handle user permissions with transparency and compliance. Its Consent and Preference Management platform enables businesses to capture purpose-based consent, build first-party data trust, and maximize user opt-ins while adhering to global privacy laws. The OneTrust solution emphasizes user empowerment by giving individuals clear control over what data they share, how it is used, and who can access it.

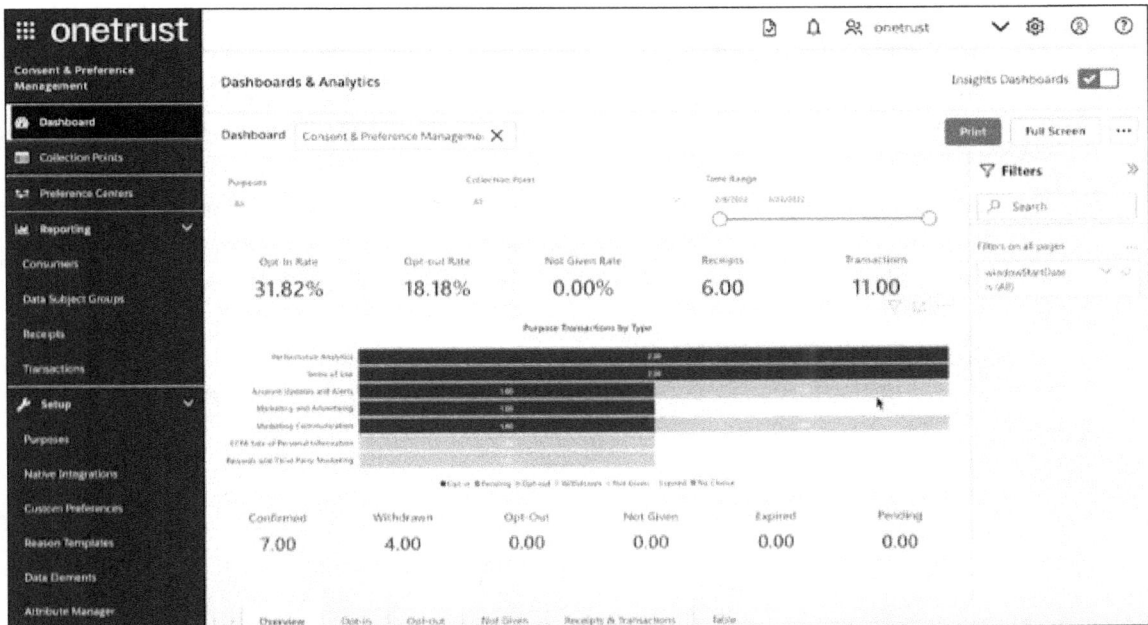

Figure 3.3: Onetrust solution dashboard

The key features and services are as follows:

- **Granular consent capture:** Gather specific consent for each purpose (e.g. marketing, analytics) so only relevant permissions are collected, aligning with privacy principles of purpose limitation.

- **Real-time consent synchronization:** Instantly update and propagate consent status across websites, apps, and connected systems. This ensures user choices are respected everywhere and reduces repetitive consent prompts.

- **Contextual consent prompts:** Trigger consent requests at the right moment in the user journey (such as during account signup or before data collection) to minimize fatigue and increase acceptance rates.

- **Audit-ready consent logs:** Maintain tamper-proof records of all consent actions (who consented, to what, when). OneTrust generates consent receipts and time-stamped logs, providing a verifiable audit trail for compliance.

- **Centralized preference center:** Provide users with a self-service portal to view and manage their consents and subscriptions. OneTrust's preference center allows granular opt-ins/opt-outs in one place, helping reduce full opt-outs by letting users tailor their experience.

- **Lifecycle management and versioning:** Track the entire lifecycle of consent from capture to withdrawal. Historical versions of consent forms and notices are retained and linked to each user's decision, ensuring transparency about what was agreed to.

- **Multilingual and geolocated experiences:** OneTrust supports consent interfaces in 100+ languages and adapts to regional laws. Pre-built templates (250+ languages) and geolocation rules ensure consent notices meet local requirements and accessibility standards.

- **Unified consent records:** Consolidate user consent across multiple channels and identities into a single profile. OneTrust unifies known and anonymous consent choices, giving organizations a 360° view of each user's preferences.

- **Seamless integrations:** Connect consent data with your tech stack. OneTrust offers APIs and pre-built integrations to sync consent signals with CRM systems, marketing platforms, tag managers, and more. This ensures downstream systems only process data with proper consent.

TrustArc at a glance

TrustArc (formerly TRUSTe) is a well-established privacy compliance technology company that helps organizations manage their data privacy obligations through software and services tailored for modern regulatory environments. Its Consent and Preference Manager is a centralized and scalable platform designed to capture, synchronize, and manage user consents and preferences across brands, digital touchpoints, and marketing ecosystems.

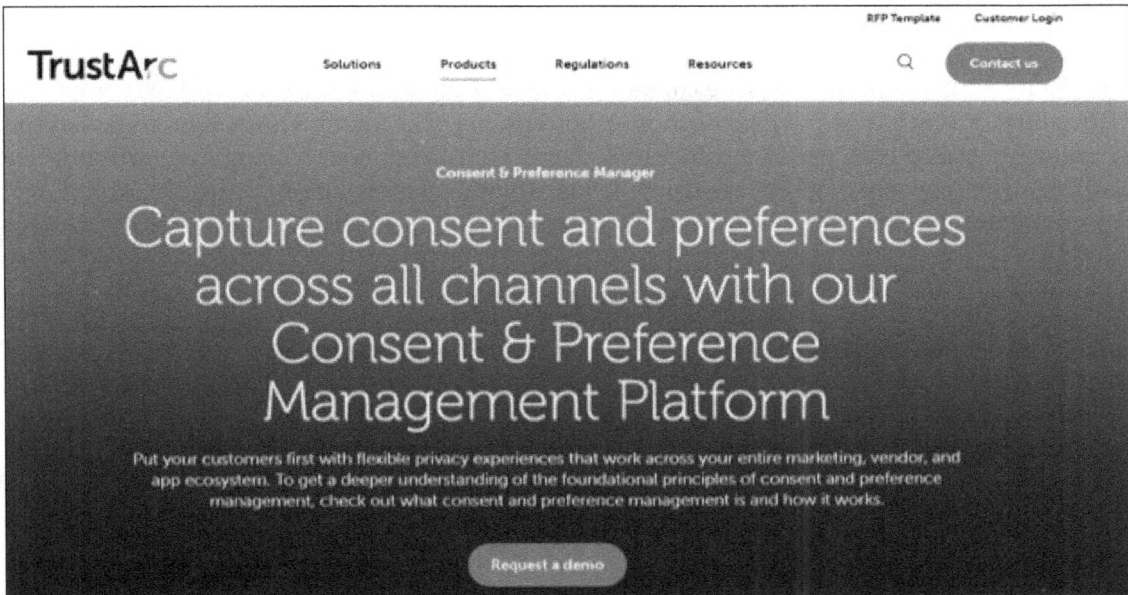

Figure 3.4: *TrustArc Consent and Preference management*

The key features of TrustArc Consent Management are as follows:

- **Centralized consent orchestration**: Consolidates user preferences from websites, apps, third-party vendors, and marketing tools into a unified control hub.

- **Real-time consent sync**: Automatically collects, syncs, and tracks consent and preference data across channels, enabling compliant processing across systems.

- **Automated updates and compliance mapping**: Continuously aligns with evolving global privacy laws (e.g., GDPR, CCPA, LGPD), using automation and behavioral analytics to optimize opt-in rates and detect anomalous behavior.

- **Transparent preference center**: Offers users a privacyfirst, accessible portal to view, update, or withdraw consent; includes full history and supports customization for advertising, analytics, and data sharing.

- **Accessibility and multilingual support**: Public-facing consent components meet WCAG 2.2 AA and ADA standards and support over 60 languages with geolocation-based adaptations.

- **Seamless integrations**: Syncs preference data with CRM and marketing platforms like HubSpot, Salesforce, Marketo, Mailchimp, enabling orchestrated consent use in campaigns.

- **Auditability and compliance reporting**: Stores secure consent logs with exportable audit trails and trending reports to demonstrate regulatory compliance

GoTrust simplified

GoTrust provides a **comprehensive consent orchestration solution** that simplifies compliance with global privacy and data protection requirements. The platform enables organizations to manage end-to-end consent processes, from capturing and storing to verifying and auditing user consents, while ensuring transparency, accountability, and alignment with legal obligations. The following figure illustrates the operational mechanism of the GoTrust solution:

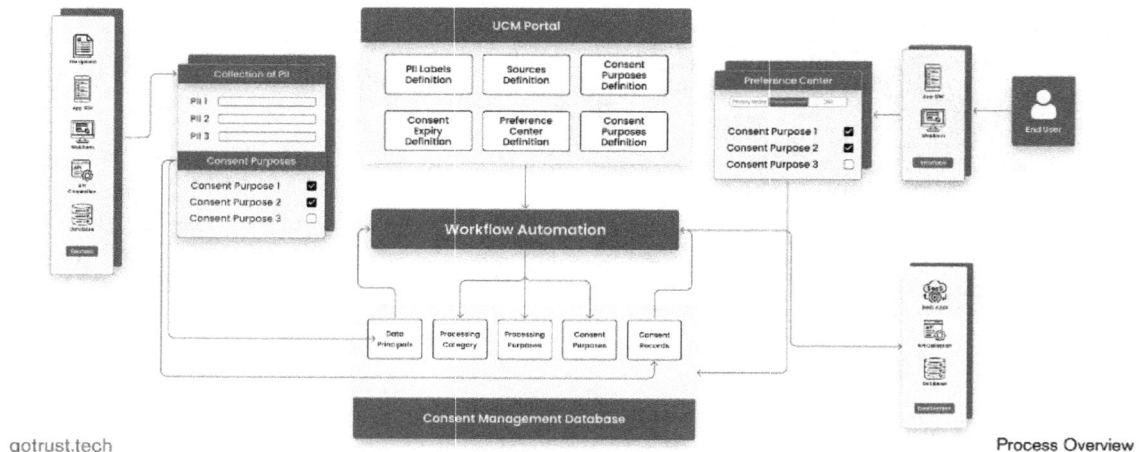

Figure 3.5: GoTrust solution components

The core management capabilities of GoTrust are as follows:

- **Granular consent management**: Capture purpose-specific consent (e.g., marketing, analytics, profiling) to ensure only relevant permissions are collected.

- **Real-time consent tracking**: Instantly update consent statuses across integrated systems to allow only authorized processing.

- **Contextual consent requests**: Trigger consent prompts at the right time and context to reduce fatigue and increase acceptance.

- **Immutable consent logs**: Maintain secure, tamper-proof, time-stamped records of all consent actions (user ID, purpose, channel, lawful basis, form version) for audit readiness.

- **Centralized preference center**: Provide a self-service portal where users can review, update, or withdraw consent anytime.

- **Consent flow visualization**: Map the full lifecycle of consent from request to withdrawal for clarity and transparency.

- **Consent expiry and renewal notifications**: Configure expiry timelines for each consent purpose and send automated alerts to users before expiry.

- **Multilingual consent capture**: Present consent forms in multiple languages to meet global compliance and accessibility requirements.

- **Dynamic consent linking**: Consolidate consents across multiple channels and identities into a unified record.

- **Automated version control**: Track and store historical versions of consent forms, linking them to user decisions.

- **Seamless system integrations**: Connect with CRMs, marketing platforms, and enterprise systems via APIs and webhooks.

So far, we have explored the world of consent management tools. However, implementing a consent solution is only the first step. Most organizations quickly realize they also need processes and tools to handle data subject requests. One such solution is Microsoft Priva, which is designed to streamline these requests. In the next section, we'll dive deeper into how it works.

It is worth noting that while Priva uses the term *'data subject'*, under India's DPDP Act, the equivalent term is *'Data Principal'*.

Handling Data Principal request with Microsoft Priva

If you are already using a dedicated consent management platform such as **GoTrust, TrustArc, or OneTrust** for DPDP compliance, you can complement it with **Microsoft Priva** to cover broader privacy operations beyond consent workflows.

Consent management tools primarily focus on **capturing, storing, and honoring user consents** in compliance with DPDP requirements. However, the DPDP Act also mandates strong capabilities for **privacy risk management** and **Data Principal Rights Requests (DPRs)**.

Here is how Priva enhances your existing consent management solution:

- **Privacy risk management**: Priva scans your Microsoft 365 environment to detect overexposed or overshared personal data. It flags risky locations and policy violations that a consent manager alone cannot address. This proactive monitoring helps reduce the likelihood of data breaches and misuse.

- **Data Principal Rights Requests (DPRs)**: While consent platforms track withdrawals or updates, Priva enables organizations to **orchestrate full DPR workflows**. For example, it can locate all instances of a Principal's personal data across Microsoft 365, assess sensitivity, and fulfill access, correction, or deletion requests within DPDP timelines.

- **End-to-end coverage**: This combined approach ensures that consent managers like GoTrust handle the **front end** (capturing and updating consents), while Priva manages the **back end** (discovering data, reducing risk, and fulfilling Principal requests). Together, they deliver a comprehensive compliance posture under the DPDP framework.

Conclusion

The significance of data collection, processing, and consent in the digital economy cannot be overstated. Data serves as the cornerstone of modern business, fueling personalized experiences, informed decision-making, and competitive advantage. As we explored throughout this chapter, the DPDP Act, 2023 and the Draft Rules, 2025 form the legal backbone, ensuring that organizations handle personal data responsibly, transparently, and lawfully.

We have discussed the various types of consent, explicit, implied, opt-in, opt-out, granular, and withdrawable, that organizations must manage to ensure compliance. Tools like Microsoft Purview, Priva, and Consent Manager facilitate this compliance, supporting organizations in aligning with the stringent requirements of the DPDP Act and the Draft Rules.

We also examined critical rights granted to Data Principals, including their right to explicit consent (Section 6, DPDP Act), access to personal data (Section 11, DPDP Act), and nominate individuals to manage their data rights in cases of incapacity (Section 14, DPDP Act). These rights empower individuals with significant control over their personal data, ensuring organizations uphold transparency, accountability, and trust.

Understanding and applying these principles not only helps businesses stay compliant but also fosters customer trust, an essential factor in the digital economy's growth. Tools such as Microsoft Purview, Priva, and Consent Manager further enable efficient management of data protection obligations, providing solutions aligned explicitly with the DPDP Act's mandates.

In the upcoming chapter titled *Data Security Measures*, we will look further into the mechanics of protecting personal data, examining essential security measures required by the DPDP Act and its rules to safeguard data from unauthorized access, breaches, or misuse, thus reinforcing compliance and maintaining trust.

Join our Discord space

Join our Discord workspace for latest updates, offers, tech happenings around the world, new releases, and sessions with the authors:

https://discord.bpbonline.com

Chapter 4

Data Security Measures

Introduction

In today's digital era, the protection of personal data is paramount, and the **Digital Personal Data Protection Act 2023** (**DPDPA 2023**) and Draft DPDP Rules 2025 address this need by imposing strict data security obligations on organizations, referred to as Data Fiduciaries and **Significant Data Fiduciaries** (**SDFs**). These entities are required to implement *reasonable security safeguards* to prevent personal data breaches, ensuring that data is protected from unauthorized access, alteration, or disclosure. The Act emphasizes the accountability of Data Fiduciaries, even when data processing is outsourced to third-party Data Processors who Act in a 'third-party' capacity, mandating that they ensure compliance with security measures through enforceable contracts. Non-compliance with these obligations can result in significant penalties, reinforcing the importance of data security as a legal and ethical responsibility. Beyond legal compliance, robust data security practices foster trust between organizations and individuals, enhancing reputational standing and ensuring the confidentiality, integrity, and availability of personal data in an increasingly data-driven world.

The law clearly states that Data Fiduciaries must maintain reasonable security. The Draft Rule 6 explains what this means, but there is still a lot of work to be done to meet this requirement. Implementing "reasonable security" involves a comprehensive approach, including conducting risk assessments, having Antivirus, **Endpoint Detection and Responses** (**EDRs**) to defend against any intrusion, deploying information protection and technologies like **data loss prevention** (**DLP**), or having data encrypted. Each of these components must be carefully designed and continuously updated to address evolving threats and vulnerabilities, making this one-line directive a complex, ongoing commitment that extends far beyond basic compliance.

Structure

In this chapter, we will cover the following topics:

- Data security in context of DPDP Act
- Interpretation in DPDP 2023 Act and Draft Rules 2025
- Operationalizing Rule 6, reasonable security safeguards
- Techniques for securing data
- Access controls and authentication
- Data security policies and training
- Data protection alert triage
- Importance of auditing
- Case study of Ananya's experience

Objectives

This chapter aims to equip readers with a comprehensive understanding of the technical and organizational measures required to secure personal data in alignment with the DPDP Act, 2023, and the Draft DPDP Rules, 2025. It explores the concept of *reasonable security safeguards* under Rule 6, including data encryption, access controls, logging, breach response, and contractual obligations with processors. Readers will learn how to secure data across its lifecycle, at rest, in motion, and in use, using practical tools such as Microsoft Purview, Defender, and Sentinel. The chapter also emphasizes the role of DLP alert triage, employee training, and continuous audits in building an accountable and resilient security framework. Through real-life scenarios and case studies, it demonstrates how to operationalize compliance while enhancing trust, mitigating breach risks, and supporting organizational transparency in a data-driven economy.

Data security in context of DPDP Act

In modern data protection, traditional security measures such as antivirus software, EDR, and network defenses play an integral role in shielding organizations from external threats. However, in the context of India's DPDP Act, 2023, and Rules 2025, these measures alone are no longer sufficient.

The DPDP Act and Draft DPDP rules necessitate a more sophisticated approach to data security, one that seamlessly integrates data classification, protection, and cross-border data protection to uphold the confidentiality, availability, and integrity of personal data, as discussed in earlier chapters. This approach brings together these critical aspects within a unified framework, ensuring comprehensive data security. Implementing each of these technologies individually is a significant challenge, but integrating them into a single, cohesive solution is essential.

To explore this approach further, we will examine how solutions like **Microsoft Information Protection** (MIP), **DLP**, **Data Security Posture Management** (**DSPM** for AI), and Microsoft Priva can assist customers with data protection, alongside traditional intrusion prevention technologies like Antivirus, EDR, and firewalls.

We will focus on Microsoft Purview, Microsoft Defender, Microsoft Entra, Microsoft Sentinel, and Azure as references to meet the needs. Readers are free to apply the same knowledge with similar products of their choice.

When considering the implications of a personal data breach under the DPDP Act, the stakes are significantly raised. Loss of data or leakage of data can lead to noncompliance. Noncompliance can lead to stringent penalties, operational disruptions, and loss of consumer trust. A comprehensive data protection strategy must, therefore, encompass not just the traditional bastions of cybersecurity but also the sophisticated mechanisms of data classification, rights management, and information governance to effectively mitigate the risk of personal data breach. This integration ensures that personal information is not only protected from malware and intrusions but also from inadvertent insider threats and data mishandling, aligning with the stringent requirements of the DPDP Act and Rules for the secure processing, handling, and storage of personal data.

Let us build on our example in the book, where Ananya wants to open a bank account. When Ananya walks into her local bank to open an account, she trusts the institution with her personal details, her basic subscriber information such as name, address, phone number, and her financial history. It is crucial for the bank to protect Ananya's data at every stage, starting with **data at rest**, the information stored in the bank's database. This data must be encrypted to prevent unauthorized access, ensuring that even if systems are compromised, the information remains unreadable.

Equally important is the security of **data in transit**. As Ananya uses mobile and internet banking, her data traverses through various networks. It must be encrypted during transmission to safeguard against interception by cybercriminals. The bank must also implement robust **physical security** to prevent data theft from its premises.

Access controls form another defense layer, ensuring that only authorized personnel can access Ananya's data, based on their roles. The bank's authentication measures, like passwords or biometric scans, must be stringent to prevent unauthorized logins to her account.

In this chapter, we will explore the depths of these critical elements, dissecting the importance of securing data at rest, encryption methods, physical security, data transmission security, and access controls. We will explore how they not only protect individuals like Ananya but also ensure that the bank complies with data protection regulations like the DPDP Act. It is not just about legal compliance; it is about maintaining the confidentiality, availability and integrity of personal data in an increasingly digital world.

Interpretation in DPDP 2023 Act and Rules 2025

Chapter II, Section 8 of the DPDP Act outlines the *general obligations of the Data Fiduciary*. It mandates that Data Fiduciaries must ensure the protection of personal data under their control, including any processing by third parties (Data Processors), by implementing robust security measures. This is crucial to prevent personal data breaches and to maintain the trust of Data Principals, the individuals to whom the data pertains. In the event of a breach, there is an obligation to notify the relevant authorities and the affected individuals.

Chapter III, section 11 of the DPDP Act also emphasizes the *Right to access information about personal data*, ensuring Data Principals can request a summary of their personal data being processed and be informed about the purpose and extent of processing. Here, Microsoft Purview Information Protection can offer transparency through trainable classifiers, allowing banks like the one Ananya uses to be transparent about how her data is processed and shared.

The following table outlines key obligations under Section 8 of the DPDP Act, focusing on data usage, sharing, and protection responsibilities of Data Fiduciaries, along with aligned security safeguard requirements from the Draft Rules:

Chapter	Section	Definition name	Narration	Solution mapping	Draft rules mapping
2	8	General Obligations of Data Fiduciary	Used to make a decision that affects the Data Principal.	Need to have SIT pre-identified with Data lineage tracking	
2	8	General Obligations of Data Fiduciary	Disclosed to another Data Processor.	Need to have agreements in place, recognized and possible visible with Trainable Classifiers	Rule 6 – Security Safeguards
2	8	General Obligations of Data Fiduciary	A Data Fiduciary shall protect personal data in its possession or under its control, including in respect of any processing undertaken by it or on its behalf by a Data Processor, by taking reasonable security safeguards to prevent personal data breach.	Need the Data Fiduciary implement SIT, extend SITs to include relevant sensitive information and have right policies like encryption, DLP offering reasonable security safeguards.	

Chapter	Section	Definition name	Narration	Solution mapping	Draft rules mapping
2	8	General Obligations of Data Fiduciary	In the event of a personal data breach, the Data Fiduciary shall give the Board and each affected Data Principal, intimation of such breach in such form and manner as may be prescribed.	Timely breach notifications to authorities and individuals	Rule 12 – Data Breach Notification
3	11	Right to access information about personal data	A summary of personal data which is being processed by such Data Fiduciary and the processing activities undertaken by that Data Fiduciary with respect to such personal data.	Bank, while using Ananya personal data for processing, is also expected to share with her what data was shared or processes.	Rule 8 – Data Access Requests

Table 4.1: *Quick view into DPDP Act chapters and sections*

Data can exist in three main states, namely data at rest, data in motion, and data in use. Each state represents a different phase in the data lifecycle and requires specific security measures to protect it. Here is an overview of each:

- **Data at rest**: Data at rest refers to inactive data that is stored physically in any digital form (e.g., databases, data warehouses, spreadsheets, archives, etc.) on a storage device. This data is not actively moving between devices or networks.

  o **Examples**: Files stored on a hard drive, data archived in a database, backups stored on cloud storage, or any data stored on devices like USB drives.

  o **Security measures:** Encryption, access control, data masking, secure backups, and physical security of storage devices.

- **Data in motion:** Data in motion, also known as data in transit, refers to data that is actively moving from one location to another, such as across the internet, through a private network, or between different systems.

  o **Examples**: Emails being sent, files being transferred over a network, streaming data between servers, or data being transmitted to a cloud storage service.

  o **Security measures:** Encryption (such as TLS/SSL), secure tunneling (VPNs), **secure file transfer protocols (SFTP)**, and data integrity checks.

- **Data in use:** Data in use refers to data that is actively being processed by an application or user. During this time, the data is often unencrypted, so it can be accessed and used for computations.

- o **Examples**: Data being processed in RAM, files open on a user's computer, data being viewed or edited in a document, or records being updated in a database.

- o **Security measures:** Access control, application security, data masking, and monitoring/logging of data access.

Why these states matter in security

While DPDP Act and Rules, expects organizations to protect data by taking reasonable safeguards, this is fundamental to data protection. Each state of data at rest, in motion, and in use has different security challenges. Protecting data at rest primarily involves securing storage systems and ensuring that data is encrypted and access controlled. For data in motion, the focus is on securing the transmission channels to prevent interception or tampering. Data in use, meanwhile, requires that systems and applications processing the data are secure and that access to data during processing is tightly controlled.

Under Rule 6 of the Draft Rules, 2025, the DPDP Act places a significant responsibility on Data Fiduciaries to implement comprehensive security safeguards. These are not only technical mandates but also foundational to building trust with Data Principals and ensuring the organization's resilience against personal data breaches. Let us unpack each clause of Rule 6 and explore how organizations can implement it effectively.

Operationalizing Rule 6, reasonable security safeguards

Rule 6(1) of the Draft DPDP Rules, 2025, mandates that Data Fiduciaries and Data Processors implement reasonable security safeguards to ensure the confidentiality, integrity, and availability of personal data. The following is a breakdown of key clauses under this rule, along with recommended approaches and supporting Microsoft toolsets:

- **Clause (a), data protection measures:** *Appropriate data security measures, including securing of such personal data through its encryption, obfuscation, or masking, or the use of virtual tokens mapped to that personal data.*

  - o **Approach**: Organizations should deploy multi-layered encryption across their environments, both at rest and in transit. Sensitive fields such as Aadhaar numbers, bank account details, or health information should be masked or tokenized when shown on interfaces. Obfuscation can be applied to logs and temporary processing environments.

  - o **Toolset**: Microsoft Purview Information Protection, Microsoft Data Loss Prevention, Azure storage service encryption.

- **Clause (b), access control mechanisms:** *Appropriate measures to control access to the computer resources used by such Data Fiduciary or such a Data Processor.*

o **Approach**: Enforce **role-based access control (RBAC)** and **Just-In-Time (JIT)** access across all cloud workloads. Administrative privileges must be tightly controlled and monitored using **Privileged Identity Management (PIM)** tools.

o **Toolset**: Microsoft Entra ID (Azure AD), Conditional Access Policies, Azure RBAC, Microsoft Defender for Identity.

- **Clause (c), logging, monitoring, and review:** *Visibility on the accessing of such personal data, through appropriate logs, monitoring, and review..."*

  o **Approach**: Implement centralized log aggregation and SIEM systems that not only store access logs but also monitor them in real-time for anomalies such as geolocation changes, after-hours access, or data exfiltration attempts.

  o **Toolset**: Microsoft Sentinel, Azure Monitor, Log Analytics Workspace, Kusto queries for advanced threat hunting.

- **Clause (d), data backup and availability:** *Reasonable measures for continued processing in the event of compromise, including by way of data backups.*

  o **Approach**: Define and test **Business Continuity Plans (BCP)** and **Disaster Recovery (DR)** protocols. Ensure geo-redundant backup storage and automated failover for mission-critical systems handling personal data.

  o **Toolset**: Microsoft SharePoint, Azure Site Recovery, Azure Backup, Zerto for multi-cloud DR.

- **Clause (e), retention of logs and personal data:** *Retain such logs and personal data for a period of one year, unless compliance with any other law requires otherwise.*

  o **Approach**: Design retention policies that preserve log data (especially access and activity logs) for at least 12 months. Secure archival storage should be used with periodic integrity checks.

  o **Toolset**: Microsoft data lifecycle management and Records Management, Immutable Blob Storage with legal hold, Microsoft Compliance Center for audit trails.

- **Clause (f), security in contracts with processors**: *Appropriate provision in the contract between the Data Fiduciary and Data Processor for taking reasonable security safeguards.*

  o **Approach**: All vendor agreements must include clauses that mirror the Data Fiduciary's obligations, especially around breach reporting, encryption standards, audit rights, and sub-processor disclosures. This should be regularly reviewed via vendor risk assessments.

  o **Toolset**: Microsoft Compliance Manager for DPDPA template, contract lifecycle management platforms like DocuSign CLM or Agiloft.

- **Clause (g), technical and organizational measures:** *Appropriate technical and organisational measures to ensure effective observance of security safeguards.*

    o **Approach**: Security must be integrated into the organization's culture and processes. Establish a Data Protection Committee, run mandatory awareness programs, and perform penetration testing regularly. Adopt frameworks like Zero Trust and NIST 800-53.

    o **Toolset**: Microsoft Defender Suite, Microsoft Purview DLP, Microsoft Priva for privacy posture management.

Techniques for securing data

In a world where data is constantly on the move across devices, networks, and borders, the ability to secure it at every stage of its lifecycle is paramount. The DPDP Act, 2023, places a legal obligation on Data Fiduciaries to adopt reasonable security safeguards to protect personal data against breaches, misuse, and unauthorized access. These obligations are reinforced in Rule 6 of the Draft Rules 2025, which outlines technical and organizational measures necessary to ensure data security.

Whether data is in transit between systems, at rest within a data center, or being accessed by an authorized user, robust security practices must be employed to maintain confidentiality, integrity, and availability. This section explores key techniques for data security, including encryption, access control, data masking, anonymization, and secure configuration of cloud services, all of which are crucial for ensuring compliance with the DPDP Act and building trust with Data Principals.

As organizations increasingly rely on hybrid and multi-cloud environments, implementing these techniques is not just best practice; it is a regulatory requirement and a foundational pillar of responsible data stewardship.

Data at rest

Now that we have a view and expectation of safeguarding data across various states, let us look at what tools are required to secure the data. **Advanced Encryption Standard (AES)** and **Rivest–Shamir–Adleman (RSA)** are two encryption techniques used to secure data, especially data at rest.

AES is a symmetric key encryption cipher, which means it uses the same key for both encrypting and decrypting data. This is the same as having keys to lock at most homes. If you have the key, you can open it. It is widely recognized for its speed and security and is commonly used to encrypt data stored on hard drives or sent over the internet. AES operates on fixed blocks of data (128, 192, or 256 bits) and is considered difficult to crack, making it a standard for securing sensitive data.

RSA, on the other hand, is an asymmetric cryptographic algorithm; it uses two keys, a public key for encryption and a private key for decryption. This key pair is generated using large prime numbers and an additional variable. RSA is often used for securing data transmissions rather than data at rest because it is computationally more intensive than AES.

Let us turn our focus to the common repositories where data is frequently stored and shared: email systems, intranet portals like SharePoint, and modern collaboration hubs, such as team chats and team sites. These platforms not only facilitate communication and collaboration but also serve as vaults for a vast amount of organizational data that organizations commonly refer to as Microsoft O365. In the context of Office 365, Microsoft uses multiple layers of encryption to protect data at rest, such as:

- **Service encryption**: By default, Office 365 uses service encryption with AES 256-bit encryption to encrypt data at rest in Microsoft's data centers.

- **BitLocker**: Microsoft employs BitLocker drive encryption to encrypt the drive where data is stored. BitLocker is designed to protect data by providing encryption for entire volumes.

- **Customer Key**: Office 365 offers a feature called **Customer Key** that allows you to control your organization's encryption keys and then configure Office 365 to use them to encrypt your data at rest in Microsoft's data centers.

With the growing sophistication of cyber threats, securing data at rest extends beyond O365 to include customer **Line of Business (LOB)** applications, which often rely on **Relational Database Management Systems (RDBMS)**, and cloud storage solutions like Amazon S3 or Azure blobs. It is crucial to implement robust security measures in these areas, as they are repositories of sensitive data that can be vulnerable to unauthorized access and potential breaches.

In RDBMS like Microsoft SQL Server and Oracle, data at rest is typically stored in structured formats, such as tables within databases. To secure this data, several common methods are employed:

- **Encryption**: Both SQL Server and Oracle provide encryption capabilities to protect data at rest. SQL Server uses **Transparent Data Encryption (TDE)** to perform real-time I/O encryption and decryption of the data and log files. Oracle provides a similar feature with Oracle Advanced Security, which includes TDE.

- **Access controls**: Both systems offer robust access control mechanisms that limit who can access data within the database. This is often managed through user roles and privileges.

- **Database auditing**: This feature tracks database events, providing a record of what data was accessed, by whom, and when, which is vital for security and compliance.

- **Data masking**: **Dynamic Data Masking (DDM)** in SQL Server and Data Redaction in Oracle hide sensitive data in the result set of a query over designated database fields, ensuring that sensitive data does not leave the database in an unencrypted form.

For Cloud Storage like Azure Blobs and Amazon S3, again, we have various technologies provided by Cloud service providers, such as:

- **Encryption**: Both Azure Blob Storage and Amazon S3 offer server-side encryption for data at rest. Azure uses Azure Storage Service Encryption, while Amazon uses S3 **server-side encryption (SSE)**.

- **Access controls**: Azure and AWS have fine-grained access controls, including Azure's RBAC and AWS's **identity and access management (IAM)**, to manage who can access storage resources.

- **Network security**: To secure data in transit to and from the cloud storage, both Azure and Amazon support the use of HTTPS to provide a secure connection using SSL/TLS.

- **Data redundancy**: Both services replicate data across multiple geographically dispersed data centers to ensure data durability and high availability, protecting against data loss in the event of failure.

Data in motion

Securing data in motion refers to protecting data as it is transmitted between systems, networks, or devices, ensuring its confidentiality, integrity, and availability during transit. Under India's DPDP Act 2023, this is critical because it mandates stringent protection of personal data, particularly when it is being transferred across borders or within digital ecosystems. Encrypting data in transit and using secure communication protocols helps safeguard it against unauthorized access, interception, or tampering, ensuring compliance with the DPDP Act's data protection obligations.

For instance, this chapter discusses special provisions regarding data security, wherein the Act stipulates that any entity managing personal data, referred to as a *Data Fiduciary*, must secure personal and sensitive data in compliance with the standards laid out by the Act. These standards would include the use of encryption to secure data both in transit and at rest, thereby aligning with the best international practices and legal requirements for data protection.

Encryption of data in transit is about securing data as it moves from one location to another, such as across the internet or through a private network. In the context of a bank with a multitude of applications, this means applying encryption when data is sent from the customer's browser to the bank's web server (in internet banking), from the mobile app to the banking API endpoints (in mobile banking), within internal bank networks transferring data between the core banking system and the CRM, and even when the call center accesses customer data remotely.

Here is how it works in different banking scenarios:

- **Core banking**: When transactions are processed through the core banking system, data must be encrypted as it travels across the network. This could be a customer's transaction data going from the teller's terminal to the central server.

- **Internet banking**: As customers log in and perform transactions, their information is encrypted using protocols such as **Transport Layer Security (TLS)** to protect their data from being intercepted by attackers.

- **Mobile banking**: Encryption in mobile banking ensures that all communications between the app on the user's device and the bank's servers are secured against eavesdropping.

- **Bank website**: When a customer visits the bank's website and enters personal information, that data is encrypted before it leaves their device, ensuring confidentiality and integrity.

- **Call center**: When call center systems access customer information or when agents assist customers through online platforms, encryption helps secure the data exchange.

- **CRM and other applications**: Data exchanges between these applications and other parts of the bank's IT environment are encrypted to prevent unauthorized access during transmission.

For a bank, encryption of data in transit is not just about technology implementation; it is also about complying with legal and regulatory standards such as those potentially outlined in the DPDP Act. This Act would stipulate that personal data must be adequately protected when it is transmitted, preventing unauthorized access or personal data breaches, and maintaining the confidentiality and integrity of customer data.

TLS and **Secure Sockets Layer (SSL)** are cryptographic protocols designed to provide secure communication over a computer network. While SSL is the predecessor to TLS, both serve a similar purpose: to encrypt data in transit, ensuring that any information sent between a client (like Ananya's computer or smartphone) and a server (such as her bank's) is protected from eavesdroppers and tampering.

In Ananya's case, these protocols work as follows:

- **Encryption of communication**: When Ananya accesses her internet banking website or uses her banking app, TLS/SSL ensures that all data exchanged between her device and the bank is encrypted. This means her login credentials, account details, transaction information, and any communication are scrambled in such a way that they can only be deciphered by her device and the bank's server.

- **Authentication**: TLS/SSL also facilitates authentication. When Ananya connects to her bank's website, the TLS/SSL protocol ensures that she is indeed communicating with her bank's legitimate server and not a malicious imposter. This is done using digital certificates issued by trusted **Certificate Authorities (CAs)**.

- **Data integrity**: Beyond encryption, TLS/SSL also guarantees the integrity of the data being transmitted. This means that any data sent by Ananya to her bank, or vice versa, cannot be altered or corrupted during transmission without detection.

Here is how the process typically unfolds:

1. When Ananya visits her bank's secure website, her browser requests a secure connection with the bank's server.

2. The server responds by sending a copy of its SSL certificate, including the server's public key.

3. Ananya's browser verifies the certificate's validity, then uses the server's public key to encrypt a session key, which is sent back to the server.

4. The server decrypts the session key using its private key, establishing a secure connection. All transmitted data is encrypted with the session key.

This encrypted communication channel ensures that sensitive financial data Ananya shares with her bank over the internet is kept confidential and secure from interception or tampering by cybercriminals, safeguarding her privacy and financial assets.

In the context of mobile banking, API-based encryption plays a critical role in securing communication between Ananya's mobile banking app and her bank's servers. API, also known as Application Programming Interfaces, allow different software applications to communicate with each other. When Ananya uses her mobile app to check her balance, transfer money, or pay bills, the app communicates with the bank's servers via APIs to conduct these requests.

Here is how API-based encryption works to protect Ananya's data:

*   **Secure API calls**: When Ananya initiates a transaction through her mobile app, the app makes a secure API call to the bank's server. This call is encrypted using TLS, ensuring that the data transmitted between her mobile app and the bank's server is protected against eavesdropping and tampering.

*   **Authentication and authorization**: Before any data is exchanged, both the mobile app and the bank's server authenticate each other. Ananya's app may also use OAuth, an open standard for access delegation, to obtain a token that grants it permission to perform actions on her behalf without revealing her authentication credentials directly to the server.

*   **End-to-end encryption**: Some banking apps implement additional layers of encryption on top of TLS for sensitive transactions. This could involve encrypting the payload data (the actual transaction information) using AES before it is sent over the API. Only the bank's server has the key to decrypting this data, adding an extra layer of security.

*   **Secured data storage on mobile**: The app ensures that any sensitive data stored on Ananya's device, like authentication tokens or transaction history, is encrypted using the device's secure storage capabilities. This protects her data even if her device is lost or stolen.

*   **Integrity checks**: To further safeguard the data, the app and the server can implement integrity checks on the data being sent and received. This could involve hashing algorithms that ensure the data has not been altered during transit.

Through API-based encryption, Ananya's mobile banking transactions are secured, providing confidentiality, data integrity, and authentication. This means that whether she is transferring funds, paying bills, or checking her account statements, her financial data remains protected, ensuring a safe and secure mobile banking experience.

The necessity of encryption under the DPDP Act cannot be overstated. It serves as a fundamental safeguard, ensuring the confidentiality and integrity of personal data as it rests within databases or traverses the digital expanse between Ananya and her bank. The DPDP Act mandates stringent protection measures for personal data, emphasizing the role of encryption in preventing unauthorized access and personal data breaches. This legal framework necessitates a comprehensive approach to encryption, encompassing distinct types of digital content from emails and documents to transaction data. Understanding the specific encryption methods applicable to several types of digital content is crucial for compliance with the DPDP Act, ensuring that personal data is protected in line with the highest security standards.

The following table categorizes types of digital content, outlines the encryption methods typically employed to secure them, and provides links for more detailed information on each encryption technique. This resource aims to guide in implementing effective encryption strategies across various digital platforms and content types, in full compliance with the DPDP Act.

Digital content type	Encryption method	More information
Emails	TLS, S/MIME	https://learn.microsoft.com/en-us/purview/email-encryption
Documents	AES, RSA	https://learn.microsoft.com/en-us/purview/data-encryption-in-odb-and-spo
Transaction data	TDE, Column-level Encryption	https://learn.microsoft.com/en-us/sql/relational-databases/security/encryption/transparent-data-encryption?view=sql-server-ver15
Mobile communications	End-to-end Encryption	https://learn.microsoft.com/en-us/mem/intune/apps/app-protection-policy
Cloud storage	Server-side encryption	https://learn.microsoft.com/en-us/azure/storage/common/storage-service-encryption
Devices	Desktops or Laptops	https://www.microsoft.com/TrustCenter/Security/Encryption

Table 4.2: Encryption methods for data in motion

This table serves as a starting point for organizations to align their data protection strategies with the requirements of the DPDP Act, ensuring that every piece of digital content is adequately protected through appropriate encryption methods.

Data in use

Encrypting data in use helps mitigate these risks by ensuring that even while data is being accessed or modified, it remains protected from unauthorized interception, malicious attacks, or accidental leaks. In line with the DPDP Act, organizations in India must adopt strong data protection strategies to maintain compliance, safeguard sensitive personal data, and avoid penalties.

Let us look at leading practices across the cloud and endpoints, which can help encrypt data even when in use:

- In Cloud, let us say if you are using Azure services:

    o **Azure policy and blueprints:** These tools help ensure security and compliance baselines for data processing activities in the cloud, ensuring that data in use is managed securely.

    o **Encryption in transit and at rest:** Even though this primarily secures data at rest and in transit, ensuring that data is encrypted across the board is crucial for overall security while being used.

- On Desktops across Windows or Mac machines:

    o **Microsoft Defender for Endpoint:** Provides real-time monitoring and protection for desktops, identifying and mitigating security threats while sensitive data is being processed or accessed.

    o **MIP, now called Purview information protection:** Prevents accidental data leakage by securing corporate data while allowing personal data to coexist on the same device. It limits how data is used within applications with its new DSPM for the AI portal.

    o **BitLocker:** Although for securing data at rest, BitLocker can also help ensure desktop data remains encrypted and secure during processing.

- **In browsers (Edge, Chrome):**

    o **Microsoft Defender SmartScreen:** Protects users against phishing attacks and malicious sites that could compromise data security while browsing, ensuring that data in use is not exposed to online threats.

    o **Microsoft Defender for Apps, or called Cloud Access Security Broker (CASB):** Provides real-time monitoring and protection of sensitive data when accessing cloud services through the browser. It enforces security policies to prevent unauthorized data access or misuse during browser sessions.

- **On mobile applications (iOS/Android):**

    o **Microsoft Intune (Mobile Device Management - MDM):** Enforces security policies, including encryption and app control, to secure corporate data in use on mobile devices. This ensures compliance with security policies and prevents data leakage.

- o **App protection policies:** These policies can restrict data sharing between apps or enforce encryption when users interact with sensitive corporate data on their mobile devices.

- o **Mobile Application Management (MAM):** Ensures that data within specific corporate apps remains secure, even on personal devices, by applying policies like selective wipe or preventing unauthorized access.

- **Across all platforms:**

  - o **Data loss prevention (DLP):** DLP policies in **Microsoft Purview Information Protection** (MIP) in M365 help monitor and prevent the accidental sharing or exposure of sensitive data in use. They can be configured to protect data across desktops, mobile apps, browsers, and cloud environments.

The **DPDP Act** mandates the need for robust data protection mechanisms, and ensuring that data in use is encrypted and properly secured is critical to compliance. M365's suite of tools helps organizations manage data securely across various platforms, mitigating risks while enhancing the security of sensitive personal data.

Encryption plays a critical role in securing data in use by ensuring that even when data is actively processed, it remains protected from unauthorized access or breaches. This safeguards sensitive personal data, which is a core requirement under the India DPDP Act.

In addition to encryption, access control is essential for limiting who can interact with data. RBAC ensures that users can only access the information necessary for their specific roles, minimizing the risk of unauthorized data exposure. The DPDP Act emphasizes the need for such stringent access controls to maintain data privacy and compliance.

Access controls and authentication

Access control and authentication form the backbone of data security, ensuring that only authorized users can access personal information. These mechanisms are especially crucial in the context of legislation like the DPDP Act, which mandates the protection of personal data through stringent measures.

When it comes to access control, Rules 2025 explains the importance of access Rule 6(1)(b) explicitly mandates Data Fiduciaries and processors to implement robust access control measures on computer resources used for processing personal data. This includes clearly defining and restricting who has access to specific data sets, thus minimizing vulnerabilities that can arise from overly permissive access rights. Proper access controls not only limit exposure but also enhance accountability, allowing organizations to enforce a principle of least privilege, where users receive only the access strictly necessary to perform their duties.

Furthermore, Rule 6(1)(c) highlights the necessity of maintaining visibility and oversight of data access through systematic logging, continuous monitoring, and regular review mechanisms. These measures are essential for promptly detecting and addressing unauthorized access attempts, facilitating rapid investigation, and ensuring appropriate remedial actions. Comprehensive audit logs provide transparency and enable detailed forensic analysis, crucial for both compliance assurance and preventing security incidents.

The need for access control and authentication is highlighted as follows:

- **Protection of personal data**: The primary goal of access control and authentication is to protect personal data from unauthorized access, misuse, or breach. In the banking sector, where sensitive financial information is managed, these controls ensure that customer data, such as Ananya's, remains confidential and secure.

- **Compliance with the DPDP Act**: The DPDP Act, through its various chapters and sections, emphasizes the need for robust data protection measures. Access control and authentication directly align with the Act's requirements to safeguard personal data against unauthorized access, contributing to an organization's compliance efforts.

- **Prevention of personal data breaches**: By implementing effective access controls and authentication mechanisms, banks can significantly reduce the risk of personal data breaches. This not only protects customers' personal data but also safeguards the bank's reputation and avoids potential penalties under the DPDP Act.

Implementing access control and authentication

In a banking environment, access control and authentication mechanisms can be implemented in several ways, such as:

- **RBAC**: Employees are granted access to information based on their role within the organization. For example, a bank teller might have access to customer account details but not to more sensitive financial data.

- **Multi-factor authentication**: For customers like Ananya using mobile and internet banking, **multi-factor authentication (MFA)** adds an additional layer of security. It requires users to provide two or more verification factors to gain access to their accounts, such as a password and a one-time code sent to their mobile device.

- **Biometric authentication**: Utilizing biometrics, such as fingerprint or facial recognition, provides a secure and user-friendly method for customers to access their banking apps.

Let us look more closely at Ananya's mobile and internet banking usage. When Ananya logs into her mobile banking app, she is first asked for her username and password (something she knows). Then, for transactions over a certain amount, the app requests fingerprint authentication (something she is), exemplifying MFA in action. This process ensures that even if her password is compromised, unauthorized access is still prevented by a biometric check.

Data security policies and training

The DPDP Act underscores the necessity of implementing stringent data security measures to safeguard personal data against unauthorized access, disclosure, alteration, and destruction. A comprehensive data security policy, as guided by the DPDP Act, forms the cornerstone of an organization's data protection strategy, ensuring compliance and fostering a culture of security awareness.

A data security policy is a formal document that outlines the rules, practices, and procedures an organization must follow to protect its data from unauthorized access, breaches, and data loss.

The importance of a data security policy is as follows:

- **Framework for protection**: It establishes a structured framework for safeguarding personal data, detailing the roles, responsibilities, and processes to prevent personal data breaches.

- **Compliance with DPDP Act**: It ensures that organizations adhere to the legislative requirements of the DPDP Act, avoiding potential legal and financial penalties associated with non-compliance.

- **Risk management**: It aids in identifying, assessing, and mitigating risks associated with the handling of personal data, aligning with the risk-based approach advocated by the DPDP Act.

Key components of a data security policy

The following are the key components of the data security policy:

- **Access control and authentication**: Policies to restrict access to personal data based on roles and responsibilities, ensuring that employees have access only to the data necessary for their job functions.

- **Data encryption**: Mandating the encryption of personal data both at rest and in transit to protect against unauthorized access.

- **Incident response plan**: Outlining procedures for responding to personal data breaches, including notification requirements as per the DPDP Act.

- **Data retention and disposal**: Defining the lifecycle of personal data, from collection to secure disposal, ensuring data is not held longer than necessary.

- **Employee training on security**: Instituting mandatory training programs to educate employees on cybersecurity best practices and the importance of data protection.

Critical role of employee training

Training employees in cybersecurity and data protection is paramount. It not only equips them with the knowledge to identify and mitigate potential threats but also instills a culture of security awareness within the organization. This is essential for building a strong security foundation and ensuring compliance across the organization. Specifically, effective training helps achieve the following:

- **Mitigating insider threats**: Educating employees on signs of phishing, social engineering, and other cyber threats can significantly reduce the risk posed by insider threats.

- **Compliance**: Training ensures employees understand their roles in complying with the DPDP Act, including the handling, sharing, and processing of personal data.

- **Fostering a culture of security**: Regular training sessions reinforce the importance of data security, encouraging employees to take personal accountability for protecting personal data.

Government of India cybersecurity training programs

The Government of India has initiated various cybersecurity training programs to enhance the nation's cybersecurity posture. These include the following:

- **Indian Computer Emergency Response Team (CERT-In)**: Offers cybersecurity training and awareness programs covering various aspects of cyber threats and countermeasures.

- **National Institute of Electronics and Information Technology (NIELIT)**: Provides courses on cybersecurity, aiming to develop skilled professionals in the field.

- **National Critical Information Infrastructure Protection Centre (NCIIPC)**: Conducts awareness and training sessions for protecting critical information infrastructure.

- **Cyber Surakshit Bharat Initiative**: Launched by the **Ministry of Electronics and Information Technology (MeitY)**, it focuses on spreading cybersecurity awareness and training among the government's IT professionals.

In addition, let us look at some links that offer a range of cybersecurity training programs and resources designed to enhance security skills and awareness across various roles and expertise levels. Here are some notable programs and resources:

- **Microsoft Learn for Security, Compliance, and Identity**: Microsoft Learn provides a comprehensive collection of training modules and learning paths specifically focused on security, compliance, and identity. These resources cover a wide range of topics from basic security concepts to advanced threat protection strategies.

https://learn.microsoft.com/en-us/training/

- **Microsoft Cybersecurity Architect Certification**: This certification is designed for professionals looking to validate their expertise in implementing security solutions across complex environments. It covers security posture assessment, designing security strategies, and recommending security solutions to protect against threats.

https://learn.microsoft.com/en-us/credentials/certifications/cybersecurity-architect-expert/

- **Microsoft Security Community**: The Microsoft Security Community offers webinars, virtual events, and discussions led by Microsoft experts and the security community. It is a terrific way to stay updated on the latest security trends and connect with other cybersecurity professionals.

https://techcommunity.microsoft.com

- **Microsoft Virtual Training Days**: Microsoft Virtual Training Days are free, in-depth training events that cover various aspects of Microsoft technologies, including security solutions like Azure Security, Microsoft 365 Defender, and Azure Sentinel. These sessions are designed to help IT professionals and developers enhance their skills and prepare for certification exams.

https://www.microsoft.com/en-ca/sites/microsoft-training-days/

- **Microsoft Security Blog**: The Microsoft Security Blog is an excellent resource for articles, security insights, and best practices from Microsoft's own security experts. Topics range from cloud security to information protection and threat intelligence.

https://www.microsoft.com/en-us/security/blog/

These resources provide valuable knowledge and skills development opportunities for individuals and organizations aiming to strengthen their cybersecurity posture.

The DPDP Act necessitates the creation of robust data security policies, with significant emphasis on training employees in cybersecurity best practices. By adhering to these guidelines and leveraging government-sponsored training programs, organizations can not only ensure compliance with the DPDP Act but also fortify their defenses against the ever-evolving landscape of cyber threats.

Data protection alert triage

In today's complex digital landscape, securing sensitive data is one of the most critical challenges faced by organizations. While investing in innovative data security software is an essential step, relying solely on software is not enough to ensure full protection. This is especially true when dealing with DLP across the entire lifecycle of data, whether at rest, in motion, or in use. DLP software plays a crucial role in flagging potential risks and vulnerabilities, but the challenge lies in efficiently managing and responding to these DLP alerts.

Again, as Rules 2025 6(e) focuses on the need of SOC and it says *for enabling the detection of unauthorized access, its investigation, remediation to prevent recurrence and continued processing in the event of such a compromise, retain such logs and personal data for a period of one year, unless compliance* with any law for the time being in force requires otherwise.

Microsoft Sentinel and Microsoft XDR serve as unified platforms for **Security Operations Centers (SOCs)**, enabling real-time detection, investigation, and response to unauthorized access attempts. Sentinel provides scalable, cloud-native SIEM capabilities with built-in AI for alert triage and correlation, while Microsoft XDR delivers cross-domain threat visibility across identities, endpoints, data, and apps. Together, they empower SOC teams to operationalize DLP alerts efficiently, in line with Rule 6(1)(e) of the Draft DPDP Rules, ensuring swift investigation, remediation, and compliance with one-year log retention mandates.

To truly safeguard data and ensure compliance with regulations like the India DPDP Act and GDPR, organizations must establish clear processes, build capable teams, and implement comprehensive monitoring frameworks. These elements help manage DLP alerts, streamline triage processes, and enforce stringent **service-level agreements (SLAs)** for timely responses. This document discusses the importance of DLP alert triage, key processes to consider, and the need for an effective team structure to support these efforts.

Role of DLP software in protecting data

Data security software that covers data in all its states, in motion, and in use, provides a solid foundation for safeguarding personal data. Here is a quick breakdown of how each state of data is protected by DLP software:

- **Data at rest**: This refers to data stored in databases, file servers, or storage media. DLP software scans personal information and prevents unauthorized access by employing encryption, access control, and monitoring tools to detect potential breaches or misuses.

- **Data in motion**: This refers to data being transferred over networks. DLP software monitors network traffic and applies encryption protocols and other security measures to prevent the interception of sensitive data during transmission.

- **Data in use**: This involves data actively being accessed or processed by applications or users. DLP software monitors access points such as endpoints and cloud applications, enforcing security policies to prevent unauthorized data handling or leakage.

While DLP software can detect and block risky actions, it generates alerts for distinct types of suspicious activities. These alerts need to be triaged efficiently to prevent personal data breaches, ensure compliance, and avoid business disruptions.

Need for DLP alert triage

DLP alert triage is the process of prioritizing, investigating, and responding to the alerts generated by DLP software. With the increasing volume of sensitive data and complex threat landscapes, the number of DLP alerts can be overwhelming. Without a structured triage process, it is easy for organizations to fall into alert fatigue, leading to missed threats and slow response times.

A well-implemented DLP alert triage process enables organizations to:

- **Prioritize alerts based on risk:** Not all alerts carry the same level of risk. By establishing a clear triage process, organizations can prioritize critical alerts that pose the most immediate danger, ensuring a swift response.

- **Improve incident response**: By having a streamlined triage process, organizations can respond to potential personal data breaches faster, minimizing the damage caused by unauthorized access or data leakage.

- **Ensure compliance**: Many regulatory frameworks, including the DPDP Act, GDPR, and HIPAA, require organizations to take immediate action when a personal data breach is detected. Efficient DLP alert triage ensures compliance with these regulations.

- **Reduce noise**: A well-structured process helps filter out false positives or low-priority alerts, allowing security teams to focus on the real risks to the organization.

Building a DLP triage process

To build an effective DLP alert triage process, organizations must establish structured workflows that ensure all alerts are investigated, prioritized, and responded to appropriately. Here is a high-level approach to building this process:

1. **Categorize alerts:** The first step is to categorize DLP alerts based on their severity and type. For instance:

   - High-severity alerts could involve unauthorized access to sensitive data or the attempted exfiltration of critical business information.

   - Medium-severity alerts might include unauthorized attempts to share sensitive files externally or violations of data handling policies.

   - Low-severity alerts could involve minor policy violations that do not pose an immediate threat but still need investigation.

2. **Prioritize based on risk:** Once alerts are categorized, it is essential to prioritize them based on the risk they pose to the organization. This requires establishing criteria such as:

   - The type of data involved (e.g., personal Data, financial data, intellectual property).

- The user or entity involved (e.g., internal employee vs. external attacker).
- The system affected (e.g., critical server vs. non-critical endpoint).

This risk-based prioritization helps teams focus their efforts on the most critical alerts.

3. **Define escalation paths:** Not all alerts can be resolved at the first level of triage. For complex or high-risk incidents, escalation paths must be clearly defined. For example, a low-risk alert may be managed by the SOC analyst, but a high-risk alert involving a potential personal data breach should be escalated to senior security engineers or incident response teams.

4. **Automate where possible:** Automation can assist in DLP alert triage by automatically categorizing and prioritizing alerts based on pre-defined rules. By leveraging tools like Microsoft 365's DLP policies and Microsoft Defender for Cloud, organizations can automate much of the triage process, allowing security teams to focus on higher-level investigations.

5. **Investigate and respond:** Once alerts are triaged, it is important to investigate them thoroughly. This could involve reviewing logs, user activity, and the context of the alert. After investigation, teams should either take immediate remediation actions (such as blocking data exfiltration) or log the incident for further review.

6. **Measure and improve:** The effectiveness of the DLP triage process must be continually measured and improved. This can be done by tracking metrics such as:

- Number of alerts triaged.
- Time taken to respond to critical alerts.
- The number of incidents escalated.

Importance of auditing

Audit plays a pivotal role in ensuring accountability, transparency, and continuous compliance under the DPDP Act, 2023, and its Draft Rules, 2025. Specifically, Rule 12 of the Draft Rules mandates that SDFs conduct annual audits to assess their adherence to the Act's provisions.

These audits are essential for systematically evaluating the effectiveness of data protection measures, including access controls, authentication mechanisms, incident response protocols, data retention practices, and logging activities. By identifying gaps and mitigating risks, organizations can demonstrate due diligence in safeguarding personal data.

Furthermore, the findings from these audits must be reported to the Data Protection Board of India, ensuring regulatory oversight and reinforcing the importance of robust data governance practices. In the event of a data breach, audit trails offer critical evidence for investigations and help establish whether appropriate measures were in place to prevent and respond to incidents.

In essence, audits serve as the backbone of a strong data governance framework, ensuring that privacy and security measures evolve in alignment with legal, technological, and organizational changes.

Audits across the DLP process

In addition to establishing a process, building a capable SOC team is critical for handling DLP alerts effectively. This team should consist of distinct roles and levels of expertise in auditing the effectiveness of the DLP process.

- **SOC Analysts (Tier 1):** Responsible for the initial triage of DLP alerts, including categorizing and prioritizing alerts, investigating low-risk incidents, and escalating high-risk ones.

- **Incident Response Team (Tier 2):** This team manages escalated alerts that require deeper investigation, forensic analysis, and incident remediation.

- **Data Protection Officer (DPO):** The DPO ensures compliance with data privacy regulations like the DPDP Act and oversees the overall data protection strategy, including DLP processes.

- **Security engineers**: These individuals are responsible for managing and maintaining the DLP software, ensuring it is up to date and properly configured to manage the latest threats.

- **Auditors**: Regular audits of the DLP triage process ensure that the organization is maintaining compliance and meeting SLA requirements. Auditors assess whether DLP alerts are being triaged effectively and whether responses are happening within the designated timeframes.

Importance of maintaining SLAs

To ensure the effectiveness of DLP alert triage, regular audits must be performed. These audits should assess the organization's ability to meet SLAs for responding to alerts. Failure to triage and resolve DLP alerts within the agreed timelines can lead to compliance violations, personal data breaches, and reputational damage.

The key areas to audit include the following:

- **Timeliness**: Are alerts being investigated and responded to within the designated SLA period?

- **Effectiveness**: Are the triage processes leading to proper resolutions, or are critical alerts being overlooked?

- **Compliance**: Is the organization meeting all regulatory requirements, such as personal data breach reporting deadlines?

Maintaining SLAs and conducting regular audits not only improves the overall security posture but also provides assurance to stakeholders that the organization is committed to protecting sensitive data.

Case study of Ananya's experience

Consider Ananya's interaction with her bank. Regular audits might reveal a need for stronger encryption for data transmitted through mobile banking, prompting a policy update. Similarly, if a new provision in the DPDP Act calls for enhanced user consent mechanisms, the bank can revise its policies accordingly, ensuring Ananya's data is managed in full compliance with the law.

Training employees in updated policies and the importance of audits ensures that everyone involved in data processing understands their role in safeguarding personal data, reinforcing a culture of security and compliance within the bank.

In summary, regular audits and policy revisions are indispensable to a bank's data security strategy. They not only ensure compliance with the DPDP Act but also strengthen the bank's defenses against cyber threats, protecting customers' personal data and maintaining the institution's reputation.

Personal data breach response and notification

Strategies for Personal Data Breach Detection and Response, coupled with the response protocols stipulated by the DPDP Act, form a critical part of an organization's cybersecurity framework. These measures are designed not only to detect and respond to personal data breaches but also to ensure compliance with regulatory requirements, thus safeguarding individuals' personal data and maintaining trust.

Strategies for personal data breach detection

The following are the strategies for data breach detection:

- **Monitoring and logging**: Continuous monitoring of network and system activities is essential. Logging these activities aids in the early detection of unusual or unauthorized actions that could indicate a personal data breach.

- **Anomaly detection systems**: Implementing advanced anomaly detection systems can help identify patterns or activities that deviate from the norm, which might signal a breach.

- **Regular security audits and vulnerability assessments**: Conducting these assessments can uncover potential weaknesses in the security infrastructure that could be exploited in a breach.

- **Employee training and awareness**: Employees should be trained to recognize the signs of personal data breaches and understand the protocol for reporting potential security incidents.

Response protocols

The DPDP Act emphasizes the importance of having a structured response plan in place to manage and mitigate the impact of personal data breaches. The key components of this plan include:

- **Immediate containment and assessment**: Once a breach is detected, immediate steps should be taken to contain it and assess the scope and impact, including which types of personal data were involved.

- **Notification procedures**: The DPDP Act requires that affected individuals and relevant regulatory authorities be notified of the breach within a stipulated timeframe. This notification should include details of the breach, the types of data involved, and the potential impact on the individuals concerned.

- **Remediation and recovery**: The organization must take steps to secure its systems from further breaches, including addressing the vulnerability that led to the breach. Plans for recovery and restoration of any compromised data should also be implemented.

- **Documentation and evaluation**: All breaches and the organization's response to them must be documented. This documentation is crucial for compliance purposes and serves as a learning tool for preventing future breaches.

Applying breach detection and response to Ananya's case

Consider Ananya's use of the internet and mobile banking. Should a personal data breach occur that compromises her personal data, the bank's detection systems would ideally identify the breach at the earliest possible stage. Following the DPDP Act's stipulations, the bank would then:

- Immediately contain the breach to prevent further data loss.

- Assess the impact, particularly concerning Ananya's compromised data.

- Notify Ananya and relevant authorities, detailing the breach's nature and advising on protective measures she can take.

- Remediate the security flaw to prevent future breaches, and support Ananya in mitigating any potential harm.

This approach underscores the necessity of proactive breach detection strategies and a well-defined response protocol in compliance with the DPDP Act. It not only helps protect individuals like Ananya but also reinforces the integrity and trustworthiness of the institution managing personal data.

Agentic world and importance of SOC

As organizations navigate increasingly complex threat landscapes, the emergence of AI-powered security agents is poised to revolutionize the operations of SOCs. Microsoft is at the forefront of this transformation, developing enterprise-grade AI agents such as Microsoft Security Copilot, Defender XDR, and AI-enhanced Priva assistants that embed intelligent capabilities into modern cybersecurity workflows.

In the agentic world of the near future, these AI agents will Act as intelligent co-defenders, augmenting human analysts and automating critical functions within the SOC. Their capabilities span a broad spectrum:

- **Autonomous threat detection**: AI agents will monitor vast volumes of telemetry data in real time, recognizing behavioral anomalies and proactively mitigating threats without human intervention.

- **Context-aware policy enforcement**: By leveraging machine learning, these agents will dynamically enforce or adapt DLP and access control policies based on contextual risk indicators such as user behavior, device posture, or geographical location.

- **Personalized privacy assistants**: Embedded AI copilots will empower Data Principals under laws like the DPDP Act by allowing them to manage consents, review data usage, and adjust privacy settings within applications, fostering transparency and digital trust.

- **Automated compliance audits**: These agents will support compliance with regulations such as Rule 6 (security safeguards) and Rule 12 (audit obligations) of the DPDP Rules, 2025, by generating real-time reports on policy effectiveness, access patterns, and incident responses.

The importance of SOC operations will only grow as AI agents scale threat detection, automate triage, and enable predictive defense models. This next generation of security operations, empowered by Microsoft's AI innovation, will transform reactive defense mechanisms into proactive and autonomous security ecosystems, ushering in a new era of resilience, compliance, and trust.

Conclusion

As we conclude this chapter, it becomes evident that securing personal data in today's interconnected digital world demands far more than traditional perimeter defenses. With the introduction of the DPDP Act, 2023, and the accompanying Draft Rules 2025, India has established a firm legal framework to ensure data fiduciaries uphold a high standard of privacy, accountability, and technical rigor in protecting personal data.

This chapter looked through the foundational pillars of data security, protecting data at rest, in motion, and in use, and how solutions like encryption, access controls, logging, authentication, and breach response planning must be woven into every facet of a data protection strategy. We also emphasized the importance of DLP alert triage, security training, and auditing to enable compliance and operational resilience.

Yet, data security is not static. Emerging technologies, particularly AI-powered agents, are poised to redefine the future of cybersecurity operations. With tools such as Microsoft Security Copilot, Defender XDR, and Priva, and the upcoming development of AI agents, threat detection, contextual policy enforcement, and real-time compliance audits are possible. These innovations will not only enhance the effectiveness of SOCs but also enable proactive data governance, delivering faster response times and more intelligent, adaptive defenses.

In the evolving digital era, organizations must not only comply but also innovate by merging legal obligations and technological foresight to create a resilient, trusted, and future-ready data protection posture.

The upcoming chapter looks into the rights granted to individuals under the DPDP Act, such as access, correction, erasure, grievance redressal, and nomination. It outlines the duties of Data Principals to Act responsibly while exercising their rights. Practical guidance on handling requests, operational challenges, and compliance tools like Microsoft Purview and Priva will also be discussed. Real-world scenarios and best practices will help organizations effectively uphold these rights.

Join our Discord space

Join our Discord workspace for latest updates, offers, tech happenings around the world, new releases, and sessions with the authors:

https://discord.bpbonline.com

CHAPTER 5

Data Principal Rights and Duties

Introduction

Data Principal Rights are central to modern data protection laws and acts, empowering individuals to control their personal data held by organizations. These rights include the ability to access, correct, delete, and restrict the processing of personal data, serving as a foundation for privacy and data protection. In today's digital world, where data is collected and processed across sectors, these rights are clearly defined in Chapter III of the DPDP Act and further elaborated in Rule 13 of the Draft DPDP Rules 2025 on the rights of Data Principal, thus serving as a cornerstone of privacy and data protection.

The **Digital Personal Data Protection (DPDP)** Act is crucial in defining and protecting these rights, offering mechanisms for resources, and requiring lawful, transparent data processing by organizations. The Act aligns with global standards, enhancing public trust in digital services. Key rights under the DPDP Act include access to personal data, correction of inaccuracies, data erasure, restrictions on processing, and reaching out to the DPO in an easy way.

To support compliance, organizations can leverage tools like Microsoft Purview Information Protection, Microsoft Priva, One Trust, and Data Grail. These solutions facilitate data governance, consent management, and automation of Data Principal requests, thereby helping organizations uphold the principles of the DPDP Act effectively.

Structure

In this chapter, we will cover the following topics:

- Understanding Data Principal Rights
- Handling Data Principal grievances
- Processing of the Data Principal request
- Challenges in Data Principal request
- Right to access information about personal data
- Right to correction and erasure of personal data
- Right of grievance redressal
- Right to nominate
- Duties of the Data Principal
- Importance of Microsoft Purview
- Implementing Data Principal Rights
- Best practices for managing Data Principal requests

Objectives

By the end of the chapter, readers will have a clear understanding of the definition and scope of Data Principal Rights under the DPDP Act and its rules, recognizing the importance of Data Principal Rights in maintaining privacy, trust, and transparency. This chapter aims to highlight the significance of empowering individuals (Data Principals) with clear rights to access, erase, restrict processing, ensuring their autonomy and privacy. Readers will explore how these rights foster transparency, build trust between individuals and Data Fiduciaries. Additionally, the chapter will discuss practical challenges organizations face in complying with Data Principal requests, such as identity verification and comprehensive data discovery. Special attention will be given to handling requests involving vulnerable groups like children and individuals with disabilities, emphasizing enhanced consent mechanisms mandated by the Act and Rules. Finally, through practical case studies and insights into leveraging tools like Microsoft Purview and Microsoft Priva, and other third-party tools. Readers will understand effective strategies and technologies available to fulfill their compliance obligations under the DPDP Act and its associated Rules.

Understanding Data Principal Rights

The previous chapters laid the foundation for understanding the DPDP Act, 2023, covering the critical need for data protection, the evolving digital landscape, the importance of consent, and the requirements for implementing reasonable security safeguards. These discussions highlighted the roles and responsibilities of various stakeholders involved in data protection. Let us look into the definitions of these covered within Chapter II, Section 2:

(f) "child" means an individual who has not completed the age of eighteen years; (i) "Data Fiduciary" means any person who alone or in conjunction with other persons determines the purpose and means of processing of personal data.

(j) "Data Principal" means the individual to whom the personal data relates, and where such individual is —

    (i) a child, includes the parents or lawful guardian of such a child.

    (ii) a person with disability, includes her lawful guardian, acting on her behalf;

The term Data Principal in the DPDP Act 2023 is defined as the individual to whom the personal data relates. This includes cases where the individual is a child, the parents or lawful guardian of such a child, and cases where the individual is a person with a disability, their lawful guardian acting on their behalf. When a Data Principal is a child under the age of eighteen, the Act mandates that their parents or lawful guardian act on their behalf to provide consent and exercise their data rights, ensuring enhanced protection for minors, which is further explained within Rule 10.

Overview of Data Principal Rights

Based on the DPDP Act 2023 Chapter III (Sections 11-14), the rights of a Data Principal (equivalent to a *Data Subject* in other jurisdictions) encompass several key areas that ensure the protection and autonomy over one's personal data. These rights aim to provide individuals with control over their personal data and how it is used by organizations. Let us explore these rights using Ananya's example to illustrate how they apply in practical scenarios.

The following is an overview of Data Principal Rights

- **Right to access information about personal data:** Ananya has the right to access the personal data that the bank holds about her. This means she can request to see what personal data the bank has collected, including account details, transaction history, and any other data linked to her. (Ch III, Sec 11).

- **Right to correction**: If any of Ananya's personal data held by the bank is incorrect or incomplete, she has the right to request its correction. For example, if her address or phone number changes, she can ask the bank to update her records accordingly. (Ch III, sec 12)

- **Right to erasure:** Ananya can request the deletion of her personal data when it is no longer necessary for the bank to hold it, or if she withdraws her consent for its processing. Suppose Ananya closes her bank account; she can ask for her information to be erased from the bank's database. (Ch III, sec 12)

- **Right of grievance redressal**: Ananya has the right to raise a grievance if she objects to the processing of her personal data for specific purposes, such as marketing or profiling.

For example, if the bank uses her data to suggest new products or services, she can file a complaint and opt out of receiving such communications. (Ch III, sec 13**)**

- **Rights to nominate:** Ananya has the right to nominate another individual who can exercise her data protection rights on her behalf in the event of her death or incapacity. For instance, Ananya may choose to nominate her spouse or a trusted family member, who would then have the authority to manage or request actions regarding her personal data held by the bank, such as accessing, correcting, or requesting the deletion of her information. (Ch III, sec 14**)**

Example scenario with Ananya

Ananya recently applied for a mortgage through her bank's online portal. Utilizing her rights under the DPDP Act, she first requests access to her personal data to ensure all information is correct and up to date. Upon noticing a discrepancy in her home address records, she exercises her right to correction, asking the bank to update her details. Concerned about the bank using her data for marketing, she objects to her information being used for any purpose other than her mortgage application. Finally, given the sensitive nature of the documents submitted, she inquires about the bank's data processing activities, affirming her right to be informed and ensuring that her data is treated with the utmost confidentiality and security.

These scenarios underscore the significance of Data Principal Rights under the DPDP Act, empowering individuals like Ananya with greater control and transparency over their personal data.

Act mapping

The DPDP Act, 2023, specifically outlines Data Principal Rights and Duties in Chapter III, through Sections 11 to 15, with detailed procedures for exercising these rights provided under Rule 13 of the Draft Digital Personal Data Protection Rules, 2025. These provisions collectively emphasize transparency, autonomy, and accountability in handling personal data:

Chapter	Section	Definition name	Narration	Solution mapping	Rule mapping
3	11	Right to access information about personal data.	Data Principals can request and obtain a summary of personal data processed by a Data Fiduciary, including data processed and identities of Data Fiduciaries or Data Processors involved.	Utilize solutions such as activity Explorer, Content Explorer, and Data Catalog.	Rule 13(2)

Chapter	Section	Definition name	Narration	Solution mapping	Rule mapping
3	12	Right to correction and erasure of personal data.	Data Principals may request correction of inaccurate or incomplete personal data and the erasure of data no longer necessary or for which consent has been withdrawn.	Implement data correction workflows and erasure protocols, supported by data governance tools.	Rule 13(2)
3	13	Right of grievance redressal.	Data Principals must have access to grievance redressal mechanisms with defined timelines for addressing and resolving complaints efficiently.	Establish clear grievance mechanisms, supported by compliance management systems.	Rule 13(3)
3	14	Right to nominate.	Data Principals have the right to nominate individuals to exercise their data rights in cases of death or incapacity, following prescribed procedures.	Provide nomination functionalities through data management platforms or apps.	Rule 13(4)
3	15	Duties of Data Principal.	Data Principals are responsible for providing accurate information and avoiding false or frivolous complaints to maintain responsible data protection practices.	Foster Data Principal awareness through continuous training and awareness programs.	

Table 5.1: Quick view into DPDP Act Chapter III and DPDP Rule 13

Handling Data Principal grievances

Handling Data Requests under the DPDP Act involves several key steps. Under the DPDP Act, 2023 and its Draft Rules, 2025, empowering individuals, referred to as Data Principals, to exercise their rights is a central obligation of every Data Fiduciary. Proper handling of these requests is critical for ensuring compliance, building trust, and fostering a transparent relationship between organizations and individuals.

The Act recognizes several rights for Data Principals, including the right to access, correct, erase personal data, raise grievances, and nominate others to act on their behalf. Rule 13 provides specific operational requirements for how Data Fiduciaries must enable the exercise of these rights.

The key requirements for handling Data Principal requests are as follows:

- **Clear communication channels (Rule 13(1)):** Data Fiduciaries must publish, on their website or app, the methods by which a Data Principal can submit a request. This could include online forms, customer portals, helpdesks, or email addresses.

    o **Example**: A bank must publish a dedicated privacy portal where customers like Ananya can submit access, correction, or grievance requests.

- **Identification mechanisms (Rule 13(1)(b)):** Data Fiduciaries must clearly inform Data Principals about any identifiers (like customer ID, account number, or user ID) that must be provided to authenticate their request.

    o **Example**: Ananya may be asked to provide her customer ID and registered mobile number when requesting correction of her data.

- **Request Handling for Access, Correction, and Erasure (Rule 13(2)):** Data Principals can submit requests for:

    o Accessing their personal data. (Chapter III, Section 11)

    o Correcting inaccurate or incomplete data. (Chapter III, Section 12)

    o Erasing data that is no longer necessary or when consent is withdrawn. (Chapter III, Section 12)

Data Fiduciaries must facilitate these requests promptly, using the means and identifiers published.

- **Grievance redressal system (Rule 13(3)):** Organizations must have a grievance redressal mechanism with a defined response timeline published clearly. They must implement technical and organizational measures to ensure grievances are resolved within the published period.

    o **Example**: If Ananya complains about unauthorized marketing communication, the bank must acknowledge and address it within the timeline they committed to on their platform.

- **Right to nominate (Rule 13(4)):** Data Principals must be enabled to *nominate* individuals who can exercise their rights if they die or are incapacitated. The nomination facility should be available according to the organization's terms of service, and users must be informed on how to complete this process.

- **Meaning of "Identifier" (Rule 13(5)):** An **identifier** refers to any unique sequence, such as customer IDs, enrollment IDs, or license numbers, that helps associate a request with the correct Data Principal.

Processing of the Data Principal request

In the context of the DPDP Act, handling requests from Data Principals requires a structured approach to ensure compliance and safeguard the rights of individuals. While the Act specifies the overarching requirements, implementing a detailed process involves several critical steps, such as:

1. **Request receipt and acknowledgment (Rule 13(1)):**

    *   **Initial contact:** Establish clear channels through which Data Principals can submit their requests, such as dedicated email addresses, online portals, or physical forms.

    *   **Acknowledgment:** Promptly acknowledge the receipt of the request to the Data Principal, providing an initial assessment of the request's scope and the anticipated timeframe for response.

2. **Verification of identity (Rule 13(1)(b)):**

    *   **Identity verification:** Before processing the request, verify the identity of the Data Principal to prevent unauthorized access to personal data. This step may involve asking for additional information or documents that can confirm the requester's identity.

    *   **Data security:** Ensure that the verification process respects the privacy and security of the Data Principal, using secure communication channels and data handling practices.

3. **Evaluation and processing:**

    *   **Assessment:** Evaluate the request to understand its nature (e.g., access, correction, and erasure) and determine the applicability and feasibility of fulfilling the request under the DPDP Act.

    *   **Execution:** Take appropriate action to process the request. This may involve accessing, correcting, or deleting personal data, or providing the requested information to the Data Principal.

4. **Communication of outcome:**

    *   **Response:** Communicate the outcome of the request to the Data Principal, including any actions taken or reasons for refusal or inability to comply with the request.

    *   **Method of communication:** Use clear, understandable language and choose a communication method that is secure and appropriate based on the initial form of request (e.g., written response for written requests).

5. **Documentation and audit trail:**

- **Record-keeping:** Maintain detailed records of all Data Principal requests, including the identity verification process, actions taken, and communications exchanged. This documentation is vital for compliance verification and audit purposes. Explained in detail within *Chapter 8, Records, Documentation, and Accountability,* of the book.

Example of handling Ananya's data request

Suppose Ananya, a bank customer, submits a request to access all personal data the bank holds about her. The bank will do the following:

- Acknowledges receipt of Ananya's request via email. The bank promptly acknowledges receipt of Ananya's request through an email or SMS, informing her that her request is being processed.

- Ask Ananya to provide a copy of her ID card through a secure portal for identity verification. To ensure that the request is genuine, the bank asks Ananya to submit a copy of her official ID (such as Aadhaar or PAN card) via a secure customer portal, matching the identifier (e.g., customer ID) already associated with her account.

- Reviews her data and compiles the information held across various departments. The bank initiates an internal review by accessing relevant systems (e.g., account management, CRM, transaction history) to compile a complete and accurate report of Ananya's personal data.

- Provides Ananya with a comprehensive report of her personal data within the stipulated timeframe. Within the published grievance handling or request processing timeframe, the bank provides Ananya a comprehensive report of her personal data, including: Account details, Transaction records, any profiling or service usage data in a secure, readable, and commonly used electronic format.

- Documents the entire process for compliance and auditing purposes. The bank documents the entire process—acknowledgment, identity verification, data compilation, and fulfillment of the request—to demonstrate compliance with the DPDP Act during audits or inspections by the Data Protection Board.

Handling Data Principal requests in compliance with the DPDP Act is not just a regulatory requirement but also an opportunity to strengthen trust and transparency with individuals concerning their personal data.

Challenges in Data Principal requests

Processing Data Principal Rights requests presents significant operational challenges for organizations, particularly when ensuring full compliance with the DPDP Act, 2023, and associated Rule 13 of the Draft Rules. These challenges impact the ability to guarantee the rights of access, correction, erasure, grievance redressal, and nomination as mandated under Chapter III of the Act. Here are the top five challenges organizations face:

- **Verification of Data Principal's identity:**
  - **Relevant Act and rule:**
    - DPDP Act, Chapter III (General Rights of Data Principals)
    - **Rule 13(1)(b):** Organizations must verify the Data Principal through specific identifiers (e.g., customer ID, enrollment number).
  - **Challenge:** Ensuring that the individual submitting the request is truly the Data Principal, or is duly authorized to Act on their behalf, is complex, especially without standardized or centralized identification mechanisms.
  - **Risk:** Failure in proper identity verification could result in unauthorized access to personal data, leading to breaches under the Act and severe penalties.

- **Comprehensive data discovery:**
  - **Relevant Act and rule:**
    - DPDP Act, Chapter III, Section 11 (Right to Access Information)
    - **Rule 13(2):** Data Fiduciary must compile and provide all personal data held about the Data Principal.
  - **Challenge:** Locating all instances of a Data Principal's personal data across multiple systems, cloud platforms, on-premises repositories, and legacy databases is operationally daunting, especially for large or decentralized organizations.
  - **Risk:** Incomplete or inaccurate fulfillment of access, correction, or erasure requests may lead to non-compliance with the Act and erode customer trust, exposing the organization to enforcement actions by the Data Protection Board.

- **Balancing transparency and security:**
  - **Relevant Act and rule:**
    - DPDP Act, Chapter III, Section 11 and Section 12 (Right to Access and Correction)
  - **Challenge:** Organizations must carefully balance their duty to provide transparent access to Data Principals without inadvertently exposing the personal data of other individuals or revealing sensitive internal security measures.
  - **Risk:** Over-disclosure could cause privacy breaches or compromise organizational security, both of which constitute violations of reasonable

safeguard requirements under the Act.

- **Resource and time constraints:**
  - o **Relevant Act and rule:**
    - ▪ DPDP Act, implied timeline expectations. (though the Act leaves detailed timelines to be notified via the Rules)
    - ▪ **Rule 13(3):** Organizations must set and disclose grievance redressal periods and implement processes to meet them.
  - o **Challenge:** Processing requests demands dedicated human resources, legal expertise, IT support, and efficient workflows, resources that many organizations, particularly smaller entities, may lack.
  - o **Risk:** Delays or procedural errors in responding to rights requests could lead to penalties under the DPDP Act, formal complaints to the Data Protection Board, and reputational damage in the market.

Addressing these challenges

Organizations can tackle these challenges through a combination of strategic planning, technological solutions, and staff training. For instance, implementing centralized data management systems can streamline data discovery, while robust identity verification processes can safeguard against unauthorized access. Additionally, investing in privacy management software can automate many aspects of handling Data Principal Rights requests, reducing the burden on resources and ensuring timely compliance.

Furthermore, fostering a culture of data protection awareness among employees and regularly reviewing and updating data security policies, considering evolving regulations, can significantly mitigate these challenges. By proactively addressing these hurdles, organizations can ensure they not only comply with laws like the DPDP Act but also reinforce their commitment to protecting individual privacy.

Case of children and the special-abled

The DPDP Act, 2023, imposes a heightened duty of care on organizations when processing the personal data of children and individuals with disabilities. Recognizing their inherent vulnerability, the Act establishes specific rights, responsibilities, and safeguards, which are operationalized through Rules 9, 10, and 11 of the Draft Rules, 2025.

This section highlights the regulatory requirements, practical handling obligations, and the challenges organizations may face.

The key regulatory requirements are as follows:

- **Verifiable consent requirement (Chapter II Section 9(1); Rule 10):**

- o **For children:** Before processing a child's personal data, the Data Fiduciary must obtain verifiable consent from the parent or lawful guardian.

- o **For special-abled individuals**: When processing the personal data of a person with a disability who cannot make legally binding decisions, verifiable consent must be obtained from a court-appointed or government-recognized lawful guardian.

- o **Illustrations (Rule 10 examples)**:

  - ▪ If a child seeks to create an online account, the platform must verify the identity of the parent either by relying on existing identity and age records or through tokens verified via trusted systems like Digital Locker services.

  - ▪ If the guardian is not previously registered, they must voluntarily submit identity and age proofs for verification before consent is accepted.

- **Prohibition on detrimental processing (Chapter II Section 9(2)):**

  - o Data Fiduciaries must not process children's personal data in any manner likely to cause harm to their well-being.

  - o Harm includes actions that may negatively impact the child's physical, emotional, mental, or social health.

- **Prohibition on tracking, behavioral monitoring, and targeted advertising (Chapter II Section 9(3)):** Data Fiduciaries are expressly prohibited from:

  - o Tracking children's online behavior.

  - o Profiling children for behavioral analysis.

  - o Sending targeted advertisements directed at children.

- **Data minimization and purpose limitation:**

  - o Only data strictly necessary for the stated, consented purpose should be collected and processed.

  - o Organizations must avoid unnecessary or excessive data collection, especially from minors and individuals with special needs.

- **Right to erasure (Chapter III Section 12):** Guardians must be allowed to request erasure of a child's or person with special needs ' personal data when it is no longer necessary or if consent is withdrawn.

- **Exemptions for specific Data Fiduciaries and purposes (Rule 11):**

  - o Certain classes of Data Fiduciaries and specific purposes are exempted from the full obligations under Chapter II Section 9(1) and 9(3) (e.g., schools processing children's data for educational delivery).

  o These exemptions are listed in Part A and Part B of the Fourth Schedule of the Draft Rules and are conditional.

Case scenario

Ananya wishes to create online learning accounts for her younger brother (a minor) and her cousin with special needs.

Under the DPDP Act and Rules, the educational platform must:

- Obtain verifiable consent from Ananya, acting as a guardian, through secure identity verification processes.
- Display a clear, child-accessible privacy notice explaining how the data will be used.
- Collect only minimal educational data necessary to operate the platform.
- Avoid tracking their behavior, profiling their usage patterns, or targeting them with ads.
- Provide Ananya with the ability to review or delete their personal data at any time.

Right to access information about personal data

One of the foundational rights granted under modern privacy laws, including the DPDP Act, 2023, is the right of a Data Principal to access their personal data held by a Data Fiduciary. This right empowers individuals to gain visibility into how their data is being collected, processed, and used. While this aligns with global privacy principles such as transparency and accountability, it is uniquely framed under the DPDP Act to give individuals meaningful control. Let us examine the Act and its provisions:

- CHAPTER III Section 11. *(1) The Data Principal shall have the right to obtain from the Data Fiduciary to whom she has previously given consent, including consent as referred to in clause (a) of section 7 (hereinafter referred to as the said Data Fiduciary), for processing of personal data, upon making to it a request in such manner as may be prescribed:*

  o *A summary of personal data which is being processed by such Data Fiduciary and the processing activities undertaken by that Data Fiduciary with respect to such personal data;*

  o *The identities of all other Data Fiduciaries and Data Processors with whom the personal data has been shared by such Data Fiduciary, along with a description of the personal data so shared; and*

  o *Any other information related to the personal data of such Data Principal and its processing, as may be prescribed.*

(2) Nothing contained in clause (b) or clause (c) of sub-section (1) shall apply in respect of the sharing of any personal data by the said Data Fiduciary with any other Data Fiduciary authorised by law to obtain such personal data, where such sharing is pursuant to a request made in writing by such other Data Fiduciary for the purpose of prevention or detection or investigation of offences or cyber incidents, or for prosecution or punishment of offences.

The right to access information about personal data is a key entitlement granted to individuals under the DPDP Act, 2023. Specifically outlined in Chapter III, Section 11, it empowers Data Principals to obtain confirmation of whether their personal data is being processed by a Data Fiduciary and to receive a summary of such data, along with details on how it is being used. This right enhances transparency by allowing individuals to understand the scope, purpose, and sharing of their personal information.

- ***Draft Rule 13***: *(5) In this rule, the expression "identifier" shall mean any sequence of characters issued by the Data Fiduciary to identify the Data Principal and includes a customer identification file number, customer acquisition form number, application reference number, enrolment ID, or licence number that enables such identification.*

Under Draft Rule 13, organizations are required to publish clear methods by which Data Principals can submit access requests and must authenticate the identity of the requester using secure identifiers such as customer IDs or enrollment numbers. Upon receiving an access request, the organization must compile and securely provide a summary of the Data Principal's personal data, including information about the categories of data being processed, the purposes of processing, and any third parties or processors with whom the data has been shared. This must be delivered in a manner that is concise, transparent, intelligible, and easily accessible, using clear and plain language.

The operational implication for organizations is significant. They must have robust systems to locate and retrieve all personal data related to a particular Data Principal across multiple repositories, structured and unstructured systems, and cloud environments. This also requires organizations to ensure that the data provided is accurate and presented in a user-friendly format. Moreover, organizations must log and retain records of access requests and their responses for a minimum of one year to demonstrate compliance with accountability obligations under Rule 13.

The right to access differs from the right to erasure in its objective and operational impact. While access focuses on transparency, enabling individuals to view and understand how their personal data is used, erasure focuses on the removal of data from organizational systems. Access requests require organizations to create mechanisms for secure data sharing, while erasure requests necessitate permanent data deletion and validation.

Right to correction and erasure of personal data

The right to correction and erasure of personal data is a privacy principle allowing individuals to have their personal data removed from certain digital records so that others cannot find it. This right empowers people to ask organizations to delete their data when it is no longer needed or if they withdraw their consent for its use. It is like having an *erase button* for your personal data on the internet or within an organization's database, ensuring your data does not linger forever in places where it was once shared or stored.

According to the DPDP Act, as stated specifically outlined in Chapter I, Section 7 *(a)* under certain legitimate uses, Chapter III, Section 12 under Right to correction and erasure of personal data, and Rule 13(2) under rights to Data Principals:

- ***Chapter I, Section 7***: *A Data Fiduciary may process personal data of a Data Principal for any of the following uses, namely:*

    o *For the specified purpose for which the Data Principal has voluntarily provided her personal data to the Data Fiduciary, and in respect of which she has not indicated to the Data Fiduciary that she does not consent to the use of her personal data.*

    A Data Fiduciary may process a Data Principal's personal data for the specific purpose voluntarily provided by the Data Principal, unless the individual has indicated otherwise (withdrawn consent).

- ***Chapter III, Section 12. (1)***: *A Data Principal shall have the right to correction, completion, updating and erasure of her personal data for the processing of which she has previously given consent, including consent as referred to in clause (a) of section 7, in accordance with any requirement or procedure under any law for the time being in force.*

    o *(2) A Data Fiduciary shall, upon receiving a request for correction, completion or updating from a Data Principal:*

        (a) Correct the inaccurate or misleading personal data;

        (b) Complete the incomplete personal data;

        (c) Update the personal data.

    o *(3): A Data Principal shall make a request in such manner as may be prescribed to the Data Fiduciary for erasure of her personal data, and upon receipt of such a request, the Data Fiduciary shall erase her personal data unless retention of the same is necessary for the specified purpose or for compliance with any law for the time being in force*

    This section grants Data Principals the explicit right to:

    - Request correction of inaccurate or outdated personal data.

- Request erasure of personal data when consent is withdrawn, or the purpose for which data was collected has been fulfilled, unless retention is mandated under another applicable law.

- **Draft Rule 13 (2):** *To exercise the rights of the Data Principal under the Act to access information about personal data and its erasure, she may make a request to the Data Fiduciary to whom she has previously given consent for processing of her personal data, using the means and furnishing the particulars published by such Data Fiduciary for the exercise of such rights.*

Under this rule, Data Fiduciaries must establish clear mechanisms for Data Principals to exercise these rights through published processes, including identity verification and timelines for fulfilling requests.

The Act mandates that a Data Fiduciary must erase personal data unless its retention is required by any currently applicable Act. Specifically, the Data Fiduciary is obliged to:

- Delete personal data once the Data Principal revokes their consent or when it is believed that the data's intended purpose has been fulfilled, whichever comes first.

- Ensure that any Data Processor who has been given personal data by the Data Fiduciary for processing also deletes this data.

To give a few examples, Ananya, an individual, signs up on an online platform provided by Contoso Cars, an e-commerce service dedicated to vehicle sales. She consents to Contoso Cars using her personal data solely for the purpose of listing her old car for sale. Once the transaction is successfully completed and the car is sold, Contoso Cars, in adherence to privacy regulations, will not retain Ananya's personal data any longer.

Ananya decides to close her savings account with Contoso Bank. Due to banking regulations, Contoso Bank is obligated to keep a record of its clients' identities for ten years after their accounts are closed. Since this retention is mandated by the Act for compliance purposes, Contoso Bank will keep Ananya's personal data for the specified duration.

When to erase data

Organizations are expected to provide clear mechanisms for Data Principals to request data erasure and to establish processes that ensure timely compliance with these requests, balancing the Data Principal's rights with any legal requirements to retain data for certain periods. The criteria under which a Data Principal can exercise the right to be forgotten typically include the following:

- **Withdrawal of consent:** If a Data Principal withdraws their consent for data processing, the Data Fiduciary must erase the data unless retention is legally required. (Ch III, Sec 12)

- **Data no longer necessary:** If the personal data is no longer needed for the original purpose of collection, it must be erased. (Ch III, Sec 12)

- **Objecting to processing**: If a Data Principal objects to data processing, and there are no overriding legitimate interests to continue processing. (Ch II, Sec 7)

- **Unlawful processing**: The processing of the data is unlawful, meaning it does not comply with legal standards or requirements.

- **Legal obligation**: The personal data must be erased to comply with a legal obligation in the jurisdiction of the Data Fiduciary. (Ch II, Sec 7)

- **Children's data**: If the data was collected in relation to the offer of information society services to a child without consent from the parent or guardian. It must be erased promptly. (Ch II, Sec 7)

Challenges involved in data erasure

The right to erasure, as stipulated under regulations like the DPDP Act, introduces several challenges for organizations, especially given the complex digital ecosystems where personal data resides. Here are some of the primary challenges and how solutions like Microsoft Purview Data Lifecycle Management and Records Management can assist:

- **Visibility across digital estates**: Modern organizations store data across a variety of locations, including on-premises applications, cloud storage (such as Azure blobs), and various **Software as a Service (SaaS)** platforms. Achieving comprehensive visibility into all these data stores to identify the Personal Data Principal to erasure requests is a significant challenge.

- **Complexity of data structures**: Data within these environments can be structured or unstructured, adding complexity to the identification and deletion process. For example, personal data might be embedded in email exchanges, documents, databases, or even log files across different environments.

- **Integration across platforms**: Many organizations use a mix of cloud services (e.g., Azure) alongside their on-premises systems. Ensuring consistent data management practices across this heterogeneous mix of platforms to effectively erase data is complex.

- **Verification and validation**: Verifying that the correct data has been erased without impacting other necessary data or system integrity requires robust validation processes, which can be resource-intensive. This, by far, is the biggest challenge and risk of deleting the wrong data.

- **Compliance and record-keeping**: Maintaining a balance between erasing data as per the right to be forgotten and retaining records for compliance with other legal or regulatory requirements presents a regulatory challenge.

Right of grievance redressal

The right of grievance redressal is a core component of the Data Principal's rights under the DPDP Act, 2023, serving as a safeguard to ensure that individuals can raise concerns or objections regarding the processing of their personal data and receive timely, structured responses. As outlined in Chapter III, Section 13 of the Act:

- **13. (1):** *A Data Principal shall have the right to have readily available means of grievance redressal provided by a Data Fiduciary or Consent Manager in respect of any Act or omission of such Data Fiduciary or Consent Manager regarding the performance of its obligations in relation to the personal data of such Data Principal or the exercise of her rights under the provisions of this Act and the rules made thereunder.*

  - *(2): The Data Fiduciary or Consent Manager shall respond to any grievances referred to in sub-section (1) within such period as may be prescribed from the date of its receipt for all or any class of Data Fiduciaries.*

  - *(3): The Data Principal shall exhaust the opportunity of redressing her grievance under this section before approaching the Board.*

Every Data Principal has the right to have their grievances addressed by the relevant Data Fiduciary, in accordance with the procedures defined under the Digital Personal Data Protection Act, 2023. This includes concerns related to data misuse, unauthorized processing, or any action that infringes upon the Data Principal's rights. Under Section 13, both Data Fiduciaries and Consent Managers are obligated to provide accessible and transparent channels for lodging complaints. They must respond to grievances within the prescribed time frame. Importantly, Data Principals are required to exhaust this redressal mechanism before approaching the Data Protection Board. This right ensures individuals have a reliable means to seek timely and effective remedies for violations of their personal data rights.

To operationalize this right, Rule 13(3) of the Draft Rules, 2025 brings further clarity, as described here:

- **Rule 13 (3):** *Every Data Fiduciary and Consent Manager shall publish on its website or app, or both, as the case may be, the period under its grievance redressal system for responding to the grievances of Data Principals and shall, for ensuring the effectiveness of the system in responding within such period, implement appropriate technical and organisational measures.*

It mandates that every Data Fiduciary and, where applicable, a Consent Manager, must publish on their website or app the period within which grievances will be resolved. This published grievance redressal timeframe must be supported by appropriate technical and organizational measures to ensure timely and effective resolution. Organizations must ensure that their grievance handling processes are accessible, secure, and transparent, and that responses are provided within the committed time period to avoid non-compliance.

From an operational standpoint, when a Data Principal, such as Ananya, raises a grievance, such as receiving unsolicited marketing emails after withdrawing consent, the Data Fiduciary must promptly acknowledge the complaint, authenticate the identity of the complainant, investigate the issue, and provide a resolution or justification within the stipulated response window. This process must be documented for accountability and audit readiness, demonstrating the organization's compliance with the DPDP framework.

The grievance redressal right is critical not only for regulatory compliance but also for establishing user trust. It ensures that Data Principals are not left without recourse when their data rights are breached. Organizations that fail to respond to grievances in a timely manner may be subject to regulatory scrutiny and penalties by the Data Protection Board of India, as empowered under the enforcement provisions of the Act.

Right to nominate

The right to nominate is a forward-looking provision under the DPDP Act, 2023, empowering individuals, referred to as Data Principals, to designate another person who may exercise their data rights in the event of their death or incapacity. This right is stated in Chapter III, Section 14 of the Act:

- *14. (1) A Data Principal shall have the right to nominate, in such manner as may be prescribed, any other individual, who shall, in the event of death or incapacity of the Data Principal, exercise the rights of the Data Principal in accordance with the provisions of this Act and the rules made thereunder.*

  - *(2): For the purposes of this section, the expression "incapacity" means inability to exercise the rights of the Data Principal under the provisions of this Act or the rules made thereunder due to unsoundness of mind or infirmity of body.*

As per Section 14 of the Act, this nominated person may exercise the Data Principal's rights in case of death or incapacity. *Incapacity* includes conditions like mental unsoundness or physical infirmity. This provision ensures continuity of data protection even when the individual cannot Act personally.

It is especially relevant in sensitive cases like medical emergencies or legal guardianship.

This right safeguards the individual's privacy preferences beyond their active control, explained as follows:

- *Rule 13(4): To exercise the rights of the Data Principal under the Act to nominate, she may, in accordance with the terms of service of the Data Fiduciary and such law as may be applicable, nominate one or more individuals, using the means and furnishing the particulars published by such Data Fiduciary for the exercise of such right.*

To operationalize this right, Draft Rule 13(4) mandates that the Data Fiduciary must publish the method by which a Data Principal can make such a nomination, typically via a website, app, or within the terms of service. This mechanism should clearly specify the process of nomination, the required identifiers or authentication measures, and any documentation needed to verify the nominee's authority. The nominated individual, once validated, shall have the authority to exercise the same rights as the Data Principal, including requesting access to or deletion of personal data, filing grievances, or withdrawing consents.

For instance, if a user like Ananya designates her spouse as her nominee while signing up with a health service provider, the provider must record and securely store this nomination. If Ananya passes away or becomes incapacitated, her spouse can then act on her behalf to manage her personal data, including exercising the right to erasure or raising a grievance if her data is mishandled. This process ensures continuity of data protection and honors the Data Principal's preferences even posthumously.

From a compliance perspective, organizations must build functionality to capture, validate, and securely store nominee details and establish clear workflows for verifying nominee claims. They must also implement safeguards to prevent unauthorized access by individuals falsely claiming nomination rights. Records of such nominations and their execution must be retained as part of the organization's accountability obligations under the Act.

By enabling the right to nominate, the DPDP Act promotes ethical data stewardship, legal continuity, and respect for individual privacy beyond one's lifetime. It reflects a maturing data protection framework that not only empowers individuals during their lifetime but also preserves their digital dignity thereafter.

Duties of the Data Principal

While the DPDP Act, 2023, provides Data Principals with significant rights to access, control, and protect their personal data, it also imposes a clear set of duties to ensure these rights are exercised responsibly and lawfully. These duties are articulated in Chapter III, Section 15 of the Act and are foundational to maintaining the integrity and balance of India's personal data protection framework.

- *Section 15: A Data Principal shall perform the following duties, namely:*
    - (a) *Comply with the provisions of all applicable laws for the time being in force while exercising rights under the provisions of this Act;*
    - (b) *To ensure not to impersonate another person while providing their personal data for a specified purpose;*
    - (c) *To ensure not to suppress any material information while providing her personal data for any document, unique identifier, proof of identity, or proof of address issued by the State or any of its instrumentalities.*
    - (d) *To ensure not to register a false or frivolous grievance or complaint with a Data Fiduciary or the Board;*

(e) To furnish only such information as is verifiably authentic, while exercising the right to correction or erasure under the provisions of this Act or the rules made thereunder.

Firstly, every Data Principal is required to comply with all applicable laws while exercising their rights under the DPDP Act. This ensures that data rights are not used in ways that obstruct or contradict other regulatory or legal frameworks. In exercising their rights, Data Principals must also not impersonate another person when providing personal data for a specific purpose. Impersonation not only violates privacy but may lead to fraudulent transactions or identity misuse, which are prosecutable under both the DPDP Act and the Indian Penal Code.

Furthermore, the Act places an obligation on individuals not to suppress material information when providing their personal data, particularly for documents such as identity cards, address proofs, or unique identifiers issued by the State or any of its instrumentalities. Suppression of such critical information compromises the accuracy of official records and undermines public trust in data systems.

The DPDP Act also discourages the misuse of grievance redressal mechanisms by making it a duty not to register false or frivolous complaints with either the Data Fiduciary or the Data Protection Board. Abuse of this process can divert attention from legitimate cases and waste regulatory resources. Finally, when exercising the right to correction or erasure, the Data Principal must ensure that they furnish only verifiably authentic information. Providing false data for correction can have far-reaching consequences, including disruption of legal obligations or services based on inaccurate records.

These duties are operationalized through Rule 13 of the Draft Rules, 2025, which mandates that Data Fiduciaries publish secure and verifiable means through which Data Principals may exercise their rights. Requests submitted under false identities or with invalid identifiers may be rejected and, in cases of willful violation, reported for further action.

Importantly, failure to adhere to these duties can result in financial penalties. As per the schedule of the DPDP Act, the filing of false or frivolous complaints by a Data Principal, whether against a Data Fiduciary or the Board, can attract a penalty of up to ₹10,000. While this penalty is modest compared to those imposed on Data Fiduciaries for serious breaches, it underscores the legislature's intention to promote responsible use of privacy rights and discourage abuse of protective mechanisms.

By upholding their duties, Data Principals contribute to a trustworthy digital environment where data protection is a shared responsibility between individuals and organizations. These duties, paired with rights, form the backbone of a fair and enforceable personal data governance model under India's emerging privacy regime.

Importance of Microsoft Purview

Microsoft Purview Data Lifecycle Management, previously known as Microsoft Information Governance, offers comprehensive tools for managing your organization's data lifecycle.

This includes retaining necessary content for compliance with regulatory requirements and discarding what is no longer useful or poses a potential risk. Eliminating redundant content not only aids in compliance but also minimizes risk and liability, effectively reducing the potential for cyber threats.

In conjunction, Microsoft Priva provides specialized tools for privacy management. Priva focuses specifically on identifying privacy risks, automating responses to privacy requests (such as Data Principal Rights requests), and ensuring data handling aligns with global privacy standards. By combining Microsoft Purview's data governance strength with Microsoft Priva's privacy-centric features, organizations can achieve comprehensive compliance, enhance transparency, and proactively manage data privacy risks throughout the entire data lifecycle.

Let us look at how Microsoft Purview and Priva services can be used to track DPR:

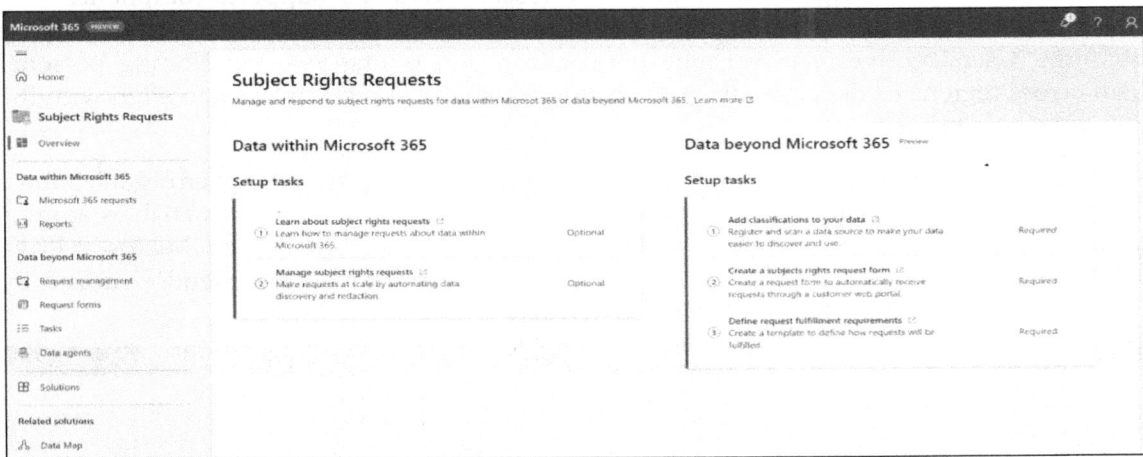

Figure 5.1: Tracking Data Principal requests

Globally, privacy laws empower individuals to request information about, or management of, their personal data held by organizations. These requests, known as **Data Subject Rights (DSRs)** requests, also known as Data Principal Rights according to the Act, **Data Subject Access Requests (DSARs)**, or consumer rights requests, present a significant challenge for organizations dealing with vast amounts of data. The process of addressing these requests is often manual, requiring considerable effort and time.

Microsoft Priva Subject Rights Requests streamlines this process by simplifying the complexity and reducing the time needed to respond to these inquiries. It leverages automation, delivers insights, and utilizes workflows, enabling organizations to manage Data Principal requests more effectively and with greater confidence. This solution is tailored to support organizations in efficiently managing and responding to the rights of individuals regarding their personal data. More of this is planned to be covered in *Chapter 9, Auditing and Compliance Monitoring*.

Implementing Data Principal Rights

Microsoft Priva offers two main products: Privacy Risk Management, which identifies privacy risks like data overexposure and helps users make informed data handling decisions, and Subject Rights Requests, which automates the processing of privacy requests with tools for data discovery and secure collaboration. Integrated with productivity tools, Priva encourages real-time, positive behaviors, such as prompting data owners to review unused data for deletion, ensuring privacy compliance without disrupting workflow.

Privacy administrators can set up policies in Microsoft Priva to detect overexposure of personal data, prompting data owners to review file access, like previous examples. This feature is particularly useful for organizations that manually audit files or site access, a time-intensive process that can leave gaps between audits. Microsoft Priva also supports compliance with data transfer requirements, particularly in Microsoft Teams, a widely used communication platform. Users receive near-real-time notifications and guidance when sharing personal data across regions or departments, with customizable transfer boundaries to align with the organization's privacy policies.

As shown in the following figure, Microsoft Priva offers an aggregated view of an organization's privacy posture, highlighting key insights into detected privacy risks. This enables admins to quickly identify privacy issues and adjust policies to better engage users. Microsoft Priva solutions follow a privacy-by-default approach, with user information pseudonymized by default in the admin interface for enhanced privacy.

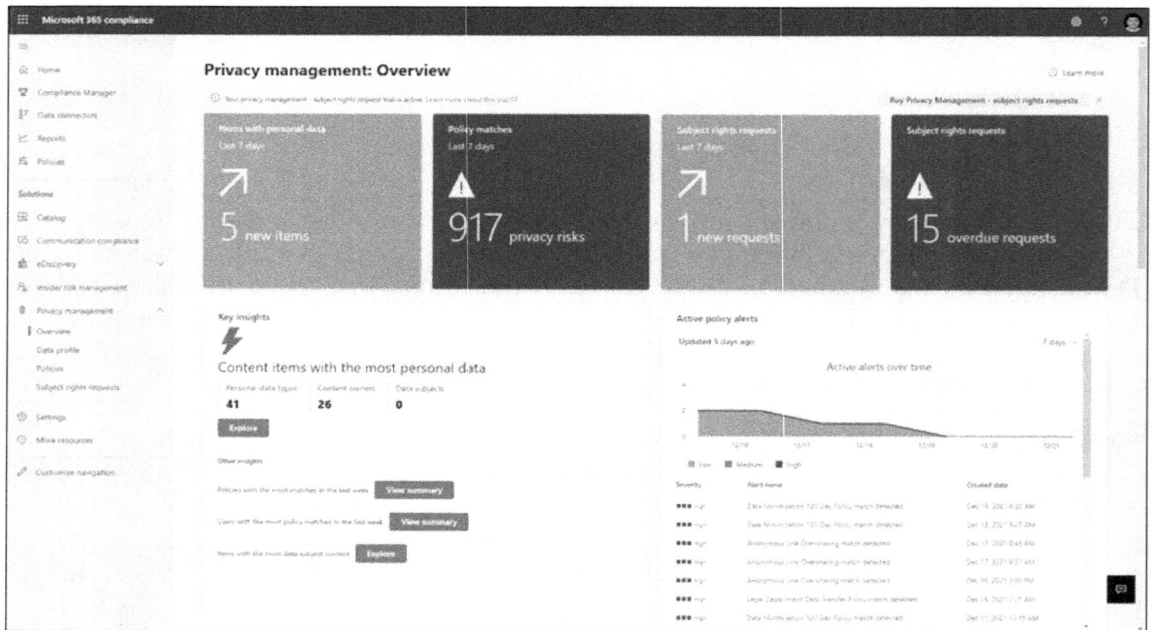

Figure 5.2: Provide an aggregated view to admins to gain visibility into privacy issues

Best practices for managing Data Principal requests

Servicing DPRs efficiently in a large organization requires a structured approach and adherence to best practices to ensure compliance with the DPDP Act and to maintain trust with Data Principals. Here are some best practices:

- **Data Fiduciary establishes clear processes**: Develop and document clear, standardized procedures for handling DPRs, including request reception, verification, processing, and response. This ensures consistency and efficiency in responding to requests.

- **Implement a centralized request management system**: Utilize technology solutions that centralize DPR management, providing a single point of control for tracking and fulfilling requests across the organization's digital estate.

- **Ensure data discoverability**: Invest in data mapping and classification tools that enhance visibility into where and how personal data is stored and processed, making it easier to access, rectify, or erase data as requested.

- **Train staff on DPR handling**: Employees directly involved in handling DPRs should receive specific training on the processes, legal implications, and the organization's policies on Data Principal Rights.

- **Maintain an audit trail**: Keep detailed records of all DPRs received, actions taken, and communications with the Data Principals, which is crucial for compliance verification and potential audits.

The **Data Privacy Officer** (**DPO**) is a cornerstone in the architecture of an organization's data protection strategy, particularly in large organizations where the scale and complexity of data processing activities are significant. The DPO ensures that the organization adheres to data protection laws and practices, providing oversight and guidance across all departments. This role involves monitoring the organization's compliance with data protection regulations, advising on data protection impact assessments, and acting as a bridge between the organization, the Data Principals, and regulatory authorities. The DPO also educates and provides necessary guidance to staff on data protection matters, ensuring that personal data is processed in a lawful, fair, and transparent manner in accordance with the applicable data protection laws.

Training and awareness programs play a vital role in embedding a culture of data protection within an organization. Such programs are essential to educate employees about the importance of protecting personal data, understanding the organization's policies on data protection, and recognizing the rights of Data Principals. Regular targeted training ensures that all employees, especially those managing personal data and involved in processing Data Principal requests, are equipped with the knowledge to perform their roles in compliance with data protection laws. Beyond formal training, ongoing awareness campaigns help to keep data protection a top priority within the organization, reminding staff of their responsibilities and updating them on any changes in legislation or internal policies. Through continuous education and fostering awareness, organizations can ensure that their workforce is not only compliant with data protection regulations but also champions the privacy rights of individuals.

Conclusion

Concluding the discussion on Data Principal Rights within the framework of the DPDP Act, it is evident that empowering individuals with control over their personal data is not just a regulatory requirement but a cornerstone of modern digital trust and privacy. The DPDP Act enshrines these rights, ensuring that Data Principals can access, rectify, erase, or manage the processing of their personal data in a manner that respects their privacy and autonomy.

In navigating the complexities of honoring these rights, organizations face significant operational challenges. From verifying the identity of requestors to efficiently locating and managing the requested data across diverse and sprawling digital estates, the task is formidable. This is where solutions like Microsoft Purview become invaluable. Microsoft Purview offers a comprehensive suite of tools designed to simplify data governance and ensure compliance. With capabilities ranging from data discovery and classification to managing consent and automating responses to Data Principal Rights requests, Purview acts as a pivotal resource in upholding the principles of the DPDP Act. It enables organizations to not only respond to Data Principal requests more efficiently but also to proactively manage the data lifecycle, ensuring data is kept secure, compliant, and utilized in alignment with the Data Principal's expectations and legal requirements.

As we look ahead to the next chapter, the focus shifts to the equally crucial aspect of data protection: Personal Data Breach Management. The DPDP Act, like many global data protection regulations, places a strong emphasis on the need for robust personal data breach detection, response, and notification mechanisms. In this evolving digital landscape, where personal data breaches can have far-reaching consequences on individuals' privacy and organizational reputation, understanding the nuances of breach management becomes paramount. The upcoming discussion will explore the strategies for effectively managing personal data breaches, the legal requirements under the DPDP Act for breach notification, and how leveraging advanced tools like Microsoft Purview can support organizations in navigating these challenges, ultimately reinforcing the trust and security that form the bedrock of the digital economy.

CHAPTER 6

Personal Data Breach Management under the DPDP Act

Introduction

With personal data breaches rapidly increasing in frequency and severity, effective breach management has become a critical necessity for organizations operating in today's digital environment. Under India's **Digital Personal Data Protection (DPDP)** Act, 2023, along with its corresponding rules, 2025, organizations are legally obligated to swiftly identify, respond to, and communicate about personal data breaches. Defined clearly under Chapter II Section 8(*6*) of the DPDP Act, a personal data breach involves unauthorized access, disclosure, misuse, or loss of personal data, posing significant risks to individual privacy and organizational integrity.

This chapter provides a comprehensive exploration of personal data breach management aligned explicitly with the provisions of the DPDP Act Chapter II section 8(6), Chapter VI section 27(1) and Chapter VIII section 33 along with The Schedule of the Act with the detailed procedural obligations outlined in the Draft Rule number 7 on the intimation of personal data breach. Readers will gain practical insights into understanding various breach scenarios, legal responsibilities of data fiduciaries and processors, critical timelines for notification as per regulatory expectations, and essential communication requirements. Real-world case studies illustrate the implications and consequences of breaches, highlighting the importance of robust prevention measures. By adopting the strategies, best practices, and technology solutions discussed, organizations can effectively navigate the complexities of breach management, ensure compliance with the DPDP Act, and strengthen their resilience against future data security incidents.

Structure

In this chapter, we will cover the following topics:

- Understanding personal data breaches
- Legal requirements for personal data breach
- Breach notification content
- Organization obligations
- Sample breach notification aligned with DPDP Rules, 2025
- Personal data breach detection and response
- Post breach activities
- Employee training and awareness programs
- Evolving into Data Security Posture Management

Objectives

This chapter aims to provide readers with an in-depth understanding of personal data breach management as mandated by the DPDP Act, 2023, and the corresponding Draft Rules, 2025. Specifically aligned with Chapter II section 8(6), Chapter VI section 27(1), and Chapter VIII section 33 along with The Schedule of the Act, as well as relevant rules, this chapter outlines organizations' obligations in the event of a personal data breach, including prompt breach detection, notification protocols, and compliance requirements. Readers will learn how to recognize different types of breaches, implement robust response strategies, and communicate effectively with regulators and affected individuals, adhering to prescribed legal timelines and notification standards. Additionally, the chapter emphasizes preventative practices such as regular security audits, employee training, and the strategic use of advanced tools like Microsoft's **Data Security Posture Management** (**DSPM**) solutions, enabling organizations to proactively mitigate risks and strengthen their overall data protection posture in line with regulatory expectations.

Understanding personal data breaches

A personal data breach occurs when confidential, personal, or protected information is accessed, disclosed, or used without authorization. Data breaches can expose an organization to significant risks, including financial penalties, reputational damage, and loss of customer trust. Effective personal data breach management is crucial for maintaining the security of personal data, complying with regulations like the DPDP Act, and safeguarding the overall integrity of the organization.

Past data breaches

Data breaches have become a significant concern globally as they increasingly affect users, businesses, and government agencies due to their heavy reliance on digital technologies. Some of the largest breaches include:

- **Yahoo (2013):** The largest recorded data breach, where approximately three billion user accounts were compromised. This incident included the theft of personal information and passwords.

- **River City Media (2017):** Lost 1.4 billion records due to a security vulnerability.

- **First American Corporation (2019):** Affected 885 million records, involving personal financial data.

- **Facebook (2019 and 2021):** Experienced multiple breaches across different years, impacting hundreds of millions of records by exposing users personal details.

- **Capita (March 2023):** The British outsourcing company Capita experienced a cyberattack impacting UK pension funds and other clients. Personal and financial data were accessed, and a ransomware group later released some stolen data, revealing its potential use in fraudulent activities.

- **Cencora (February 2024):** Pharmaceutical services provider Cencora (formerly AmerisourceBergen) reported a breach where data, including some personal information, was stolen from its systems. Cencora took quick measures to contain the breach, which did not impact core operations but led to increased security reviews.

- **Tangerine Telecom (February 2024):** The Australian ISP Tangerine had over 200,000 customer records compromised due to unauthorized database access. Stolen data included personal details, but not financial or password information. A contractor's credentials were used in the breach, suggesting an insider-related vulnerability.

These breaches are documented in Visual Capitalist's report *Visualizing the 50 Biggest Data Breaches from 2004–2021*, on The Pensions Regulator website, in Reuters reports, and on Tangerine's official site (*tangerine.com.au*). The above examples highlight the broad and significant impact of personal data breaches across various sectors, underlining the critical need for robust security measures to protect personal information.

Common causes of personal data breaches

In the complex world of personal data breaches, human error often plays a key role, with simple mistakes like sending personal information to the wrong recipient or misconfiguring databases leading to significant vulnerabilities. Additionally, cybercriminals exploit these openings through sophisticated phishing and malware attacks, which trick employees into handing over confidential data.

Insider threats add another layer of risk, with privileged users potentially misusing their access, whether intentionally or accidentally.

Moreover, outdated software and physical theft expose organizations to further threats, while third-party vendors can also become weak links in data security. This intricate scenario underscores the critical importance of advanced security strategies, ongoing vigilance, and rigorous training to protect personal data effectively.

Legal requirements for personal data breach

As listed out in Chapter II section 8(6), *In the event of a personal data breach, the Data Fiduciary shall give the Board and each affected Data Principal intimation of such breach in such form and manner as may be prescribed.*

Let us say Ananya has an account with a bank, and the bank experiences a personal data breach where her personal information might have been accessed by unauthorized parties. According to the DPDP Act, specifically mentioned in Chapter II section 8(6), the bank, acting as a Data Fiduciary, is required to promptly inform both the authorities (referred to as the Board in the Act) and Ananya, the affected individual, about the breach. The law mandates that this notification should be done in a specific way, though the exact details of how it should be formatted and communicated will be provided by the regulatory guidelines. If Ananya's data is compromised, she has the right to be informed about it as soon as possible, so she can take necessary actions like changing passwords or monitoring for potential identity theft.

Overview of personal data breach notification

The **Data Protection Board (DPB)** of India, under the DPDP Act, is responsible for enforcing data protection regulations, investigating data breaches, and ensuring that individuals' rights over their personal data are upheld. The DPB has the authority to direct organizations to take corrective measures, impose penalties, and enforce compliance standards.

Understanding the DPB's powers is crucial because it helps organizations anticipate regulatory expectations and be better prepared for compliance. Knowing the Board's enforcement mechanisms also highlights the importance of proactive data protection practices, as non-compliance could result in significant penalties and reputational damage.

To meet these regulatory requirements, organizations need to establish clear breach management processes. This includes implementing robust detection mechanisms, preparing incident response plans, and ensuring timely notifications to both the Board and affected individuals in the event of a breach. By doing so, organizations demonstrate accountability and strengthen consumer trust in data protection practices.

In addition, Chapter VI, Section 27 talks about expectations, interactions, and the power of the DPB. It reads as follows:

1. The Board shall exercise and perform the following powers and functions, namely:

    a. On receipt of an intimation of a personal data breach under sub-section (6) of section 8, the authority shall direct any urgent remedial or mitigation measures in the event of a personal data breach, and inquire into such personal data breach and impose a penalty as provided in this Act.

    b. On a complaint made by a Data Principal in respect of a personal data breach or a breach in observance by a Data Fiduciary of its obligations in relation to her personal data or the exercise of her rights under the provisions of this Act, or on a reference made to it by the Central Government or a State Government, or in compliance of the directions of any court, to inquire into such breach and impose penalty as provided in this Act.

    c. On a complaint made by the Data Principal in respect of a breach in observance by a Consent Manager of its obligations in relation to her personal data, to inquire into such a breach and impose penalties as provided in this Act.

    d. On receipt of an intimation of breach of any condition of registration of a Consent Manager, to inquire into such breach and impose a penalty as provided in this Act.

    e. On a reference made by the Central Government in respect of the breach in observance of the provisions of Chapter IX, section 37, by an intermediary, to inquire into such breach and impose a penalty as provided in this Act.

What this means is, in the context of Ananya as a Data Principal, Chapter VI, section 27 of the DPDP Act outlines the powers and functions of the DPB, which serves as an oversight and enforcement body for data protection laws in India. If Ananya's personal data were to be breached, she has several protections and recourse options under the Act, facilitated by the Board:

*   **Immediate action and inquiry**: If the Board receives information about a personal data breach affecting Ananya's personal information, it has the authority to direct urgent remedial or mitigation measures to address the breach. It can also conduct an inquiry into the incident and, if necessary, impose penalties on those responsible as dictated by the Act. The DPB conducts inquiries into breaches and is empowered to impose penalties as stipulated in the Act and detailed under Rule 7 of the Draft DPDP Rules 2025.

*   **Complaints by Ananya**: If Ananya's data rights are violated, she must first use the internal grievance mechanism of the responsible entity. For a **Significant Data Fiduciary (SDF)**, this includes a designated DPO as the grievance contact, acknowledgment of her complaint within 72 hours, resolution within 30 days, and maintenance of a grievance register with outcomes. If the SDF fails to resolve her complaint, Ananya may escalate it to the DPB under Chapter III Section 13(3), which can investigate and impose penalties per Chapter VI Section 27(1)(b).

- **Oversight of Consent Managers**: If a Consent Manager fails in its duty to protect or correctly manage Ananya's data, Ananya can also report this issue. The Board will investigate and can impose penalties based on the severity and nature of the breach.

- **Government and court references**: In cases where a government body or a court directs the Board to investigate a particular issue related to personal data breaches or non-compliance by data fiduciaries, including intermediaries like internet service providers or social media platforms, the Board is empowered to investigate and take appropriate action, including levying penalties.

This framework ensures that Ananya and individuals like her are not only protected by stringent data protection norms but also have a robust mechanism to seek redressal and ensure accountability from those managing their personal data. This contributes to a trustworthy environment where Data Principals can feel secure about the privacy and security of their personal information.

Chapter VIII, section 33 of the DPDP Act grants the DPB the authority to impose penalties for significant breaches of data protection regulations. When a breach occurs, the Board first conducts a detailed inquiry to ascertain the specifics and impact of the incident. Those accused of violating the Act are given a chance to present their defense, ensuring fairness in the enforcement process. If a violation is confirmed, the Board can levy monetary penalties, the amount of which is predetermined by a specific schedule within the Act.

In determining the penalty, the Board considers several key factors: the nature, gravity, and duration of the breach; the sensitivity of the affected personal data; whether the breach was a repeated offense; any financial gain or loss prevention resulting from the breach; the actions taken by the offender to mitigate the damage; and the timeliness and effectiveness of these actions. Additionally, the penalty's proportionality to the breach and its potential impact on the violator are also assessed. This methodical approach ensures that penalties are just appropriate to the scale of the breach, and effective in promoting compliance with the Act.

Section 33 along with The Schedule of the DPDP Act outlines a structured penalty schedule for violations of the data protection regulations. The penalties vary significantly based on the severity and nature of the breach, with the potential fines ranging as follows:

- The maximum penalty can go up to 250 crore rupees for the most severe breaches, with up to of 50 crore rupees for data fiduciaries.

- Smaller infractions can attract fines as minimal as ten thousand rupees and mostly for the responsibility of Data Principal.

In determining penalties, the DPB considers several factors:

- Nature, gravity, and duration of the breach.
- Sensitivity of the affected personal data.
- Repeat offenses.

- Financial implications of the breach (gains or avoided losses).
- Remedial actions and timeliness in addressing breaches.

This structured approach ensures that penalties are proportional to the severity of the breach, providing a deterrent effect to ensure compliance with the data protection laws.

Act mapping, personal data breach

The following table outlines key DPDP Act provisions and Draft Rules mapping related to personal data breach notification, with corresponding compliance solutions and relevant draft rule references:

Chapter	Section	Definition name	Narration	Solution mapping	Draft rules mapping
2	8(6)	Personal Data Breach Notification	Data Fiduciary must notify both the DPB and affected Data Principals immediately upon knowledge of a personal data breach, detailing the breach nature, potential risks, and mitigative actions.	Implement automated breach detection and response solutions, maintain detailed incident logs, and establish clear incident reporting workflows.	Rule 7 – Format and procedure for breach notification.
6	27(1)(a)	Urgent Remedial and Mitigation Measures	Upon notification of a personal data breach, the DPB can direct immediate remedial or mitigation measures, investigate the breach thoroughly, and impose relevant penalties.	Deploy incident response platforms integrated with security systems and conduct periodic mock drills to prepare for rapid mitigation actions and regulatory compliance.	Rule 7 – Obligations concerning breach notification and remedial actions.
6	27(1)(b)	Complaints by Data Principal	Data Principals can file complaints about breaches involving their data, prompting investigations and penalties by the DPB.	Establish grievance redressal systems and internal escalation mechanisms to manage Data Principal complaints promptly and transparently.	Rule 13(3) – Grievance redressal timelines and mechanisms.

Chapter	Section	Definition name	Narration	Solution mapping	Draft rules mapping
6	27(1)(c)	Consent Manager Accountability	The DPB investigates breaches caused by Consent Managers and may impose penalties accordingly.	Implement clear contractual agreements defining security obligations and responsibilities with Consent Managers, supplemented by regular audits.	Rule 4 – Registrations and Obligations of Consent Managers.
6	33	Penalties and Enforcement actions	DPB imposes penalties based on the severity, nature, and duration of breaches, considering mitigation actions taken by the fiduciary and the sensitivity of breached data.	Maintain comprehensive compliance records, incident documentation, and robust forensic capabilities for effective representation and mitigation during regulatory inquiries.	

Table 6.1: Personal Data Breach Act Mapping

Reporting time frame

The DPDP Act of India specifies that in the event of a personal data breach, the Data Fiduciary (the entity handling the data) must report the breach to the relevant authority *as soon as such breach comes to the knowledge of the Data Fiduciary*. The promptness of the report is emphasized without a precise deadline, which suggests that it should be done without unreasonable delay.

Since the DPDP Act does not establish specific timelines for reporting personal data breaches, organizations should adhere to the directives issued by the **India Computer Emergency Response Team (CERT-In)**. The CERT guidelines mandate that cybers security incidents, including unauthorized access to IT systems or data, must be reported within six hours of detection or notification. This serves as a critical fallback guideline for timely incident reporting in the absence of explicit timelines under the DPDP Act.

Additionally, according to Rule 7(2) of the Draft DPDP Rules, 2025:

On becoming aware of any personal data breach, the Data Fiduciary shall intimate to the Board, as per the following instructions:

(a) Without delay, a description of the breach, including its nature, extent, timing, and location of occurrence, and the likely impact;

(b) Within seventy-two hours of becoming aware of the same, or within such longer period as the Board may allow on a request made in writing in this behalf:

(i)   Updated and detailed information in respect of such description;

(ii) The broad facts related to the events, circumstances, and reasons leading to the breach;

(iii) Measures implemented or proposed, if any, to mitigate risk;

(iv) Any findings regarding the person who caused the breach;

(v) Remedial measures taken to prevent recurrence of such breach;

(vi) A report regarding the intimations given to affected Data Principals.

In summary, under the DPDP Act, a Data Fiduciary must notify the Board of any personal data breach without unreasonable delay. In practice, organizations follow CERTIn's six-hour reporting guideline when no statutory deadline exists. Draft DPDP Rules 2025 Rule 7(2) then requires immediate intimation with basic breach details and a full, 72-hour update covering the breach's nature, scope, mitigation measures, responsible party findings, and notifications sent to affected individuals.

Breach notification content

Under the DPDP Act, a breach notification must include the details of the breach's nature, the types of personal data affected, and the likely consequences of the breach. Additionally, the notification should clearly describe the measures that the Data Fiduciary has taken or proposes to take in response to the breach. According to Rule 7 of the DPDP Draft Rules, 2025, the notification must specifically include:

- The nature and extent of the personal data breach, clearly indicating the categories and approximate number of Data Principals involved.

- The type of personal data impacted, specifying the sensitivity and potential risks associated with the breach.

- A description of the likely consequences and potential harm to the affected Data Principals.

- Immediate actions taken by the Data Fiduciary to mitigate the breach, including containment measures and protective actions.

- Further proposed actions and recommendations were provided to Data Principals for minimizing potential harm.

This comprehensive notification requirement ensures transparency, enabling both authorities and affected individuals to understand the breach thoroughly and take timely, appropriate actions to mitigate potential harm.

Organization obligations

Under the DPDP Act, data fiduciaries and Data Processors have defined obligations in the event of a personal data breach. These roles are tasked with implementing robust measures to prevent data breaches and to manage them effectively should they occur.

Data Processors: Data Processors, handling personal data on behalf of a Data Fiduciary, should adopt security measures that comply with the DPDP Act standards. They should notify the Data Fiduciary immediately upon detecting a personal data breach, ensuring timely remediation. All these mandates should be explicitly mentioned in the data protection agreement/clause entered into between the Data Processor and Data Fiduciary.

Continuing the bank example, if a cloud service provider managing the bank's data experiences a breach, it must promptly inform the bank. The bank will then evaluate the breach impact, report it to the DPB, and inform affected customers, clearly outlining breach details, potential consequences, and mitigation measures.

In summary, both Data Fiduciaries and Data Processors not only prevent personal data breaches through stringent security measures but also have clear procedures in place for quick action and transparent communication in the event of a breach. This ensures timely remediation and compliance with legal requirements, thus minimizing harm to data principles and reducing the liability of the organizations involved.

Sample breach notification aligned with DPDP Rules, 2025

Under the DPDP Act and the DPDP Draft Rules, 2025, breach notifications serve distinct purposes for affected users and regulators, and both must adhere to specific requirements outlined by these regulations.

> Note: **Neither the DPDP Act nor its Draft Rules prescribe a specific template or format for breach notifications. Organizations are free to tailor their messages so long as they cover the required elements.**

Notification to Users (Rule 7(1))

In the event of a personal data breach, the Data Fiduciary is required to notify affected individuals clearly and promptly. According to **Rule 7(1)** of the DPDP Draft Rules, 2025, the notification must include:

- **Nature:** A concise description of what happened (e.g., unauthorized access to customer records).
- **Extent:** The categories of personal data exposed (e.g., names, email addresses, payment details).

- **Timing:** When the breach occurred or was discovered (e.g., detected on 12 April 2025 at 09:30 IST).

- **Location:** Where in the system or network the breach took place (e.g., the customer database hosted in Mumbai).

This *NETL* notice empowers users to take protective steps, such as changing passwords or enabling fraud alerts, to mitigate harm. The primary goal of notifying users is to empower them with actionable information to minimize potential harm resulting from the breach.

Notification to Regulators (Rule 7(2))

Notifications to regulatory authorities, specifically the DPB, are governed by **Rule 7(2)** of the DPDP Draft Rules, 2025, and must include detailed, technical information, as discussed in the upcoming sections.

Initial intimation, without delay

Without delay, a description of the breach, including its nature, extent, timing, and location of occurrence, and the likely impact. (Rule 7(2)(a)). These details include:

- **Nature:** A succinct summary of what went wrong (e.g., "Unauthorized access to customer email database").

- **Extent:** The broad categories of data exposed (e.g., names, contact details, payment tokens).

- **Timing:** When the breach was detected or believed to have occurred (e.g., "Detected on 20 April 2025 at 14:45 IST").

- **Location:** The system or network component compromised (e.g., "CRM server hosted in Mumbai region").

- **Consequences:** A high-level view of potential risks to affected individuals (e.g., "Possibility of phishing attempts using stolen emails").

Why? This rapid summary lets the Board triage the incident and, if needed, issue immediate directives under Chapter VI Section 27(1)(a) of the Act.

Detailed report, within 72 hours

Within seventy-two hours of becoming aware of the same (or such longer period as the Board may allow). (Rule 7(2)(b)).

Within this window, the Data Fiduciary must submit:

- **Updated NETL detail**s: Any refinements to the initial description of nature, extent, timing, and location as more facts emerge.

- **Full facts and timeline:** A chronological account of how the breach unfolded, from initial intrusion to discovery.

- **Immediate mitigation actions:** Steps already taken to contain the breach (e.g., revoked credentials, applied security patches).

- **Findings on responsible parties:** If known, the identity or profile of the individual(s) or process that caused the breach.

- **Remedial and preventative steps:** Planned measures to harden systems and prevent recurrence (e.g., enhanced monitoring, staff retraining).

- **Notification confirmation:** Evidence that affected Data Principals have been informed, including dates and communication channels used.

Extensions: The Board may grant a longer period for this detailed report if a written request demonstrates genuine need.

Sample breach notification for the user

Here is a sample personal data breach notification letter that complies with typical requirements under data protection laws such as the DPDP Act:

Contoso Bank

20th April 2025

To: Ananya

Dear Ananya,

Subject: Urgent Security Notification Regarding Your Personal Data

We are writing to inform you about a security incident that may have involved your personal data held by Contoso bank. Protecting your information is important to us, and we apologize for any concern this may cause you. This notice explains what happened, measures we have taken, and some steps you can take in response.

What Happened

On 20th April 2025, we detected unauthorized access to our system that occurred . We immediately launched an investigation with the assistance of cyber security experts and discovered that personal data stored in our system may have been accessed without authorization.

Information Involved

The following types of personal data related to your account may have been involved:

- Name – Address - Email address - Telephone number

- [Other potentially affected personal data]

Steps We Are Taking

Upon discovering the issue, we took immediate steps to secure our systems and mitigate any further unauthorized access. These actions include:

- Isolating and securing the affected systems.

- Implementing additional security measures to prevent future breaches.

- Notifying relevant authorities as required by law.

Steps You Can Take

We encourage you to remain vigilant by reviewing your account statements and monitoring free credit reports. Additionally, you may consider the following actions:

- Changing your account passwords and security questions and answers.

- Using two-factor authentication on your accounts.

- Monitoring your accounts for any suspicious activity.

For More Information

We understand that you may have questions or concerns regarding this incident. Please contact our dedicated helpline at [Contact Information], available from [hours] on [days]. Alternatively, you can email us at [Email Address] for further assistance.

Your Right to Data Protection

You have the right to make a complaint or inquire more about the handling of your personal data by contacting our Data Protection Officer at [DPO's Contact Information].

Again, we apologize for any inconvenience this incident may have caused. We are committed to ensuring the safety and security of all personal data entrusted to us and are taking this matter very seriously.

Thank you for your understanding and cooperation.

Sincerely,

[Your Name] [Your Title]

[Company Name] [Company Address]

[Company DPO Contact Information]

This template is designed to comply with notification requirements, providing affected individuals with clear, concise, and useful information about the breach and steps they can take to protect themselves. Adjustments might be needed based on local laws and the specifics of the personal data breach.

Sample breach notification for regulator

Here is a sample template for a personal data breach notification to a regulator, formatted to convey essential information clearly and professionally:

Contoso Bank

Personal Data Breach Notification

Date: [Insert Date]

To:

The Regulatory Authority

[Insert the specific office or department if applicable]

[Address]

[City, State, Zip Code]

Subject: Notification of Personal Data Breach under Compliance with the Digital Personal Data Protection Act 2023

Dear [Regulator's Title/Name],

We are writing to inform you of a data security breach at [Your Company Name], which we identified on [Date of Discovery]. This breach potentially affects personal data related to approximately 200,000 of our users, including personal information such as credit card details and Aadhaar numbers.

1. Description of the Breach:

The breach was first noticed on [specific date] and involved unauthorized access to our [describe the system, e.g., "online payment processing system"]. The breach was detected by our internal security systems on [date], and immediate steps were taken to secure the system and halt further unauthorized access.

2. Types of Data Involved:

- Credit Card Information

- Aadhaar Numbers

- Names and Contact Details

- [Any other types of affected data]

3. Cause of the Breach:

Preliminary investigations suggest that the breach was caused by [describe cause, e.g., "a sophisticated cyber-attack exploiting a vulnerability in our database software which has since been patched"].

4. Steps Taken Post-Breach:

Upon detecting the breach, we initiated the following response:

- Immediate isolation and securing of the compromised systems.

- Engagement of an independent cybersecurity firm to conduct a thorough investigation.

- Notification of all affected stakeholders and implementation of remedial actions to mitigate potential harm.

5. Current Status of the Breach:

As for [today's date or the date of the last assessment], we have:

- Contained the breach to prevent any further unauthorized access.

- Initiated comprehensive identity protection services for the affected individuals.

- Enhanced our security measures to prevent future occurrences.

6. Potential Impact on Data Principal:

Unauthorized access could potentially lead to misuse of the affected personal data. We are currently working with cyber team to monitor affected accounts for any suspicious activity

7. Contact Information for Further Inquiry:

Please direct any inquiries or requests for further information to our designated Data Protection Officer:

Name: [DPO's Name]

Email: [DPO's Email]

Phone: [DPO's Phone Number]

We deeply regret any inconvenience this incident may cause and are committed to rectifying the situation swiftly and transparently. Please let us know if there is any further information we can provide or actions we can undertake that would be helpful to your investigation.

Thank you for your attention to this serious matter. We will keep you updated as our investigation progresses and more information becomes available.

Sincerely,

[Your Name] [Your Position]

[Your Company Name] [Contact Information]

This template ensures that all relevant details are covered and that the communication remains clear and formal, aligning with regulatory expectations.

Personal data breach detection and response

Using technologies for personal data breach detection and response involves implementing various software tools and systems designed to identify, monitor, and mitigate unauthorized access to or theft of personal information. This process is critical for ensuring that personal data is protected and that organizations can react swiftly and effectively in the event of a security incident. Here is a breakdown of how technologies contribute to each stage of personal data breach management:

- **Detection**:
  - **Monitoring tools**: Technologies like **Intrusion Detection Systems (IDS)** and **Security Information and Event Management (SIEM)** solutions continuously

monitor network traffic and system activities for unusual behavior that might indicate a breach.

- o **Data loss prevention (DLP)**: DLP tools scan and monitor data at rest, in use, and in motion to ensure that personal information is not lost, misused, or accessed by unauthorized individuals.

- o **Endpoint Detection and Response (EDR)**: EDR platforms monitor end-user devices for malicious activity signs, providing detailed forensic data and the ability to respond quickly to threats.

- **Response:**
  - o **Incident response platforms**: These tools help security teams manage and coordinate their response to a breach, providing workflows and automated processes to address the incident effectively.

  - o **Automated security orchestration**: Automated response solutions can initiate actions to contain a breach, such as isolating infected devices or blocking suspicious IP addresses, reducing the potential impact and spread of the breach.

  - o **Forensics and analysis tools**: After a breach, these technologies help analyze how the breach occurred, the extent of the data compromised, and the methods used by attackers. This analysis is crucial for preventing future incidents and for fulfilling legal and regulatory obligations to report and investigate security incidents.

- **Ongoing improvement**:
  - o **AI and machine learning**: These technologies are increasingly used to improve breach detection by identifying patterns and anomalies that may elude traditional detection methods.

  - o **Threat intelligence platforms**: These systems provide ongoing insights into new and emerging threats, allowing organizations to update their defense strategies based on the latest information about cyber threats.

By integrating these technologies, organizations can create a layered defense strategy that not only detects and responds to breaches more effectively but also adapts and evolves in response to the changing cybersecurity landscape. More tools are covered in the *Technology* section at the end of this chapter.

Implementing a personal data breach response plan

A personal data breach response plan is a comprehensive strategy and set of procedures that an organization puts in place to manage and mitigate the impact of a personal data breach. The plan is crucial for ensuring that an organization can Act swiftly and efficiently in the face of a security incident, minimizing both the damage and the recovery time.

The following are the key elements of a personal data breach response plan:

- **Identification and classification of data**: Understanding what data is most sensitive and at risk helps prioritize security efforts and responses.

- **Roles and responsibilities**: Clearly defined roles and responsibilities for the response team, including who leads the effort, who communicates with stakeholders, and who manages technical aspects.

- **Notification procedures**: Guidelines on how to notify all impacted parties, including regulatory bodies, affected individuals, partners, and potentially the public, depending on the severity and nature of the breach.

- **Containment and eradication**: Steps to immediately contain the breach to prevent further data loss and to eradicate the cause of the breach to prevent recurrence.

- **Investigation and assessment**: Procedures for investigating the breach to determine its cause and scope. This includes forensic analysis to understand how the breach occurred and which vulnerabilities were exploited.

- **Recovery plans**: Processes to restore and secure IT systems to normal operation, ensuring that all vulnerabilities are addressed to prevent future breaches.

- **Post-incident analysis**: After-action review to assess the response effectiveness and to learn from the incident. This includes revising the personal data breach response plan based on what was learned to strengthen future responses.

- **Compliance and legal factors**: Ensuring all actions taken comply with relevant data protection laws and regulations, which may dictate specific actions like the timing of breach notifications.

Creating a personal data breach response plan involves careful planning, regular training, and periodic testing to ensure it remains effective and relevant to the organization's needs. This proactive approach is essential in today's digital landscape, where the risk of personal data breaches is continually evolving.

Post breach activities

When a personal data breach is detected, the immediate priority is to contain the breach and minimize its impact. Here are the top three steps that should be taken:

- **Containment**: The first step is to contain the breach to prevent further unauthorized access to systems or data. This may involve isolating affected systems, disabling compromised accounts, or temporarily shutting down affected services or applications.

- **Notification of response team**: Immediately notify the designated response team or **Incident Response Team (IRT)**. This team typically includes representatives from IT, cybersecurity, legal, communications, and executive leadership. They will coordinate the organization's response efforts.

- **Preservation of evidence**: Preserve evidence related to the breach for forensic analysis and investigation. This may involve taking snapshots of affected systems, capturing log files, and documenting any suspicious activity.

Communicating with stakeholders

As for communication, it is essential to inform the relevant stakeholders promptly and accurately. This typically includes the following:

- **Internal communication**: Notify internal stakeholders such as senior management, IT teams, legal counsel, and HR to ensure everyone is aware of the breach and their roles in the response effort.

- **External communication**: Depending on the nature and severity of the breach, external communication may be necessary. This includes notifying affected individuals, customers, partners, regulators, and law enforcement authorities as required by applicable laws and regulations.

- **Regulatory bodies**: In many jurisdictions, organizations are required to report personal data breaches to regulatory bodies within a specified timeframe. Ensure compliance with relevant regulations by promptly reporting the breach to the appropriate authorities.

- **Legal counsel**: Engage legal counsel to provide guidance on compliance obligations, potential liabilities, and communication strategies. Legal advice is crucial in navigating the legal complexities associated with personal data breaches.

By promptly taking these steps and communicating effectively with all relevant parties, organizations can minimize the impact of personal data breaches and demonstrate their commitment to transparency and accountability in data protection.

Preventative measures and best practices

To effectively prevent personal data breaches under the **Digital Personal Data Protection Act, 2023 (Section 8)** and associated **Draft DPDP Rules, 2025 (Rule 6)**, organizations must adopt proactive and comprehensive measures across their data management practices:

- **Regular risk assessments and audits (Rule 6):** Organizations are required to periodically conduct assessments to identify vulnerabilities within IT infrastructure, systems, and data processing activities. These assessments ensure compliance with the security standards outlined in Rule 6, prioritizing remediation of potential weaknesses and enhancing overall security posture.

- **Implementation of robust security controls (Section 8(5), Rule 6(1)(b)):** Data fiduciaries and processors must establish robust technical and organizational measures, including encryption, **multi-factor authentication (MFA)**, firewalls, and **intrusion detection/**

prevention systems (IDS/IPS), to safeguard personal data against unauthorized access, alteration, or misuse as mandated by Section 8(5) of the DPDP Act and Rule 6.

- **Timely software updates and patching (Rule 6):** Ensuring regular updates and patches of software and systems addresses known vulnerabilities and protects against evolving cyber threats, aligning with the "reasonable security safeguards" requirement of Rule 6.

- **Access control and least privilege principles (Rule 6):** Enforcing stringent access controls and adhering to the principle of least privilege ensures that only authorized personnel have access to personal data necessary for their roles. This minimizes the risk of insider threats and unauthorized data access as required under Rule 6.

- **Employee training and awareness:** Conducting ongoing training and awareness programs is crucial. Employees should be educated on security best practices, data handling guidelines, and recognition of common threats, such as phishing and social engineering attacks.

- **Incident response planning and testing (Rule 6):** Organizations should develop, implement, and regularly test comprehensive incident response plans. These plans enable rapid identification, containment, and mitigation of personal data breaches, fulfilling obligations under Rule 6.

- **Vendor risk management:** Organizations must manage third-party vendors rigorously by including contractual obligations for maintaining security standards consistent with the DPDP Act and Rules. This ensures Data Processors meet the same robust security standards as data fiduciaries.

- **DLP and continuous monitoring (Rule 6):** Leveraging advanced DLP tools, continuous monitoring systems, and threat intelligence platforms enables real-time detection and prevention of potential breaches, aligning with the standards required under Rule 6.

By systematically adopting these preventative measures in alignment with the DPDP Act (particularly Section 8) and the DPDP Draft Rules, 2025 (especially Rule 6), organizations can significantly reduce the risk of personal data breaches, ensuring robust protection of personal data and achieving full regulatory compliance.

Role of audit

Regular audits play a crucial role in identifying vulnerabilities and preventing personal data breaches by providing organizations with a systematic way to assess their security posture and compliance with relevant regulations and standards. These audits involve comprehensive reviews of IT systems, networks, applications, and data handling processes to uncover weaknesses, misconfigurations, and potential gaps in security controls. By examining access controls, encryption practices, patch management procedures, and employee training programs, audits help organizations pinpoint areas of improvement and prioritize remediation efforts.

Identifying vulnerabilities through audits allows organizations to take proactive measures to address security risks before they can be exploited by malicious actors. This may involve implementing security patches, updating software and firmware, configuring systems to follow security best practices, and strengthening access controls. Additionally, audits help organizations ensure compliance with regulatory requirements and industry standards, reducing the risk of penalties and legal liabilities associated with non-compliance.

Audits also play a key role in breach response preparedness. By evaluating incident response plans and conducting mock breach exercises, audits help ensure that the team is well-prepared to detect, contain, and mitigate any breach quickly. This preparedness is essential in minimizing the impact of any potential breach and fulfilling notification requirements effectively.

Employee training and awareness programs

Training and awareness programs for both IT staff and general users play a pivotal role in preventing personal data breaches by fostering a culture of security consciousness and empowering individuals to recognize and respond effectively to potential threats. IT staff can benefit from specialized training on cybersecurity best practices, emerging threats, and incident response procedures, enabling them to proactively identify and mitigate security risks within the organization's infrastructure. On the other hand, educating general users about the importance of data security, common attack vectors such as phishing and social engineering, and proper handling of personal information can significantly reduce the likelihood of human error-related breaches. By promoting a shared responsibility for cybersecurity and equipping both IT professionals and users with the knowledge and skills needed to identify and address security threats, training and awareness initiatives serve as invaluable defense mechanisms in safeguarding organizational data and assets.

Tools for managing personal data breach management

To effectively manage personal data breaches, many organizations leverage existing investments in SIEM systems.

This approach centralizes threat detection and streamlines breach response by integrating multiple security solutions. When a potential breach occurs, the SOC team is responsible for detecting the incident and gathering initial details, often from alerts generated by DLP tools, antivirus software, or identity monitoring systems. These tools provide critical insights into the nature of the breach, helping to identify factors such as data sensitivity, scope, and potential impact.

For example, consider a breach scenario where an unauthorized party accesses personal financial records within an organization. The SOC team detects this activity through the SIEM system, which flags unusual patterns, such as attempts to access restricted files or repeated login attempts from unusual locations. Alerts from the EDR system, such as Defender or CrowdStrike, might provide additional details about the compromised endpoint or malicious processes.

Once this information is gathered, the SOC team promptly informs the DPO, who leads the next steps in breach evaluation and notification.

The DPO's role is critical, as they must assess the breach's severity and determine whether the organization is required to notify regulatory bodies and affected individuals. The DPO's evaluation considers several key factors, including:

- **Data sensitivity**: Was personal data, such as financial or health records, involved?
- **Data volume**: How much data was exposed, and how many individuals are affected?
- **Breach source and impact**: Is the breach accidental or malicious? What are the potential consequences for those impacted?

If the breach is determined to be severe, the DPO may initiate notifications to comply with legal and regulatory requirements. This involves reviewing legal obligations to understand penalties and coordinating a communication plan to mitigate damage. For instance, under regulations like the GDPR or the India DPDP Act, organizations have strict timelines for reporting breaches to regulatory bodies and notifying individuals if there is a risk to their privacy or security.

DLP alerts, EDR solutions alerts, and alerts on phishing or compromised accounts offer real-time visibility into potential incidents and support a systematic approach to identifying, analyzing, and calling out for incident triage by collating data into a SIEM or a standalone incident management tool. This layered approach, led by the SOC team and coordinated with the DPO, helps organizations navigate breach incidents efficiently while ensuring compliance with regulatory requirements and minimizing risk.

Additional points for employee training and awareness programs are listed as follows:

- **Role-specific training:** Ensure training programs are tailored to the roles and responsibilities of employees, distinguishing clearly between general users and those with privileged access (e.g., system administrators, DPOs).

- **Regular refresher courses:** Conduct ongoing and periodic refresher training sessions to update employees on emerging threats, changes in data protection regulations, and the organization's evolving security practices.

- **Training record maintenance:** Keep comprehensive records documenting participation and completion of training sessions to demonstrate regulatory compliance and facilitate internal audits or investigations by the DPB.

- **Incident simulation and drills:** Include practical incident simulations (e.g., mock breach exercises, phishing simulations) to improve employee readiness, enabling them to identify and respond quickly to actual incidents.

- **Feedback mechanisms:** Implement feedback loops where employees can report potential risks, suspicious activities, or provide suggestions on improving data security practices. This reinforces an organizational culture of proactive security awareness.

By using existing tools and implementing clear communication between the SOC and DPO, organizations create a robust breach management framework that allows them to quickly and effectively respond to incidents, helping to protect both the organization's reputation and the individuals whose data may be impacted.

Evolving into Data Security Posture Management

In recent years, organizations have shifted from a reactive approach to data security to a more proactive one, actively monitoring their data security posture rather than waiting for an incident to occur. This evolution is part of the broader trend toward DSPM, where businesses continuously assess and strengthen their security measures to mitigate potential breaches before they happen. By employing DSPM strategies, organizations ensure that they are not only aware of their security vulnerabilities but are also equipped to address them swiftly, should they arise.

A multi-layered approach to security, incorporating various tools and technologies, is key to establishing a robust data security posture. By combining endpoint detection, network monitoring, and threat intelligence, organizations can create a more complete view of potential security incidents, ensuring that breaches are detected and mitigated at multiple points in the attack chain. For example, deploying endpoint detection tools alongside advanced network monitoring and threat intelligence platforms can significantly enhance breach detection capabilities, enabling faster and more accurate responses to potential incidents.

The deployment of these tools should always be informed by an organization's unique environment and threat landscape. Regular updates and ongoing training for security teams are essential to ensure that these tools are being utilized effectively, keeping the organization's defenses up to date against emerging threats.

Early peek at Microsoft DSPM tools

As organizations increasingly embrace DSPM strategies, **Microsoft Information Protection** (**MIP**) plays a pivotal role in both the prevention and detection of personal data breaches. MIP allows businesses to proactively monitor, classify, and protect personal data across its lifecycle, extending across both Microsoft and third-party platforms.

One of the key benefits of MIP is its Content Explorer, which offers a granular view into data across an organization's environment. This tool enables security teams to locate and analyze personal content in real time, providing critical insights into where data resides, who has access to it, and how it is being used. By using MIP to classify and label data based on its sensitivity, organizations can ensure that protection policies are automatically enforced, safeguarding data from unauthorized access and exposure.

In addition, DLP capabilities within MIP ensure that personal data is not shared or accessed inappropriately, whether within the organization or with external partners. MIP's DLP policies span across Microsoft 365 services like Teams, Exchange, SharePoint, and OneDrive, preventing accidental or malicious data leaks.

Another important aspect of MIP is its Policy Enforcement mechanism. By applying encryption and access controls that are aligned with the sensitivity of the data, MIP ensures that even if data is mistakenly or maliciously exported, it remains protected. This feature is essential for maintaining compliance and preventing costly personal data breaches.

Looking to the future, Microsoft is introducing the DSPM for AI in preview, which is set to become a foundational tool for enhancing an organization's data security posture. This AI-driven hub will leverage advanced machine learning and analytics to identify weak data points, provide actionable insights, and help organizations adopt a proactive stance toward potential vulnerabilities. By using AI to continuously analyze data and behavior patterns, the DSPM for AI will enable security teams to anticipate risks and reinforce weak areas in their data posture before breaches occur.

Together, these tools within MIP and the upcoming DSPM for AI will provide a comprehensive and proactive approach to data security, ensuring organizations not only protect personal data but also identify and mitigate risks early.

Conclusion

Effective management of personal data breaches has become a critical necessity for organizations, reinforced by the detailed provisions of India's DPDP Act, 2023, and its accompanying Draft Rules, 2025. This chapter has comprehensively addressed the essential elements organizations must consider in managing personal data breaches, highlighting the significance of prompt detection, timely notification, and robust response mechanisms. Through clear delineation of the obligations of data fiduciaries and Data Processors, as well as illustrating practical procedures for breach notifications to both affected individuals and regulatory authorities, organizations are now equipped to meet their compliance requirements effectively.

By exploring real-world cases, common causes, and potential consequences of breaches, this chapter emphasizes the imperative of proactive measures. Regular risk assessments, thorough audits, stringent access controls, advanced security technologies, and ongoing employee training form the foundation of robust preventative strategies. Additionally, tools such as Microsoft's DSPM have been highlighted as instrumental in enhancing proactive security measures, enabling organizations to identify vulnerabilities and mitigate risks before breaches occur.

Ultimately, adherence to the structured requirements of the DPDP Act and Draft Rules not only ensures legal compliance but also fortifies organizational resilience, fosters consumer trust, and protects individual privacy. Organizations that integrate these comprehensive strategies into their data management practices will not only reduce the risk and impact of future breaches but also demonstrate their commitment to data protection excellence and regulatory responsibility.

In the next chapter, we look into building a true data-protection culture. We will look further into the need of implementing a data protection culture throughout the organization, and how leaders set the tone and back it with resources, and how role-based training turns every employee into a data steward. In the upcoming chapter, we will look further into the evolution of cloud computing, how cross-border data transfer under DPDPA, and how to achieve compliance by complying with the DPDPA and its Draft Rules, 2025, using Microsoft Security capability.

Join our Discord space

Join our Discord workspace for latest updates, offers, tech happenings around the world, new releases, and sessions with the authors:

https://discord.bpbonline.com

CHAPTER 7

Taking Data Overseas and Using Cloud

Introduction

Having explored the foundational elements of data protection, we now turn to a critical and evolving landscape, the cloud. The **Digital Personal Data Protection (DPDP)** Act applies uniformly across the cloud ecosystem, whether you are using **Software as a Service (SaaS)**, **Infrastructure as a Service (IaaS)**, or **Platform as a Service (PaaS)**. This chapter delves into the intersection of cloud computing and regulatory compliance, offering insights for both technical leaders and business executives.

Quick review on cloud terminology, cloud computing refers to the delivery of computing services, including storage, processing power, databases, and software over the internet. Instead of managing physical servers, organizations can leverage cloud platforms on demand, paying only for what they use.

This chapter outlines how the DPDP Act impacts the use of global cloud services like Microsoft Azure, AWS, and other cloud service providers. It examines cross-border data transfer rules, consent responsibilities, and the role of privacy-enhancing tools such as Microsoft Purview and Priva.

Whether you are a CISO, CIO, or a business leader shaping digital strategy, this section equips you with a practical understanding of cloud compliance, data sovereignty, and privacy-first governance in an increasingly connected world.

Structure

In this chapter, we will cover the following topics:

- Evolution of cloud computing
- Data transfers and cloud services
- Cross-border data transfer under DPDPA
- Necessity of cross-border data transfers
- Achieving compliance with the DPDP Act and Rules
- From event logs to audit logs for compliance
- Microsoft security capabilities
- Data residency role in regulatory compliance
- Priva's role in reducing data residency risk

Objectives

By the end of this chapter, it aims to equip readers with a practical understanding of how the DPDP Act, 2023, and Draft Rules, 2025, apply to cloud computing and cross-border data transfers. As organizations increasingly rely on cloud services such as Microsoft Azure, AWS, and others, understanding the regulatory expectations around data residency, international processing, and security safeguards becomes essential. The chapter provides clarity on different cloud service models (SaaS, PaaS, IaaS), outlines the legal and operational implications of transferring personal data across borders, and introduces privacy-enhancing tools like Microsoft Purview and Microsoft Priva. Through real-world use cases and guidance on implementing compliance controls, this chapter helps CISOs, CIOs, and business leaders navigate the intersection of digital transformation and regulatory compliance. Ultimately, it fosters a privacy-first approach while leveraging cloud scalability, interoperability, and collaboration across geographies, ensuring data is protected, lawful, and secure in a globally connected environment.

Evolution of cloud computing

The concept of cloud computing dates back to the 1960s, with the introduction of the idea of utility computing. At the time, visionaries imagined a future where computing power and applications could be delivered just like public utilities, on-demand and pay-as-you-go. However, due to the limitations in networking and computing infrastructure, this vision remained largely theoretical for several decades.

In the late 1990s and early 2000s, significant progress in grid computing and virtualization technologies laid the foundation for what we now recognize as modern cloud computing. Grid computing enabled resource sharing across distributed systems, allowing organizations to pool computing power from different locations. At the same time, virtualization technology advanced to allow multiple **virtual machines** (**VMs**) to operate independently on a single physical server. This innovation significantly improved hardware utilization and introduced the flexibility that modern cloud services rely upon.

Together, these developments marked a turning point, transforming cloud computing from a theoretical concept into a practical and scalable model that would redefine how businesses and individuals access technology.

The rise of cloud computing

The early 2000s marked the emergence of true cloud computing services. In 2006, **Amazon Web Services** (**AWS**) launched Amazon EC2 and S3, offering scalable compute and storage resources over the internet. This revolutionized IT operations by eliminating the need for heavy upfront infrastructure investment.

Since then, the cloud market has matured with key players such as Microsoft Azure. Today, cloud computing powers organizations of all sizes and sectors, enabling agility, cost-efficiency, and digital transformation.

Understanding the types of cloud services is critical for compliance under the DPDP Act, which applies to all forms of data processing, regardless of whether it is done via IaaS, PaaS, or SaaS models:

- **IaaS:** Provides on-demand compute, storage, and networking.
    - o **Example***:* Microsoft Azure's Virtual Machines and Blob Storage.
- **PaaS:** Offers a platform to build, deploy, and manage applications without dealing with infrastructure.
    - o **Example***:* Azure App Service for scalable web and API apps.
- **SaaS:** Delivers software applications over the internet on a subscription basis.
    - o **Example***:* Microsoft Office 365 for productivity tools like Word, Excel, and Outlook.

The major cloud providers and their impact are as follows:

- **Microsoft Azure** offers a complete suite of cloud services with deep integration into enterprise ecosystems, extensive compliance support, and global data centers. It is widely adopted by regulated sectors due to its strong privacy and security posture.
    - o **Key services***:* Azure VMs, Azure SQL, Azure DevOps, and Azure AI.
- **AWS** is one of the market players in terms of scale and diversity of offerings. With a strong ecosystem and an innovation-first mindset, AWS supports businesses of all sizes.
    - o **Key services***:* EC2, S3, Lambda, RDS, and SageMaker.

The Act makes it essential for organizations using any of these platforms to implement safeguards around data localization, cross-border transfers, consent, and access controls. Cloud providers offer tools to support these needs, but responsibility lies with the Data Fiduciary to ensure compliance.

By understanding the architecture and responsibilities associated with each cloud model, organizations can adopt a Privacy by Design approach, leveraging cloud capabilities while staying aligned with India's data protection laws.

Data transfer and cloud services

In today's interconnected digital landscape, most organizations utilize multiple cloud service providers to support their business operations. As data flows across borders, platforms, and hybrid architectures, ensuring secure and compliant data transfer becomes crucial, especially in light of the regulatory framework introduced by the DPDP Act, 2023, and Draft Rules, 2025.

The Act recognizes the increasing complexity of data exchange in a multi-cloud environment and sets strict guidelines to protect the rights of Data Principals while enabling legitimate data use.

Interoperability in cloud environments

Interoperability is the ability of disparate systems and services to communicate, exchange, and effectively utilize shared data, and enables businesses in cloud computing to integrate diverse environments (public, private, and hybrid) into a unified ecosystem. For example, a multinational enterprise might run its infrastructure on Microsoft Azure, manage customer relationships in Salesforce, and coordinate projects in Zoho; seamless data integration across these platforms ensures real-time access and collaborative efficiency. Tools like Azure API Management bridge on-premises and cloud environments, providing automated, secure data synchronization and consistent governance. Beyond enhancing operational agility, interoperability also reinforces lawful dataprocessing principles, ensuring transparency, accountability, and compliance with relevant regulations.

Interoperability not only supports operational efficiency but also aligns with the principles of lawful data processing.

Collaboration across geographies

Modern business operations demand real-time collaboration across globally distributed teams and locations, with platforms like Microsoft Teams, SharePoint, and Azure DevOps facilitating such interactions through shared access to data and repositories. For instance, a global development team using Azure DevOps may include developers in India, the US, and Germany working simultaneously on the same codebase. These cross-border data transfers must align with Chapter IV Section 16 of the DPDP Act and Rule 14 from the Draft Rules 2025, which requires robust protection mechanisms to ensure data security and uphold national data sovereignty. Similarly, cloud collaboration tools like OneDrive enable file sharing via public or private links, but without appropriate safeguards, such activities could unintentionally lead to unauthorized international data flows, posing compliance and privacy risks.

Cross-border data transfer under DPDPA

The DPDP Act takes a cautious yet enabling approach to data transfers beyond Indian borders. It introduces clear conditions under which data may or may not be sent overseas:

- **Chapter IV, Section 16: Transfer of personal data outside India:**
    - *16. (1): The Central Government may, by notification, restrict the transfer of personal data by a Data Fiduciary for processing to such country or territory outside India as may be so notified.*
    - *(2): Nothing contained in this section shall restrict the applicability of any law for the time being in force in India that provides for a higher degree of protection for or restriction on transfer of personal data by a Data Fiduciary outside India in relation to any personal data or Data Fiduciary or class thereof.*
- **Rule 14: Processing of personal data outside India:**
    - *Transfer to any country or territory outside India of personal data processed by a Data Fiduciary:*
        - *(a) Within the territory of India; or*
        - *(b) Outside the territory of India in connection with any activity related to offering of goods or services to Data Principals within the territory of India, is subject to the restriction that the Data Fiduciary shall meet such requirements as the Central Government may, by general or special order, specify in respect of making such personal data available to any foreign State, or to any person or entity under the control of or any agency of such a State.*
- **Rule 12: Additional obligations of Significant Data Fiduciary (Draft Rules, 2025):**
    - *12 (4) A Significant Data Fiduciary shall undertake measures to ensure that personal data specified by the Central Government on the basis of the recommendations of a committee constituted by it is processed subject to the restriction that the personal data and the traffic data pertaining to its flow is not transferred outside the territory of India.*

An Indian financial services company leverages Microsoft Azure to host customer data for better performance, high availability, and disaster recovery. To ensure business continuity and meet global latency requirements, it considers storing personal data in Azure's Singapore and European data centers.

To remain compliant with the DPDP Act, 2023, and Draft Rules, 2025, the company must adhere to the following safeguards and legal obligations:

- **Check for Government restrictions**: Under Chapter IV Section 16(1) of the DPDP Act, the Central Government may notify specific countries or territories where cross-border transfers of personal data are either restricted or permitted.

  The company must validate that Singapore and the European region are not listed as restricted destinations, as notified under Section 16 or the Fourth Schedule of the Draft Rules.

- **Ensure additional safeguards (for Significant Data Fiduciaries (SDFs))**: If the company is designated as a Significant Data Fiduciary, it must comply with Rule 12(4) of the Draft Rules, which may prohibit the transfer of specified categories of personal and traffic data outside India.

  The company must verify whether the type of customer data it processes is subject to localization requirements, as recommended by the committee formed under the Act.

- **Comply with processing conditions for overseas transfers**: According to Rule 14 of the Draft Rules, any transfer of personal data outside India, whether for internal processing or service delivery to Indian citizens, is subject to conditions set by the Central Government, particularly regarding sharing with foreign states or entities under their control.

- **Implement technical and organizational safeguards**: While not explicitly mandated under Chapter IV, Section 16, the intent of general obligations of Data Fiduciary and Rule 6 (Reasonable Security Safeguards) strongly suggests that it is a best practice for the company to:

  o Use encryption to secure data in transit and at rest.

  o Ensure that Microsoft Azure offers equivalent or stronger privacy protections in line with Indian standards.

- **Establish legal grounds for processing**: The company must also satisfy a valid legal basis for processing the data under Chapter II Section 7 of the DPDP Act, such as obtaining the explicit consent of the Data Principal or relying on a legitimate purpose.

This approach enforces accountability and transparency, ensuring the Data Fiduciary remains liable for protection even when data crosses borders. Data transfer across cloud services is inevitable in today's digital enterprise landscape. However, the DPDP Act and its accompanying rules place the onus of compliance squarely on the Data Fiduciary. Through interoperability, collaboration, and secure transfer protocols, organizations must architect cloud strategies that balance innovation with data sovereignty.

By leveraging governance and privacy-enhancing tools like Microsoft Purview and Priva, businesses can ensure compliant data transfers while empowering operational excellence across borders.

Necessity of cross-border data transfers

Cloud computing delivers unmatched scalability and operational efficiency, enabling organizations to handle large volumes of data and adapt to dynamic workloads in real time. However, to realize these benefits, especially in distributed or multi-cloud environments, data must often traverse geographical boundaries. In such cases, compliance with the DPDP Act, 2023, becomes a core consideration.

Scalability enabled by the cloud

Scalability refers to the dynamic ability to scale IT infrastructure up or down based on fluctuating operational demands. Cloud service providers such as Microsoft Azure offer elastic computing environments that are particularly valuable in data-intensive sectors like retail, healthcare, and finance, where rapid scaling ensures business continuity, responsiveness, and cost-efficiency.

This operational flexibility aligns with Chapter II Section 7(a) of the DPDP Act, 2023, which permits the processing of personal data when it is voluntarily provided by the Data Principal, who has not indicated that they do not consent to such processing. In essence, when a Data Principal explicitly requests a service, such as real-time access to financial statements or appointment booking in a healthcare app, the cloud's scalability enables the Data Fiduciary to fulfill the request effectively, while remaining compliant under lawful grounds of processing.

Efficiency through seamless data transfer

Efficiency in the cloud is achieved through optimized resource allocation, automation, and real-time access. Efficient data transfers reduce latency, enable timely analytics, and streamline operations. For example, a multinational firm can use Azure Data Factory to orchestrate **Extract, Transform, Load** (**ETL**) operations across distributed data sources. Timely access to analytics-ready data improves decision-making and business responsiveness.

These processes must be designed with Chapter IV Section 16 of the DPDP Act in mind, which regulates cross-border data transfers, ensuring that data sent to foreign jurisdictions meets required privacy and protection standards.

Achieving compliance with DPDP Act and Rules

As organizations increasingly adopt cloud infrastructure to scale operations, enhance agility, and reduce costs, they must also address the regulatory expectations laid out in the DPDP Act and its Draft Rules, 2025. These laws emphasize accountability, security, and sovereignty in the handling of personal data, making it essential for Data Fiduciaries to design cloud strategies that prioritize both performance and compliance. To reap the benefits of cloud scalability and efficiency while remaining compliant, organizations must implement:

- **Define clear cross-border transfer policies:** Under Chapter IV, Section 16 of the DPDP Act, the Central Government may restrict or permit personal data transfers to specific countries or territories via official notification. Organizations must ensure that personal data is only transferred to jurisdictions that have not been restricted by such notification. As of now, no definitive list of permitted or restricted countries has been released.

- **Respect data localization requirements for SDFs:** As per Rule 12(4) of the Draft Rules, **SDFs** may be required to process certain categories of personal or traffic data exclusively within India, based on Government notifications and expert committee recommendations. Cloud architectures must be configured accordingly to avoid the cross-border flow of such restricted data.

- **Follow conditions for international processing:** According to Rule 14, if personal data is processed outside India, either as part of a domestic operation or for services offered to Indian Data Principals, it must meet additional requirements prescribed by the Central Government. This includes controls around making such data available to foreign states or their affiliated entities, safeguarding sovereignty and privacy.

- **Implement strong security controls:** As required by Rule 6, Reasonable Security Safeguards, Data Fiduciaries must put in place technical and organizational measures such as encryption, access restrictions, and audit logging to protect data in transit and at rest, including when using cloud services.

Hybrid and multi-cloud environments

In the modern enterprise landscape, many organizations are increasingly adopting hybrid and multi-cloud strategies to optimize performance, control costs, and meet growing regulatory compliance requirements. A hybrid environment combines on-premises infrastructure with public or private cloud platforms, while a multi-cloud approach involves using services from multiple cloud vendors such as Microsoft Azure and AWS.

While these environments provide flexibility and resilience, they introduce complexities in managing data transfers across different infrastructures and jurisdictions, especially when dealing with personal data governed by the DPDP Act, 2023.

Real-world example of a manufacturing use case

Consider an international manufacturing company with operations in India, the United States, and Germany. The company relies on Microsoft Azure for hosting critical services, storage, compute, analytics, and regularly transfers design files and research data between locations for product development and innovation. In this context, the Indian operations must comply with the DPDP Act, which imposes strict controls over cross-border data transfers.

The key data transfer considerations are as follows:

- **Chapter IV Section 16**: Government notification for cross-border transfers:
  - Cross-border transfer of personal data is permitted only to countries or territories approved by the Central Government via official notification. The Government may restrict transfers to jurisdictions it deems insufficient in terms of privacy safeguards. No list has been officially published yet, but organizations must remain alert to future notifications.

- **Rule 14:** Additional conditions for international processing:
  - If personal data is processed outside India, whether within the scope of services offered to Indian Data Principals or otherwise, the Data Fiduciary must meet any additional requirements set by the Central Government. These could relate to data access by foreign Governments or entities, especially those under state control, and are intended to protect national interest and data sovereignty.

- **Rule 6:** Reasonable security safeguards:
  - All data transfers, whether domestic or international, must be protected by reasonable security safeguards, as defined in Rule 6 of the Draft Rules. This includes encryption, role-based access control, audit logging, and incident response mechanisms to prevent unauthorized access or breaches during data movement.

- **Chapter IV Section 17**: Exceptions to processing restrictions:
  - This section provides that the Central Government may exempt certain Data Fiduciaries or classes of Data Fiduciaries from provisions of the Act, including restrictions under Chapter IV section 16, for reasons such as national security, prevention of offences, or public order. These exemptions must be explicitly notified by the Government and are generally narrow in scope, typically applying to Government bodies or strategic functions.

Data collaboration scenario

In this example, the company's R&D team in India shares personal documents with its counterparts in the US and Germany. This includes design blueprints, customer prototype feedback, and performance metrics, all of which may contain personal data.

To ensure compliance with the DPDP Act, keep the following in mind:

- The company uses Microsoft Purview Information Protection to classify, label, and encrypt documents.
- Only authorized users from approved geographies can access the information.

Enforcing data boundaries in IaaS

For organizations using IaaS, enforcing data residency and transfer controls is critical. Tools such as:

- **Azure policy:** Used to enforce regional data storage and restrict outbound transfers.
- **Firewall and content gateways**: Monitor and block unauthorized data exfiltration.

Collaboration and SaaS usage

When employees collaborate using Microsoft Teams, SharePoint, or OneDrive, documents and messages can traverse global networks. Monitoring this flow is essential:

- Microsoft Priva plays a key role here. It monitors collaborative data use, identifies overexposure, and enforces cross-border transfer restrictions.

  https://learn.microsoft.com/en-us/privacy/priva/risk-management-policy-data-transfer

- Data-sharing via Teams messages or email attachments is analyzed for potential boundary violations and flagged for administrator action.

  https://learn.microsoft.com/en-us/privacy/priva/risk-management-policy-data-overexposure

Organizations operating in **hybrid and multi-cloud models** must:

- Assess which cloud platforms handle personal data.
- Apply strict controls for **data residency**, **classification**, and **transfer boundaries**.
- Regularly review and audit data transfer logs.

By doing so, businesses can remain compliant with the DPDP Act, uphold privacy expectations, and maintain operational flexibility.

Common protocols to transfer data

In the modern cloud ecosystem, understanding the various protocols used for data transfer is crucial for maintaining compliance with privacy regulations like the DPDP Act, 2023. These protocols Act as the *vehicles* for data to move between systems, applications, and geographical locations, often across borders. The protocols are as follows:

- **File Transfer Protocol (FTP):** FTP is one of the earliest methods used for transferring files over a network. It uses separate control and data channels to exchange information between the client and the server.
  - o **Pros**: Supports large file transfers; widely available.
  - o **Cons**: Lacks encryption; vulnerable to packet sniffing and man-in-the-middle attacks.

Under Rule 6 of the Draft Rules (2025), organizations must implement reasonable security safeguards. Therefore, transferring personal data using unsecured protocols like FTP without encryption would violate this obligation.

- **HTTP and HTTPS: Hypertext Transfer Protocol (HTTP)** is the foundation for data communication on the web. However, it lacks encryption.

    o   HTTPS is the secure version, incorporating SSL/TLS to encrypt the data.

    o   **Compliance impact**: According to Chapter II Section 8(5) of the DPDP Act, Data Fiduciaries must protect personal data using appropriate safeguards; thus, HTTPS should always be used for data exchange involving personal information.

- **APIs (REST and SOAP): Application Programming Interfaces (APIs)** are widely used by developers to allow systems and applications to communicate and transfer data.

    o   REST APIs use standard HTTP methods.

    o   SOAP APIs offer structured messaging with built-in security standards like WS-Security.

    o   **Best practice**: APIs should use HTTPS endpoints and authentication tokens. Logging API usage and applying throttling are key to meeting Rule 6 compliance.

- **Collaboration tools and data leakage risk:** Modern collaboration platforms like Microsoft Teams, Outlook, and SharePoint Online enable easy sharing of documents, messages, and screen content. However, this convenience brings risks:

    o   Files shared through Teams or Outlook can be accessed via global links, possibly crossing jurisdictional boundaries.

    o   Microsoft OneDrive and SharePoint links can be distributed beyond intended users, resulting in inadvertent international data transfer.

    o   WhatsApp, Telegram, Signal, and other messaging apps allow file sharing that may bypass organizational controls.

Organizations must implement content inspection, boundary enforcement, and **data loss prevention (DLP)** tools. Under Chapter IV, Section 16 and Rule 14, such requirements are mandatory to ensure that personal data does not get transferred to unauthorized or blacklisted jurisdictions.

From event logs to audit logs for compliance

In the digital age, every user interaction, whether it is logging into an email account, accessing a file, or initiating a transaction, generates a corresponding log. These entries, known as event logs, capture activity within systems and applications. However, when logs are specifically configured to record and monitor sensitive actions such as data access, modifications, deletions, and transfers, they become audit logs, a cornerstone of data governance and compliance frameworks.

Importance of audit logs in data protection

The DPDP Act, 2023, recognizes the necessity of audit mechanisms to uphold the principles of transparency, accountability, and security in personal data handling:

- **Chapter II Section 8(4)** mandates that Data Fiduciaries implement technical and organizational measures to ensure compliance with the provisions of the Act, including traceability of data processing activities.

- **Rule 6(1)**(e) of the Draft Rules, 2025 *for enabling the detection of unauthorised access, its investigation, remediation to prevent recurrence and continued processing in the event of such a compromise, retain such logs and personal data for a period of one year, unless compliance with any law for the time being in force requires otherwise.*

  This emphasizes the requirement for reasonable security safeguards, which explicitly includes mechanisms for logging, audit trails, and regular monitoring of data processing activities for a period of one year.

- **Rule 4, Part B Under obligations of Consent Managers:** *The Consent Manager— (a) shall give the Data Principal using such platform access to such record; (b) shall, on the request of the Data Principal and in accordance with its terms of service, make available to her the information contained in such record, in machine-readable form; and (c) shall maintain such record for at least seven years, or for such longer period as the Data Principal and Consent Manager may agree upon or as may be required by law.*

  It further mandates that registered Consent Managers must maintain and make available audit trails of consents managed on behalf of Data Principals, ensuring verifiability and transparency, and maintain the records for at least seven years.

Importance of audit logs

Audit logs are essential for the following reasons:

- **Security monitoring and breach detection**: Audit logs track user behavior and system operations, enabling organizations to quickly detect unauthorized access or suspicious activities. For example, if personal data is accessed outside of standard business hours or from an unusual location, it triggers alerts for further investigation.

- **Compliance and legal proof**: Logs act as legal evidence of responsible data handling. In the event of an audit, regulatory inquiry, or dispute, organizations can present these records to demonstrate compliance with the provisions of the Act, 2023, and the associated Rules, 2025. These logs are especially vital when an organization receives a notice from the **Data Protection Board (DPB)** or a request from a Data Principal under their rights (such as access, correction, or grievance redressal). Logs provide traceable proof of consent, processing actions, and security events, thereby reinforcing transparency, accountability, and legal defensibility.

- **Forensic analysis and incident response**: In the event of a security incident, audit logs enable forensic teams to trace the sequence of actions, identify root causes, and assess the extent of the breach.

- **Operational insights and system optimization**: Log analysis helps in identifying patterns, diagnosing performance bottlenecks, and improving user experience through better system configuration.

Alignment with the DPDP Act

Audit logs are not optional; they form a required **technical safeguard** under Rule 6. They are instrumental in fulfilling duties outlined in:

- **Chapter II Section 8(4):** Requires Data Fiduciaries to implement technical and organizational measures to ensure compliance with the Act. Maintaining traceability of processing activities, which audit logs enable, is fundamental to this obligation.

- **Rule 4, Part B of the First Schedule:** Obligations of Consent Managers:
    - Mandates registered Consent Managers to maintain verifiable records and audit trails of consents obtained and managed on behalf of Data Principals. These logs must be available upon request to ensure transparency and verifiability.

- **Rule 6 (1)(c) and (1)(e):** Reasonable security safeguards:
    - Visibility on the accessing of such personal data, through appropriate logs, monitoring, and review, for enabling detection of unauthorized access, and in the event of such a compromise, retain such logs and personal data for a period of one year.

Organizations should implement centralized log management and automated alerting systems to ensure compliance with the DPDP Act. Use native tools like Microsoft Purview, Azure Monitor, Microsoft Sentinel, and Priva to manage and review audit trails effectively.

By incorporating audit logging into their data governance strategy, organizations not only enhance operational resilience but also build trust with Data Principals and regulatory authorities alike.

Microsoft security capabilities

In a world where data security is foundational to trust, Microsoft offers a robust security ecosystem tailored to safeguard organizational assets, especially digital personal data governed by laws under the DPDP Act, 2023, and the accompanying 2025 Draft Rules. At the heart of this ecosystem lies Azure Security Center, a unified infrastructure security management system that strengthens the security posture of data environments, both in Azure and across hybrid clouds. Cloud platforms like Microsoft Azure offer advanced audit logging features through:

- **Azure Monitor:**
  - o **Activity logs**: Capture control-plane operations (e.g., creation/deletion of resources).
  - o **Diagnostic logs**: Provide in-depth visibility into the behavior of Azure services (e.g., API calls, data access).
  - o **Log analytics**: Allows real-time querying, alerting, and visualization of logs to support proactive monitoring.

The following figure is a snapshot of the Azure Monitor service:

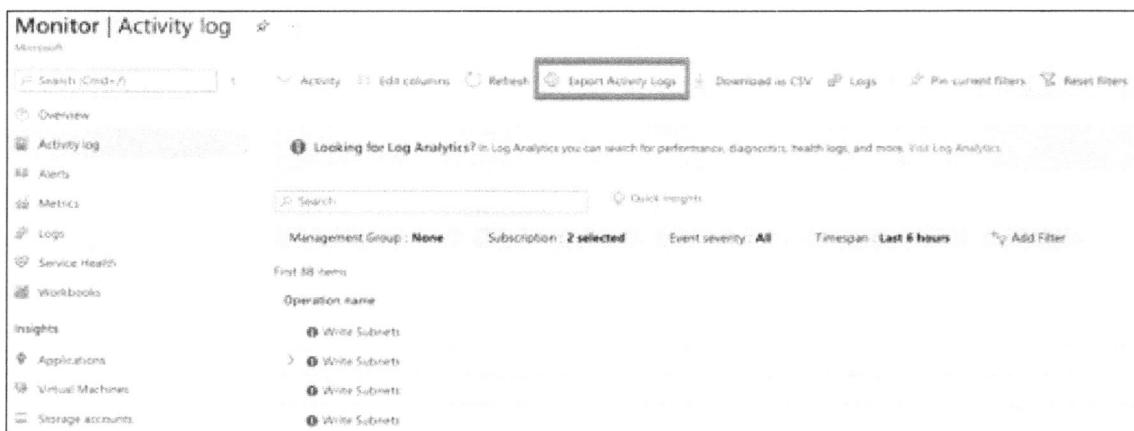

Figure 7.1: Azure activity log

Azure Security Center

Azure Security Center provides end-to-end visibility and control over security configurations and risks, enabling organizations to meet stringent compliance mandates under **Rule 6** of the DPDP Rules.

The key capabilities are as follows:

- **Security alerts and incident response**: Azure Security Center uses advanced threat intelligence, machine learning, and behavioral analytics to detect potential intrusions and generate security alerts. These alerts help security teams investigate and respond to threats in real time, reducing dwell time and damage.
  - o **Examples**: Unauthorized login attempts, malware detection on VMs, or lateral movement indicators.

      o **DPDPA alignment**: Helps meet **Rule 6(1)(c)**, ensuring visibility, logging, and detection of unauthorized access.

- **Security recommendations and hardening guidance**: The platform continuously assesses your Azure resources and recommends best practices to close security gaps. This includes remediation suggestions for:

      o Misconfigured storage

      o Open ports

      o Outdated systems lacking patches

        These recommendations support proactive defense and help organizations **harden their digital perimeter**.

      o **DPDPA Alignment**: Fulfills **Rule 6(1)(a) and (1)(g)** by enforcing technical safeguards and promoting effective observance of security controls.

- **Compliance reports and posture management**: Azure Security Center supports built-in regulatory compliance dashboards. These are mapped to various standards, including ISO 27001, SOC, and NIST, and are now increasingly aligned with custom frameworks like the DPDP Act.

      o **Real-time reporting** allows auditors and regulators to verify that the organization complies with **data security mandates**, such as encryption, logging, backup, and retention policies.

      o **DPDPA Alignment**: Enables compliance demonstration for **Rule 6(1)(e)**, ensuring retention of logs for at least one year, and **Rule 6(1)(f)**, audit readiness for contracts involving Data Processors.

Integrated compliance tools

Microsoft also integrates other compliance and security products to ensure organizations can fulfill obligations under the DPDP Act:

- **Microsoft Defender for Cloud**: Adds layered protection across cloud-native services.

- **Microsoft Purview Compliance Manager**: Helps assess and manage compliance risk with a **DPDPA template**, offering control mapping, scorecards, and action plans.

- **Microsoft Sentinel**: A scalable SIEM and SOAR solution that centralizes logging from Azure and non-Azure sources, ideal for advanced threat detection and triage.

Microsoft Purview, Audit Portal

Within **Microsoft Purview**, the **Audit (Standard and Premium)** solution offers end-to-end tracking of activities across Microsoft Purview's Audit Search feature, which gives you interactive, flexible querying of your organization's audit log data, whether you are troubleshooting an incident, preparing for an audit, or simply investigating user activity. Key capabilities include the following:

- SharePoint, OneDrive, Exchange, Teams, Power BI, and Defender tools.
- Tracks 1,000+ user and admin operations with detailed metadata (user ID, IP, object affected, time, action, outcome).

Retention options

Microsoft Purview offers two audit log retention tiers to meet Rule 6(1)(e) of the Draft DPDP Rules, which requires retaining logs for at least one year: Audit (Standard) retains logs for 180 days by default (extendable up to two years with custom policies) and is included with most Microsoft 365 plans (E3, Business Premium, etc.), while Audit (Premium), available with Microsoft 365 E5 Compliance or as a Purview Audit Premium add-on, retains core service logs for one year (and up to ten years if needed), giving you the required one-year retention plus extra headroom for long-tail investigations or legal holds. These options are listed here:

- **Standard audit**: Retain logs for 180 days.
- **Audit (Premium)**: Retain audit logs for **up to 10 years** (DPDP Act only requires **1 year**, so this provides ample headroom).

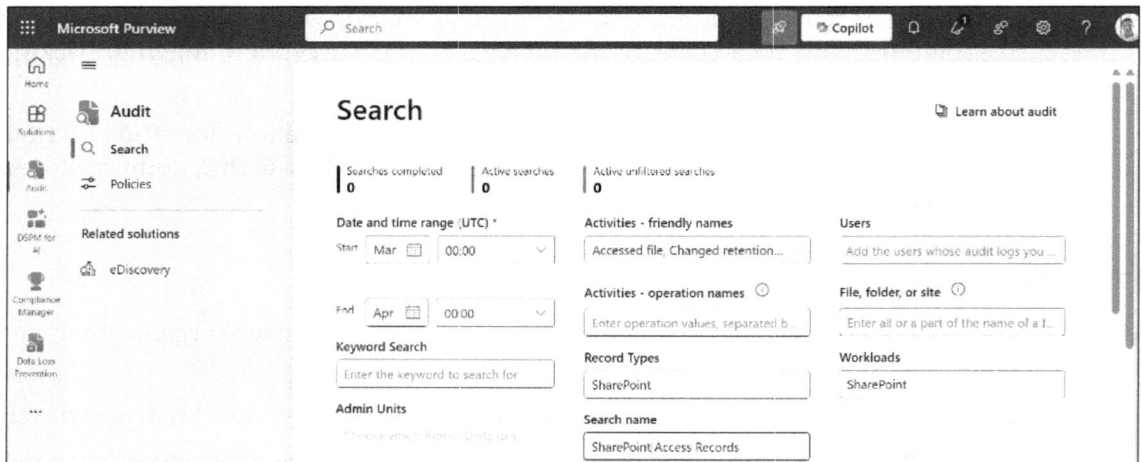

Figure 7.2: Microsoft Audit solution

Log retention and legal holds

To fulfill **Rule 6(1)(e)** of the Draft DPDP Rules:

- **Log retention:** Under **Rule 6(1)(e)** of the Draft DPDP Rules, all audit events (access, modification, deletion attempts, etc.) must be retained for at least one year. In Microsoft Purview Records Management, you achieve this by applying an immutable retention label (e.g. "AuditLogs-1Year") to the audit-log store (Azure Blob or SharePoint library). This label blocks any delete operation—manual or automated, until 365 days have elapsed, then surfaces records for defensible disposition review.

- **Legal hold:** A Purview eDiscovery legal hold places a preservation tag on specified content sources (including audit logs). Any log entry in scope is copied into the **Preservation Hold Library** (**PHL**) and locked by the hold, making it undeletable regardless of retention label expiry. Even after the one-year retention period, the PHL copy remains until the hold is explicitly released, ensuring critical evidence persists through investigations or litigation.

Now, let us examine a case example. When Ananya's team published their quarterly report in SharePoint, they anticipated regulatory scrutiny. The compliance officer, therefore, placed the entire document library on legal hold using a Microsoft Purview eDiscovery case. From that moment on, no file subject to the hold could be deleted. One afternoon, Ananya realized she had uploaded an outdated draft of `Contract-Q1.docx` and clicked **Delete**. However, the file was not removed because it was protected by the legal hold policy. The system recorded every detail of Ananya's attempt, her user ID, the file name, the timestamp, the site URL, and the fact that the deletion was blocked and the file preserved. This audit entry joined the ledger of events, where it will remain intact for at least one year in compliance with **Rule 6(1)(e)** of the Draft DPDP Rules. Months later, if a DPB investigator, or Ananya herself, asked what happened to that file, the audit log would state: *On 2025-04-15 10:42 AM, Ananya attempted to delete Contract-Q1.docx; action blocked; file preserved in PHL.* That record would still be there, unaltered and an indisputable testament to how legal hold, immutable storage, and meticulous auditing work together to protect both data and compliance.

Legal hold enforcement for Ananya:

- The Purview eDiscovery case applies a "legal hold" tag to Ananya's mailbox and associated SharePoint site.

- When Ananya attempts to delete `Contract-Q1.docx`, the item is copied into the PHL in her SharePoint site.

- The PHL copy is immutable and cannot be removed until the legal hold is lifted.

Audit logging Ananya's delete attempt (Rule 6(1)(e) Compliance):

- An audit event is generated with these details:
    - **Actor**: Ananya's user principal name (e.g., *ananya@company.com*)
    - **Operation**: DeleteFile attempted on **Contract-Q1.docx**
    - **Object**: `/sites/Finance/Contract-Q1.docx`
    - **Timestamp**: e.g., `2025-04-15T10:42:00Z`
    - **Outcome**: Blocked; file preserved in PHL

- This audit record is stored in Purview Audit for at least one year, satisfying Rule 6(1)(e).

The immutable storage configuration includes:

- The PHL uses Azure Blob Storage with a legal-hold retention policy to lock Ananya's preserved files.
- Even global administrators cannot delete these items until the hold is removed.

Verification via Audit Search includes:

- Administrators query Purview Audit Search for DeleteFile events filtered by user "Ananya" and date range.
- The search returns the blocked deletion event, which can be exported as CSV for compliance reporting or legal review.

Data residency role in regulatory compliance

Data residency refers to the specific geographic location where data is stored and processed. In the modern digital economy, where data is not only a strategic asset but also a regulatory responsibility, data residency has emerged as a fundamental pillar of data governance and privacy compliance.

With the increasing enforcement of data protection laws globally, countries are asserting their Digital Sovereignty by requiring that certain categories of data, particularly personal data, remain within their national borders. This regulatory stance aims to prevent unauthorized access by foreign entities, ensure enforceability under domestic laws, and enhance national security and privacy protections.

Data residency matters for the following reasons:

- **Regulatory compliance**: Ensures organizations meet the **legal mandates** under the DPDP Act and sectoral laws like those from RBI, SEBI, and IT Act. Non-compliance could result in:
  - Suspension of services by the DPB.
  - Financial penalties (up to ₹250 crore under the DPDP Act).
  - Reputational damage and loss of consumer trust.

- **Security and sovereignty:** Keeping personal data within national borders ensures it remains under the jurisdiction of Indian law, reducing the risk of unauthorized foreign surveillance or access. This aligns with India's Digital Sovereignty goals.

- **Customer trust**: Organizations that adhere to data residency rules demonstrate their commitment to protecting customer privacy. This not only fulfills compliance expectations but also becomes a differentiator in competitive markets like banking, telecom, and healthcare.

Indian regulatory frameworks that require data residency

Several sectoral regulators also enforce data localization and residency obligations:

- **Reserve Bank of India (RBI):** Circular on data storage (April 6, 2018):
    - Mandates that **all payment data** must be stored **only in India**.
    - Includes transaction data, end-to-end details, and payment instructions.
    - Requires RBI-approved **System Audits** to validate compliance.
    - **Link to the regulation**: **https://aka.ms/RBI-CS-Framework.**

- **Securities and Exchange Board of India (SEBI):** Cybersecurity framework:
    - Requires **market infrastructure institutions (MIIs)** to **retain data in India** and ensure its availability to Indian regulators upon request.
    - Encourages **geo-fencing, data access control**, and **audit trail maintenance**.
    - **Link to the regulation**: **https://www.sebi.gov.in/legal/circulars/aug-2024/ cybersecurity-and-cyber-resilience-framework-cscrf-for-sebi-regulated- entities-res-_85964.html.**

- **Information Technology Act, 2000:**
    - Read with Section 43A and associated IT (Reasonable Security Practices and Procedures) Rules, mandates that organizations adopt **local security controls** and **data protection measures**.
    - This Act serves as a complementary framework to the DPDP Act and still governs areas not yet transitioned to the new law.
    - **Link to the regulation**: **https://aka.ms/IT-Act-2000.**

You can access these regulation links directly within the Microsoft Compliance Manager solution:

1. In the **Overview** section, open the **About** dropdown.
2. You will see a list of all supported regulations (390+ globally).
3. Clicking any regulation displays a brief description and a direct link to the official text.

This library not only covers India's RBI, SEBI, and IT Act requirements but also provides visibility into global regulatory frameworks.

Data transfer policies

In modern organizations, vast amounts of unstructured data are continuously created, consumed, shared, and reshared by employees, partners, and external stakeholders. Ensuring that personal data does not inadvertently cross geographic or compliance boundaries is a significant challenge, particularly in the context of the DPDP Act, 2023, and the Draft Rules 2025 in India.

Addressing this challenge involves two primary aspects: data discovery/classification and enforcing compliance boundaries. While previous chapters extensively covered the intricacies of data discovery and classification, this section focuses specifically on enforcing geographic compliance boundaries, particularly through policies and technological solutions. The key question organizations face is: once personal data is identified and classified, how can it be effectively managed and controlled to ensure compliance with geographic or jurisdictional boundaries?

According to the DPDP Act, organizations must adhere to stringent rules concerning data transfers, especially to countries or regions defined as *restricted* or *hostile states* by the Government. Effective compliance requires organizations to develop comprehensive data transfer policies that clearly articulate:

- **Data classification**: Categorizing data clearly according to sensitivity, such as personal data and critical personal data.

- **Transfer conditions**: Explicitly defining circumstances under which data may be transferred, emphasizing consent and legitimate legal bases.

- **Security controls**: Enforcing robust security measures such as encryption (both in transit and at rest), rigorous access control mechanisms, and thorough audit logging.

- **Geographic and jurisdictional boundaries**: Clearly identifying permissible and prohibited regions for data transfers to comply with Indian regulatory requirements.

- **Monitoring and compliance reporting**: Regular monitoring of data movements and generating audit reports to verify compliance with the DPDP Act.

Priva's role in reducing data residency risk

Microsoft Priva is a privacy management solution designed explicitly to help organizations proactively manage privacy risks associated with data transfers and data exposure. Leveraging artificial intelligence and machine learning, Microsoft Priva provides advanced capabilities for:

- **Data usage insights**: Understanding how personal data is being accessed, shared, and potentially overexposed.

- **Policy enforcement**: Automatically applying privacy controls to personal data.

- **Compliance with regulations**: Assisting organizations to meet specific requirements set forth by the DPDP Act, such as preventing unauthorized cross-border data transfers and managing data exposure.

In essence, Microsoft Priva integrates seamlessly into the Microsoft 365 ecosystem, providing built-in support for data residency compliance. This integration is crucial because most organizational data, including emails, SharePoint files, OneDrive documents, and Teams communications, resides within Microsoft 365.

Data overexposure occurs when personal information is accessible beyond necessary roles, creating vulnerabilities for unauthorized access and breaches. Microsoft Priva specifically addresses this risk by identifying instances of data overexposure and enabling automated remediation:

- **Overexposure detection**: Priva scans SharePoint, OneDrive, Teams, and other Microsoft 365 repositories, highlighting scenarios where personal data is excessively accessible.

- **Automated access reviews**: It proactively prompts reviews and adjustments to access permissions, ensuring data visibility is confined strictly to required individuals.

For example, employees frequently create and share SharePoint or OneDrive links containing personal data. Over time, these links often remain active beyond their intended use, potentially being shared further without appropriate oversight.

Priva identifies such cases where personal customer data, perhaps stored in SharePoint, is inadvertently accessible to all employees rather than restricted to a limited group who require access for legitimate business functions. Administrators can then take corrective action, reducing the risk of unauthorized access or data breach incidents.

Automated remediation and continuous monitoring

Once overexposed data is identified, Microsoft Priva can automate remediation actions to reduce exposure effectively. This includes adjusting access controls, removing unnecessary permissions, and notifying data owners of potential risks. For instance, Priva can automatically adjust permissions to ensure that financial records are accessible only to authorized personnel, significantly mitigating breach risks.

Priva continuously monitors data usage and access patterns, ensuring persistent protection against overexposure. It generates alerts for unusual activities indicative of potential privacy risks, enabling organizations to respond swiftly and effectively.

Data minimization and compliance

Data minimization is another essential principle enforced by Microsoft Priva, emphasizing that organizations should collect and retain only data essential to their operations. Priva identifies **redundant, obsolete, or trivial (ROT)** data and suggests actionable strategies to reduce unnecessary data storage.

For example, Priva can identify outdated customer records no longer required for business operations and recommend their deletion or archival. It supports enforcing retention policies that automatically delete or anonymize personal data after a specified period, directly aligning with the DPDP Act's data minimization mandates.

Need to identify personal data during data transfer

Microsoft Priva integrates seamlessly with other Microsoft security tools, particularly **Microsoft Information Protection (MIP)**. This integration enables the automated application of sensitivity labels on documents, further reinforcing compliance by ensuring that personal documents cannot be shared beyond designated geographic or organizational boundaries. Data classification in Microsoft Purview uses automated scanners (including on-demand for cold-storage SharePoint part of pay-as-you-go model) to detect sensitive types (e.g., financial data, PII) and apply predefined sensitivity labels (Confidential, Highly Confidential) with persistent protections. In Microsoft Priva Privacy Risk Management, you then define data transfer policies that block or alert on any attempt to share labeled data with unapproved regions or external parties. This end-to-end workflow, discovery, labeling, and policy enforcement secures personal information at rest and in motion.

Example: Consider a scenario where an employee attempts to share confidential financial documents with a partner located in a country explicitly defined as a restricted or hostile jurisdiction by Indian authorities. Priva, together with MIP, applies sensitivity labels to prevent the unauthorized sharing of such documents, enforcing compliance with data residency and transfer requirements.

Conclusion

In today's digital era, cloud computing presents immense opportunities alongside complex regulatory challenges, especially under the DPDP Act, 2023, and its Draft Rules, 2025. Organizations must navigate rules on cross-border data transfers, data residency, and security safeguards, making compliance a strategic necessity. This chapter explored how businesses can manage data security and regulatory compliance while leveraging cloud technologies responsibly. Tools like Microsoft Azure, Purview, and Priva help enforce data residency, control transfers, and minimize risk through automation and governance. These solutions not only simplify compliance but also strengthen data protection and build trust. Looking ahead, intelligent automation and AI-driven privacy tools will become central to compliance, enabling real-time risk detection, context-aware policies, and proactive privacy management. As cloud adoption rises, embedding privacy into cloud strategies, backed by advanced tools and strong governance, will be vital. This approach ensures sustainable compliance, operational resilience, and lasting confidence among customers and regulators.

In the upcoming chapter, we will explore how organizations can implement effective records keeping management, thorough documentation, and well-defined accountability structures, which are essential pillars of DPDPA compliance.

CHAPTER 8

Records, Documentation, and Accountability

Introduction

In the era of stringent data privacy laws, meticulous record-keeping, comprehensive documentation, and clear accountability structures have become pivotal for organizations. This chapter explores critical practices mandated under India's **Digital Personal Data Protection (DPDP)** Act, 2023, and its Draft Rules, 2025. It highlights essential activities such as maintaining accurate records of data processing, conducting mandatory **Data Protection Impact Assessments (DPIAs)**, appointing qualified **Data Protection Officers (DPOs)**, and demonstrating ongoing compliance through robust accountability frameworks. Organizations are now required to systematically document their data processing activities, enabling swift responses to regulatory inquiries, audits, and data subject requests. The DPDP Act emphasizes not just compliance, but proactive transparency and accountability, demanding clear roles and responsibilities, particularly the appointment and active engagement of a DPO. By understanding and applying the principles outlined in this chapter, organizations can effectively manage risks, maintain compliance, and foster trust among stakeholders, ensuring that privacy becomes a foundational element of their operational excellence.

Structure

In this chapter, we will cover the following topics:

- Record keeping explained
- Necessity of effective record-keeping
- Accountability under the DPDP Act and Rules
- Breach risk reduction
- Accountability in third-party processing and data sharing
- DPIAs under the DPDP Act and Rules
- DPO appointment and responsibilities under the DPDPA
- Role of eDiscovery in accountability under DPDP Act
- Technologies enabling accountability and records compliance

Objectives

This chapter aims to equip organizations with a practical and comprehensive understanding of how to fulfill key obligations under the DPDP Act, 2023, and its Draft Rules, 2025, through effective record-keeping, documentation, and accountability measures. It highlights the importance of maintaining verifiable records of data processing, consent, third-party engagements, and breach responses. The chapter explores the legal requirement for **DPIAs**, the mandatory appointment and role of **DPOs**, and how tools like Microsoft Purview can operationalize compliance through automation, auditability, and lifecycle management. It emphasizes the necessity of demonstrating compliance through structured documentation, transparent data handling, and continuous oversight, especially during audits, data subject requests, or regulatory inquiries. By adopting the principles and best practices discussed, organizations can reduce legal and reputational risks, improve regulatory readiness, and foster a culture of accountability, thereby aligning privacy with operational excellence and stakeholder trust.

Records keeping explained

Records keeping involves systematically organizing, maintaining, and preserving records within an organization, regardless of whether those records exist digitally or in physical form. These records encompass various forms of information, such as contracts, employee details, emails, meeting minutes, and operational reports. Effective records keeping ensures that critical information remains organized, accessible, and reliably retrievable throughout its lifecycle. It goes beyond merely organizing records neatly; it is essential for uninterrupted business operations and adherence to legal and regulatory mandates.

In the context of the DPDP Act and its Draft Rules, there is a strong emphasis on records keeping, preserving contents, and adhering to standard documentation to demonstrate organizational compliance. This includes requirements such as appointing a DPO and conducting DPIAs (For only designated SDFs). A robust records management system enables organizations to swiftly access and provide information during legal inquiries or compliance audits, significantly reducing the risk of penalties, litigation, or reputational harm due to misplaced or inaccessible documentation. Furthermore, effective records management safeguards organizational knowledge, facilitates continuity during personnel changes, and ensures that critical institutional insights and information are preserved.

Electronic Document and Records Management Systems

An **Electronic Document and Records Management System** (**EDRMS**) is a type of software that helps organizations manage both documents and records electronically. It enables the classification, storage, retrieval, and secure disposal of records, ensuring compliance with data management regulations and standards. EDRMS solutions typically fall into the following categories:

- **On-premises EDRMS**: Installed and hosted within the organization's own infrastructure, giving the organization full control over security and data management.

- **Cloud-based EDRMS**: Hosted by third-party service providers, offering scalability, remote accessibility, and reduced upfront investment.

- **Hybrid EDRMS**: Combines on-premises and cloud solutions, allowing flexibility to manage records internally while leveraging cloud benefits.

To maintain and demonstrate compliance over time, you must use a records management system to save your data and maintain organizational compliance adherence. Microsoft's cloud-native **Data Lifecycle Management** (**DLM**) and **Records Management** (**RM**) solutions in Microsoft Purview together form an EDRMS that helps you automate retention, disposition, and proof-of-compliance for all your Microsoft 365 data.

Necessity of effective record keeping

Effective records management is crucial under the DPDP Act, 2023, and the Draft Rules, 2025, in India, but it does not explicitly mandate the implementation of a formal *records management solution*. However, they impose critical obligations on Data Fiduciaries, particularly **Significant Data Fiduciaries** (**SDFs**), which make effective record-keeping indispensable for demonstrating compliance. Under Chapter II, Section 10 of the Act, SDFs must undertake measures such as conducting DPIAs, maintaining records of processing activities, and implementing grievance redressal mechanisms. Additionally, Chapter II Section 5 and Section 6 emphasize principles like notice and consent, necessity, and limitation, requiring organizations to maintain clear and verifiable records to demonstrate the lawful basis for processing personal data, whether through valid consent, legal obligation, or other legitimate grounds.

Further operational requirements under Rule 4 and Rule 6 of the Draft Rules, 2025, necessitate the documentation of the consent lifecycle (including obtaining and withdrawing consent), the grounds for processing where consent is absent, the outcomes and recommendations of DPIAs, records of responses to DPR requests, and details of breach notifications made to the Data Protection Board of India and impacted individuals. Without a systematic and auditable approach to managing these records, organizations would struggle to prove compliance during regulatory audits, investigations, or enforcement actions.

Although the DPDPA does not prescribe a specific technological solution, effective records management becomes a practical necessity. It is essential for establishing legal defensibility, fulfilling accountability obligations under Chapter II Section 8 (General Obligation of Data Fiduciary), responding adequately to regulatory authorities and Data Principals, and mitigating financial and reputational risks associated with non-compliance. In practice, organizations must adopt a structured, secure, and auditable record keeping framework that integrates policies, procedures, technological tools, and audit trails to ensure that all personal data processing activities are accurately recorded, readily retrievable, and reviewable as required under the law.

Records keeping and legal duties of Data Fiduciaries

The DPDP Act, 2023, along with its Draft Rules, 2025, primarily emphasizes that personal data must be retained only for as long as it is necessary to fulfill the purpose for which it was collected, or as required by law. However, the Act and Rules do not explicitly define rigid criteria or durations for such retention in every case, instead placing accountability on Data Fiduciaries to manage this responsibly under Chapter II Section 8 (General obligations of Data Fiduciary). This open-ended requirement creates a significant legal risk: in the event of litigation, regulatory investigations, or audits, the ability to produce appropriate evidence becomes critical. Therefore, having an effective and secure records management solution is not only a best practice but a strategic necessity for compliance. It is also pertinent for the Data Fiduciary to review their own sectoral laws, which may require it to retain data. Data Retention mandates of other applicable laws have to be reconciled with the provisions of the DPDPA. Systems like Microsoft Purview Data Lifecycle Management and Records Management ensure that vital documents remain under enforceable retention policies. Even if someone attempts to tamper with or delete records internally, tools like SharePoint automatically preserve an immutable copy of the file until the end of its defined retention period within a hidden site Preservation Hold Library, ensuring the integrity and availability of evidence when needed.

Moreover, under the DPDP Draft Rules, 2025, organizations must maintain a verifiable record of Data Principal consent for a minimum of seven years from the date of withdrawal or cessation of processing based on such consent. This applies to all categories of Data Principals, including customers and employees, reinforcing the need for a systematic approach to consent record retention. Records Keeping system ensures that evolving consent preferences are accurately captured, stored securely, and retrievable for compliance audits or dispute resolution.

In addition, third-party risk management and supply chain governance are integral compliance areas under the DPDPA framework. Organizations are expected to perform and document DPIAs, supply chain assessments, DPO appointments, and adherence to other regulatory requirements. Leveraging a solution like Microsoft Purview Data Lifecycle Management and Records Management enables organizations to centralize, update, and retain these critical compliance records over extended periods. Furthermore, when personal data or related records must be deleted promptly to meet compliance needs (for instance, after fulfilling a Data Principal's right to erasure under Chapter III Section 12 of the Act), features within the Microsoft Purview Data Lifecycle Management and Records Management enable the immediate and irreversible deletion of targeted information while maintaining audit trails of the deletion action.

In conclusion, while the DPDPA emphasizes necessity and proportionality in data retention, the practical necessity of maintaining a defensible, tamper-evident, and compliant records management system is paramount. Solutions like Microsoft Purview not only simplify compliance with India's evolving data protection landscape but also future-proof organizations against operational, legal, and reputational risks.

Accountability under the DPDP Act and Rules

Accountability forms the backbone of modern data protection frameworks globally, and India's DPDP Act, 2023, is no exception. The Act adopts a principle-based approach to data governance, emphasizing that Data Fiduciaries, entities that determine the purpose and means of processing personal data, must not merely comply with the law but be able to demonstrate that they have complied.

The accompanying Draft Rules, 2025, provide additional operational clarity, reinforcing the expectation that organizations take ownership of their data handling practices. Accountability under the DPDPA is not a passive requirement; it is a proactive, continuous obligation that must permeate every layer of an organization's data lifecycle management.

Defining accountability under the DPDPA

The Act's Chapter II, Section 8 explicitly outlines the Duties of Data Fiduciaries, setting the foundation for accountability obligations. These include ensuring data security, processing personal data lawfully, handling consent appropriately, providing transparent privacy notices, facilitating the exercise of Data Principal Rights, and notifying authorities in case of personal data breaches. However, accountability under the DPDPA is broader than mere adherence to these duties; it also demands proof of compliance.

In practice, this means that organizations must maintain comprehensive internal documentation, establish auditable records of data processing activities, and implement safeguards that evidence the organization's commitment to responsible data governance.

Core accountability requirements

Several sections of the DPDPA and its Draft Rules reinforce the core pillars of accountability:

- **Chapter II Section 8** mandates that processing must be necessary and proportionate to the stated purpose, and organizations must be ready to justify this necessity if challenged.

- **Chapter II Section 8(5)** requires that reasonable security safeguards be put in place to prevent breaches and unauthorized processing. It also mandates Data Fiduciaries to ensure that their Data Principals are also complying with the mandate of implementing reasonable security safeguards.

- **Chapter II Section 10** lays out additional obligations for SDFs, including:
  - Conducting and retaining DPIAs.
  - Appointing a **DPO.**
  - Undertaking periodic audits of compliance.

- **First Schedule Part B under Draft Rule 4** requires that the consent manager must be able to demonstrate that consent was obtained, managed, and withdrawn lawfully and that consents are retained for **seven years** after cessation of processing.

- **Consent Manager Requirement**: As per First Schedule Part B under Draft Rule 4, organizations must recognize and facilitate Data Principal Rights exercised through authorized Consent Managers. A Consent Manager is an entity registered with the Data Protection Board of India that acts as a custodian for managing an individual's consents across various Data Fiduciaries. Data Fiduciaries are required to interact with these Consent Managers, accept instructions regarding consent withdrawals, and ensure that the processing of personal data reflects the updated consent status communicated via the Consent Manager. Organizations must, therefore, maintain system integrations and auditable logs of all consent actions routed through Consent Managers, further reinforcing the accountability framework.

Accountability towards Data Principals

The DPDPA, 2023, places significant emphasis on the accountability of organizations not only towards regulatory authorities but critically towards the individuals whose data they process, the Data Principals. One of the fundamental obligations under the Act is transparency at the time of data collection. Chapter II, Section 5 and Section 6 of the DPDPA explicitly require that consent must be obtained from the Data Principal only after providing a clear and comprehensive notice describing the intended processing activities.

The Draft DPDP Rules, 2025, further elaborate this obligation. Draft Rule 3 specifies that notices must be provided in clear, plain language and must be standalone, that is, understandable without requiring reference to any other documents or terms. At a minimum, these notices must clearly list:

- The categories of personal data being collected,
- The specific purposes for which the data will be processed,
- The manner in which the Data Principal can withdraw consent,
- And how they can exercise their broader rights under the Act, such as access, correction, grievance redressal, and erasure.

To operationalize this transparency and accountability towards Data Principals, most organizations will deploy a consent management system. This software must be capable of capturing the entire lifecycle of consent, from initial grant to withdrawal, modification, and historical auditing. However, customer expectations will extend beyond a single channel. Data Principals may seek to manage or update their consent using multiple modes, including:

- Email requests
- Call center interactions
- Web portals
- Mobile applications
- In-person branch visits

In large organizations, particularly in sectors like banking, there are often different systems managing various interaction channels, separate systems for call center management, online banking platforms, mobile applications, and physical branch operations. Given this diversity, it becomes critical for organizations to reconcile consent updates across all systems into a single, tamper-evident repository that maintains the chronological integrity of all Data Principal interactions.

Solutions such as enterprise-grade records management systems (e.g., Microsoft Purview Records Management) can support this requirement, but they must be properly configured to capture and preserve:

- Consent-related interactions from disparate systems.
- Changes or updates to consent.
- Withdrawal requests.
- Any other communications relevant to the Data Principal's data rights

These records must be immutable; once created, they cannot be altered or deleted without a trace, and should be securely retained for auditability and regulatory scrutiny.

Thus, under the DPDPA, companies must ensure full accountability towards Data Principals by maintaining systems that can accurately track and manage consent changes across all points of interaction, email, chat, call centers, web portals, mobile apps, and branch visits, and by consolidating this data into a secure, compliant, and auditable framework.

Demonstrating compliance through record keeping duty

A key aspect of accountability is the ability to demonstrate compliance. The DPDP Act explicitly places the burden of proof on the Data Fiduciary in certain cases. If consent is the legal basis for processing personal data, the Fiduciary must be able to prove that a proper notice was given, and that valid consent was obtained from the Data Principal. This legal requirement means organizations must maintain records of the consent lifecycle, what notice was shown, when and how consent was given, and if it was withdrawn. Without such records, an organization cannot meet its obligation if a dispute arises about whether a person was informed or agreed to the use of their data. Thus, even by law, record-keeping is intertwined with accountability and transparency.

Demonstrating compliance for consent management records

Every instance of consent obtained from a Data Principal should be logged and stored securely. This includes the content of the consent notice presented, the date/time of consent, the specific purposes consented to, and any consent withdrawal. The Draft Rules recognize the importance of this by regulating *Consent Managers*, entities or platforms that intermediaries can use to manage user consents. In case a Significant Data Fiduciary or a Data Fiduciary has been replaced, Consent Manager is required to maintain a record of all consents given, denied, or withdrawn, as well as the corresponding notices presented to the individual. It must also log any sharing of the individual's data that it facilitates. These records must be accessible to the Data Principal, and they must be retained for at least seven years.

Even if your organization is not using an external *Consent Manager* service, you should implement similar practices internally. For instance, if you collect consent via a website form, ensure that your systems capture and store the exact version of the privacy notice or consent text shown and link it to the user's record. This way, you mirror the standard of compliance expected of formal Consent Managers.

Demonstrating compliance for records of data collection and use

Beyond consent, organizations should document what personal data is collected, the purpose associated with each collection (which should align with what was told in the notice), and how that data is used internally. Each dataset or system containing personal data ideally should have an entry in an ROPA. While the DPDP Act does not literally use the term "ROPA", the principle still applies; accountability is greatly aided by having a living inventory of personal data processing. Include details like data categories, storage location, retention period, and any applicable legal basis or consent ID. This internal record ensures that at any point, the organization can answer: *What personal data do we have on individual X? Where is it stored? For what purpose? Who can access it? Until when will we keep it?* Such documentation directly supports transparency and is invaluable if a Data Principal exercises their rights or if regulators inquire.

Data sharing and processor records

If personal data is shared with any third parties, whether they are vendors, service providers (Data Processors), or other Data Fiduciaries, those flows should be logged. Data sharing records should note which data was shared, with whom, on what date, for what purpose, and under what security measures or agreements. This is critical for transparency (the DPDP Act's Right to Information for Data Principals includes knowing the identities of all entities with whom their data has been shared) and for accountability (to show you have control over downstream use). In practice, organizations can maintain a register of all third-party data processing agreements and data transfer logs. For example, if an organization (Data Fiduciary) shares customer data with a marketing analytics firm (Data Processor), it should record the scope of data shared and confirm that the processor is contractually bound to use it only for the defined purpose. Later, if a user asks, *who has my data?* or if a breach at the processor occurs, the organization can quickly retrieve this record. The Draft Rule 6(1)(c) reinforces this need by requiring *visibility on the accessing of such personal data, through appropriate logs* to monitor all access and detect unauthorized activity. Moreover, Rule 6 requires that logs of data access and other security-relevant events be retained for at least one year for forensic purposes. Together, these suggest that maintaining an audit trail of *who accessed or received personal data and when* is part of expected practice. The rule is as follows:

6. Reasonable security safeguards.(1): A Data Fiduciary shall protect personal data in its possession or under its control, including in respect of any processing undertaken by it or on its behalf by a Data Processor, by taking reasonable security safeguards to prevent personal data breach, which shall include, at the minimum:

(f) appropriate provision in the contract entered into between such Data Fiduciary and such a Data Processor for taking reasonable security safeguards;

(g) appropriate technical and organisational measures to ensure effective observance of security safeguards.

Under Rule 6 of the Draft DPDP Rules, 2025, a Data Fiduciary must ensure that when personal data is shared with a Data Processor, the processor is contractually bound to implement reasonable security safeguards (Clause f). Additionally, the Fiduciary must adopt technical and organizational measures to actively monitor and enforce these safeguards (Clause g). Maintaining contracts, data sharing records, and access logs becomes essential to demonstrate control, ensure security, and fulfill accountability obligations under the Act.

Data retention and disposal records

The DPDP Act, 2023, places clear obligations on organizations to manage the lifecycle of personal data responsibly, from collection to eventual disposal. A critical component of this obligation is the management of data retention and the secure disposal of records.

Chapter II Section 8(7) A Data Fiduciary shall, unless retention is necessary for compliance with any law for the time being in force, —

(a) erase personal data, upon the Data Principal withdrawing her consent or as soon as it is reasonable to assume that the specified purpose is no longer being served, whichever is earlier; and

(b) cause its Data Processor to erase any personal data that was made available by the Data Fiduciary for processing to such Data Processor.

It specifically mandates that Data Fiduciaries must cease retaining personal data once the purpose for which it was collected is fulfilled, unless further retention is required under another applicable law. In other words, organizations cannot hold onto personal data indefinitely *just in case;* they must justify continued retention either by demonstrating an ongoing lawful purpose or by referencing a specific legal requirement.

In contexts where other laws require longer retention, for example, tax laws, labor regulations, or sector-specific compliance standards, the DPDP Act permits continued storage. However, retention decisions must be explicitly tied to these laws and clearly documented. For instance, if financial regulations mandate retaining transactional data for seven years, the organization must record this legal basis in its records retention schedule.

Regarding consent records, the Draft Rules, 2025 specify that consent given by Data Principals must be retained for a minimum of seven years after withdrawal of consent or cessation of processing based on consent. Consent Manager platforms must not only store consents securely but must also evaluate the risks of retaining data beyond this period. Excessive storage of personal data, even when consent exists, increases the exposure to future data breaches, leading to potential loss of customer trust, reputational harm, and hefty penalties under the DPDPA's enforcement framework.

Thus, a comprehensive records management program must go beyond simple retention. It must actively track:

- Retention periods for each data category (e.g., customer profiles, employee files, marketing consents).
- Expiry dates for lawful purposes.
- Timely erasure or anonymization actions when data is no longer required.

Importantly, each deletion or anonymization action should be logged, creating an auditable trail that demonstrates compliance with both internal policies and regulatory mandates. For instance, a deletion log should record the data set deleted, the date of deletion, the responsible system/user, and the justification for disposal.

The Draft Rules, 2025, also contemplate sector-specific timeframes. For example, large e-commerce platforms may be instructed to delete customer data three years after the last recorded interaction for that given purpose. Having a formal data retention and disposal schedule, aligned with both the DPDP Act and any industry-specific regulations, will ensure defensible, compliant operations.

Beyond legal compliance, careful management of data retention reduces operational risks by:

- Limiting the volume of personal data exposed in the event of a breach.
- Demonstrating good faith and responsible stewardship to customers.
- Showing regulatory bodies that the organization practices proactive risk management.

In summary, maintaining lifecycle records, from consent collection to processing activities, to data flows, and finally to disposals, allows an organization to demonstrate accountability at any point in time. These records become the backbone of operational transparency, enabling organizations to fulfill the spirit and the letter of the DPDPA, thereby strengthening customer trust and ensuring regulatory resilience.

Breach risk reduction

One important aspect of accountability is managing risks to personal data, particularly the risk of breaches. **Breach Risk Reduction (BRR)** refers to the set of practices aimed at minimizing both the likelihood of a data breach and the impact if one occurs. Two major strategies under BRR are:

- Data retention and minimization.
- Security safeguards and monitoring.

Data retention and minimization

Reducing the amount of personal data an organization holds and deleting it as soon as it is no longer needed directly reduces breach impact. If an attacker or unauthorized person gains access, there will simply be less data available to potentially leak. The DPDP Act builds this principle into law by prohibiting indefinite retention. Organizations are required to erase personal data once the initial purpose is fulfilled and the data is no longer actively needed.

Rule 8. Time period for the specified purpose to be deemed as no longer being served.— (1) A Data Fiduciary, who is of such class and is processing personal data for such corresponding purposes as are specified in Third Schedule, shall erase such personal data, unless its retention is necessary for compliance with any law for the time being in force, if, for the corresponding time period specified in the said Schedule, the Data Principal neither approaches such Data Fiduciary for the performance of the specified purpose nor exercises her rights in relation to such processing.

If a Data Principal has not interacted further for that purpose for a certain period, it should be deemed that the purpose is over. The Draft Rules 2025 are expected to specify these time periods for different contexts (as seen in draft Rule 8 and its third Schedule). For example, for some large online platforms, *3 years of inactivity* may be defined as the cutoff after which user data must be deleted. Organizations should *proactively enforce data retention schedules* in line with such rules and their own business needs. This means inventorying data to know when it was collected or last used, and automating deletion or archiving processes to trigger at the appropriate time. Every deletion should be documented (for accountability, as mentioned). By systematically purging stale personal data, an organization shrinks its *attack surface*; even if a breach happens, the attackers cannot steal what is not stored.

Security safeguards and monitoring

Preventing personal data breaches is one of the core objectives of the DPDP Act, 2023. Under Chapter II Section 8(5) of the Act, Data Fiduciaries are obligated to implement reasonable security safeguards to protect personal data against unauthorized access, loss, or misuse. The Draft Rules, 2025, particularly Rule 6, elaborate on these safeguards by requiring organizations to adopt measures such as data encryption, access controls, continuous monitoring, and, critically, the logging of data access and processing activities.

Records keeping plays an essential role within this security framework. Maintaining detailed audit logs of user actions and system activities is not merely a compliance requirement; it is a foundational breach risk reduction measure.

By systematically recording who accessed, edited, shared, or deleted a document and when, organizations can:

- Detect suspicious behaviors early, such as unauthorized internal access or external infiltration attempts.
- Limit the impact of breaches through swift identification and containment.
- Provide forensic evidence during incident investigations.
- Demonstrate to regulators that effective monitoring and detection capabilities were in place, potentially reducing regulatory penalties in the event of a breach.

Draft Rule 6 mandates that organizations retain audit logs for at least one year, ensuring that forensic investigation capabilities extend well beyond the immediate incident timeframe. These logs should be securely stored, tamper-proof, and readily accessible if requested by the Data Protection Board of India during investigations or audits.

Modern EDRMS and data governance platforms (such as Microsoft Purview Data lifecycle management and Records management) offer integrated audit trail capabilities. Such systems automatically capture and retain comprehensive logs that record:

- User identities
- Timestamps of actions
- Type of activity (view, edit, download, delete)

- Source devices and IP addresses
- Changes to document metadata or permissions

By monitoring audit trails proactively, organizations can not only detect unauthorized access but also prove accountability under the DPDPA's transparency and security obligations. Effective monitoring builds an evidentiary chain showing that the organization exercised due diligence in protecting personal data, thereby strengthening its defense posture in regulatory inquiries.

In the context of breach risk reduction, comprehensive audit logging and monitoring help organizations in two vital ways:

- **Early breach detection**: When unusual access patterns are identified (e.g., a large volume of downloads at unusual hours), security teams can respond swiftly to mitigate potential damage.

- **Post-incident forensics**: If a breach does occur, retained audit logs enable forensic analysts to reconstruct the timeline of events, identifying the entry point, the scope of compromised data, and the steps taken in response, thereby fulfilling notification obligations under Chapter II section 8(6) and defending the organization's compliance standing.

In summary, record-keeping through audit trails is not optional; it is a strategic necessity for enforcing security safeguards, monitoring access, reducing breach risks, and demonstrating legal accountability under the DPDP Act. Organizations that embed robust monitoring and audit practices within their records management frameworks position themselves not only for compliance success but also for resilient, trustworthy operations in today's evolving data protection landscape.

Accountability in third-party processing and data sharing

Modern organizations often rely on third-party processors or service providers to handle personal data. For example, cloud hosting services, payment processors, marketing agencies, or outsourced customer support. Under the DPDP Act, using a third-party does not absolve a company of responsibility. The primary organization (Data Fiduciary) remains accountable for personal data processing carried out on its behalf. Section 8(1) of the Act explicitly states that *A Data Fiduciary shall, irrespective of any agreement to the contrary or failure of a Data Principal to carry out the duties provided under this Act, be responsible for complying with the provisions of this Act and the rules made thereunder in respect of any processing undertaken by it or on its behalf by a Data Processor.* This is a direct alignment with the accountability principle: you can delegate work, but you cannot delegate accountability.

To implement this in practice, organizations should take a lifecycle approach to managing third-party relationships:

- **Due diligence before sharing:** Before transferring any personal data to a vendor or partner, assess their capability to protect the data. This includes reviewing their security measures, privacy policies, breach history, and compliance posture. If the third-party will have access to personal data, consider requiring them to fill out a security questionnaire or to demonstrate certifications (like ISO 27001, etc.). Essentially, *know your processor*. The DPDP Act empowers the government to classify some entities as SDFs based on risk factors, which must undergo independent data audits. Even if your organization is not classified as such, adopting a similar mindset for critical vendors (e.g., running privacy impact assessments on a new data processing arrangement) is a good way to show accountability.

- **Contracts with clear obligations:** The Act requires that any engagement of a Data Processor be under a *valid contract*. That contract should clearly stipulate the processor's obligations regarding personal data, including confidentiality, using the data only for the specified purpose, and not further sharing it without permission. The Draft Rules add that the contract must include clauses obligating the processor to implement reasonable security safeguards. In other words, your vendor agreements should mirror the protections you are expected to have. Key terms to include:

  o **Purpose limitation:** The processor may only process the personal data for the explicit purposes instructed by the Fiduciary.

  o **Security requirements:** The processor must protect the data with at least the same standard of care as the Fiduciary (encryption, access control, etc.), and ideally adhere to industry standards or specific measures (as listed in Draft Rule 6).

  o **Breach notification:** The processor should be required to notify the Data Fiduciary immediately if they suspect or experience a data breach. This ensures the Fiduciary can take action and notify authorities/Data Principals as required by law.

  o **Assistance with Data Principal Rights:** If a Data Principal exercises a right (like access or deletion), the processor must cooperate in providing or deleting any data they hold, upon request from the Fiduciary.

  o **Audit rights:** The Fiduciary should have the right to audit the processor's data protection practices or receive regular compliance reports, especially for significant or processing operations.

  o **Sub-processor restrictions:** The processor should not sub-contract further (or only with consent and similar contractual flow-down of obligations); in fact, the Draft Rules for Consent Managers explicitly forbid them from sub-contracting their obligations, reflecting the regulator's intent to keep accountability clear and unbroken.

By solidifying these points in contracts, organizations create legal evidence of the shared understanding of responsibilities, which can be crucial if a breach or dispute arises. For example, if a processor misuses data in violation of the contract, the contract is the basis for the Fiduciary to take legal action against that processor (and possibly claim damages or indemnification). It will also be a key piece of evidence to present to the Data Protection Board or courts to show that the organization *did its due diligence and imposed necessary safeguards*, reinforcing that the Fiduciary took reasonable steps (which might influence penalty decisions).

- **Liability and indemnity planning:** In line with accountability, organizations should prepare for handling incidents in third-party scenarios. While an organization cannot escape its regulatory liability by blaming a vendor, it can *contractually* arrange indemnification, e.g., the processor agrees to cover losses or fines arising from their negligence. Ensure such clauses are present and clear. This is more of a legal safety net, but it underscores the need to formally assign responsibility. Again, any such legal steps would rely on evidence, which goes back to maintaining records of what went wrong and why.

In essence, accountability in third-party processing means extending your governance to your partners. One practical approach is to treat external processors almost like an internal department when it comes to compliance: incorporate them into your data flow maps, include them in your risk assessments, and get routine assurance of their controls. When a Data Principal asks *"Who has access to my data?"*, you should be able to answer not just with names, but with confidence that those parties are held to the same standard as you are. This closes the loop of transparency as well, because the DPDP Act's Right to access information regarding processing of personal data, compels disclosing *"identities of all other Data Fiduciaries and Data Processors"* involved, and no organization wants to list a partner that is a weak link. By carefully managing third-party processors, organizations protect Data Principals' interests across the entire ecosystem of processing.

DPIAs under the DPDP Act and Rules

A DPIA is a systematic process that organizations use to identify and mitigate privacy risks arising from data processing activities. DPIAs involve a detailed examination of how personal data is processed, assessment of potential privacy impacts on Data Principals, and implementation of appropriate risk mitigation measures. DPIAs ensure compliance with data protection laws, safeguard privacy rights, and demonstrate organizational accountability, thereby fostering trust among Data Principals and regulatory authorities.

The importance of conducting DPIAs is as follows:

- **Risk identification:** DPIAs enable organizations to proactively identify potential privacy risks, particularly when adopting new technologies or processing large volumes of personal data.

- **Mitigation measures:** By recognizing risks early, organizations can implement targeted mitigation strategies, substantially reducing the likelihood of data breaches and regulatory non-compliance.

- **Compliance assurance:** Regularly conducting DPIAs helps organizations maintain continuous compliance with evolving data protection regulations, thereby avoiding potential penalties and reputational harm.

- **Transparency and trust:** DPIAs reinforce an organization's commitment to data protection, promoting transparency and building trust with both Data Principals and regulators.

DPIAs as mandated by the DPDP Act

The DPDP Act, particularly in Chapter II Section 10, mandates DPIAs for SDFs. The key obligations include:

- **Mandatory assessments:** SDFs must perform DPIAs before initiating data processing involving new technologies or presenting high privacy risks.

- **Assessment scope:** DPIAs must thoroughly evaluate privacy impacts, considering the nature, scope, context, and processing purposes.

- **Risk management protocol:** Where DPIAs reveal significant unmitigable risks, fiduciaries are required to consult the Data Protection Board before proceeding.

- **Ongoing evaluations:** DPIAs should be periodically updated to reflect new risks and evolving processing activities, ensuring continual compliance.

Further, additional obligations of an SDF are clarified within Rule 12:

(1) A Significant Data Fiduciary shall, once in every period of twelve months from the date on which it is notified as such or is included in the class of Data Fiduciaries notified as such, undertake a Data Protection Impact Assessment and an audit to ensure effective observance of the provisions of this Act and the rules made thereunder.

The purpose of this requirement is to ensure that SDFs proactively assess their personal data processing activities for potential risks to the rights and freedoms of Data Principals, and continuously verify that they are complying with the DPDP Act and applicable Rules.

This regular exercise supports early detection of compliance gaps, risk exposure, and technical vulnerabilities, strengthening overall governance and accountability.

(2) A Significant Data Fiduciary shall cause the person carrying out the Data Protection Impact Assessment and audit to furnish to the Board a report containing significant observations in the Data Protection Impact Assessment and audit.

This provision introduces external oversight and transparency: the Board is not solely reliant on organizational self-reporting but receives independent assessment outcomes.

It enables the Board to monitor high-risk processing activities more closely and intervene if critical issues affecting Data Principals' rights are identified.

(3) A Significant Data Fiduciary shall observe due diligence to verify that algorithmic software deployed by it for hosting, display, uploading, modification, publishing, transmission, storage, updating, or sharing of personal data processed by it is not likely to pose a risk to the rights of Data Principals.

This address concerns automated decision-making, AI-based processing, profiling, and content management. Organizations must validate that the algorithms they deploy are transparent, fair, unbiased, and secure, preventing discrimination, unfair profiling, or data misuse. Algorithm testing, validation reports, and risk assessments become critical for fulfilling this obligation.

(4) A Significant Data Fiduciary shall undertake measures to ensure that personal data specified by the Central Government on the basis of the recommendations of a committee constituted by it is processed subject to the restriction that the personal data and the traffic data pertaining to its flow are not transferred outside the territory of India.

This introduces a data localization obligation for personal data, meaning SDFs must process and store specific personal data strictly within Indian territory. It emphasizes national data sovereignty, addresses security concerns, and ensures that critical datasets remain under Indian jurisdiction, subject to Indian regulatory oversight. SDFs will need to adapt their infrastructure, cloud storage solutions, and data sharing models to comply with this localization requirement once the government defines the specific data types.

DPO appointment and responsibilities under the DPDPA

The DPO is formally defined under Chapter I, Section 2(i) of the Digital Personal Data Protection Act, 2023:

Data Protection Officer" means an individual appointed by the Significant Data Fiduciary under clause (a) of sub-section (2) of section 10

This DPO is not optional for an SDF; an appointment is mandatory once the organization is classified as an SDF by the government, based on the volume and sensitivity of data processed, risk factors, etc.

Chapter II Section 8 (9) A Data Fiduciary shall publish, in such manner as may be prescribed, the business contact information of a Data Protection Officer, if applicable, or a person who is able to answer on behalf of the Data Fiduciary, the questions, if any, raised by the Data Principal about the processing of her personal data.

This requires Data Fiduciary to publish the business contact information of their DPO, if appointed, or alternatively, the contact details of a designated person who can respond to questions about the processing of personal data. This ensures that Data Principals (individuals whose data is being processed) have a clear and accessible point of contact to raise queries or concerns regarding their personal information. The information must be made available in a prescribed manner, typically by being prominently published on the organization's website or app and included in responses to Data Principal Rights requests. The objective of this requirement is to promote transparency, accountability, and ease of communication between individuals and organizations, helping Data Principals exercise their rights effectively and fostering trust in the organization's data handling practices.

Chapter II *Section 10 (2) The Significant Data Fiduciary shall:*

(a) *appoint a Data Protection Officer who shall —*

(i) *represent the Significant Data Fiduciary under the provisions of this Act;*

(ii) *be based in India;*

(iii) *be an individual responsible to the Board of Directors or similar governing body of the Significant Data Fiduciary; and*

(iv) *be the point of contact for the grievance redressal mechanism under the provisions of this Act*

An SDF is required to appoint a DPO to ensure a strong compliance and accountability framework within the organization. The DPO's role is multi-faceted: they must represent the Significant Data Fiduciary in all matters relating to compliance with the provisions of the Act, act as a central figure for regulatory communications, and ensure that the organization upholds the rights of Data Principals. Importantly, the DPO must be based in India to facilitate jurisdictional oversight and accessibility and must report directly to the Board of Directors or an equivalent governing body to maintain independence and seniority. Additionally, the DPO serves as the primary point of contact for grievance redressal, meaning they are responsible for receiving, managing, and resolving complaints from Data Principals regarding the processing of their personal data. Through these duties, the DPO plays a crucial role in strengthening internal governance, safeguarding personal data, and maintaining the organization's compliance with the DPDP Act.

Rule 9. Contact information of person to answer questions about processing. Every Data Fiduciary shall prominently publish on its website or app, and mention in every response to a communication for the exercise of the rights of a Data Principal under the Act, the business contact information of the Data Protection Officer, if applicable, or a person who is able to answer on behalf of the Data Fiduciary the questions of the Data Principal about the processing of her personal data.

This rule mandates that every Data Fiduciary must prominently publish the business contact information of their DPO, if appointed, or of an authorized individual capable of answering queries regarding personal data processing. This information must be made available on the organization's official website or app and must also be included in every communication issued in response to a Data Principal exercising their rights under the Act, such as access, correction, or erasure requests. The rule ensures that individuals are not left without a clear channel to raise questions or concerns about the use of their personal data. By requiring a publicly available and easily accessible point of contact, Rule 9 enhances transparency, facilitates the effective exercise of Data Principal Rights, and strengthens organizational accountability in managing personal data under the DPDPA framework.

Supporting tools and systems

Tools like Microsoft Purview data lifecycle management and records management system automate retention and deletion processes, maintain compliance records, and provide audit reports. These solutions assist DPOs in effective oversight and compliance.

Demonstrating accountability through Board commitment and DPO oversight

Effective data protection demands strong leadership from executive management and the Board. A committed leadership team ensures that data privacy is integrated into organizational strategies and supported by necessary resources. The DPO operationalizes this vision by conducting DPIAs, ensuring robust consent management, and leveraging compliance management tools such as Microsoft Purview. Regular audits and eDiscovery practices further demonstrate accountability and transparency, reinforcing compliance and trust.

Role of eDiscovery in accountability under DPDP Act

Under the DPDP Act, 2023, organizations are required to uphold transparency, demonstrate accountability, and respond effectively to regulatory audits and Data Principal Rights. Electronic discovery (eDiscovery) systems, particularly Microsoft's new Purview eDiscovery (Premium) experience, play a pivotal role in fulfilling these obligations:

- **Efficient data retrieval for audits and rights requests:** Sections 11 to 14 of the DPDP Act empower individuals to request access, correction, or erasure of their personal data. To meet these demands within statutory timelines, organizations must locate and retrieve relevant data quickly.

  o **Microsoft Purview's new eDiscovery search experience** enables contextual, federated search across Microsoft 365 workloads (Outlook, Teams, SharePoint, etc.), surfacing both content and metadata. This allows organizations to extract complete, accurate, and defensible data records with minimal delay, critical during audits or Board inquiries.

- **Ensuring compliance with rights under Sections 11–14:** The DPDP Act obliges Data Fiduciaries to provide clear, timely responses to rights requests. eDiscovery tools enable:

  o Mapping and exporting all personal data associated with a Data Principal.

o   Confirming lawful bases for processing.

o   Maintaining audit trails to prove transparency.

Purview's updated case workflow lets administrators search using custodians, specific queries, or sensitive information types, streamlining regulatory compliance and reducing response times.

- **Breach investigation and notification support:** Draft Rule 7 requires that upon detecting a personal data breach, the Data Fiduciary must notify the Data Protection Board and affected Data Principals "without delay." eDiscovery aids breach response by:

    o   Identifying impacted individuals.

    o   Mapping compromised content.

    o   Preserving and exporting incident logs for forensic review Microsoft Purview enables evidence preservation via legal holds and maintains immutable collections, aligning with Draft Rule 6(1)(c) on secure storage and visibility.

- **Internal investigations and integrity assurance:** eDiscovery platforms support:

    o   Investigation of internal misuse or unauthorized access.

    o   Logging of every user interaction with personal data (aligned with Rule 6(1)(e)).

    o   Demonstrating the fulfillment of Data Principal complaints (Section 14).

With Microsoft's unified audit and eDiscovery integrations, organizations can compile defensible records for DPIAs and periodic compliance reviews.

- **Continuous monitoring and legal readiness:** DPDPA emphasizes proactive governance. eDiscovery helps organizations establish:

    o   Detailed audit trails on who accessed what data, when, and for what purpose.

    o   Logs of exports, deletions, or edits—crucial for audits or litigation.

Purview eDiscovery supports full auditability, integrating with Microsoft 365 compliance features such as DLP, Insider Risk Management, and activity Explorer. This ensures unified risk posture visibility across the data lifecycle.

Technologies enabling accountability and records compliance

Implementing the above principles can be challenging without the right tools, especially for organizations dealing with large volumes of data. Fortunately, there are **modern software solutions** that help operationalize accountability and transparency requirements:

- **Data lifecycle management and records management systems:** Solutions like Microsoft Purview provide integrated capabilities to map, manage, and protect data across an enterprise. For example, Microsoft Purview's Data lifecycle and Records Management module helps an organization manage legal obligations and *"provides the ability to demonstrate compliance with regulations"* by enforcing retention schedules and disposal of records. Such a system allows you to define policies (e.g., *delete customer data 3 years after account closure*) and then automatically apply them across emails, documents, databases, etc. It also maintains an audit trail of what was deleted and when, which can serve as evidence of compliance. Purview's data cataloging features can help build the inventory of processing activities, scanning, and classifying personal data in disparate systems, which is invaluable for answering Data Principal requests or breach analyses. Many EDRMS or specialized privacy management platforms similarly let you catalogue data flows and even simulate the impact of removing or restricting a data set (useful for evaluating responses to access or deletion requests). The following figure shows how Microsoft Records management tool looks like:

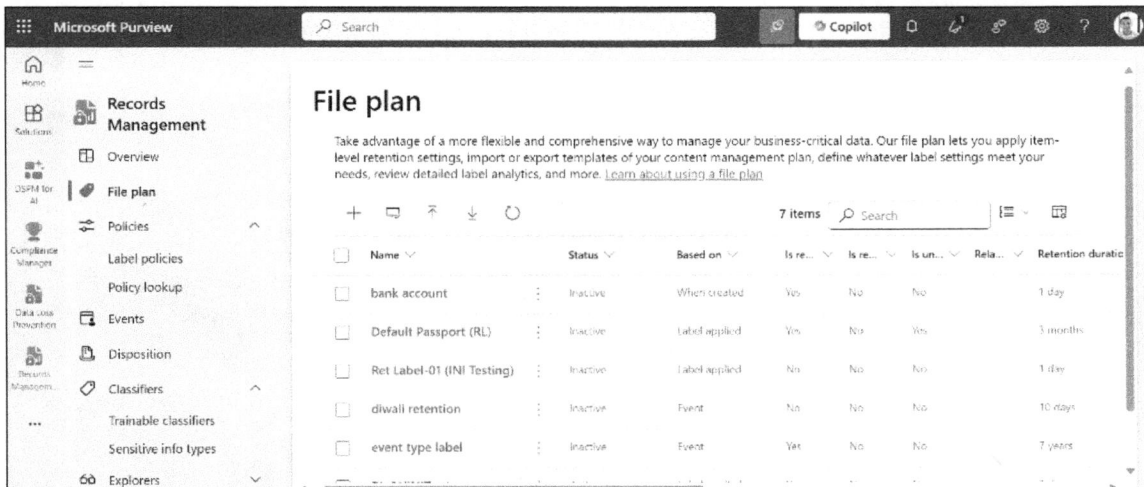

Figure 8.1: Microsoft records management solution

- **Consent management platforms:** If an organization has to handle a lot of user consents (for instance, a consumer-facing app or website with millions of users), using a dedicated consent management tool can simplify compliance. These tools present standardized consent prompts, capture the user's choice along with a timestamp and context, and store that in a centralized ledger. Some consent managers (possibly those registered as per the DPDPA framework) can also integrate with downstream systems so that if a user withdraws consent, all connected systems automatically stop processing that user's data for the withdrawn purpose. Even for smaller operations, a basic database or CRM extension can be used to log consents. The key is to ensure every piece of personal data in your systems can be linked to a valid consent or other legal basis, a task made feasible by technology. If audited, pulling up a user's record and showing the associated consent form and history will strongly demonstrate accountability.

- **Data Principal Rights management:** Managing individual rights requests at scale calls for automation. There are tools (often part of privacy management software or even built into platforms like Microsoft 365 via Microsoft Priva) that help track and fulfill these requests. For example, Priva's Privacy Risk Management can alert administrators or even end-users when data might need attention, it can send notifications if an employee's mailbox contains personal data that should be deleted or if files are shared too widely, effectively prompting compliance actions in real-time. Some systems offer portal solutions where Data Principals can log in to request access to their data or deletion, and the backend will gather the data from various sources and provide a consolidated report or execute erasures. This not only improves efficiency but also consistency, reducing the chance of human error in missing some data. When integrated with an EDRMS or data inventory, the tool can ensure that, say, a *delete my data* request triggers workflows to every department or system that has the individual's data. All such actions are logged. The following figure shows what the Microsoft Priva tool looks like:

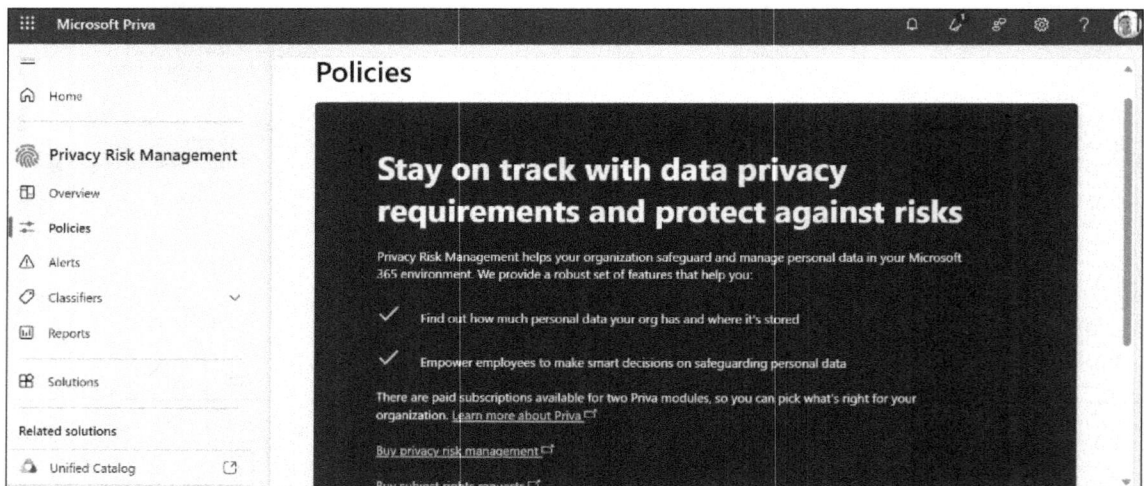

Figure 8.2: Microsoft Priva risk management solution

- **Security and risk monitoring tools:** Accountability is not only about documentation; it is also about preventing active issues Microsoft Sentinel, a cloud-native SIEM and **Security Orchestration, Automation, and Response** (**SOAR**) solution, allow organizations to collect, correlate, and analyze security data across all systems, cloud, network, and endpoints, Complementing SIEM solutions, DLP systems like those in the Microsoft Purview DLP suite enforce organizational policies directly where data resides or moves, user activity monitoring can all tie into the transparency/ accountability framework by ensuring any inappropriate access or sharing of personal data is flagged. For instance, data loss prevention policies can block or warn against emailing large sets of personal data outside the company. This enforces the rules you set and provides a log of attempts. In the case of Microsoft Priva, it actually empowers employees by notifying them if they are *holding onto personal data for too long* or making it too broadly accessible, and prompts them to take corrective action. This kind of tool turns internal transparency into a culture: employees become aware of data protection in their day-to-day work, and the organization can show that it has controls in place even at the human layer. The following figure shows how Microsoft DLP tool looks like:

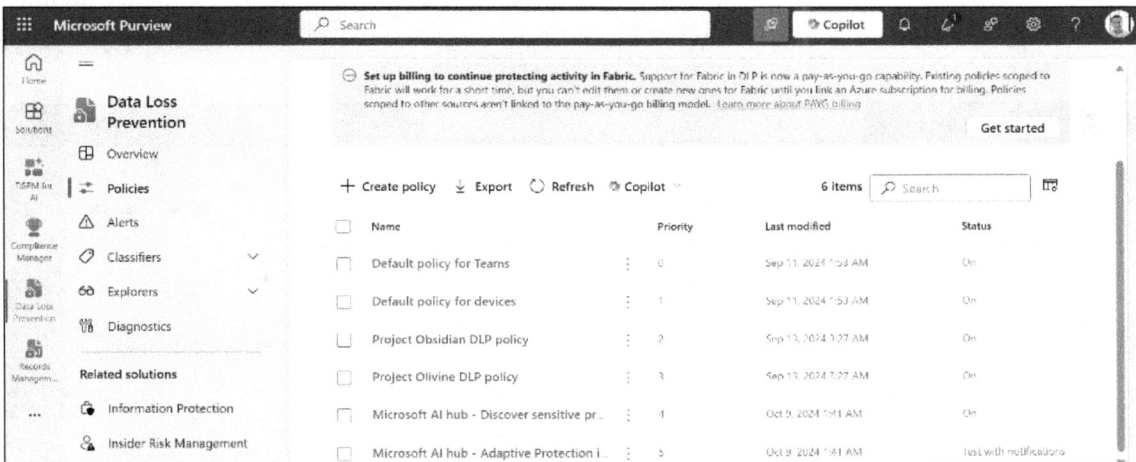

Figure 8.3: Microsoft data loss prevention solution

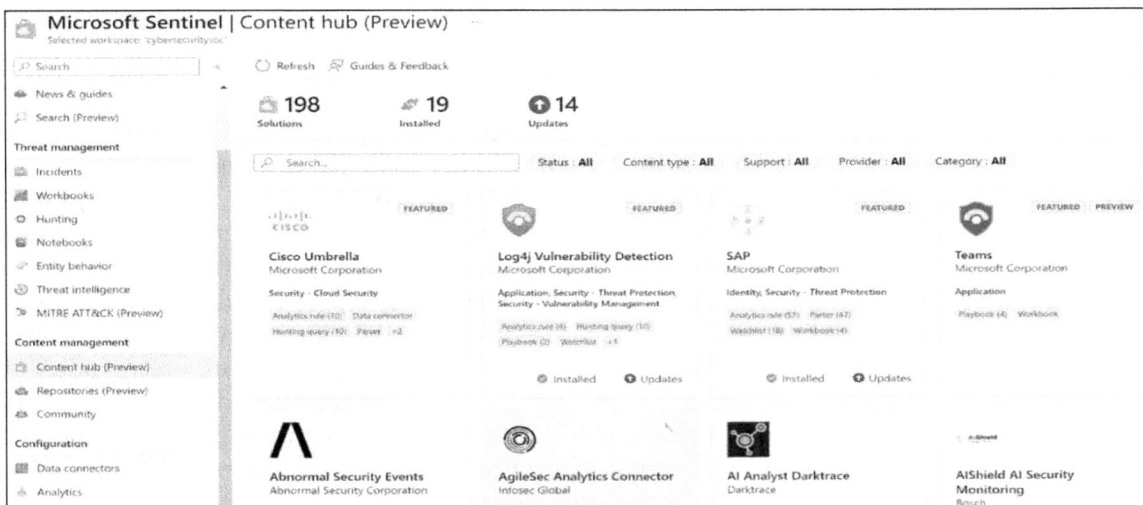

Figure 8.4: Microsoft sentinel solution

- **Audit and compliance reporting:** Many compliance suites (including Purview) have dashboards and reporting functions specifically to demonstrate compliance status. For example, an admin could pull a report of all retention policy actions in the last year, or all user access requests fulfilled and the time taken. These reports are very useful when engaging with regulators or during internal audits. They essentially compile the records we have discussed into management information, highlighting areas of strength or needed improvement. An Electronic DMS often includes *audit trail reports;* as one reference notes, *"audit trails serve as essential evidence during regulatory audits or investigations, showcasing compliance with data protection regulations and reinforcing data governance practices.".* By leveraging these features, organizations can more easily *prove their accountability.* The following figure shows what the Microsoft audit solution looks like:

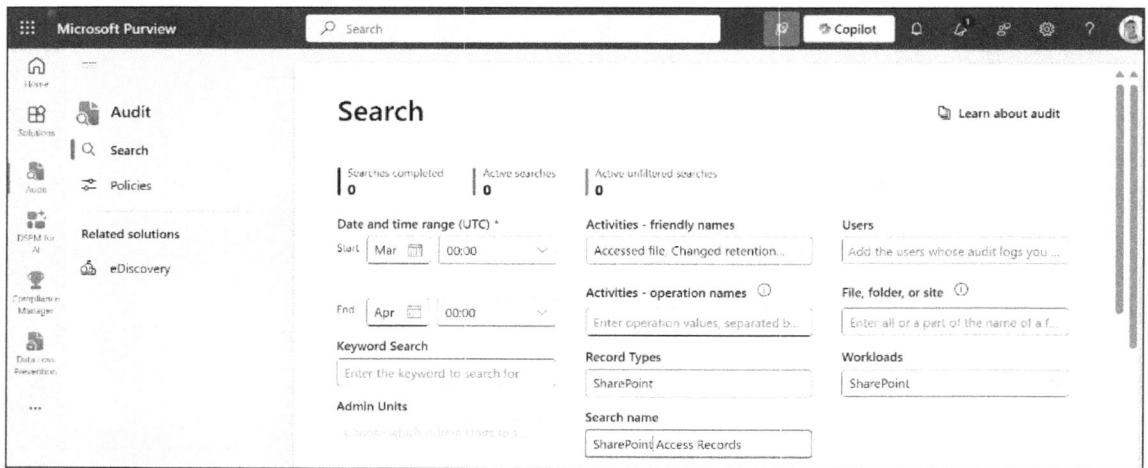

Figure 8.5: Microsoft audit solution

- **Microsoft Purview eDiscovery:** Key capabilities aligned with DPDPA requirements built to support compliance with the DPDP Act, 2023, by delivering a robust and intuitive platform for legal and regulatory response. Its contextual search and graph-based navigation allow teams to conduct relevance-ranked searches across vast enterprise data, enabling faster and more accurate responses to Data Principal Rights requests under Sections 11 to 14 of the Act. The platform's legal hold feature ensures that records under investigation are protected from deletion or tampering, directly supporting compliance with Draft Rule 6(1)(c), which requires secure preservation of audit and access logs. Additionally, collections and review sets allow data to be exported in tamper-evident formats, complete with full metadata, ensuring that organizations can provide verifiable documentation during audits or breach investigations. The insights dashboard offers visual, real-time summaries of case activity and user actions, enhancing transparency and simplifying internal or regulatory reporting. Integrated seamlessly with Microsoft's broader compliance ecosystem, including Records Management, Priva, Sentinel, and DLP, Purview eDiscovery forms a unified solution for end-to-end governance. Overall, this new experience operationalizes complex DPDPA requirements through automation, precision, and transparency, helping organizations stay audit-ready and accountable. The following figure shows how Microsoft eDiscovery tool looks like:

Figure 8.6: *Microsoft eDiscovery*

It is important to note that tools need to be configured correctly to align with the DPDPA requirements. Buying software alone does not guarantee compliance; it must be set up with the proper policies (e.g., the correct retention period, the right classifications for personal data types relevant under DPDPA, etc.). However, once configured, these tools significantly reduce the manual effort and risk of error in enforcing policies. They also provide *consistency* across an organization, crucial for large enterprises where multiple departments might otherwise implement the principles unevenly.

Any industry can benefit from these solutions. Whether it is a bank, a hospital, an e-commerce company, or a small startup, the fundamental tasks, knowing what personal data you have, keeping records of processing, securing the data, honoring individual rights, and managing vendor obligations, are the same. The scale and complexity might differ, but the DPDP Act's principles apply uniformly. A healthcare provider, for instance, might use an EDRMS to manage patient consents for treatment and data sharing with labs, ensuring that each consent is tied to a record of which medical data was shared with which lab. A tech startup might use cloud-based privacy management SaaS to handle user consent for analytics cookies and to automate the deletion of user data if the user closes their account. The end goal is that transparency (being open and clear with individuals about their data) and accountability (taking responsibility for protecting that data at every step) become ingrained in the organization's processes.

Conclusion

In implementing accountability and transparency under the DPDP Act 2023, organizations essentially build a robust data governance program: one that keeps detailed records of data processing activities, enables individuals to exercise their rights, minimizes data to only what is necessary, and extends oversight to all parties involved in processing. The law provides the *what* and *why*, mandating clear notice, consent, data quality, security, and rights, but it is up to each organization to execute the *how*. By aligning internal policies with specific sections of the Act and Draft Rules, businesses can ensure they meet legal requirements. More importantly, these practices build trust with customers and partners. When an organization can readily show what data it has, why, where it flows, how it is protected, and that it will respect the individual's wishes, compliance becomes an enabler of credibility and efficiency rather than a box-ticking exercise. The DPDP Act's focus on accountability and transparency thus nudges organizations toward data stewardship excellence, something that is achievable with careful planning, cultural commitment, and the smart use of technology. By following the principles and measures outlined in this section, organizations in any industry can create a strong evidence-backed compliance posture, be prepared for the DPDPA regime, and significantly reduce the risks associated with personal data handling.

In the upcoming chapter, we will examine how IT audits are evolving from point-in-time reviews to continuous compliance. The discussion will cover audit planning, execution, reporting, follow-ups, assessing third-party compliance, and ways to leverage Microsoft solutions to stay compliant.

Join our Discord space

Join our Discord workspace for latest updates, offers, tech happenings around the world, new releases, and sessions with the authors:

https://discord.bpbonline.com

CHAPTER 9

Auditing and Compliance Monitoring

Introduction

Auditing and compliance monitoring are core components of the accountability framework established by India's **Digital Personal Data Protection Act**, 2023 (**DPDP Act**) and its Draft DPDP Rules, 2025. These mechanisms ensure that organizations (Data Fiduciaries) not only achieve compliance with the law but also maintain it over time through continuous oversight. In the DPDPA context, compliance monitoring refers to the ongoing processes, audits, and assessments that verify adherence to the Act's provisions and the rules made under it, thereby protecting the rights of Data Principals (individuals). This chapter provides a comprehensive examination of auditing and compliance monitoring as required by the DPDP Act and Rules, including both mandatory and best-practice measures. It covers the journey of getting compliant (initial implementation of the law's requirements) and staying compliant (ongoing monitoring and improvement), with a focus on specific provisions like annual data audits, **Data Protection Impact Assessments** (**DPIAs**), continuous monitoring, documentation, and the roles of internal teams versus third-parties. The goal is to highlight how organizations can establish robust compliance programs aligned strictly with DPDPA 2023 and the Draft Rules 2025, emphasizing continuous compliance and proactive risk mitigation.

Structure

In this chapter, we will cover the following topics:

- Power of continuous monitoring under the DPDP Act
- Point-in-time to continuous compliance
- Ongoing audits protect data and foster trust
- Audit planning, execution, reporting, and follow-up
- Assessing third-party compliance
- Internal data protection reviews
- Tools and technologies

Objectives

The objective of this chapter is to provide a comprehensive understanding of the auditing and compliance monitoring obligations introduced by the DPDP Act, 2023, and its Draft Rules, 2025. It aims to equip readers with practical knowledge on how organizations, especially **Significant Data Fiduciaries (SDFs)**, can establish, implement, and sustain robust compliance programs through structured audits, ongoing monitoring, and proactive risk mitigation. This chapter explores mandatory legal requirements such as annual data audits and DPIAs, while also highlighting best practices for continuous compliance, including the use of modern tools and technologies. By mapping auditing practices to key sections of the Act, the chapter helps organizations operationalize compliance, strengthen data protection controls, and demonstrate accountability to regulators and stakeholders. Ultimately, this chapter emphasizes that compliance under DPDPA is not a one-time obligation but a continuous governance process that must evolve alongside the organization's data landscape and risk environment.

Power of continuous monitoring under the DPDP Act

Achieving and maintaining compliance with the DPDP Act, 2023, is not a one-time initiative; it is a sustained operational responsibility. The Act, along with the Draft Rules 2025, embeds the principle of continuous oversight into its very framework. Rule 6(1)(c) of the Draft Rules mandates that all Data Fiduciaries must ensure *monitoring and review of logs to detect any unauthorized access to personal data*, reflecting the legal requirement for continuous compliance monitoring, not merely a best-practice recommendation.

To effectively meet both initial and ongoing compliance obligations under the DPDPA framework, organizations must implement mechanisms that monitor compliance posture in real-time. This section explores the critical importance of compliance monitoring, not just for adhering to legal obligations, but for proactively managing risk and demonstrating accountability when called upon by the Data Protection Board of India.

Getting compliant by building the monitoring foundation

Establishing compliance starts with aligning business processes to the core provisions of the DPDP Act by ensuring valid consent mechanisms, appointing grievance redressal contacts, applying reasonable security safeguards, and, if applicable, fulfilling **Significant Data Fiduciary** (**SDF**) obligations. A key enabler in this phase is the deployment of compliance monitoring tools that help track and validate:

- Whether consent has been captured and stored properly.
- If access logs are maintained for all personal data processing systems.
- If data minimization, purpose limitation, and retention policies are being enforced.

Tools like Microsoft Purview Compliance Manager, which offer control mapping, task assignment, and a real-time compliance score dashboard, can help organizations map each DPDPA control requirement to an operational activity and continuously monitor its status.

Staying compliant by operationalizing continuous monitoring

Once compliance controls are implemented, the focus must shift to maintaining compliance over time, in line with the dynamic nature of IT systems, business practices, and legal expectations.

Key aspects of continuous monitoring include:

- **Security monitoring (Rule 6(1)(c)):** Organizations are required to monitor system access logs for anomalies that may indicate unauthorized access to personal data. This can include **Security Information and Event Management** (**SIEM**) solutions, **data loss prevention** (**DLP**) tools, or Microsoft's Audit and Advanced Audit tools within Purview. Real-time alerts help mitigate the risk of data breaches, a core concern under Chapter II Section 8 of the Act.

- **Operational compliance monitoring:** Regular checks must ensure that operational controls, such as consent withdrawal mechanisms, **data subject access request** (**DSAR**) response times, and privacy notice disclosures, are functioning as expected. Solutions like eDiscovery tools can verify whether a user's data has been removed upon request or identify lingering data across distributed systems.

- **Automated workflows and review cycles:** Compliance should be embedded into daily business operations. For example, automated triggers can ensure a **Data Processing**

Agreement (DPA) is in place before onboarding a vendor (aligning with Chapter II Section 8(2)), or can notify teams to conduct a DPIA if a new high-risk processing activity is introduced (required annually for SDFs per Rule 12).

- **Audit trail and evidence retention**: Draft Rule 6 requires organizations to retain logs and evidence of data processing for a minimum of one year. Monitoring tools should be configured to retain audit trails of access, deletion, correction, or data sharing events, which can be later presented to regulators or used during internal/external audits. This reinforces Chapter II Section 10(2)(b) and (c), which require SDFs to conduct and report on data audits annually.

Why a compliance snapshot matters

A live, consolidated compliance snapshot enables organizations to:

- Quickly identify control gaps and high-risk areas.
- Demonstrate due diligence to auditors or the Data Protection Board.
- Track remediation actions are tied to audit or DPIA findings.
- Avoid compliance decay between formal audit cycles.

This real-time visibility is especially crucial for SDFs, who must submit annual audit and DPIA findings to the Board (Rule 12(2)). However, even non-SDFs benefit from a compliance monitoring program that surfaces issues before they escalate into reportable breaches or penalties under Schedule I of the Act.

Point-in-time to continuous compliance

Traditional IT audits or compliance audits are often seen as point-in-time assessments. An audit team might come once a year, review policies, inspect systems and records, and produce a report of compliance status at that moment. Under the DPDP Act regime, such audits remain very important, especially given the Act's requirement for periodic audits for SDFs. However, there is a clear trend to integrate these audits into a more continuous compliance approach.

This section explores how organizations can transition from treating audits as isolated checkups to making them part of an ongoing compliance cycle:

- **Role of point-in-time audits:** Point-in-time IT audits provide a snapshot of your compliance. They are invaluable for formally assessing whether the organization meets DPDP Act requirements at a given time. For example, an annual compliance audit might check: are all required notices and consents properly obtained? Is personal data (like children's data) being handled with requisite extra protections? Has the organization implemented all "reasonable security safeguards" listed in Rule 6 (encryption, access controls, etc.)? These audits are often structured and rigorous, sometimes performed by independent parties (as mandated for SDFs via an independent data auditor). They might result in certifications or formal reports to management. In the DPDPA context, an SDF's independent data auditor will likely do a point-in-time audit each period (say yearly) and provide an audit report evaluating compliance across all aspects of the Act.

- **Limits of point-in-time audits:** While essential, a once-a-year audit has limitations. Compliance is not static; an organization might pass an audit in January, but by July, new data processing activities or a lapse in procedures could put it out of compliance. If one waits until the next audit to discover this, the damage (to individuals or the organization) could be done. Also, auditors sample and spot-check; they might not catch every issue. This is where continuous compliance efforts fill the gap. Continuous monitoring (as discussed earlier) works in between audits to maintain standards. Think of point-in-time audits as the exams, and continuous monitoring as the daily homework and corrections. Both are needed: you do homework to be ready for the exam, and the exam validates that the homework was effective.

- **Integrating audits into continuous compliance:** How can organizations merge these concepts? One way is to treat **audit findings as the start of a new cycle** rather than the end. After an IT audit or compliance audit, the findings and recommendations should feed into an action plan (we will cover reporting and follow-up later). That action plan should be implemented through continuous monitoring: if the audit said "improve access control for database X," then new controls are put in place and thereafter monitored continuously (e.g., monthly user access reviews, alerts on permission changes). Then, when the next audit happens, it will verify that those controls are effective. In essence, each audit becomes a checkpoint in a continuous improvement loop. Additionally, many organizations now use *continuous controls monitoring tools* that can be configured to check controls in real-time. For example, a tool might continuously validate that backups of personal data are encrypted (a security safeguard), something an audit would normally check annually, and can now be checked every day automatically. So when auditors arrive, they find fewer issues because compliance has been self-checked continuously.

- **"Always-on" auditing with technology:** Modern technology and processes allow a shift toward what some call "always-on auditing." While a fully continuous audit in real-time is hard to achieve in practice, elements of it are feasible. For instance, internal audit teams might do *rolling audits* focusing on different areas in different quarters, rather than everything once a year. Q1: they may audit consent and notice processes, Q2: focus on data security controls, Q3: on third-party management, and Q4: on Data Principal Rights handling. This way, each area gets audited at least once a year, but staggered, ensuring that no area goes unchecked for too long. This rolling approach also reduces audit fatigue and allows deeper dives into each area. Furthermore, using compliance software, some audit checks can be partially automated, e.g., a script to check if all required privacy notices on the company's apps have the latest mandated content per the Draft Rules can run monthly. In case of a deviation, it can flag the privacy office to fix it without waiting for an official audit.

In summary, IT audits under the DPDP Act should be viewed as part of a continuum. The Act explicitly requires periodic audits for significant players, which formalizes the need for point-in-time evaluations. However, to truly comply 24/7, organizations must embrace continuous compliance practices that complement these audits. Done right, by the time an external or independent auditor comes in, the organization's internal monitoring should have already identified and addressed most issues, making the formal audit more of a validation exercise than a discovery mission. This not only leads to better audit results but, more importantly, ensures that personal data is consistently protected and the principles of the Act are upheld every day.

Ongoing audits protect data and foster trust

A compliance audit under India's DPDPA framework is a formal, systematic review of a Data Fiduciary's practices to verify adherence to legal requirements. In the DPDPA context, such audits examine key areas including: the mechanisms for obtaining valid consent (Chapter II Section 6 requires consent to be "free, specific, informed, unconditional and unambiguous", with a clear notice of what data is collected and why); the processes that enable Data Principal Rights (such as access, correction, deletion, nomination and grievance redress under Chapter III Sections 11–14); the organization's breach-response and the technical and organizational safeguards in place (for example, encryption, access controls, logging and backups as specified in Draft Rule 6). A thorough audit will verify that consent logs and notices comply with the Act, that Data Principal requests are handled correctly, that incident response procedures are tested, and that security measures are in place. The key principles are listed as follows:

- **Consent and notice:** Audits check that Data Fiduciaries present a clear privacy notice (including an itemized description of data and purpose) and obtain "specific and informed consent" in line with Section 6. Auditors verify that consent withdrawal is as easy as giving consent, and that systems record and honor consent accurately.

- **Data Principal Rights:** Audits confirm that procedures exist to fulfill rights (access, correction, erasure, grievance, and nomination) and that requests are processed within prescribed timelines.

- **Breach readiness:** Audits evaluate breach detection and response plans. This includes verifying that the organization can promptly detect unauthorized access (through logs and monitoring), and that it has policies to notify both affected individuals and the Data Protection Board without delay, as required under Chapter II Section 8 and Rule 7.

- **Security safeguards:** Audits ensure that the organization has implemented the "reasonable security safeguards" mandated by Rule 6. These include technical controls (encryption or obfuscation of data, strong access controls on systems, logging and monitoring of access events, routine backups, and disaster recovery) and organizational measures (training, vendor controls, incident response processes).

By covering these areas, a compliance audit provides an **independent assessment** of whether an organization's data processes live up to the DPDP Act's requirements.

Role of compliance audits in ongoing compliance

Compliance audits are not just one-time checklists; they are integral to sustaining lawful data practices as a business grows and changes. Once an organization has implemented the DPDPA requirements (e.g., updated policies and systems), audits serve to maintain that standard. Regular audits catch drift or new gaps that arise as the organization's operations evolve. For example, if a company launches a new service, onboards additional technology (like AI systems), acquires another business, or changes vendors, an audit will identify whether the data flows introduced by these changes are properly documented and compliant. Audits also help incorporate updates when the law or rules change (such as new regulations on algorithms or data localization). In practice, a periodic audit ensures continuous improvement: it prompts updates to policies, retraining of staff, and enhancements to security controls in response to audit findings. By benchmarking compliance at regular intervals, an organization can address issues long before they become violations. Over time, this process builds a culture of accountability: management sees audit reports and takes corrective actions, demonstrating to regulators and the public that the Fiduciary is proactive about privacy. In short, audits help an organization remain compliant not just at a single point-in-time, but throughout its lifecycle.

Mandatory audit requirements for Significant Data Fiduciaries

The DPDP Act imposes **extra obligations** on **SDFs**, entities processing large volumes of personal data. Chapter II, Section 10 of the Act grants the government power to designate classes of fiduciaries as SDFs. Once notified, an SDF must meet additional requirements, including rigorous audit obligations:

- **Independent data auditor:** Under Section Chapter II 10(2)(b), every SDF must *appoint an independent data auditor to carry out a data audit, who shall evaluate the compliance of the Significant Data Fiduciary in accordance with the provisions of this Act; and* of its compliance with the Act. This means the audit must be performed by an external qualified auditor or audit firm with no conflicts of interest, ensuring an unbiased evaluation. The auditor's task is to examine the SDF's policies, processes, and records to confirm compliance with all DPDPA obligations.

- **Periodic DPIAs and audits:** Section 10(2)(c) explicitly requires SDFs to conduct periodic DPIAs and periodic audits. As defined by the Act, a DPIA involves documenting the rights of Data Principals, the purposes of processing, and assessing and mitigating risks to those rights. A periodic audit complements the DPIA as a systematic review of observance of the law. Together, these ensure that as processing evolves, risk assessments and compliance checks occur regularly.

- **Annual requirements (Draft Rule 12):** The Draft DPDP Rules 2025 provide detailed timing for these obligations. Draft Rule 12(1) mandates that *"once in every period of twelve months"* from being notified as an SDF, the organization must undertake a DPIA *and* an audit. In practice, this means at least an annual full-scope compliance audit, with the DPIA integrated as part of that process.

- **Reporting to the Data Protection Board:** Crucially, Draft Rule 12(2) requires the SDF to have the person who conducted the DPIA and audit submit a report to the Data Protection Board containing the *"significant observations"* from those exercises. This creates accountability: audit results (including any gaps found) are formally shared with the regulator.

- **Other SDF Safeguards:** In addition, SDFs must appoint a **Data Protection Officer** (**DPO**) (as per Section 10(2)(a)) and take specific measures such as algorithmic due diligence (Rule 12(3)) and data localization checks (Rule 12(4)). But the audit and DPIA requirements are the core compliance tools.

Together, Section 10 and Rule 12 ensure that SDFs maintain a strong, independent audit regime, appointing an independent external auditor, performing annual risk assessments and audits, and sharing results with the regulator.

Importance of regular audits

Regular compliance audits offer multiple benefits for an organization and for privacy governance:

- **Early detection of non-compliance:** Audits uncover gaps and violations before they cause harm. For example, an audit might reveal outdated consent records, lapses in breach notification procedures, or security weaknesses. Detecting these issues early lets the Fiduciary fix them proactively, rather than waiting for a complaint or a data breach that could trigger fines and reputational damage.

- **Adaptation to change:** As laws, rules, or organizational processes change, audits help ensure the compliance program keeps up. If new categories of data are collected, audits verify that the notice and consent processes cover them. If rules are updated (e.g., clarifications on DPIA or new retention limits), audits check that new requirements have been integrated. In fast-moving industries, regular audits are the "canary in the coal mine" for compliance.

- **Accountability and governance:** Compliance audits create documentation and metrics of privacy governance. Audit reports are reviewed by senior management or the Board, ensuring accountability at the highest level. This oversight can be mandated in corporate governance policies, holding privacy compliance to executive responsibilities. When management sees audit findings, they are compelled to Act, reinforcing a culture of accountability. In the event of legal scrutiny, an organization can show regulators evidence that it conducts regular audits and takes corrective action.

- **Building public trust:** From a stakeholder perspective, publicizing a commitment to regular audits (even without disclosing specifics) signals that an organization is serious about protecting personal data. Customers and partners are more likely to trust a company that can demonstrate independent oversight of its privacy practices. In sectors where data is sensitive, an audit regime can even become a competitive advantage.

In short, audits are not just an internal tool; they are a statement of trustworthiness. They catch non-compliance, ensure the privacy program evolves with the business, and provide evidence to stakeholders and regulators that the organization is accountable.

Periodic audit schedule and consequences of non-compliance

To institutionalize the above benefits, organizations should establish a periodic audit schedule, for example, conducting full compliance audits on an annual or biannual basis. Maintaining a regular schedule ensures that audits are not missed or rushed. In practice:

- Organizations often align audit cycles with business planning and budgeting for an annual review. Some may choose biannual audits if operations change rapidly or risk is high.

- Between full audits, lighter ongoing monitoring (e.g., quarterly risk reviews) can catch smaller issues early, feeding into the formal audit cycle.

By scheduling audits periodically, an organization systematically updates its compliance controls, rolls out training as needed, and continuously refines policies. Each audit acts as a compliance checkpoint. Moreover, for SDFs, the law itself effectively mandates a yearly cycle, so aligning with that is not just best practice but a legal requirement as specified in Rule 12(1) of the Draft DPDP Rules,2025.

Failing to conduct required audits or failing to remedy issues they uncover has serious consequences under the DPDP Act. Section 33 empowers the Data Protection Board to initiate inquiries and impose penalties for *"breach of the provisions of this Act or the rules"* if found significant. In other words, if an SDF ignores its audit obligations (a breach of Sections 10 or Rule 12), that is a contravention of the Act. The penalty schedule provides for steep fines: up to **₹250 crore** for a general violation (up to **₹50 crore)**. These sums are among the highest in any privacy law, reflecting the Act's emphasis on compliance.

Even for non-SDF fiduciaries, failing to comply with duties (such as neglecting breaches or rights obligations revealed by an audit) can trigger penalties as mentioned under Section 33. In determining the fine, the Board will consider factors like the *nature, gravity, and duration of the breach, the data affected, and steps taken to mitigate harm.* Importantly, under Section 33, the Board is supposed to impose *effective and proportionate penalties* to deter non-compliance.

Beyond monetary fines, repeat or egregious offenders risk regulatory orders (the Board can make a reference before the Central Government for blocking of services if violations recur) and reputational damage. In short, skimping on audits is a high-risk strategy. Regular audits serve as a preventive mechanism: by fixing issues early, a Fiduciary avoids the *"significant breaches"* that would invite the Act's severe penalties.

In conclusion, regular compliance audits are the bedrock of an ongoing data protection program under India's DPDPA law. By systematically reviewing consent processes, rights facilitation, breach readiness, and safeguards, and by fulfilling the explicit audit mandates for SDFs, organizations not only stay legally compliant but also foster transparency, accountability, and trust in their data practices. The discipline of periodic audits, annual or more frequent, helps detect lapses, adapt to change, and demonstrate to both regulators and the public that the organization takes its privacy obligations seriously. Critically, it protects the organization from the heavy penalties the Act provides for any failure of compliance.

Audit planning, execution, reporting, and follow-up

An effective audit program under the DPDP Act involves careful audit planning, thorough audit execution, and diligent reporting and follow-up on findings. Each phase should align with the Act's requirements and Draft Rules, ensuring that all key obligations, from obtaining valid consent and providing proper notices to implementing security safeguards and breach response mechanisms, are evaluated and enforced. This section provides a comprehensive guide to auditing for DPDP Act compliance in a formal, step-by-step manner.

Audit planning

Audit planning under the DPDP Act begins with defining clear objectives and mapping the audit criteria to the Act's provisions and associated Rules. The primary objective is to evaluate the organization's compliance with all relevant obligations in the DPDP Act and Draft Rules, and to ensure that any non-compliance risks are identified for remediation. For SDF-classified organizations, the stakes are higher: The Act explicitly requires SDFs to appoint an independent data auditor to assess DPDP Act compliance and to undertake periodic audits of data protection measures. These legal requirements inform the scope, frequency, and depth of the audit plan.

Setting objectives and criteria: The audit's scope and criteria should be directly derived from the DPDP Act's provisions and the 2025 Draft Rules. This means each audit checkpoint or question corresponds to a specific legal requirement. For example, Section 5 of the Act requires that any request for a Data Principal's consent be preceded or accompanied by a comprehensive notice, informing the individual of the personal data to be collected and the purpose of processing, as well as how to exercise their rights or file a complaint. Likewise, Section 6 defines that valid consent must be *free, specific, informed, unconditional, and unambiguous,* given through a clear affirmative action. These provisions become audit criteria: the auditor will check that the organization's consent forms and processes indeed meet the *free, informed, unambiguous* standard, and that privacy notices include all mandated information. The Draft Rules add further specificity; for instance, Rule 3 stipulates that notices must be in clear, plain language and itemize the personal data and purposes involved. Thus, the audit criteria should map each key requirement (consent, notice content, etc.) to what evidence or observation would confirm compliance. Many organizations find it useful to build an audit checklist or matrix that links each DPDP Act section or Rule to specific controls or practices; some compliance management tools (such as Microsoft Purview Compliance Manager) even provide templates for the DPDP Act to facilitate mapping of these requirements.

Identifying key areas of compliance: A DPDPA audit plan must cover all *major obligation areas* that the law imposes on Data Fiduciaries. The following are critical focus areas to include in the audit scope:

- **Consent and notice mechanisms:** Proper consent collection and notice are foundational requirements. The auditor should verify that the organization only processes personal data for lawful purposes (either with the Data Principal's consent or under a specified lawful use) and that consent is obtained in compliance with the Act. Key checkpoints include whether every request for consent is accompanied by an adequate privacy notice and whether that notice contains all required details (description of personal data being collected, the specific purpose of processing, the nature of goods or services involved, etc.). The notice must also inform individuals how they can withdraw consent, exercise their data rights, and lodge complaints with the Data Protection Board. Audit planning should ensure sampling of these consent notices and records. Additionally, the method of obtaining consent should be reviewed to confirm it results in a clear affirmative action (for example, unchecked opt-in boxes or explicit consent buttons) in line with Section 6's definition of valid consent. Any use of "deemed consent" or other non-explicit bases (if allowed under the Act's legitimate uses) must be scrutinized against the conditions laid out in the law.

- **Data security safeguards:** The DPDP Act mandates that Data Fiduciaries protect personal data by implementing "reasonable security safeguards" to prevent data breaches. Rule 6 of the Draft Rules, 2025, enumerates minimum security measures expected: for instance, **encryption or pseudonymization** of personal data, strict **access controls** on systems, and monitoring through **audit logs**. The audit plan should include verification that these controls are in place and functioning. Auditors will review security policies and configurations to ensure that personal data is encrypted or masked in databases and during transmission. They will also check access management, confirming that only authorized personnel can access personal data, and that an access log is maintained to detect and investigate any unauthorized access. Additional safeguards outlined in the rules, such as maintaining backups and continuity measures to protect data integrity / availability, should be part of the criteria.

In planning, it is useful to identify all systems and processes handling personal data, so that a representative sample of each can be tested for these security controls.

- **Personal data breach response:** Another key area is the organization's preparedness and process for handling data breaches, as defined by the Draft DPDP Rules. Rule 7 requires Data Fiduciaries to notify affected Data Principals *"without delay"* upon becoming aware of a personal data breach, providing details of the breach and guidance to the individual on protective measures. Simultaneously, the Data Fiduciary must inform the Data Protection Board of India of the breach, including an initial notice with a description and impact, followed by a comprehensive report within **72 hours** with further details on the causes and remedial actions. Audit planning should therefore cover the review of the incident response plan: Is there a defined procedure to detect and report breaches internally? Does the organization have templates and mechanisms to send timely breach notifications containing all required information (nature of breach, extent, timing, likely consequences, measures taken, and contact information) to both individuals and the Board? The auditor might plan to examine past incident logs or conduct a tabletop exercise to assess whether the breach response process meets the DPDP requirements.

- **SDF specific obligations:** If the organization has been designated or is likely to be designated as an SDF (based on criteria such as volume and sensitivity of data, or risk to individuals), the audit must include the additional obligations that apply to SDFs under Section 10 of the DPDP Act and the Draft Rules. SDFs are required to appoint a DPO who is based in India and accountable to the organization's Board – the audit should confirm that a qualified DPO is in place and that their appointment meets the Act's criteria (e.g., reporting line to the Board, serving as point of contact for grievances). SDFs must also appoint an **independent data auditor** and conduct **periodic data audits** of their processing activities. In planning, it should be determined whether the audit at hand fulfills this requirement (i.e., if this is the mandated annual audit being performed by an independent auditor). Furthermore, SDFs need to perform regular DPIAs for high-risk processing and **submit a summary of DPIA and audit findings to the Data Protection Board**. Thus, the audit scope for an SDF should include checking that DPIAs have been conducted on schedule and that any insights from DPIAs (such as identified risks and mitigation plans) are being acted upon. Other SDF obligations to include are the requirement to exercise due diligence in case of **algorithmic decision-making** (ensuring that any AI/ML algorithms used do not unfairly impact Data Principals' rights) and compliance with restrictions on transferring certain personal data abroad as notified by the government. By enumerating these SDF-specific items in the plan, the auditor ensures a comprehensive evaluation of all heightened duties of a significant data handler.

- **Scheduling and frequency (risk-based approach):** The frequency and timing of DPDPA compliance audits should be planned based on statutory requirements and the organization's risk profile. The Draft Rules 2025 specify that SDFs must carry out a

DPIA *and a Data Protection Audit at least once every 12 months*, with the results furnished to the Board. In practical terms, most SDFs will adhere to an *annual audit cycle* to meet this mandate. The audit plan should schedule these audits well in advance (for example, aligning with a particular quarter each year) and allow time for management to address findings before the next cycle. For organizations that are not SDFs (i.e., regular Data Fiduciaries), the law does not prescribe a fixed audit interval; however, a *risk-based approach* is advisable. This means scheduling audits or compliance reviews at a frequency commensurate with the volume and sensitivity of personal data processed and the potential impact of non-compliance. Higher-risk environments (for instance, a company processing large amounts of personal data or one that has experienced incidents) may warrant more frequent audits or continuous monitoring, whereas a smaller entity with limited data processing might conduct full-scale audits less frequently but perform targeted mini-audits in specific areas periodically. The plan should document the rationale for the chosen frequency, for example, referencing that the organization considered factors like data breach probability, changes in business processes, or updates in the law. Importantly, audits should be timed such that critical compliance deadlines are met; for instance, if new Draft Rules come into effect on a certain date, an audit soon after can verify that the organization implemented any new requirements. By using a risk-based schedule, the organization remains agile in its compliance oversight, focusing audit resources where they are needed most. Regardless of frequency, each audit's timing should be communicated to relevant stakeholders (management and operational teams) as part of planning so that they can prepare and ensure the availability of information to the auditors.

Audit execution

Once the audit plan and scope are defined, the next phase is **execution**, carrying out the audit activities to gather evidence, assess controls, and identify any compliance gaps. Audit execution under the DPDP Act should follow a structured process to ensure thorough coverage of all areas identified in the planning phase. Typically, an audit will progress through stages such as kickoff, fieldwork (evidence collection and testing), analysis, and preliminary reporting of findings. Throughout these steps, maintaining an **audit trail** (record of evidence and procedures performed) is crucial, both for the integrity of the audit and to demonstrate compliance efforts if required by regulators.

Conducting the audit, steps and methodology: At the outset, the auditor (or audit team) will hold an opening meeting with key stakeholders, including the organization's Privacy Officer or DPO, relevant IT and security managers, and business process owners for functions like marketing or customer data management. In this meeting, the audit objectives, scope, and schedule (as determined in the planning stage) are confirmed. Then the fieldwork begins, generally following an approach of reviewing documentation, interviewing personnel, and performing technical and operational tests:

- **Documentation review**: The auditor collects and reviews all relevant policies, procedures, and records. This includes the privacy policy and privacy notices given to Data Principals, standard consent forms or consent screens, records of consent obtained, data retention policies, security policies, incident response plans, training materials, and any previous internal audit or assessment reports. For each key area (consent, security, etc.), there should be documented procedures that the auditor evaluates against the DPDP Act requirements. For example, the organization has a standard operating procedure for handling personal data breaches. In that case, the auditor will compare its content to the Rule 7 requirements (e.g., does the procedure instruct staff to notify affected individuals "without delay" with all required details? Does it mandate notifying the Board within 72 hours?) and note any discrepancies.

- **Interviews and walkthroughs**: A vital technique in execution is interviewing staff and walking through processes to assess how procedures are implemented in practice. The auditor might interview the team responsible for onboarding new customers to understand how they present the consent notice and obtain consent. During the walkthrough, the auditor might follow the user journey: e.g., seeing the actual screens a user interacts with, to verify that the notice is presented "independently" and not bundled with other terms (a Draft Rule 3 requirement), and that the consent mechanism requires an explicit opt-in. Similarly, for data security, the auditor may meet with IT security personnel to discuss how access to personal data is controlled, and may observe a demonstration of the access control system or review a sample user access list. Walkthroughs can also involve tracing the "life cycle" of personal data: from collection, to storage, usage, sharing, and deletion. By tracing a few sample data flows, the auditor can confirm compliance at each stage (for instance, checking that when data is shared with a third-party processor, there is a contract in place requiring the processor to also implement DPDP Act safeguards, as implied by the Act's provisions on processors and Rule 6(f) on contracts with processors).

- **Sampling and testing:** Given the potentially large scale of data processing operations, auditors will use sampling techniques to test compliance. For example, rather than reviewing every single consent record, the auditor might sample a reasonable number, say, 50 consent records from different points in time or different services, and verify that each has an associated notice and an explicit consent captured (and that no personal data was processed without consent or a valid legal basis). If Data Principal Rights (such as the right to access or erase data) are in scope, the auditor could sample recent requests from Data Principals and evaluate how they were handled: Was the response given within a reasonable timeframe? Were any refusals compliant with the limited grounds allowed by the Act? Another area for sampling is security logs; the auditor might inspect log entries or incident tickets to see if any unauthorized access was detected and how it was remedied. Importantly, the samples should be chosen to cover a cross-section of the organization's activities, including different departments or systems, to get a representative view of compliance. If weaknesses are found in the sample, the auditor may expand testing in that area to determine if it is an isolated case or a systemic issue.

- **Technical verification:** Compliance audits under the DPDP Act often require technical assessment techniques to validate security controls. For instance, the auditor might perform a **configuration review** of databases to check if encryption at rest is enabled for tables storing personal data (aligning with Rule 6's expectation of encryption or obfuscation for data security). They might also examine user access permissions in critical applications to ensure the principle of least privilege is followed (only necessary access). Some audits may include vulnerability scanning or penetration testing results review to ensure that known security risks are being addressed. This ties into the DPDPA mandate for "reasonable safeguards," which implicitly includes keeping systems secure from known vulnerabilities. Another technique is reviewing audit logs and monitoring systems: e.g., checking if the system is configured to log events of personal data access and if those logs are retained for at least the minimum period (Draft Rule 6(1)(e) prescribes retaining relevant logs and data for one year for forensic purposes). The auditor will seek evidence that security monitoring is active and that any anomalies are flagged and investigated promptly. Tools like data discovery or data mapping software might also be employed to verify that the organization knows what personal data it has and where it flows, which is fundamental to ensuring all such data is within the Purview of DPDPA compliance controls.

Throughout the execution, evidence collection is critical. Auditors will gather copies of documents (or document excerpts) as evidence, for example, a screenshot of a sample consent form showing the language of the notice and consent button, or an export of user access roles from a system as evidence of access control. Interview notes and observations from walkthroughs are documented. If the organization uses automated compliance tools (for instance, Microsoft Purview Compliance Manager or similar solutions), the auditor may also review the outputs of those tools. Such tools can provide mappings of DPDP Act requirements to controls and indicate the status of implementation; for example, Compliance Manager might show a control for "Breach notification process in place" and whether the organization marked it as implemented. The auditor can use this as a reference, but will validate the truth of it via independent testing. It is important to note that while automation and software can greatly aid in gathering and organizing compliance data, they do not replace the auditor's judgment. The auditor should independently verify compliance rather than rely solely on self-assessments. For instance, if a tool indicates that encryption is in place, the auditor should still ask to see the encryption settings or policies to confirm. In practice, compliance tools are extremely useful for risk assessment and for tracking remediation tasks, but the audit execution should include manual verification steps for all critical requirements.

Maintaining independence and rigor: The DPDP Act requires that the data audit, especially for SDFs, be carried out by an *independent* auditor. This principle means that the person or team executing the audit must not have direct involvement in the operational areas being audited. In an internal audit scenario, the organization should ensure the auditors are from a separate department (e.g., an internal audit or compliance team that is not under the operational IT or business units). Many SDFs may opt to engage external firms or certified professionals to perform the annual DPDPA compliance audit for objectivity. During execution, auditors should adhere to professional standards, evidence-based evaluation, completeness, and fairness in assessing compliance. Every finding or potential non-compliance noted should be backed by evidence (e.g., a particular section of the Act that is unmet and the observed situation that violates it) and discussed with the relevant staff to ensure accuracy of understanding. Regular communication during the fieldwork (e.g., daily debriefs or updates) can help address any confusion and keep the audit running smoothly. By the end of the execution phase, the auditor will compile a list of observations, positive compliance practices, and any gaps, which will then be analyzed and formalized in the reporting phase.

Reporting and follow-up

After completing the audit fieldwork, the auditor must compile the findings into a clear and structured report. **Reporting** is a critical phase, as it translates the technical and legal assessment into actionable information for management and creates a record that may be shared with regulators if required. Under the DPDP framework, reporting has an added dimension for SDFs: a summary of the audit results must be furnished to the Data Protection Board of India. This means the audit report may eventually be scrutinized by the regulatory authority, so it should be meticulously prepared, accurate, and aligned with the law.

Documenting audit findings with references

Each compliance gap or finding identified should be described in the audit report with sufficient detail. A typical way to structure findings is to include: (a) a description of the issue, (b) the reference to the specific DPDP Act section or Rule that is violated or not adequately met, (c) the evidence observed, and (d) the auditor's recommendation for remediation. For example, a finding might read: *"Finding: Consent notices do not include an easy means for Data Principals to withdraw consent. Requirement: Section 5 of the DPDP Act and Rule 3(c)(i) require that the notice provide a clear method for withdrawal of consent. Observation: The current privacy notice on the website, while describing data collected and purpose, has no mention of how a user can revoke consent, and there is no link or interface for withdrawal. Recommendation: Implement a visible 'Withdraw Consent' link in the user account settings and update the notice text to comply with the law."* By tying each finding to the legal requirement, the report not only informs internal stakeholders but also serves as evidence of due diligence if authorities review the audit. It is equally important to document areas of *compliance strength* or controls that are working well, as this provides a balanced view and helps the organization understand what is effective in its privacy management program. The report should have an Executive Summary highlighting the overall compliance status and key risks (e.g., noting if any high-severity issues were found, or if the organization appears in material compliance aside from a few improvements). Following that, a section detailing the *audit scope and methodology* is useful – it can list which departments were reviewed, how many samples were taken, etc., to give context to the findings. Then the detailed findings can be listed, grouped by area (consent, security, etc.) or priority.

Audit report structure

In a book chapter context, one can outline the recommended structure as follows:

- **Executive summary:** A high-level overview of the audit's purpose, scope, dates, and a summary of major findings and conclusions. Management will look here for a snapshot of whether the organization is compliant or if there are significant gaps needing attention. If the audit is an annual required audit for an SDF, the summary should explicitly state whether the company meets DPDP Act obligations or not, and may be used to communicate with the Board (regulator).

- **Scope and objectives:** Clearly state what was covered in the audit (which business units, systems, processes, time period of data, etc.) and the objectives (e.g., "to assess compliance with Chapters II, III, and IV of the DPDP Act and associated Rules, including consent management, data security, and breach notification processes"). Also note any areas not covered (if any were excluded) to avoid ambiguity.

- **Methodology:** Describe the approach, documents reviewed, interviews conducted, sampling methods, and any tools used. For instance, mention if automated compliance checks were used, or if technical testing was performed. If the audit was performed by an independent external auditor, that can be stated here as well.

- **Findings and observations:** This is the core of the report. It can be organized by thematic areas (as identified in planning). Each subsection (e.g., **Consent and Notice Compliance**, **Security Safeguards**, **Breach Response**, **Data Principal Rights handling**, **SDFs obligations**) would list the findings relevant to that topic. Use bullet points or tables for clarity if there are many points. Each finding should indicate its **severity level** (e.g., low, medium, high-risk). High-severity issues are those that could lead to significant harm to Data Principals or large penalties, for example, failing to honor opt-outs or a lack of any breach notification mechanism would be high, whereas a minor omission in a notice might be low or medium. Wherever possible, reference the exact Rule or Section as done in the example above. This not only reinforces the legal basis but also helps the organization prioritize, for example, non-compliance with an explicit legal obligation carries the risk of regulatory action (the DPDP Act has an associated penalty schedule for various violations).

- **Recommendations and action plan:** Alongside each finding, or in a separate section after listing all findings, the auditor should provide recommendations. These should be specific and practical steps to achieve compliance. For instance, if encryption was found lacking, the recommendation might be to implement encryption for databases X and Y using industry-standard algorithms by a certain timeline. In some cases, refer to best practices or relevant standards (like ISO/IEC 27001 for information security) to strengthen the recommendation. The report can include a column for **management response** to each finding. While the initial draft of the report is by the auditor, it is good practice to allow management to formally respond, agreeing with the finding and committing to an action or providing clarification if they disagree. This makes the report a living document that feeds into the remediation process.

After the report is finalized, the **follow-up** phase begins. Follow-up is about ensuring that the agreed recommendations are implemented and that the issues are resolved within a reasonable timeframe. The audit report should ideally include a section on *"Corrective action Plan"* or *"Management action Plan,"* summarizing all remediation tasks, owners (responsible persons), and target deadlines. For example, it might list that by *Q3 2025, the IT team will deploy a consent withdrawal feature on the website; by next audit, the legal team will have updated all privacy notices to include missing elements; within 1 month, the security team will enable encryption on the backup tapes*, etc. Tracking these actions is crucial; many organizations use a tracking tool or spreadsheet where each audit finding is logged, and periodic status updates are provided by the owners. The DPO or Compliance Manager typically oversees this remediation tracker to ensure momentum is maintained.

To truly close the loop, a **remediation validation** or follow-up audit is often conducted. This might not be as extensive as the original audit, but it is a targeted review to verify that each high-risk finding was fixed. For instance, if the audit found that breach notifications were not being sent to Data Principals, once the organization claims to have fixed this by updating their incident response process, the auditor (or an internal compliance function) would perform a check, maybe simulate a minor incident or inspect the revised procedure and even carry out a drill, to confirm the fix is effective. In the case of SDFs, since audits are annual, the next yearly audit will automatically include reviewing past findings; however, waiting a full year to confirm critical fixes is not advisable. Therefore, follow-up reviews in 3-6 months are recommended for major issues.

Another aspect of follow-up under the DPDPA regime is *regulatory communication*. As noted, SDFs must submit a summary of the audit and DPIA results to the Data Protection Board. Typically, this would involve extracting the salient points of the audit report (or perhaps an attestation from the independent auditor) and sending it to the Board. If the Board has questions or requires additional information, the organization (and auditor, if needed) should be prepared to provide it. If an audit uncovers a serious compliance failure (for example, a systemic violation of consent requirements), the organization might have a legal obligation to self-report it to the Board or risk a penalty if it remains unaddressed. While the DPDP Act's enforcement provisions focus mainly on responding to complaints and breaches, a proactive approach in follow-up can demonstrate good faith. Ensuring remediation and closure of audit findings not only moves the organization toward full compliance but also is an important part of demonstrating **accountability**, which is a core principle underlying the DPDP Act.

In conclusion, audit planning, execution, reporting, and follow-up form a continuous cycle of compliance management under India's DPDP Act, 2023. A well-planned audit with clear criteria aligned to the Act and Rules will illuminate whether an organization's practices around consent, notice, data security, breach handling, and other obligations are in line with the law. Thorough execution using a variety of audit techniques will gather the evidence needed to support conclusions. Comprehensive reporting, complete with legal references and actionable recommendations, translates those conclusions into a roadmap for compliance improvement. Finally, rigorous follow-up ensures that the audit is not a one-time exercise but leads to real enhancement of privacy protections. By adhering to this cycle, organizations subject to the DPDP Act can maintain continuous compliance and be prepared for scrutiny by the Data Protection Board, thereby minimizing legal risks and reinforcing trust with Data Principals through robust data protection practices.

Assessing third-party compliance

Organizations often rely on third-party service providers (vendors) to process personal data on their behalf. Under the DPDP Act, such vendors are considered Data Processors, defined as any person who processes personal data on behalf of a Data Fiduciary. Ensuring these third-parties comply with data protection requirements is critically important. The DPDP Act explicitly holds the Data Fiduciary (the principal entity determining purpose and means of processing) accountable for all personal data processing carried out "on its behalf by a Data Processor," regardless of any contracts to the contrary. In other words, even if an organization outsources data processing, it cannot escape liability; ultimate responsibility for protecting personal data remains with the Data Fiduciary.

Given this clear allocation of accountability, third-party compliance becomes a key pillar of an effective data protection program. If a vendor fails to safeguard personal data or violates the Act, the Data Fiduciary may face legal consequences, including investigations and penalties by the Data Protection Board of India. Moreover, non-compliance by vendors can erode trust with customers and damage the Fiduciary's reputation. Therefore, organizations must treat third-party compliance as equally important as internal compliance, ensuring that all external partners uphold the same standards of data protection mandated by the DPDP Act.

Risks associated with third-party data processing

When engaging third-parties to handle personal data, Data Fiduciaries should be mindful of several inherent risks. Key risks associated with third-party data processing include:

- **Data security breaches:** Vendors may become the weak link in security, potentially leading to unauthorized access or leaks of personal data. Under the DPDP Act, any *"unauthorised processing…or accidental disclosure"* of personal data that compromises its confidentiality or integrity constitutes a personal data breach. A breach at a third-party can thus directly trigger the Fiduciary's breach notification obligations and expose it to penalties.

- **Regulatory non-compliance:** Third-parties that do not understand or implement DPDP Act requirements (for example, obtaining valid consent or honoring data retention limits) can cause the Data Fiduciary to unknowingly violate the law. Since the Fiduciary is legally accountable for all processing on its behalf, any compliance failure by the vendor is effectively a compliance failure of the Fiduciary. This can lead to regulatory action even if the lapse occurred outside the Fiduciary's organization.

- **Loss of control over data:** Outsourcing processing means personal data is stored or handled in systems not directly controlled by the Fiduciary. This can result in reduced visibility into how data is used, who accesses it, and whether it is further shared. Without proper oversight, there is a risk of data being processed beyond the agreed purpose or retained longer than necessary, contravening the Act's principles.

- **Sub-processor and supply chain risks:** A vendor might engage its own sub-contractors (sub-processors) to carry out portions of the processing. Each additional link in the chain introduces further risk, as data may pass through multiple hands. Suppose sub-processors are not disclosed or not held to the DPDP Act standards, the risk of misuse or breach increases. The Data Fiduciary could be unaware of vulnerabilities deep in the supply chain.

- **Reputational damage and liability:** Regardless of where a data incident originates, the public and regulators will hold the primary organization responsible. A privacy incident at a third-party processor can lead to loss of customer trust, negative publicity, and civil liability for the Data Fiduciary. The DPDP Act empowers the Data Protection Board to inquire into breaches and impose penalties on the Fiduciary, which can be significant. In summary, poor vendor practices can directly translate into financial and reputational harm for the principal organization.

By recognizing these risks, Data Fiduciaries can take proactive steps (through due diligence, contracts, and oversight) to mitigate third-party threats and ensure compliance throughout the data processing lifecycle.

Legal obligations under the DPDP Act

The Digital Personal Data Protection Act, 2023, lays down clear legal obligations that Data Fiduciaries must fulfill when engaging third-party processors. Accountability for compliance always remains with the Data Fiduciary. Section 8(1) of the Act states that *"A Data Fiduciary shall, irrespective of any agreement to the contrary or failure of a Data Principal to carry out the duties provided under this Act, be responsible for complying with the provisions of this Act and the rules made thereunder in respect of any processing undertaken by it or on its behalf by a Data Processor."*. In essence, the law does not allow a Fiduciary to contract out of its duties – any personal data handled by a vendor is deemed to be handled by the Fiduciary itself for compliance purposes.

To lawfully engage a third-party, the DPDP Act requires a valid contract between the Data Fiduciary and the Data Processor. Section 8(2) specifies that a Data Fiduciary may involve a Data Processor to process personal data "only under a valid contract." This legal requirement ensures that the obligations and limits of processing are documented. At a minimum, the contract should bind the processor to process data only on the instructions of the Fiduciary and for no other purpose.

Security safeguards are another critical obligation. The Act mandates that Data Fiduciaries protect personal data in their possession or *under their control,* including data processed by a third-party, by adopting reasonable security measures. In fact, Section 8(5) explicitly extends the duty of implementing "reasonable security safeguards to prevent personal data breach" to processing carried out on the Fiduciary's behalf by a Data Processor. This implies that the Fiduciary must ensure vendors also implement appropriate technical and organizational security controls. The Draft Rules, 2025, reinforce this by requiring a specific contract clause obligating the Data Processor to maintain such safeguards.

The DPDP Act also addresses *personal data breaches* in the context of third-party processing. If a breach occurs (be it within the Fiduciary's systems or at a vendor), the Data Fiduciary has a legal duty to notify of the event. Section 8(6) requires the Fiduciary to inform both the Data Protection Board of India and each affected Data Principal of the breach in the manner prescribed. In practice, this means that even if a vendor's negligence caused the incident, the Fiduciary must take the lead on breach notifications and bear responsibility before the law. The Draft Rules specify that notice to the Board must be given "without delay" and within *72 hours* of becoming aware of the breach, and the notice to individuals should include details of the nature of the breach, likely consequences, and measures taken in response.

Additionally, the Act imposes obligations related to *data retention and erasure* that extend to third-party processors. Under Section 8(7), when a Data Principal withdraws consent or the purpose of processing is fulfilled, the Data Fiduciary must erase the personal data (unless retention is required by law) and *"cause its Data Processor to erase any personal data"* that was provided to that processor. This provision makes it clear that vendors are expected to delete or return personal data once the Fiduciary no longer has a legal basis to retain it. The Fiduciary should thus ensure that its processors have procedures to securely delete data on request and do not hold on to personal data beyond the authorized period.

Finally, if personal data is processed or stored outside India by a third-party, Data Fiduciaries must heed the Act's provisions on cross-border data transfers. The Act (as elaborated in Draft Rule 14) stipulates that personal data may be transferred to a foreign country or entity only if the conditions or restrictions set by the Central Government are met. While the government will specify the allowed jurisdictions or safeguards via notification, it is the Fiduciary's obligation to ensure that any offshore vendor processing does not violate these transfer restrictions.

In summary, under the DPDP Act, a Data Fiduciary must: use vendors under a binding contract, ensure third-parties implement necessary security controls, remain prepared to handle breach notifications, enforce data lifecycle requirements (like deletion), and comply with any cross-border transfer rules. All these legal obligations underscore that *outsourcing processing does not dilute responsibility*; the Data Fiduciary is expected to extend its compliance program to cover any third-parties involved in handling personal data.

Due diligence for selecting vendors

Selecting the right vendor is the first line of defense in third-party compliance. Before entrusting personal data to a third-party Data Processor, a Data Fiduciary should conduct thorough due diligence to vet the vendor's capability to meet the Act's requirements. This due diligence process typically includes:

- **Security and privacy practices:** Evaluate the vendor's information security measures and privacy program. Does the vendor follow industry standards (for example, ISO/IEC 27001 certification for security)? Do they have robust access controls, encryption, and incident response plans in place? A vendor should be able to demonstrate that it can *protect personal data* with appropriate technical and organizational measures, as the DPDP Act would require.

- **Legal and regulatory compliance:** Assess the vendor's familiarity with the DPDP Act and readiness to comply. The vendor should ideally have internal policies addressing data protection, confidentiality, and breach handling aligned with Indian law. If the vendor has experience handling data under privacy regulations, it is more likely to understand and fulfill obligations such as obtaining consent where needed, honoring deletion requests, and restricting processing to defined purposes. Vendors that process sensitive or large volumes of personal data may even fall under "SDF" categories themselves, in which case they would have additional compliance obligations (e.g., appointing a DPO).

- **Past performance and reputation:** Investigate the vendor's track record. Any history of data breaches or security incidents should be a red flag. Similarly, check for any prior regulatory penalties or legal disputes related to data handling. A vendor with a clean record and positive references provides more confidence. Publicly available information or audits can be useful – for instance, a SOC 2 report or past audit summaries can indicate the maturity of the vendor's controls.

- **Data handling capabilities:** Confirm that the vendor can support the Data Fiduciary's compliance needs operationally. This includes the ability to *adhere to data retention requirements* and delete or return data when instructed (critical for compliance with Section 8(7)), as well as mechanisms to assist with Data Principal Rights. For example, if a Data Principal requests erasure or correction of data, the vendor should be capable of promptly locating and updating or deleting the data on their systems. During due diligence, asking how the vendor would handle such requests is prudent.

- **Sub-processors and location of data:** Inquire whether the vendor intends to further subcontract any processing or store data with cloud providers. If yes, those sub-processors should be identified and held to the same standards. Importantly, verify **where** the personal data will be processed or stored. If the data will leave Indian territorial jurisdiction, the Fiduciary must ensure this is permitted under the DPDP Act's cross-border transfer rules. It may be necessary to choose a vendor with data centers in India or in jurisdictions approved by the Indian government to avoid legal complications.

- **Financial and organizational stability:** Given that compliance is an ongoing endeavor, the vendor should be stable enough to be a reliable partner. A financially unstable vendor might not invest in security or might even go out of business, jeopardizing the data. Reviewing the company's stability and commitment to privacy (for example, do they have a dedicated privacy team or officer?) can be part of the due diligence.

By performing such due diligence, a Data Fiduciary can select vendors who are capable and trustworthy, thereby significantly reducing the risk of downstream compliance failures. This front-end scrutiny sets the stage for incorporating appropriate protections in the contract and managing the relationship to maintain compliance.

Contracts and agreements

A well-drafted contract is the cornerstone of third-party data protection compliance. The DPDP Act makes a contract *mandatory* for any engagement of a Data Processor, but beyond this formality, the contract (often termed a DPA) is the tool by which the Data Fiduciary extends its data protection policies to the vendor. It should clearly define the *scope of processing*, allocate responsibilities, and provide mechanisms for oversight and redress.

Key clauses to include in such contracts encompass the following areas:

- **Purpose limitation and instructions**: The agreement should specify that the Data Processor will process personal data only for the purposes explicitly stated by the Data Fiduciary and only on its documented instructions. This ensures the vendor does not use or disclose the data for any unauthorized purpose. It operationalizes the Act's requirement that processing on behalf of the Fiduciary be strictly controlled by contract. Any data use beyond the contract's scope (e.g., for the processor's own analytics or marketing) should be prohibited.

- **Confidentiality and authorization of personnel:** There should be a clause requiring the processor to keep the personal data confidential and to ensure that any staff or sub-contractors who access the data are bound by appropriate confidentiality obligations. Only authorized personnel with a need-to-know should handle the data. This helps maintain the secrecy of personal data and accountability within the vendor's organization.

- **Security measures:** Given the Fiduciary's duty to implement security safeguards even for outsourced processing, the contract must obligate the vendor to apply reasonable security practices. Draft Rule 6(1)(f) explicitly calls for *"appropriate provision in the contract…for taking reasonable security safeguards."*. The contract might reference specific security standards the vendor must follow (encryption standards, access control measures, regular vulnerability assessments, etc.). Including a right for the Data

Fiduciary to *verify* or obtain evidence of the vendor's security measures (such as audit reports or certifications) is also advisable.

- **Sub-processor restrictions:** If the vendor may engage any sub-processors, the contract should require that the Data Fiduciary be informed and ideally give prior approval. It should also stipulate that any sub-processor will be held to the same contractual standards. This creates a chain of accountability so that all downstream parties protect the data appropriately.

- **Data subject rights assistance:** The agreement should require the processor to assist the Data Fiduciary in fulfilling obligations to Data Principals. For instance, if an individual submits an access or erasure request, the processor should promptly provide relevant data or delete data, as needed, to enable the Fiduciary's compliance with the Act. This ties into the obligation under Section 8(7)(b) that the processor erase data upon the Fiduciary's instruction. Similarly, processors should agree to support the correction or porting of data if those rights are invoked.

- **Breach notification and incident response**: A crucial clause is that the Data Processor must notify the Data Fiduciary immediately (or within a very short specified timeframe) if it becomes aware of a personal data breach or any security incident involving the personal data. Since the Fiduciary has legal obligations to notify the Board and individuals within strict timelines, it must contractually ensure it will be alerted by the vendor without delay. The contract can also require the processor to cooperate in investigating and remediating the breach, including providing all necessary information about what was compromised.

- **Data return/deletion on termination**: The contract should clearly state that upon completion of the services or upon termination of the contract, the Data Processor will return all personal data to the Fiduciary or securely delete it, as instructed. It should mirror the Act's requirement that data be erased when it is no longer required and ensure no copies are retained by the vendor (aside from any legal record-keeping copies, which should be agreed upon). This prevents unauthorized retention of data post-contract.

- **Audit and monitoring rights**: To enforce the above clauses, the Data Fiduciary may include a right to conduct audits or inspections of the vendor's data processing operations or to request third-party audit certifications. For example, the contract might allow an annual security audit or require that the processor supply an independent audit report attesting to its compliance. This clause ensures transparency and provides a mechanism for the Fiduciary to verify adherence to the contract and the law.

- **Service levels and penalties:** Often, Data Fiduciaries will also incorporate **service level agreements (SLAs)** related to data protection. For instance, an SLA might set a maximum time for the processor to respond to a data deletion request or to report a breach (e.g., within 24 hours of discovery of an incident). Non-compliance with these requirements can be tied to penalties or the right to terminate the contract. While the DPDP Act does not dictate specific SLAs, including them helps translate legal obligations into measurable operational requirements.

- **Indemnity and liability:** Finally, the contract can include indemnification clauses where the processor agrees to indemnify (compensate) the Fiduciary for losses arising from the processor's breach of the agreement or violation of the law. This is a risk-sharing mechanism. Although the Fiduciary will be directly liable to regulators under the DPDP Act, an indemnity ensures the vendor bears financial responsibility if its actions caused the non-compliance. Clear liability caps and insurance requirements for the processor can also be detailed.

By incorporating these clauses, the Data Fiduciary creates a strong contractual framework that not only fulfills the DPDP Act's requirement of a valid contract but also operationalizes compliance. The contract sets expectations and provides remedies if the third-party falls short. It is effectively an extension of the Fiduciary's privacy policy and security program, tailored to the vendor relationship. Both parties should review such agreements carefully and ensure understanding of their obligations. The contract management process should also track that agreements with all vendors processing personal data are in place and kept up-to-date (especially if laws or circumstances change).

Ongoing monitoring and auditing

Signing a comprehensive agreement is not the end of the compliance journey; Data Fiduciaries must actively **monitor and audit** third-party compliance on an ongoing basis. Continuous oversight is essential because it helps verify that the vendor is living up to the promises in the contract and adhering to the DPDP Act in practice throughout the duration of the engagement.

Regular monitoring can take several forms. First, the Data Fiduciary should require *periodic reports or attestations* from the Data Processor. For example, the vendor might be asked to provide an annual compliance report, the results of any security tests, or updates on any sub-processors used. Many organizations institute quarterly or annual vendor reviews, where key aspects like incident reports, access logs, and any difficulties in responding to Data Principal requests are reviewed. This ongoing dialogue keeps the Fiduciary aware of emerging issues and allows for timely corrective action.

Secondly, exercising *audit rights* (as provided in the contract) is a powerful way to ensure third-party adherence. Audits can range from desk reviews of policies to on-site inspections or penetration testing of the vendor's systems (where appropriate). In some cases, independent third-party audits or certifications can substitute for direct audits; for instance, reviewing the vendor's ISO 27001 certification report or SOC 2 Type II report can provide assurance of control effectiveness. The Draft DPDP Rules emphasize the importance of audits for larger data handlers: SDFs are required to *"undertake a Data Protection Impact Assessment and an audit"* every 12 months to ensure compliance. While this specific mandate is for SDFs, it signals the overall regulatory expectation that *periodic auditing* is a best practice for data protection. A

Data Fiduciary, even if not formally classified as "Significant," would benefit from adopting a similar approach for its high-risk processing activities and vendors.

Effective monitoring also involves keeping track of any changes in the vendor's circumstances. If a Data Processor undergoes a major business change (such as a merger or acquisition) or a significant systems change (like a migration to a new platform or a new sub-processor), the Data Fiduciary should reassess the risk and possibly update the contract or seek re-certification of controls. Maintaining an up-to-date inventory of all third-parties handling personal data, along with details of what data they process and where, is a fundamental part of governance. This inventory helps in ensuring coverage of all vendors in the monitoring schedule.

In addition, the Data Fiduciary should ensure there is an internal *owner* for each vendor relationship, such as a Privacy Officer or a business relationship manager, who is responsible for overseeing that vendor's compliance. This person would liaise with the vendor's team, schedule compliance checkpoints, and handle any issues that arise. For organizations that are SDFs, the appointed DPO will typically have, among their duties, the task of monitoring all processing (including by vendors) and advising on compliance. The DPO or similar function can implement a vendor compliance assessment checklist to be reviewed at set intervals. It is also advisable for the Data Processor to appoint a DPO to ensure effective data protection practices.

When audits or monitoring activities reveal gaps or non-compliance, the Data Fiduciary should Act quickly. Minor issues may be addressable by requiring the vendor to implement a remediation plan (for example, improving encryption or providing additional staff training within a set timeframe). Serious breaches of contract or law might necessitate stronger responses, such as suspending data transfers to the vendor until issues are fixed, invoking penalty clauses, or ultimately terminating the contract and engaging an alternative provider. The contract's provisions will guide what remedies are available. Throughout, it is important to document these oversight activities and any remediation, as this evidence can be crucial to demonstrate the Fiduciary's own compliance (especially if ever scrutinized by the Data Protection Board).

In summary, ongoing monitoring and auditing operationalize the accountability principle: it is how Data Fiduciaries ensure effective observance of the DPDP Act over time, as required by Chapter II Section 8(4). By continuously verifying third-party compliance, organizations can catch and address issues early, maintain the integrity and security of personal data, and uphold their obligations under the law.

Handling data breaches involving third-parties

Despite robust precautions, data breaches can occur even at well-vetted vendors. When a personal data breach involves a third-party processor, the Data Fiduciary must respond swiftly and decisively, fulfilling legal requirements and protecting Data Principals. A clear breach response plan that includes third-party incidents is essential. The points to keep in mind are as follows:

- **Immediate notification and containment:** The moment a Data Fiduciary becomes aware (either through the vendor or by its own detection) that a breach has occurred at a third-party, it should activate its incident response procedure. As emphasized, the contract should oblige the vendor to inform the Fiduciary without delay in the event of any incident. Upon such notice, the Fiduciary's incident response team should work with the vendor to understand the scope and impact of the breach. Key details include what personal data was compromised, how and when the incident happened, whether the breach is ongoing, and what remediation steps are being taken to contain it. The Fiduciary may dispatch its own security experts to assist or require the vendor to take specific immediate actions (like shutting down a system, rotating credentials, etc.) to contain the damage.

- **Legal notifications (Data Protection Board and Data Principals):** The DPDP Act imposes explicit breach notification duties on the Data Fiduciary. As soon as practicable, and "without delay," the Fiduciary must notify the Data Protection Board of India about the breach. Draft Rule 7(2) sets a timeline of no later than 72 hours from becoming aware of the breach for notifying the Board, unless a longer period is allowed in exceptional cases. This notification typically requires information about the nature of the breach, its extent, the categories of personal data affected, and a preliminary assessment of impact. Simultaneously, the Fiduciary is obligated to inform each affected Data Principal about the breach. The notification to individuals should be in clear language and include details such as a description of the breach, likely consequences for the individual, measures taken by the Fiduciary to mitigate harm, and advice on what the individual can do (e.g., reset passwords, be vigilant for fraud). It should also provide contact information for a person or helpdesk that the Data Principal can reach out to. Even though the incident occurred in the systems of the Data Processor, the Data Fiduciary must take ownership of these communications, maintaining transparency and trust.

It is critical that the Data Processor supplies all necessary information to facilitate these notifications. If details are incomplete within 72 hours, the Fiduciary should still send an initial notice to the Board with available information and follow up as more facts emerge. The DPDP Act's requirement to notify "to the best of its knowledge" indicates that good faith reporting is expected even if an investigation is ongoing. The contract's breach clause should align with this by requiring the vendor's full cooperation in forensic analysis and in drafting notification content.

- **Engagement with the Data Protection Board:** Once notified, the Data Protection Board may exercise its authority to inquire into the breach. Under the Act, upon receiving intimation of a breach under Chapter II Section 8(6), the Board can direct urgent measures to mitigate the breach and will inquire into it, with the power to impose penalties as provided in the Act. The Data Fiduciary should be prepared to demonstrate to the Board that it had exercised due diligence in choosing and overseeing the vendor, and that it responded appropriately to the incident. All correspondence and actions taken should be documented. The Fiduciary may also need to coordinate with the vendor to provide additional information requested by the Board during its inquiry. Notably, penalties can be imposed on the Fiduciary for failing to protect personal data or failing to notify in time, even if the fault originated at the processor, reinforcing why breach handling is a non-delegable duty.

- **Remediation and lessons learned:** After the immediate crisis is handled, the Data Fiduciary (in partnership with the vendor) should focus on remediation to prevent recurrence. This might involve requiring the vendor to fix vulnerabilities, increase security controls, or undergo additional training. In severe cases, the Fiduciary might cause suspension of data processing by that vendor until fixes are verified or consider transitioning the work to a more secure provider. An internal post-incident review is useful: evaluating what went wrong, how effective the response was, and what improvements can be made in vendor management. Perhaps the breach revealed a gap in the contract or oversight processes, for example, maybe the vendor had a sub-processor that experienced the breach, unknown to the Fiduciary. Such insights should lead to stronger contractual clauses or monitoring steps going forward.

Throughout breach handling, an overarching principle is clear: The Data Fiduciary retains accountability to those affected and to regulators. The third-party's role does not diminish the Fiduciary's responsibility to Act swiftly and decisively. With a solid incident response plan, clear contractual requirements for vendor cooperation, and an understanding of DPDP Act timelines, the Fiduciary can effectively manage breaches involving third-parties and mitigate harm to individuals as well as to its own compliance standing.

Internal data protection reviews

While formal audits (whether internal or external) are crucial, organizations can also benefit from more frequent and less formal **internal data protection reviews**. These are typically conducted by the organization's own privacy or compliance team on an ongoing basis. The idea is to regularly "check the pulse" of various processes for compliance outside of the structured audit cycle. In this section, we clarify what internal reviews are, how they differ from audits, and how they complement the overall compliance monitoring program.

Review vs audit

The terms "review" and "audit" are sometimes used interchangeably, but there are distinctions in practice:

- **Formality and rigor:** An *audit* (especially an independent or formal internal audit) is generally more rigorous, follows a defined standard or framework, and results in an official report. Audits often have a wider scope and occur at defined intervals. A *review*, on the other hand, is usually less formal. It might be focused on a specific area or a single process, and can be done more frequently. Reviews might not produce a formal report, but rather a summary of observations or a checklist of compliance status that is used internally to quickly fix issues.

- **Conducted by:** Audits are frequently conducted by auditors who are independent of the process (e.g., an internal audit department or external auditor). Reviews are often done by the process owners themselves or by the privacy/compliance team that works closely with those processes. For example, a Privacy Officer might review the marketing team's new campaign for compliance with consent requirements, which is a review. It might not involve all the evidence gathering an auditor would do, but it leverages the Privacy Officer's expertise to flag any issues.

- **Scope and depth:** Audits usually cover a broad scope with depth (they will dig in and verify evidence). Reviews might either be broad and shallow (just a quick health check across many things) or narrow and deep (focusing on one topic thoroughly). For instance, an internal monthly review could simply be a checklist: "Have we received any Data Principal complaints? Have all last month's data deletion requests been completed?" That's broad but shallow. Or a review could be, "This month, let us deeply review how our HR department is handling employee personal data." That is narrow (one department) but deeper.

- **Frequency:** Internal reviews are typically more frequent. They could be monthly, quarterly, or even ad-hoc before launching new initiatives. Audits might be annual or semi-annual. The frequency of reviews provides a continuous oversight mechanism. In fact, Chapter II Section 10's emphasis on "continuous compliance" through measures like DPIA and periodic audit suggests an environment of ongoing checking – internal reviews are a way to achieve that in between formal audits.

- **Outcome:** The outcome of an audit is an audit report with findings and required actions, often to be addressed with a formal management response. The outcome of a review might simply be some recommendations or an action list that the team can implement right away. As per draft Rule 12(2) of the draft rules 2025, the audit related details have to be furnished to the DPB. For example, a review might find that a particular data retention schedule is not being followed; the reviewer could then immediately work with that team to purge the old data, rather than documenting it as a formal finding first.

- **Perspective:** Audits usually take a point-in-time snapshot and often have an element of independence, meaning they can provide assurance to external stakeholders. Reviews are more of an *internal management tool*, used to maintain or improve compliance on a rolling basis. They might not satisfy an external requirement, but are invaluable for internal governance.

In essence, think of *audits as the exam* and *reviews as the regular quizzes or homework*. Both are needed for a good study regime, but they serve slightly different purposes.

The benefits of internal reviews are as follows:

- They catch issues early (before an audit or regulator might).
- They keep the topic of data protection active within teams (since someone is checking regularly).
- They can be more collaborative and educational. When a privacy team reviews something, they often educate that business unit about best practices in the process, which raises overall awareness and compliance culture.

Possible structure for reviews

Many organizations create a schedule for internal privacy reviews. For example:

- **Q1**: Review consent and preference management processes.
- **Q2**: Review data retention and deletion practices.
- **Q3**: Review third-party agreements and any new vendors.
- **Q4**: Review user rights request handling and record-keeping.

This rotational review ensures each area is looked at least once a year, aside from audits. If something is high-risk, it might be reviewed more often.

Another kind of review is event-triggered: whenever a new project starts that involves personal data, the privacy team does a **Privacy Impact Assessment (PIA)** (similar to DPIA), which is essentially a review of that project's design to ensure compliance. This might not be called an audit; it is a proactive review.

Tools and technologies

Technology has become a linchpin in effective auditing and compliance monitoring. With the scale of data and complexity of modern IT systems, manual compliance checks are not sufficient. Fortunately, a range of *tools and technologies* is available to automate and streamline data protection compliance tasks. In this section, we will discuss some key tools, many of which have been touched upon in earlier sections, and how they assist in auditing and monitoring. We will also discuss concepts like audit personas (roles), AI integration, and workflow automation for compliance tasks.

Microsoft Purview Compliance Manager

This is a flagship tool for compliance management in Microsoft 365 and broader Microsoft cloud environments. It provides an **assessment framework** with templates for various regulations (over 300 regulations, including global ones and likely the DPDP Act soon). How it works is explained as follows.

The Compliance Manager can **automate some of the evidence collection**. For instance, it can automatically detect if you have DLP policies enabled (which might map to a control about preventing unauthorized data sharing) or if multifactor authentication is enabled for all users (mapping to a security control). These automations feed into a **compliance score**, giving a quantitative indicator of compliance completeness. As a result, it provides a real-time or near-real-time view of compliance. Auditors can look at Compliance Manager and quickly see strengths and weaknesses. It also allows exporting reports that can be used in audit documentation. It is essentially a continuous self-audit tool. The following are a few examples of using Compliance Manager:

- Lists out control requirements and lets you assign implementation status to each. For example, a control might be "Ensure personal data is encrypted at rest" – you can mark it implemented and attach documentation or notes.

- It gives a compliance score that shows how much of the compliance framework you have completed. This quantification can help track progress and also highlight gaps that need attention.

- Compliance Manager is also often linked to Microsoft 365 configuration checks. For instance, it might automatically detect if audit logging is turned on, or if multi-factor authentication is enabled for admins – things relevant to security best practices.

- In essence, it acts as a project management tool for compliance, guiding organizations on what actions to take for various regulations. For the DPDP Act, one could input all the Act's obligations and use it to monitor that each is addressed (like a live Act mapping tool).

The Compliance Manager also supports *task assignment and tracking*, effectively functioning as a project management tool for compliance activities. Suppose an audit finds a gap, you could create an action in Compliance Manager to address a control, assign it to someone with a deadline, and track it to closure. This aligns well with the follow-up needs mentioned earlier.

Microsoft Purview eDiscovery

Electronic Discovery (eDiscovery) tools were originally developed for legal proceedings (to find relevant documents/emails), but they are incredibly useful for privacy compliance, too. Purview eDiscovery (Premium and Standard) allows you to:

- Search across emails, SharePoint, OneDrive, Teams chats, etc., for specific information. For privacy, you might search all content for a particular person's name or identifier to fulfill an access or deletion request.

- Place holds on data (which can be relevant for preserving evidence during an investigation of an incident).

- *Do keyword searches and content filtering.* For example, you can search for files containing personally identifiable information like credit card numbers or Aadhaar numbers to locate where personal data is stored. This helps in data mapping and detecting policy violations (if such data appears where it should not).

- In an audit context, eDiscovery can be used to quickly gather samples or verify that certain data no longer exists (post-deletion). It is like your X-ray machine to see inside all unstructured data stores.

- eDiscovery is also crucial in investigating incidents or compliance issues. If there is a suspected misuse of data, you can search communications or files to piece together what happened (e.g., did someone share data they should not have?). In the context of DPDPA, if a complaint arises or an audit is investigating something, eDiscovery can quickly gather the needed records.

- It also helps in legal compliance in case of litigation, but from the DPDPA perspective, think of it as a powerful search engine across your corporate data, invaluable for both internal review and demonstrating compliance (you can show, if needed, that you can retrieve and manage user data effectively).

Microsoft Purview Audit

Purview Audit (formerly Office 365 Unified Audit Log) captures user and admin activity logs across many Microsoft services. It is invaluable for investigating "who did what, when." In compliance monitoring, Purview Audit can be used to:

- Check if privileged accounts are doing unusual activities (like an admin accessing a lot of user mailboxes, which could indicate misuse).

- Verify certain controls, e.g., confirm that when a user requested data deletion, no one accessed that data afterward.

- Purview offers an "Advanced Audit" option with longer retention and more detailed logs (including things like mailbox read access events).

- Auditors or investigators with proper permissions can query these logs in real-time. This is often part of security operations, but it doubles as a compliance tool. For example, demonstrating compliance with an "access on need-to-know basis" control might involve showing logs that access to a sensitive database is only by service accounts and DBAs and is audited.

Identity and access management, Microsoft Entra ID

Ensuring only authorized access to data is fundamental. Azure AD (now part of the Entra brand) provides:

- **Access reviews:** You can regularly trigger access reviews for critical groups or apps (Azure AD will prompt the group owners to certify who still needs access). This is a kind of continuous audit of access rights. It aligns with compliance needs to ensure the timely removal of access for those who no longer need it (say, someone moved departments).

- **Conditional access policies:** These enforce conditions (like multi-factor auth, trusted device, location) for accessing certain data. They contribute to compliance by reducing the risk of unauthorized access; often, a finding in audits is "excessive access" or "weak authentication"; conditional access and MFA solve that.

- **Logs and reports:** Azure AD provides sign-in logs and risky sign-in detections that compliance or security can monitor.

Having a strong IAM in place is often an audit requirement; Azure AD's features help demonstrate that.

Microsoft Security Copilot

This is an AI assistant that can help parse and summarize security and compliance data. For example, Copilot could be asked: "Have there been any unusual data access events in the last week that I should worry about?" and it will analyze your logs and highlight anomalies. This helps compliance officers focus on real issues quickly rather than combing through thousands of log lines. It can also answer questions about compliance posture by summarizing information from different tools. Essentially, AI can Act as a smart analyst, reducing the grunt work.

Microsoft DSI

Microsoft's DSI is a relatively new solution that uses AI-driven tools to help investigate data security incidents and risks. It is part of the Microsoft Purview suite as well:

- DSI can quickly search through large volumes of data (emails, messages, documents) to find content related to a security incident. For example, if there is a suspected data leak, DSI might help pinpoint all messages containing a certain confidential project name or personal data elements to trace the leak's scope.

- It leverages AI to identify patterns or connections that might not be obvious in a manual search. For instance, it might correlate a leaked file to all the places the file was stored or sent.

- Essentially, it accelerates forensic analysis. In DPDPA terms, if a personal data breach occurs, DSI could be used to rapidly assemble the facts needed for notification, like whose data was impacted, how, and when, thus enabling the Data Fiduciary to inform Data Principals more accurately and quickly.

- It can also be used proactively by running investigations to see if any personal information is circulating where it should not. It complements DLP by not just preventing but also analyzing what's happening with data.

- High-level, think of DSI as a specialized search and analysis tool tailored for data security scenarios, using AI to handle the big data problem of searching through potentially millions of records in an investigation.

Conclusion

Auditing and compliance monitoring are pivotal for sustaining robust data protection practices, especially under India's DPDP Act 2023 and its Draft Rules 2025. As explored, achieving initial compliance marks only marks the beginning of a perpetual process. Organizations must embed vigilance and accountability into their operational DNA, proactively conducting regular audits, DPIAs, and third-party assessments to ensure continuous alignment with evolving regulatory expectations. Leveraging advanced technologies such as Microsoft Purview and automated compliance solutions enables organizations to manage compliance efficiently at scale, adapting swiftly to emerging threats. Rather than viewing audits as periodic burdens, progressive organizations recognize them as essential feedback loops, fostering continuous improvement. Ultimately, a mature compliance culture does not merely prevent breaches or fines; it builds trust with regulators, partners, and customers alike. By prioritizing ongoing compliance efforts and integrating best practices into everyday business operations, organizations will secure their data protection posture, demonstrate an unwavering commitment to privacy, and confidently navigate the future of digital trust.

The upcoming chapter is a practical guide to working with India's Data Protection Board under the DPDP Act. It outlines a Data Fiduciary's key duties, from prompt breach notification and five-step complaint handling to maintaining eDiscovery-ready records. You will learn the DPO's central liaison role, the IT team's investigation playbook, and what the Board expects under the Draft Rules 2025. Finally, we break down the Board's enforcement powers and tiered penalty regime so you can build a cooperative, compliance-first relationship with regulators.

Join our Discord space

Join our Discord workspace for latest updates, offers, tech happenings around the world, new releases, and sessions with the authors:

https://discord.bpbonline.com

CHAPTER 10

Dealing with Regulatory Authorities under the DPDP Act

Introduction

In the field of data protection, how an organization engages with regulators can make all the difference between a cooperative resolution and a costly sanction. Under India's **Digital Personal Data Protection (DPDP)** Act 2023, the Data Protection Board of India (the regulatory authority) plays a pivotal role in enforcement. Data Fiduciary of the organizations that determine the purpose and means of processing personal data; must be prepared to work constructively with this Board at every step. Imagine a scenario where a company faces a personal data breach: the clock starts ticking as soon as the breach is discovered, and the company must swiftly notify the Board and affected individuals, launch an internal investigation, and fully cooperate with regulators. This chapter provides an instructional roadmap, with a narrative touch, on how to effectively deal with such regulatory authorities under the DPDP Act. We will explore the duties of Data Fiduciaries when interacting with the Board, outline breach notification procedures and complaint handling workflows, and discuss how organizations can gear up for inquiries through robust internal processes. By the end, you will see that dealing with regulators is not just about avoiding penalties; it is about building trust through accountability and transparency.

Structure

In this chapter, we will cover the following topics:

- Data Protection Board of India oversight
- Data Fiduciary Duties for Board Engagement
- Complaint handling process from grievance to Board inquiry
- Expectations from the Board
- Ensuring eDiscovery readiness, a 6-step approach
- Role of the DPO in regulatory engagement
- IT department preparedness for investigations
- Enforcement, penalties, and sanctions under DPDP Act

Objectives

This chapter aims to equip readers with a practical understanding of how to effectively engage with the Data Protection Board of India under the DPDP Act, 2023, and its Draft Rules, 2025. As data protection oversight in India becomes more structured and rigorous, organizations must go beyond surface-level compliance and be prepared for active regulatory engagement. Whether it is responding to a data breach, handling a complaint from a Data Principal, or cooperating in a formal inquiry, this chapter provides a step-by-step guide to managing interactions with the regulator.

You will learn about the Board's structure, powers, and expectations, the responsibilities of Data Fiduciaries, how to prepare for audits and investigations using tools like eDiscovery, and the vital role of the **Data Protection Officer** (**DPO**) in regulatory communications. We will explore how to build a compliance posture that is proactive, transparent, and resilient. Ultimately, this chapter empowers organizations to handle regulatory scrutiny professionally, minimize penalties, and reinforce trust through consistent, accountable data governance.

Data Protection Board of India oversight

The **Data Protection Board** (**DPB**) of India is the central regulatory authority established by the DPDP Act 2023 to enforce India's data protection law. It is the body that individuals (Data Principals) can turn to for grievances, and it is empowered to oversee and ensure organizations' compliance with the Act. The DPDP Act envisions the Board as an independent agency, though it is constituted by the Central Government. According to the Act, the Board's mandate includes monitoring compliance, imposing penalties for violations, and directing remedial measures in case of personal data breaches. Importantly, the Board cannot take action when a personal data breach occurs; it has the power to issue immediate remedial or mitigation directions to contain the breach's impact. This proactive power means that once you report a breach, the Board might quickly order you to implement certain fixes or safeguards (for example, to shut down a compromised system or inform stakeholders) even before any formal inquiry is completed.

The DPB also acts as an adjudicatory body for complaints. Data Principals who feel that a Data Fiduciary has violated their rights or not complied with obligations can approach the Board for redress. The Board can conduct inquiries into such complaints and issue binding decisions. In doing so, it is vested with the powers of a civil court; it can summon and inspect documents, issue orders, and hear testimony. The Board is expected to operate as a "digital office," meaning much of its complaint intake, hearings, and interactions will happen through online platforms. This digital-by-default approach aligns with India's broader push for tech-driven governance and should make it easier for organizations to engage with the regulator without physical appearances.

The constitution of the Board (as outlined in the Draft DPDP Rules 2025) ensures a mix of expertise and oversight. A Chairperson will head the Board, selected through a high-level committee (led by the Cabinet Secretary) to ensure independence and capability. Members of the Board are likewise chosen for their knowledge or experience in fields relevant to data protection. Once operational, the Board will publish procedures and may issue guidelines to clarify how organizations should comply with the law. Data Fiduciaries should stay abreast of any regulations or guidelines the Board releases, as these will detail practical aspects (for example, the format for breach notices or the process for submitting compliance reports).

In summary, the DPB is the chief regulator and enforcer of data protection norms in India. Its role encompasses: overseeing breach responses, adjudicating complaints, guiding implementation via rules, and penalizing non-compliance. Understanding the Board's powers and expectations is the first step for any organization aiming to maintain a good standing under the DPDP regime. Next, we turn to what *you*, as a Data Fiduciary, are responsible for when dealing with this regulatory authority.

Data Fiduciary Duties for Board Engagement

Under the DPDP Act, Data Fiduciaries carry significant responsibilities in their interactions with the DPB. These responsibilities can be viewed as an extension of an organization's overall compliance obligations; they ensure that if and when the regulator comes knocking, the organization is ready to respond appropriately. The key responsibilities include:

- **Establishing a grievance redressal mechanism:** Every Data Fiduciary must establish an effective internal grievance redressal mechanism for Data Principals (individuals). This means setting up a clear process (e.g., a helpdesk or portal) through which data subjects can lodge complaints about the Fiduciary's data practices or any violation of their rights. The DPDP explicitly requires that Data Principals exhaust the Data Fiduciary's grievance process before approaching the Board. In practice, a Fiduciary should ensure complaints are addressed within a reasonable timeframe and resolved to the Data Principal's satisfaction. The Draft Rules 2025 even mandate that organizations publicly publish their typical grievance resolution timelines on their website/app, underscoring the importance of timely redress. To fulfill this responsibility, Data Fiduciaries should designate a suitable officer or team to handle data protection complaints. For Significant Data Fiduciaries (those classified based on volume/sensitivity of data and risk levels), the law requires the appointment of a DPO who will serve as the point of contact for grievance redressal. It is advisable to ensure the DPO is a CxO level officer. Other fiduciaries must at least provide the contact information of a person (sometimes referred to as a "privacy officer") who can answer data subject queries and assist in grievance resolution. By proactively resolving issues through an internal mechanism, Data Fiduciaries demonstrate compliance and reduce the likelihood of escalations to the Board.

- **Cooperating with investigations**: If a complaint is escalated or the Board initiates an inquiry (for instance, into a data breach or violation), Data Fiduciaries are expected to fully cooperate with the investigation. The Board operates with powers akin to a civil court; it can summon individuals, call for documents, and take evidence on oath. In engaging with the Board, a Data Fiduciary must promptly comply with any notices or summons for information that are issued to them. This includes producing relevant records (audit logs, data processing records, policies, etc.) and allowing examination of systems or documents as needed. The DPDPA requires that the DPB follow the principles of natural justice (e.g., the Fiduciary will get an opportunity to be heard), but it is incumbent on the Fiduciary to respond truthfully and swiftly to the Board's queries. Cooperation also means facilitating any on-site inspections or assisting any officers deputed to investigate. Notably, the Board may co-opt police or government officials to aid in inquiries, so obstructing an investigation is not an option. A prudent Data Fiduciary will maintain transparency with regulators, for example, by voluntarily providing incident reports or audit findings, to show a collaborative stance. Being responsive and organized during investigations not only helps resolve issues faster but also reflects well on the Fiduciary's compliance culture, potentially mitigating penalties.

- **Appointing required roles (e.g., DPO) and maintaining records**: To engage effectively with the Board, Data Fiduciaries must have the right compliance roles and records in place. The DPDP Act introduces the concept of a **Significant Data Fiduciary (SDF)**, who has additional obligations. An SDF is required to appoint a DPO based in India and accountable to the Fiduciary's Board or governing body. The DPO represents the Fiduciary under the Act and is effectively the liaison for all data protection matters, including communications with the Board. SDFs must also appoint an independent data auditor and undertake measures like periodic Data Protection Impact Assessments, bolstering their compliance readiness. All Data Fiduciaries, whether significant or not, should maintain comprehensive records of their data processing activities and protection measures. This includes keeping logs of data access and transfers, records of consent and withdrawal, and documentation of security safeguards implemented.

In fact, the Draft Rules enumerate minimum security practices (such as encryption and access controls) and require maintaining logs for at least one year. Having these records readily available is crucial when the Board asks for evidence of compliance or during audits and investigations. Moreover, as per the rules, every Data Fiduciary must prominently publish the contact details of their DPO (or designated officer) on their website and in all privacy communications. This ensures that the Board (and the public) knows who to reach out to for any data protection concerns. In summary, by appointing the mandated personnel and diligently documenting compliance efforts, Data Fiduciaries can confidently engage with the Board and demonstrate accountability.

- **Notifying and updating the Board on data breaches:** One of the most critical obligations in the DPDP Act is the duty to report personal data breaches. Chapter II Section 8(6) of the Act requires that upon becoming aware of a personal data breach, the Data Fiduciary must inform *both* the Board *and* the affected Data Principals without undue delay. In practice, this means if a breach (e.g., a leak or unauthorized access of personal data) occurs, the organization should promptly send an intimation to the Board and notify individuals, following the prescribed format. The Draft Rules 2025 (Rule 7) provide detailed guidance on this process. Immediately, a brief notice should go out to impacted users in plain language describing the breach, its likely consequences for them, measures being taken, and advice on protecting themselves, along with a contact for further inquiries. Concurrently, the Fiduciary must inform the Board about the breach "without delay" with an initial description of its nature, scope, timing, and likely impact. Furthermore, within 72 hours of becoming aware of the breach (or within an extended period allowed by the Board), the Fiduciary is obligated to submit a more detailed report to the Board. This follow-up should include an explanation of the events that led to the incident, any identified causes or perpetrators, the remedial actions taken to contain and fix the issue, and steps being implemented to prevent future occurrences. It should also confirm that affected Data Principals have been notified as required. Proactive breach notification is not only a legal duty but also a sign of good faith; it allows the Board to monitor large-scale incidents and guide the Fiduciary on mitigation if needed (the Board can direct urgent remedial measures upon receiving a breach intimation). Failing to notify the Board or individuals about a breach can attract severe penalties (up to ₹200 crores as per the Schedule). Therefore, Data Fiduciaries must have internal breach response plans that include immediate Board communication. Keeping the Board updated on such key developments ensures transparency and can significantly influence the regulatory outcome.

- **Adhering to Board decisions and directions:** When the Board issues a decision, order, or direction to a Data Fiduciary, compliance is not optional; it is mandatory. The Board has broad authority to issue binding directions to ensure Data Fiduciaries fulfill their obligations under the Act. For example, the Board may direct a Fiduciary to take urgent mitigation action in response to a breach or to cease a certain processing activity found unlawful. Before issuing such directives, the Board will typically give the affected

Fiduciary an opportunity to be heard and will record its reasons in writing (reflecting natural justice). Once issued, however, the Fiduciary must promptly implement the instructions. This could involve making technical changes, providing specified information to Data Principals, or improving compliance processes as ordered. Data Fiduciaries should note that the Board can also impose conditions, modify, or cancel its directions based on new information or representations. If a Fiduciary believes a direction is unwarranted, it has the right to appeal the Board's order to the designated Appellate Tribunal (TDSAT) within 60 days. However, during the interim, unless a stay is obtained, the expectation is that the Fiduciary will adhere to the Board's decision. Ignoring or willfully disobeying a Board order not only breaches the law but could be treated as a fresh violation, inviting additional enforcement action. In essence, respect for the Board's rulings is a key responsibility. Data Fiduciaries should integrate the Board's feedback and directions into their operations and governance. This cooperative posture will help avoid compounding regulatory issues.

- **Consequences of non-compliance and repeat violations:** The DPDPA's enforcement framework makes it clear that non-compliance with the above responsibilities can lead to significant consequences. The Board is empowered to levy hefty monetary penalties for various failures, for instance, not providing a grievance mechanism, not cooperating with inquiries, or violating any provision of the Act, which can result in fines (the Act outlines tiered penalties up to ₹250 crore for certain breaches of obligations). Each incident (such as a data breach or failure to furnish information to the Board) may be counted separately for penalties. Beyond fines, repeated violations escalate the seriousness of enforcement. If a Data Fiduciary has been penalized more than twice for flouting data protection requirements, the Board may make a formal recommendation to the Central Government for stricter measures. Notably, Chapter IX, Section 37 of the Act empowers the Government to issue blocking orders in the interest of the general public. Upon receiving the Board's references (one confirming multiple penalties on the same Fiduciary, and another advising that blocking is necessary), the Central Government can direct intermediaries or agencies to block public access to the offending Data Fiduciary's information or services. In plain terms, a company that persistently disregards the law could find its app or website made inaccessible in India as a last resort. Before such an extreme step, the Fiduciary is given a chance to be heard, ensuring some procedural fairness. Nonetheless, the prospect of a blocking order underscores how critical compliance is; continuous defiance can literally put a business offline.

In summary, engaging with the Board is not merely a formality but a core part of a Data Fiduciary's compliance lifecycle. By proactively instituting grievance redressal channels, cooperating with investigations, appointing the required officers, staying transparent about breaches, and faithfully executing the Board's directives, Data Fiduciaries can maintain a constructive relationship with the regulator. This not only avoids penalties and drastic actions but also builds trust with users and regulators alike, ensuring that data protection obligations are met in both letter and spirit.

Complaint handling process from grievance to Board inquiry

Beyond data breaches, another primary function of the DPB is to address **complaints** from Data Principals (individuals). These complaints could be about anything; an individual might allege that a Data Fiduciary violated their rights (e.g., denied an access request unfairly), processed their data unlawfully, or otherwise not complied with the DPDP Act. Understanding the *flow of how a complaint is handled* will help organizations anticipate what to do at each stage. We will outline a six-step model, aligning it with both the DPDP framework and global practices.

1. Internal grievance redressal by the Data Fiduciary

The first step is in-house resolution. The DPDPA mandates that every Data Fiduciary (the entity handling personal data) establish an effective grievance redressal mechanism. A Data Principal who feels her data rights are infringed must initially lodge a complaint with the Data Fiduciary's designated officer or helpdesk. Under Chapter III, Section 13 of the Act, the Data Principal has a *"right to have readily available means of grievance redressal"* provided by the Fiduciary. The Fiduciary is legally obliged to respond to such grievances within a prescribed period. While the Act itself leaves the exact timeline to be prescribed by rules, the Draft DPDP Rules 2025 require Fiduciaries to publish clear timelines for resolving complaints and to implement technical and organizational measures to meet those deadlines. This ensures that complaints are not ignored or indefinitely delayed, reinforcing accountability. For example, a social media company might promise to resolve data deletion requests within 15 days and must have processes in place to achieve that. Importantly, the Data Principal must exhaust this internal remedy before approaching the Board; a legal prerequisite that encourages amicable resolution at the source. In practice, Data Fiduciaries should maintain a grievance register and appoint a DPO or dedicated contact (as required by Section 8) to handle complaints. Clearly published help channels (email, portal, etc.) and prompt, reasoned decisions on complaints not only fulfill legal duties but also serve as evidence of good faith if the matter escalates.

2. Filing a complaint with the DPB

If the Data Fiduciary's response is unsatisfactory or the prescribed time lapses without resolution, the Data Principal may escalate the issue to the Data Protection Board of India. Chapter III Section 13(3) explicitly allows the Data Principal to approach the Board after the internal route is tried. The DPDPA envisions the Board as an independent digital office for enforcement. Complaints to the Board are filed in writing (likely via an online portal, since the Board's operations are *"digital by design"* for receiving complaints and conducting hearings). The complaint should detail the grievance, for instance, how the Fiduciary violated obligations (e.g., wrongful denial of a correction request or a personal data breach). Under Chapter VI Section 27(1)(b), the Board is empowered to Act *"on a complaint made by a Data Principal in respect of a personal data breach or a breach in observance by a Data Fiduciary of its obligations... or the exercise of her rights under the Act"*. In essence, any failure by the Fiduciary to meet its duties (whether not fulfilling a data rights request, lacking a valid consent, or causing a data breach) can be brought before the Board. The Draft Rules 2025 are expected to prescribe the manner of filing (as indicated by the Act's requirement that consent notices inform individuals *"the manner in which the Data Principal may make a complaint to the Board"*. Upon a proper complaint, the Board will notify the concerned Data Fiduciary (or other opposite party) and prepare to assess the case.

Example*:* A user whose request to erase her data was ignored by a fintech app could file a complaint to the Board. She would submit evidence of her request and the company's inaction. The Board's digital system would register the complaint and send a notice to the fintech company, initiating the formal process.

3. Initial assessment by the Board

Upon receiving a complaint (or a referral, or data breach report), the Board undertakes a prima facie assessment. By law, the Board must determine whether the complaint has "sufficient grounds" to proceed with an inquiry. This acts as a filtering stage to weed out baseless or non-jurisdictional issues. If the Board finds the complaint lacks merit or does not fall under the Act, it can close the matter with recorded reasons in writing. For instance, if a complaint is about a non-personal data issue or filed against an entity not covered by DPDPA, the Board may dismiss it at this stage. The Act emphasizes that every decision not to proceed must be justified in writing, ensuring transparency and allowing the complainant to see why it was closed. Conversely, if the Board finds the grievance credible and within scope, it will formally initiate an inquiry, documenting the grounds for proceeding. All actions of the Board must adhere to principles of natural justice, meaning both sides get a fair chance to be heard, and all orders are reasoned. Notably, the law builds in a safeguard against abuse of process: if at any stage a complaint appears to be false or frivolous, the Board may warn the complainant or impose costs for misusing the system. This deters bad-faith complaints while encouraging genuine grievances to be raised without fear.

Best practice*:* For a smooth assessment, the Data Principal should present clear facts and any evidence (e.g., copies of emails with the Fiduciary) in the complaint. Data Fiduciaries, on their part, should be prepared to demonstrate that they addressed the grievance properly. Prompt cooperation at this stage can sometimes lead the Board to resolve the issue without a protracted inquiry (for example, the Fiduciary might offer to settle or comply upon notice, potentially leading the Board to close the case with a warning or advice).

4. Formal inquiry and investigation by the Board

When the Board proceeds with a complaint, it conducts a formal inquiry akin to a quasi-judicial proceeding. The Board has robust investigative powers, almost mirroring a civil court. Under Chapter VI Section 28(7), the Board can summon and examine witnesses under oath, demand affidavits or document production, and inspect any relevant data or records.

In practice, the Board may issue notices to the Data Fiduciary (or other involved parties) to submit information, produce logs, agreements, or any evidence required to ascertain compliance. The proceedings remain guided by principles of natural justice; the accused party is given due notice of the allegations and an opportunity to respond at every stage. Both the complainant and the opposite party can present their arguments, and any material the Board relies on is typically shared or made part of the record. The DPDPA explicitly requires that the Board record reasons for its actions during the inquiry, which means interim decisions (like extending the inquiry or requiring certain evidence) are documented, ensuring accountability.

During inquiries, the Board can also issue interim orders if necessary to prevent further harm. For example, if a major data breach is ongoing, the Board might direct the Data Fiduciary to immediately cease certain processing or take containment measures while the investigation continues. Before any interim order, the affected person or company is given a chance to be heard, and the order must be reasoned. This balances urgency with fairness.

Crucially, the Board's authority has limits to protect against overreach. The Act clarifies that the Board (or its officers) cannot raid premises or seize equipment on its own. Unlike a police investigation, the Board cannot, for instance, barge into a company's office and confiscate servers. If such enforcement action is needed (said, to prevent evidence destruction), the Board must enlist the help of law enforcement or other government officers. Chapter VI Section 28(9) empowers the Board to request assistance from police or government officials for executing its inquiry, and those officials are legally bound to assist. This means the Board can ensure compliance with its investigation (like securing digital evidence) through proper channels while respecting the rule of law; the Board itself remains a civilian body focusing on adjudication.

Throughout the inquiry, the Board maintains an impartial stance, functioning digitally (hearings might be via video conference or online submissions) and following a predefined procedure (the Draft Rules detail aspects like how meetings are recorded, etc., under a "techno-legal" framework). This stage ends when the Board is satisfied, it has all the facts, and both sides have been heard.

Example: Suppose a Data Principal complained that a healthcare app violated her rights by selling her data without consent. In the inquiry, the Board may summon the app's management to testify under oath, require production of data-sharing contracts, and inspect the app's data logs. If needed, the Board could issue an interim order for the app to stop sharing any personal data during the investigation. The Board might also ask a government forensic expert to assist in analyzing whether a data transfer took place, rather than seizing the company's servers itself. All through this, the app operators get to present their defense (perhaps claiming consent was taken), and the complainant can provide rebuttals or additional evidence.

5. Decision, enforcement, and appeal

After the inquiry, the Board deliberates and reaches a final decision. If no violation is found, the Board will close the proceedings and document the reasons for exoneration. However, if the inquiry establishes that the Data Fiduciary (or other party) breached the law, the Board will proceed under Chapter VIII Section 33 to impose remedial orders and penalties. The DPDPA empowers the Board to levy monetary penalties according to a tiered Schedule based on the nature of the violation. For instance, failing to implement reasonable security safeguards (leading to a data breach) can attract a fine of up to ₹250 crore, reflecting the seriousness of cybersecurity lapses. The Board's order will typically specify the provision violated (e.g., Section 8 on security, or Section 9 on children's data), the penalty amount or corrective action required, and a deadline for compliance. All penalties are payable to the government (credited to India's Consolidated Fund as per Section 34). The decision may also include directions like requiring the Fiduciary to cease a violating process, delete unlawful data, or adopt certain measures to prevent future harm. Due process is evident in this final stage as well: the order is a written, reasoned document issued to all parties, and the Board cannot exceed the maximum penalty limits set by law. If the Data Principal's complaint is upheld, she receives a sense of vindication (though notably, the Act provides for penalties payable to the state, not direct compensation to individuals). If the complaint is rejected or only a warning is given, the Data Principal is informed of the outcome and reasons.

Enforcement of the Board's order is backed by legal force. While the Board itself is not a court, its penalties and directions are binding. A non-compliant Fiduciary could face further legal action or increased penalties. The Act also has a concept of "voluntary undertaking" (Section 32), at any stage, even post-decision, a Data Fiduciary might propose a compliance plan which, if accepted by the Board, halts further proceedings. For example, a company might voluntarily pledge to overhaul its data security within 60 days under Board supervision. If the Board accepts this undertaking, it is recorded and enforceable; failure to fulfill it would itself count as a breach with its own penalties. This mechanism encourages remedial compliance over adversarial punishment.

Both Data Principals and Data Fiduciaries are given the right to appeal the Board's decision. Under Chapter VII Section 29, any person aggrieved by an order of the Board can approach the designated Appellate Tribunal (the **Telecom Disputes Settlement and Appellate Tribunal,** **(TDSAT)**) within 60 days of receiving the Board's order. The appeal process is designed to be user-friendly and digital as well; filings can be online, and hearings via video, mirroring the Board's digital approach. The Appellate Tribunal re-examines the case, affording both parties a fresh opportunity to present their arguments. It has the power to confirm, modify, or set aside the Board's order after hearing both sides in accordance with the law. Importantly, the law urges swift justice: The Tribunal is expected to endeavor to dispose of the appeal within six months, and if it cannot, it must record reasons for the delay (to discourage slow attrition of justice). The Tribunal's orders are given teeth by treating them as equivalent to a civil court decree for execution purposes (meaning, for example, any fine upheld by the Tribunal can be recovered as if it were a court judgment).

After the Tribunal's decision, a further *appeal to the Supreme Court of India* is available on specific legal grounds. The Act channels this through Section 18 of the TRAI Act, 1997, which typically allows a final appeal on *substantial questions of law*. In practice, this means that if either party believes the Tribunal made a legal error (for instance, misinterpreted a definition in the Act), they can petition the Supreme Court. The Supreme Court appeal must usually be filed within 90 days of the Tribunal's order, and the Court will decide if the question raised is significant enough to be heard. No further appeal lies from the Supreme Court's judgment, making it the conclusive end of the journey.

Throughout this 5-step journey, the DPDPA and its rules build in *due process and compliance best practices*: clear timelines and responsibilities at the Fiduciary level, an empowered yet accountable Board with investigative powers tempered by natural justice, and a multi-tiered review system (Tribunal and Supreme Court) to ensure fairness. Data Principals are advised to follow the steps in order, first contact the Fiduciary, then escalate, and to maintain records of all communications. Data Fiduciaries, on the other hand, should treat internal grievances with utmost seriousness (both to comply with the law and possibly to avoid the escalated scrutiny of the Board). By adhering to this structured process, both individuals and organizations contribute to an ecosystem where digital personal data is protected through *responsive grievance handling and rule-of-law-based enforcement*. Each step in this journey reinforces trust in the system, from prompt resolution of minor issues to rigorous inquiries into serious violations, ultimately upholding the data protection rights envisioned by the DPDPA 2023.

Expectations from the Board

The DPB of India is vested with sweeping powers under the DPDPA, acting as the chief compliance overseer. The key powers include:

- **Inquiry into data breaches:** The Board can initiate inquiries on a written complaint about any personal data breach, summoning the accused Fiduciary for clarification.

- **Urgent remediation directions:** In an ongoing breach or crisis, the DPB may order immediate containment or mitigation measures by the Data Fiduciary (including interim orders) to protect affected Data Principals.

- **Inquiry into personal data breaches:** One of the Board's core mandates is to probe breaches of personal data and determine compliance with the Act.

- **Impose penalties:** Under Chapter VIII Section 33, the Board can levy fines on Data Fiduciaries or Data Principals for non-compliance. In doing so, the Board must consider factors like severity of the offense, cybersecurity safeguards, breach notification, and validity of consent.

- **Oversight of Consent Managers:** On complaint, the Board can investigate failures or inconsistencies by registered Consent Managers (entities managing opt-in consents) in observing duties or registration conditions and impose penalties if needed.

- **Enforce intermediary cooperation:** If directed by the Central Government, the Board may require an intermediary (e.g., social media platform) to furnish information or even penalize it under the Act.

Each DPB action must follow the principles of natural justice, both parties get a hearing and written reasons are recorded, and every order can be appealed (ultimately to TDSAT under the TRAI Act). In sum, the Board is empowered to investigate complaints, summon evidence, direct remedies or penalties, and oversee consent infrastructure, making it the central hub for enforcing data compliance. The following are the key operational themes in the Draft Rules that flesh out how the Board shall apply these principles in practice:

- **Timeline for implementation:** The Draft Rules stipulate a phased rollout. The establishment of the Board itself takes effect immediately upon notification of the Rules in the Official Gazette. In practice, this means the Board will be constituted promptly, even if other provisions are delayed. Reports indicate the government plans a long transition, on the order of roughly two years, for businesses to achieve full compliance. In other words, while the Board and basic framework kick in at once, many obligations (e.g., updated notices, privacy processes) may have later compliance dates. Data Fiduciaries should therefore prepare their programs now, but note that enforcement is being phased in.

- **Digital and efficient operations:** Consistent with a *digitalbydesign* ethos, the Rules explicitly require the DPB to operate as a fully electronic office. Rule 19 states *The Board shall function as a digital office, which, without prejudice to its power to summon and enforce the attendance of any person and examine her on oath, may adopt techno-legal measures to conduct proceedings in a manner that does not require the physical presence of any individual.* In practical terms, all hearings, complaints, and orders will be handled electronically. Parties can participate virtually; evidence and filings move through secure portals; and the Board can issue directives online. This digital-first approach aims to make DPB processes faster and more accessible (saving travel and wait times). Data Fiduciaries should expect all interactions with the Board, from breach notifications to hearings, to be handled through online systems and portals.

- **Natural justice and fair hearings:** Both the Act and Rules underscore that DPB proceedings will be fair and transparent. Every inquiry must follow *principles of natural justice*. In practice, this means: The Board must give affected parties notice and a chance to be heard, record its findings in writing, and explain any decision or order. Chapter VI Section 28(6) of the Act explicitly requires that the Board *"shall conduct such inquiry following the principles of natural justice and shall record reasons for its actions"*. Moreover, during an inquiry, the Board may issue interim orders (e.g., for mitigation) *after* giving the party a hearing. Ultimately, when the investigation concludes, the Board will again hear the concerned party before finalizing whether to impose sanctions or close the case. Data Fiduciaries should therefore plan for a formal adjudication process with written submissions, the opportunity to contest evidence, and prompt written decisions.

- **Civil court powers and non-intrusive inspections**: For fact-finding, the DPB wields robust investigative powers akin to a civil court. Under Chapter VI Section 28(7), the Board can summon individuals, enforce their attendance, administer oaths, and require the production of affidavits and documents. It can also inspect data, books, registers, accounts, or any documents relevant to a case. In short, the Board can compel witnesses and sift through records to uncover compliance gaps. Importantly, however, these inspection powers are *non-intrusive*. The Act flatly prohibits the Board or its officers from seizing premises or taking custody of equipment that would disrupt an entity's normal operations. If necessary, the Board can requisition assistance from police or other government officers to carry out inspections or enforce orders. Compliance officers should prepare to answer lawful summons and to furnish requested records electronically, while maintaining operational continuity.

- **False or frivolous complaints:** The DPDP Act discourages baseless complaints. Chapter VI Section 28(12) empowers the Board to penalize complainants for misusing the process: if the Board deems a complaint *false or frivolous*, it may issue a warning or impose costs on the complainant. (Data Principals also bear a duty not to lodge spurious grievances under the Act.) This means the Board will critically vet every complaint. Data Fiduciaries should note that vexatious or unfounded claims may backfire; conversely, genuine complaints will be treated seriously. In practice, complainants will need to show credible evidence of a breach or non-compliance. The possibility of cost awards should encourage Data Fiduciaries to maintain clear records and transparent practices (so that meritless claims can be swiftly dismissed).

- **Mediation and Alternative Dispute Resolution (ADR):** The Act actively encourages early resolution of disputes. Chapter VII Section 31 authorizes the Board to refer cases to mediation or similar ADR mechanisms whenever a complaint appears amenable to such resolution. In other words, if both parties agree, the DPB can direct them to attempt a negotiated settlement under its auspices. This provision aims to save time and resources by steering straightforward disputes away from full adjudication. For example, if a Data Principal complains about minor nonnotice issues, the Board might suggest a one-time corrective undertaking rather than a drawn-out hearing. Data Fiduciaries should therefore be prepared to engage constructively in mediation through the Board, and to propose or accept voluntary undertakings (binding promises to fix a problem) when appropriate. The availability of ADR means that not all issues will end in penalties; many may be resolved with agreed-upon remedies.

- **Coordination with other laws and agencies:** The DPB does not operate in a vacuum. The Act preserves the primacy of other legal frameworks and enables cross-agency cooperation. For one, appeals from DPB orders go to the TDSAT under the TRAI Act, integrating with the existing regulatory structure. The Board may also cooperate with law enforcement and sector regulators as needed. Notably, the Act explicitly allows the Board to seek help from police or any government officer in its inquiries. Thus, if a cybercrime or national security issue overlaps with a privacy complaint, the DPB can coordinate with agencies like CERT-In or police cyber units. Likewise, the government can direct the Board or intermediaries under certain conditions (e.g., blocking orders). Data Fiduciaries should ensure that their compliance teams can also navigate other applicable laws (IT Act, sectoral regulations, etc.) and coordinate with external authorities when DPB inquiries touch on those domains.

- **Quality of notices and consent mechanisms:** One clear theme of the Draft Rules is greater transparency and granularity in notices and consent management. Data Fiduciaries will have to meet higher standards: the privacy *notice* must be a standalone document written in plain language, separate from other terms. It must clearly itemize each category of personal data collected and explicitly tie each to its specified purpose and the related goods or services. In effect, notice content is not an afterthought; it must give Data Principals a fair, easy-to-understand account of *what* and *why* (with each data type linked to each purpose). The Rules also require including a simple, accessible mechanism (e.g., a web link) for a Data Principal to withdraw consent and exercise rights. Similarly, Consent Managers (if used) will have to be properly registered and will face audit-like obligations. Overall, the Board will expect that notices and consent processes are robust, precise, and user-friendly. Data Fiduciaries should audit their notices and consent flows now, ensuring they meet the draft prescriptions (itemized data lists, clear purposes, easy opt-outs) and be ready to publish the required contact information for the DPO.

In summary, the Board under the DPDPA will be a powerful, digitally enabled regulator. The Draft Rules signal that it will act quickly (via immediate establishment and online operations) but also fairly (hearing all sides, allowing **Alternate Dispute Resolution (ADR)**). It will wield civilcourt–style powers to investigate breaches, yet may resolve many complaints through mediation or corrective orders. Data Fiduciaries should align their compliance programs to these expectations: prepare clear notices and consent records, build electronic reporting channels (especially for breaches), maintain organized audit trails, and get ready to engage with the Board's online processes. Doing so will ensure smoother interactions with the regulator and avoid penalties or enforcement surprises.

Ensuring eDiscovery readiness, a 6-step approach

Electronic discovery (eDiscovery) refers to the process of identifying, collecting, and producing electronically stored information for legal or regulatory purposes. Organizations of all sizes, from large enterprises to small firms, must be prepared to handle regulatory investigations under India's DPDP Act, 2023, and its Draft Rules 2025. A robust eDiscovery readiness plan ensures that if the DPB or other authorities inquire into your data practices, you can respond quickly, completely, and in compliance with the law. The following six steps, identification, preservation, collection, processing, review and analysis, and production, provide a structured approach to navigate a DPB investigation or data breach inquiry while upholding due process, maintaining the chain of custody, and safeguarding data security and privacy at every stage. Here is a six-step eDiscovery process tailored for regulatory investigations:

1. **Identification:** Long before any issue arises, know your data landscape. This means mapping out what types of data you have, where they reside, and who the "custodians" of that data are. For example, customer personal data might be in a CRM database, HR data in an HRMS system, emails on an Exchange server, and logs in an IT logging system. Identification also involves determining what data might be relevant to different types of inquiries. If a complaint is about consent, relevant data might include consent records in your database, the consent form text, and any related emails. If it is a breach inquiry, relevant data includes incident logs, security audit reports, and communication with affected users. Essentially, step 1 is about creating a data map and an index of potential evidence sources. When the Board's notice comes, you will use this map to pinpoint where to collect information. Many companies perform periodic drills or tabletop exercises to practice this identification step, which can reveal gaps (e.g., "We realize we have no easy way to search chat messages for relevant info; maybe we need a tool for that."). Modern data governance solutions and data inventories also help. The bottom line: you cannot gather what you have not first discovered exists. As the saying goes, *If you do not know where your data is, protecting it becomes a significant challenge,* and by extension, finding it for an investigation is equally challenging.

2. **Preservation:** Once you know what data might be relevant, the next step is preservation. This means making sure that data is not accidentally deleted or altered once an investigation is anticipated. In legal terms, this is often called issuing a "legal hold." For example, if a complaint triggers an inquiry, you might need to instruct your IT team to preserve all emails between certain dates or not to purge certain logs that would normally be overwritten. Under DPDP, there is no explicit concept of legal hold, but failing to preserve evidence could lead to trouble (like not being able to demonstrate compliance, or worse, being seen as destroying evidence). So, treat the moment you receive a notice from the Board as the moment to freeze relevant data. Many email and document management systems have features to place content on hold (preventing deletion). Coordinating with IT is critical here: let us say logs rotate every seven days; you might ask IT to immediately back up the current log set and stop rotation until you have made copies. Preservation can also include snapshots of databases or systems as of a certain date. By preserving in step 2, you create a safety net so that when you move to collection and analysis, you are not missing pieces due to routine data lifecycle processes.

3. **Collection:** Now comes the gathering of the preserved data. In the collection phase, you pull together all the identified information into a centralized repository or a review platform. This can be a technical task, for instance, exporting emails to PST files, querying databases for relevant records, downloading system logs, etc. It is important to maintain a chain of custody, document what you collected, from where, and when, to show the data's integrity. In a regulatory context, you might not need to prove chain of custody as formally as in a court, but it is still wise to maintain rigor (the Board could question authenticity if something seems odd). A common challenge is volume:

raw collections can be huge (thousands of emails or millions of log lines). This is where having eDiscovery tools or specialists helps. Microsoft Purview, for example, includes eDiscovery tools that can search across email, Teams chats, SharePoint, etc., and collect responsive data. Aim to collect broadly but also try to filter obvious irrelevance if you can (for example, by date range or keyword). However, be careful not to filter too narrowly and miss something. It is better to over-collect and then cull down in the next step. For example, if a complaint concerns events in March, you might still collect data from February and April if context is needed. All collected items should be securely stored, as they may contain personal data. Limit access to this raw data to your core investigation team.

4. **Processing:** After raw data collection, processing involves organizing and reducing the data to make the review manageable. This can include de-duplication (removing duplicate files or emails), converting files into readable formats (like turning proprietary log formats or email archives into PDF or text), and indexing for search. For instance, if you collected 10GB of email data, processing might weed out duplicate email threads and only keep unique content, then index the text for keyword searches. Processing can also entail applying filters like date ranges or keywords to narrow down the dataset if that was not fully done during collection. Specialized eDiscovery software or services often handle this step, ensuring that the data set you have is both comprehensive and not cluttered with wholly irrelevant material. Think of it as preparing the evidence; you are creating a focused library of the information that matters. In some regulatory cases, you might also be asked to produce data in a specific format (e.g., "Provide logs in CSV format" or *Provide communications in chronological order*). During processing, you can organize data to meet such requirements. For example, you might separate documents into categories: one folder for policy documents, one for communications, one for system logs, etc., to help the Board (and yourself) navigate them.

5. **Review and analysis:** With a refined data set, your internal team (often legal, compliance, and relevant subject matter experts) reviews the material. The goal here is twofold: *find the facts and assess your position.* You are looking at the evidence to piece together what happened in the case of an incident, or to check what was done in the case of a compliance issue. For example, reading through email threads might reveal who knew what and when during a breach response, or why a decision was made that is being challenged. At this stage, it is crucial to maintain the attorney-client privilege for any sensitive analysis. If your legal counsel is involved, their analysis documents should be kept privileged (not shared with the regulator unless necessary) so you can candidly assess risks. However, objective facts (like an email from one employee to another about disabling a security setting) are not privileged and would likely need to be disclosed if relevant. During review, flag the items that are key evidence, maybe a particular email is a "smoking gun," or a log entry shows exactly when unauthorized access happened. It is often useful to create a *chronology* of events from the evidence, which can then be the basis of your report or response to the Board. Analysis may also reveal areas where you lack evidence, which is itself a finding (e.g., "We do not have

logs from that period because none were kept"; the Board will want to know why). Identifying those gaps allows you to prepare explanations for them.

6. **Production (reporting to the Board):** This final step is delivering the relevant information and documents to the regulator. After your review, you should have a clear idea of what the Board would find important. You then produce (submit) the evidence as part of your official response or during the inquiry process. This could be in the form of a written *investigation report* summarizing findings, accompanied by exhibits (supporting documents, communications, screenshots, etc.). It is often effective to present the Board with a well-structured report that tells the story (if it is a breach, outline timeline, cause, impact, actions taken; if it is a compliance issue, explain what happened and why, and what you are doing to fix it) and reference the evidence. For example, we received the data deletion request on Jan 5, and due to an internal ticketing error, it was not processed (See Exhibit B: Incident ticket screenshot). On discovering this, we immediately deleted the data on Mar 1 and have since revised our process. We apologize for the delay. By doing this, you help the Board quickly see the facts with proof. When handing over documents, follow any format guidelines the Board gives (they might say "submit all documents in PDF" or use their portal to upload). Keep an index of what you provided. Importantly, produce *only what is asked or what is necessary to demonstrate compliance*; do not overshare unrelated confidential information. However, do not *hide* anything that is directly relevant, as that could backfire if the Board discovers it by other means or perceives you as withholding. After production, be ready for follow-up questions.

By following these six steps, an organization can systematically tackle any information request from the regulator. To make this concrete, consider a quick example: The Board asks, *Provide evidence that you obtained consent from Mr. X before processing his data, and detail your processing of his data.* Using the steps: You identify that Mr. X's data and consent records are in your database and emails (step 1), preserve his records so nothing gets deleted (step 2), collect his consent form and data records (step 3), process by exporting them in a readable format (step 4), review them to ensure they show proper consent and usage (step 5), and produce a small report to the Board with those records attached (step 6). Being adept at eDiscovery will also impress upon the Board that you are organized and control your data; it reflects well on your overall governance.

Role of the DPO in regulatory engagement

Under India's DPDP Act, 2023, SDFs must appoint a DPO to oversee data compliance. The DPO serves as the central liaison between the organization's leadership, its data teams, and external regulators. As the named representative under Chapter II Section 10, the DPO is based in India and is explicitly responsible to the Board of Directors or similar governing body. In practice, this means the DPO briefs senior management on privacy risks and regulatory developments, reporting directly to the Board on data governance. By law, the DPO also acts as the official point of contact for Data Principals (customers) to raise grievances or queries.

This central role is visualized in *Figure 10.1* with the DPO at the center linking to internal and external stakeholders:

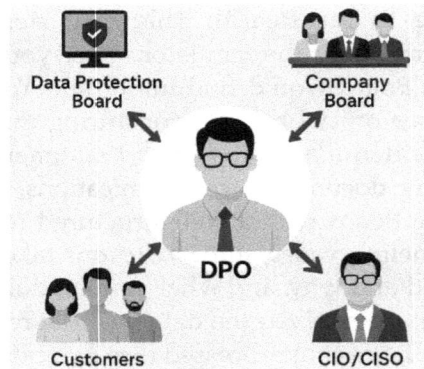

Figure 10.1: DPO Interaction across internal and external stakeholders

The explanation is as follows:

- **Primary point of contact with the Board:** The DPDPA explicitly makes the DPO the organization's representative under the Act. In regulatory terms, the DPO is the primary point of contact with the DPB and other authorities. Whenever the DPB issues notices, directions, or inquiry orders (for example, on a data breach), the DPO coordinates the response. This includes promptly notifying the DPB of any data breach as required by the law and then working with senior management to implement any urgent remedial or mitigation measures ordered by the Board. By acting as the "face" of the company in dealings with the DPB, the DPO ensures that all communications are accurate, timely, and approved by the Board. The DPO must keep the Board of Directors informed of any major regulatory correspondence or compliance lapses, fulfilling the statutory mandate that the DPO be answerable to the governing body.

- **Internal coordinator for investigations:** When a privacy incident or regulatory inquiry arises, the DPO takes charge of the internal investigation. The DPO convenes cross-functional teams, including IT, security, and legal, to gather facts and evidence. For example, in the event of a suspected breach, the DPO works with the CIO/CISO and IT staff to collect system logs, identify affected data, and reconstruct events. At the same time, the DPO engages legal and privacy teams to assess regulatory obligations. This is because the Data Protection Board has the power to inquire into breaches or noncompliance, and the DPO's coordination is crucial. The DPO makes sure that internal investigations are thorough and documented so the organization can satisfy any DPB inquiries or audits. In dealing with complaints from Data Principals (customers), the DPO also manages or oversees internal grievance procedures and escalates unresolved issues to the Board if needed. By bridging between operational teams and compliance/legal functions, the DPO ensures that investigations and evidence gathering are conducted under professional and legal standards.

- **Ensuring eDiscovery and documentation:** A key part of regulatory readiness is **documentation**. The DPO establishes and enforces processes for recordkeeping, so that all data processing activities are logged and retrievable. This includes maintaining an inventory of personal data holdings, records of processing activities, and evidence of compliance, such as consent records and DPIA results. In practice, when a Data Protection Board inquiry or court process demands disclosure of documents, the DPO ensures the organization can perform eDiscovery, quickly locating and producing the relevant data and files. For example, if a Data Principal appeals or complains about a breach, the DPO oversees the collection of the relevant notices, policies, and technical logs to respond to the complaint. Maintaining a culture of documentation also helps the DPO track past incidents and remedial steps, which is important if the DPB issues repeat inquiries. Although the Act focuses on outcomes rather than mandatory formats, the DPO typically implements internal guidelines (and in many cases, the Draft Rules will later specify details) to retain logs of access, audit reports, and breach notifications. By ensuring all investigations, the Board communications, and breach responses are fully documented, the DPO helps the company demonstrate accountability in any regulatory review.

- **Driving remediation and compliance improvements:** Beyond reactive tasks, the DPO proactively drives compliance improvements. Under Chapter II Section 10, Significant Data Fiduciaries must conduct periodic **Data Protection Impact Assessments (DPIAs)** and audits. In practice, the DPO often leads these exercises or oversees outside auditors, then reports the findings to the Board. When audits or DPB feedback reveal gaps, for example, inadequate access controls or unclear consent processes, the DPO ensures that remedial action plans are developed and implemented. The DPO works with the CIO/CISO and IT teams to improve security measures and with business owners to update policies and training. Since the DPO reports to senior management, they can push for resources and attention to fix compliance issues. In short, the DPO translates regulatory and audit requirements into operational changes: tightening system protections, revising privacy notices, enhancing user consent flows, and improving **incident response (IR)** procedures. By closing the loop on every internal finding or DPB directive, the DPO helps the organization continually advance its data protection maturity.

- **Advocate for Data Protection within the organization:** Finally, the DPO serves as an **internal champion** of privacy and data protection culture. This means educating and advising all levels of the organization, from developers and data analysts up to executives and the Board, about legal obligations under the DPDPA. The DPO coordinates regular training with HR and legal to ensure employees understand data handling rules and breach protocols. With legal and privacy operations teams, the DPO also develops or updates policies, such as consent frameworks and data retention policies, to stay aligned with the Act. DPO's advocacy includes working closely with the CIO/CISO on privacybydesign: for example, embedding data minimization into new IT projects or ensuring vendors meet the Act's standards. By highlighting the importance of data protection at Board meetings and leadership forums, the DPO helps secure executive buy-in. In all these ways, the DPO ensures that compliance is not siloed but is a strategic priority.

Throughout all responsibilities, the DPO engages with both internal stakeholders (Senior Management/Board, CIO/CISO, Legal/Privacy teams) and external stakeholders (Data Protection Board, Data Principals). This central coordination role, shown in the diagram above, reinforces the DPO's mandate to represent the organization under the DPDPA and to enable continuous regulatory compliance.

IT department preparedness for investigations

When facing a regulator's questions, much of the heavy lifting often falls on the IT and information security teams. They are the ones who possess the keys to the data vault, so to speak. The IT department's preparedness can significantly influence how quickly and accurately you can respond to the Data Protection Board. We will discuss the key aspects of IT readiness in the coming sections.

Robust logging and monitoring

IT should ensure comprehensive logging of all critical events (user access, admin actions, application usage, and security alerts). Each log entry should capture *who* performed the action, *what* was done, *when* (timestamp), and the outcome (success/failure). These audit trails provide *system transparency and accountability* by recording *who did what and when*. In practice, this means enabling built-in logging in databases, servers, cloud platforms, and security appliances. To operationalize robust logging and monitoring, focus on the following essential elements:

- **Log types and content:** Record user logins, permission changes, file access/ modifications, configuration changes, and system errors. Include details like user ID, IP address, event type, and timestamps.

- **Retention policies:** Define log retention based on legal requirements. For example, Microsoft Purview Audit (Premium) retains key audit logs (Exchange, SharePoint, Azure AD, etc.) for at least one year by default, with options to retain up to ten years. (As a rule of thumb, many regulations call for retaining logs a year or more.) Use tiered storage or archiving as needed.

- **Real-time monitoring:** Use SIEM or log analytics tools to continuously analyze logs and trigger alerts on unusual patterns (multiple failed logins, abnormal data transfers, etc.). Automated anomaly detection helps spot potential issues early.

- **Searchable audit trail:** Aggregate logs into a central audit system. For Microsoft 365, for example, the Microsoft Purview Audit solution captures thousands of user and admin activities across Teams, Exchange, SharePoint, OneDrive, etc., and retains them in a unified, searchable audit log. Investigators can query this log to trace user actions across the organization.

Incident response capability

IT must work within a documented IR program that includes the steps, roles, and timelines for handling breaches. This plan should be written, approved by management, and aligned with legal obligations (e.g., DPDPA breach-notification rules). For example, the law requires notifying the Data Protection Board within 72 hours of discovering a personal data breach, so the IR plan must enable rapid detection, analysis, and reporting. Key building blocks of an effective incident-response program include the following:

- **Formal IR plan:** Develop an IR policy and playbook covering detection, analysis, containment, eradication, and recovery. Define clear roles and responsibilities (including IT, security, DPO, legal, PR, etc.) at each phase. Specify communication paths (internal and external) and approval processes, so no time is lost figuring out who does what.

- **Cross-functional team:** Establish a response team that spans IT, security operations, legal/compliance, communications, and senior management. Cross-team collaboration reduces delays and confusion. As one guide notes, an incident *affects more than just the engineering team, [it] puts customer trust, legal standing, and financial stability on the line,* so involving stakeholders early is crucial.

- **Drills and exercises:** Test the IR plan with regular tabletop and live simulations. Conducting mock incidents, phishing exercises, or red-team drills helps the team practice coordination and identify gaps. Industry best practices recommend *running regular IR drills and simulations*, and forming an incident team in advance. It is far better to find workflow errors in an exercise than during a real breach.

- **Post-incident reviews:** After any real or simulated incident, hold a post-mortem to document what happened, analyze root causes, and update procedures. NIST and IR experts emphasize capturing *lessons learned* and improving the IR plan iteratively. This continuous improvement ensures the IR capability matures over time.

- **Regulatory workflows:** Prepare to manage multiple concurrent actions. After a breach, IT may need to preserve forensic evidence, notify authorities (and affected users), fulfill audit obligations, and assist law enforcement or the Data Protection Board, all on a tight deadline. Predefined processes and checklists (digital evidence preservation, legal notifications, breach reporting, etc.) help IT coordinate these complex workflows.

Data inventory and discovery tools

For quick responses to investigations or data requests, IT should maintain an up-to-date inventory of where personal data resides. This involves using data-mapping tools and classification: scanning data stores, labeling personal data, and cataloging systems. For example,

Microsoft Purview's data map can automatically scan on-premises and cloud data sources (databases, file shares, SaaS apps, etc.) and index their metadata for search and classification. Keeping this metadata current means the organization can quickly answer questions like *In which systems is XYZ's personal data stored?* To keep investigations swift and defensible, your data-inventory strategy should address the following essentials:

- **Real-time data mapping:** Continuously update a data inventory (a "map") with data locations, types, and sensitivity. An automated catalog (e.g., Azure Purview / Microsoft Purview) ensures new data sources or changes are recorded.

- **Metadata and lineage:** Record who owns each data asset and how it flows between systems. This helps trace data back to its source if needed. Data lineage and tagging (e.g., marking columns as personal information) further speed up discovery.

- **Search and eDiscovery:** Use content search tools for targeted retrieval. For instance, Microsoft Purview eDiscovery allows IT to run search queries across Exchange mailboxes, Teams chat, SharePoint/OneDrive files, and more. Investigators can identify and export all content that matches keywords or metadata filters. eDiscovery tools can also place holds on relevant content to prevent deletion.

- **Responding to Board inquiries:** When the Data Protection Board asks for specific data (e.g., records of a Data Principal or evidence of controls), an up-to-date data map and eDiscovery search enable quick, precise results. This is far more efficient (and defensible) than manual data hunts.

Access controls and audit trails

Strict access management limits who can see or modify personal data. Use **role-based access control (RBAC)** and the principle of least privilege so users only have the permissions needed for their job. Review these permissions regularly (e.g., quarterly) to remove old or excessive access. Require **multi-factor authentication (MFA)** for all privileged and remote accounts to prevent credential theft. Each access event (successful or failed) should be logged in detail. Adopt these core practices to build DPDP-compliant access controls and tamper-evident audit trails:

- **Role-based access:** Assign permissions by role, not by individual requests. For example, only HR staff can access employee records, and only finance can see payroll data. Periodically audit user roles and remove unused accounts. Such reviews help detect orphaned privileges (e.g., a former employee still having access).

- **MFA and identity:** Enforce strong authentication (MFA), especially for admins and high-privilege users. This ensures a password breach alone is not enough to gain entry. Coupled with MFA, each login event provides an extra layer of proof of identity.

- **Audit logging:** Enable audit logs for all access control changes (role assignments, permission grants/revokes) and for access attempts to critical data. For instance, enable logging of all Azure AD sign-ins and file access in SharePoint/OneDrive. Every access event becomes an audit trail that can be reviewed.

- **Accountability:** By design, audit trails support accountability. As one expert notes, these logs play a vital role in compliance and fraud prevention by making user activity transparent. In a breach investigation, audit logs help determine exactly who accessed which data and when. For example, with comprehensive audit logging enabled, IT can produce a report of all times a given user account accessed files.

- **Internal misuse detection:** Use the audit trails to look for insider risks (e.g., large bulk downloads, use of admin privileges at odd hours). Alerts or periodic reviews can flag these behaviors. This complements external threat detection by catching misuse even from legitimate accounts.

Collaboration with DPO/legal

IT readiness also means clear coordination with the organization's DPO and legal/compliance teams. Establish formal workflows so that any regulatory request is handled efficiently. The DPO or legal team should know exactly which IT person to contact for logs or data extracts, and vice versa. Likewise, IT should briefly lead on where key data is stored and how to interpret system logs. Effective collaboration across IT, DPO, and legal teams relies on the following coordination mechanisms:

- **Request/response workflow:** Define a process (ticket system or rapid-response channel) for compliance/legal to submit data requests to IT. For example, a Board inquiry might trigger a *Privacy Incident Request* that automatically notifies the IT incident manager. This avoids ad-hoc queries getting lost.

- **Shared data knowledge:** Ensure compliance and IT have a common data dictionary. If legal asks for *consent records* or *customer IP logs*, IT must know which database or log file stores those. Regular joint reviews of data sources help build this shared understanding.

- **Real-time coordination:** In a crisis or tight investigation timeline, IT staff should be on standby to work directly with the DPO and legal counsel. For example, while legal prepares the formal response, IT can simultaneously gather and package the raw data. Pre-establishing who in IT has clearance to communicate with the Board (and through which channels) prevents delays.

- **Policy alignment:** As NIST advises, legal and management should define information-sharing policies with IT *before* incidents occur. For instance, IT and legal can pre-agree on what types of data or logs will be released (and in what form) to investigators, subject to Board direction. This pre-planning ensures compliant, consistent responses.

- **Regulatory triggers:** Train IT on the triggers for involvement. Under the DPDPA rules, DPO/legal might request IT help for Data Principal Rights requests or Board audits. For example, if a Board summons specific records, IT must know to treat them with the highest priority and legal oversight.

Use of forensic and compliance tools

Finally, leverage specialized tools for breach investigation and ongoing compliance assurance. IT should be equipped for forensic analysis and continuous control validation. To strengthen breach investigations and prove ongoing compliance, ensure your IT team deploys the following specialized forensic and validation tools:

- **Digital forensics:** Maintain a *jump kit* of forensic hardware and software (NIST recommends having a workstation for disk imaging, trusted analysis tools, write-blockers, etc.). In a suspected breach, IT can use this kit to create bit-for-bit disk images of compromised systems, preserving evidence. Use forensic tools to analyze logs, malware, and file copies without altering originals (for instance, using write-once media). Following forensic best practices ensures data integrity for any legal proceedings.

- **Endpoint Detection and Response (EDR):** Deploy EDR or SIEM solutions that can record detailed process and network activity. When investigating a breach, these tools can trace an attacker's steps through endpoints and servers.

- **Continuous compliance tools:** Use compliance management platforms to track and document controls. Microsoft Purview Compliance Manager, for example, provides built-in assessments and a compliance score. It maps regulatory controls to actual configurations and collects evidence of implementation. For actions managed by Microsoft, it even shows *implementation details and audit results* automatically.

- **Evidence cataloging:** Compliance Manager and similar tools keep an evidence library. This means if a Board investigator asks, *show that we encrypt data at rest*, IT already has a saved report or screenshot demonstrating the encryption policy is active. The tool can continuously scan system settings and award points for compliant configurations.

- **Policy enforcement:** Use automated compliance checks. For instance, continuous control assessment features in Compliance Manager will detect if a required security setting (like MFA or disk encryption) is turned off, alerting IT to fix it. This proactive monitoring closes gaps before they become violations.

- **Audit trails for controls:** Document every change in security posture. When IT implements a new control (e.g., a data loss prevention policy, a firewall rule), record it in the compliance system. Over time, this creates an audit trail of the organization's security governance efforts, valuable evidence when regulators review your practices.

By combining thorough logging, tested response plans, detailed data inventories, strict access governance, and the right forensic/compliance tools, the IT department can support any Data Protection Board investigation with confidence. These practices ensure transparency and readiness: if regulators knock on the door, IT has the records and processes to respond quickly and accurately, turning a potential crisis into a managed compliance exercise.

Enforcement, penalties, and sanctions under DPDP Act

The DPDP Act establishes an administrative penalty regime enforced by the Data Protection Board of India ("the Board"). Under Chapter VI Section 27, the Board may investigate breaches on its own motion (for example, on receiving a breach intimation under Chapter II Section 8(6)) or upon complaints or references, and, after an opportunity to be heard, impose penalties *as provided in this Act*. Section 27 explicitly authorizes the Board to direct urgent remedial or mitigation measures in the event of a personal data breach. Further, Section 27(2) empowers the Board to issue binding directions (after hearing) to persons in breach, subject to modification on review. Chapter VIII (Sections 33–34) then sets the penalty framework: after a significant breach is established, the Board: *If the Board determines on conclusion of an inquiry that breach of the provisions of this Act or the rules made thereunder by a person is significant, it may, after giving the person an opportunity of being heard, impose such monetary penalty specified in the Schedule.*. The Schedule (appended to Section 33(1)) lists tiered fines for specific violations. The penalties for breaches under the Act highlight the seriousness of non-compliance. Unlike other jurisdictions that may impose relatively lenient fines, the DPDP Act prescribes substantial penalties. These are illustrated in *Figure 10.2*:

THE SCHEDULE

[*See* section 33 (*1*)]

Sl. No.	Breach of provisions of this Act or rules made thereunder	Penalty
(1)	(2)	(3)
1.	Breach in observing the obligation of Data Fiduciary to take reasonable security safeguards to prevent personal data breach under sub-section (*5*) of section 8.	May extend to two hundred and fifty crore rupees.
2.	Breach in observing the obligation to give the Board or affected Data Principal notice of a personal data breach under sub-section (*6*) of section 8.	May extend to two hundred crore rupees.
3.	Breach in observance of additional obligations in relation to children under section 9.	May extend to two hundred crore rupees.
4.	Breach in observance of additional obligations of Significant Data Fiduciary under section 10.	May extend to one hundred and fifty crore rupees.
5.	Breach in observance of the duties under section 15.	May extend to ten thousand rupees.
6.	Breach of any term of voluntary undertaking accepted by the Board under section 32.	Up to the extent applicable for the breach in respect of which the proceedings under section 28 were instituted.
7.	Breach of any other provision of this Act or the rules made thereunder.	May extend to fifty crore rupees.

DR. REETA VASISHTA.
Secretary to the Govt. of India.

Figure 10.2: *Penalties according to Chapter VIII Section 33(1)*

The explanation is as follows:

- **Tiered penalty structure.** The Act's Schedule creates a hierarchy of fines for different breaches. The key categories include:

    o **Chapter II Section 8(5)** (failure to implement reasonable security safeguards to prevent data breach): penalty *"may extend ₹250 crore rupees."*.

    o **Chapter II Section 8(6)** (failure to notify the Board and affected individuals of a personal data breach): up to *₹200 crore*.

    o **Chapter II Section 9** (processing of children's data without required safeguards): up to *₹200 crore*.

    o **Chapter II Section 10** (obligations of a "Significant Data Fiduciary"): up to *₹150 crore*.

    o **Chapter III Section 15** (duties of Data Principals): up to *₹10,000*.

    o **Chapter VII Section 32** (breach of a voluntary undertaking accepted by the Board): up to the amount applicable for the underlying breach (per Schedule item 6).

    o **Any other violation** of the Act or Rules: up to *₹50 crore*.

    This structured scheme makes clear which obligations carry the highest penalties. In practice, the Board can impose a fine for each instance of a breach. The Schedule caps are "per violation", for example, failing to secure data (Sec 8(5)) could draw up to ₹250 crore in one case, and a separate fine for a second breach. Indeed, Chapter VII Section 33(2)(c) directs the Board to consider the *"repetitive nature of the breach"* when setting penalties. Thus, multiple breaches (or breaches affecting many individuals) may lead to cumulative penalties without a single aggregate cap.

- **Board's penalty powers.** The Board's authority to impose these fines derives from Sections 27 and 33. Upon finding a "significant" breach after inquiry, Chapter VII Section 33(1) permits the Board to levy the Schedule's monetary penalty. The Board must consider factors such as the breach's nature, gravity, and duration, the sensitivity of data involved, any gain or loss, mitigation efforts, and proportionality. In all cases, the Board must give the person an opportunity to be heard before imposing any fine. All penalties collected are credited to the Consolidated Fund of India (Section 34).

    The Act ties the Board's penal powers to the specific provisions breached. For example, Sections 8(5) and 8(6) impose core data security and breach-notification duties on Data Fiduciaries. A contravention of either provision falls under Schedule items 1 or 2, with fines up to ₹250 crore or ₹200 crore, respectively. Similarly, violations of Section 9 (children's data) or Section 10 (Significant DF obligations) invoke Schedule items 3 and 4. Breach of any duty by a Data Principal under Section 15 is comparatively minor (only up to ₹10,000, item 5). The Board may act on breach intimation, complaint, or government/court reference, and can penalize any person (Data Fiduciary, intermediary, Consent Manager, etc.) for non-compliance *as provided in this Act.*

- **Non-monetary enforcement and remedies.** In addition to fines, the Board can issue various orders and accept commitments to ensure compliance. Chapter VI Section 27(1) (a) specifically allows the Board, on a breach intimation under Section 8(6), to direct urgent remedial or mitigation measures for a data breach. In practice, this means the Board can order a Fiduciary to fix security flaws, notify additional parties, or take other steps to limit harm. Moreover, Section 27(2) empowers the Board to issue binding directions (after hearing) to any noncompliant party, who *shall be bound to comply.* For example, the Board might direct a Data Fiduciary to suspend disputed processing or update policies to meet the law. If such a direction is challenged, Section 27(3) allows the Board to review or modify its own orders.

  Under *Chapter VII Section 32,* the Board may also accept voluntary undertakings to cure a breach. At any stage of proceedings, a party can offer an undertaking *in respect of any matter related to the observance of the provisions of this Act.* Such undertakings can include specific actions and timelines, and once accepted, they form a bar to further proceedings on the same issue. If the party later fails to honor the undertaking, the Board treats that failure as a breach of the Act and may then initiate formal proceedings for penalties.

- **Appeals and blocking orders.** All Board orders (whether penalties or directions) are appealable. Any aggrieved person may appeal to the Telecom Disputes Settlement and Appellate Tribunal within 60 days. The Appellate Tribunal has all the powers of a civil court in hearing the appeal. Notably, an order of the Tribunal is executable as a civil court decree. If an appeal is delayed, the Tribunal can condone delays for sufficient cause.

  In extreme cases, Chapter IX Section 37 introduces a form of *cascading* enforcement. If the Board notifies the Central Government that a Data Fiduciary has been penalized in *two or more instances,* the government may, after hearing the Fiduciary and for public interest reasons, direct any intermediary (e.g., an ISP or hosting provider) to *block public access* to the Fiduciary's online services. An intermediary receiving such a direction *shall be bound to comply.* This ensures that repeated violators can be effectively shut out of providing digital services if necessary.

- **No criminal sanctions or compensation orders.** The DPDP Act's enforcement is entirely administrative and civil. Nowhere does the Act create a criminal offense or imprisonment for data breaches. Likewise, it does not authorize the Board to award monetary compensation to Data Principals. All penalties under the Act are fines levied by the Board (per the Schedule). Data Principals who suffer loss must seek redress under other laws or contracts; the DPDP Act itself does not provide a compensatory remedy.

In summary, organizations subject to the DPDP Act face a clear, tiered penalty regime enforced by the Data Protection Board. The Board can impose very large fines for violations of core duties (especially Sections 8–10), and also issue remedial directions or accept undertakings to achieve compliance. Understanding the statutory Schedule and Sections 27–37 is crucial: every breach can trigger a separate fine (with factors like repetition considered), and non-monetary remedies may also be applied. No criminal or automatic compensation sanctions exist under the Act, but civil claims remain an option outside this statutory scheme.

Conclusion

Navigating the regulatory landscape under the DPDP Act, 2023, requires organizations to go beyond checkbox compliance. As detailed in this chapter, engaging constructively with the Data Protection Board of India is both a legal necessity and a strategic opportunity to demonstrate accountability. Whether dealing with a breach, a complaint, or a formal inquiry, success hinges on transparency, preparedness, and prompt action. By establishing robust grievance redressal mechanisms, maintaining accurate records, enabling swift eDiscovery processes, and empowering the DPO as a central coordinator, organizations can minimize disruption and mitigate risks. The DPDP Act introduces a detailed, tiered penalty regime and emphasizes cooperative compliance over adversarial enforcement. Key takeaways include the importance of internal readiness, proactive communication, and leveraging digital tools like Microsoft Purview to manage investigations efficiently. With the Board expected to function as a digital-first, fair, and tech-savvy authority, organizations must align their operations accordingly. Ultimately, dealing with regulators under the DPDP Act is not just about avoiding penalties; it is about building resilience, earning trust, and embedding data protection into the organization's core values and culture.

In the next chapter, we look into building a true data protection culture. You will learn what *privacy by instinct* looks like, how leaders set the tone and back it with resources, and how role-based training turns every employee into a data steward.

Join our Discord space

Join our Discord workspace for latest updates, offers, tech happenings around the world, new releases, and sessions with the authors:

https://discord.bpbonline.com

CHAPTER 11

Building a Data Protection Culture

Introduction

In today's data-driven world, personal information is a prized asset and, simultaneously, a significant vulnerability. As organizations increasingly leverage data to drive innovation, enhance services, and compete globally, protecting this information has become a strategic imperative. High-profile breaches and privacy scandals serve as stark reminders of the devastating consequences, both in financial loss and trust erosion, when personal data is mishandled. With penalties for non-compliance under India's **Digital Personal Data Protection (DPDP)** Act, 2023 reaching up to ₹250 crore, the legal and reputational risks have never been higher.

This chapter explores how building a robust data protection culture is essential not only for compliance but also for sustaining business success. A culture of privacy goes beyond policies and technology; it requires that every employee, from leadership to the front line, understands the value of data and their role in safeguarding it. By integrating privacy into everyday operations and decision-making, organizations can transform data protection into an inherent business strength, earning trust from customers, empowering staff, and fostering resilience in an ever-evolving digital landscape.

Structure

In this chapter, we will cover the following topics:

- What a data protection culture means
- Leadership accountability and tone at the top
- Educating and empowering employees
- Embedding privacy in all organizational processes
- Implementing data protection procedures and guidelines
- Role of DPO's communication with Data Principals
- Role played by finance when engaging with vendors

Objectives

The primary objective of this chapter is to illustrate the critical importance of cultivating a robust data protection culture within organizations in the context of India's DPDP Act, 2023. It aims to demonstrate that achieving compliance extends beyond policies and technological solutions, requiring a fundamental shift in organizational attitudes, values, and behaviors. By emphasizing leadership accountability, employee empowerment through continuous training, the integration of **Privacy by Design** (**PbD**) principles, clear and enforceable policies, and strategic use of technological safeguards, the chapter outlines a comprehensive approach to embedding data privacy into everyday operations. Furthermore, it underscores the necessity of continuous monitoring, auditing, and improvement to sustain and enhance compliance efforts over time. Ultimately, the chapter seeks to equip organizations with actionable insights and best practices that enable them not only to meet legal obligations but also to build enduring trust, achieve competitive advantage, and foster resilience in the face of evolving privacy challenges.

What a data protection culture means

A data protection culture is an organizational mindset in which protecting personal data is a fundamental value, not just a checkbox exercise. In a private conscious culture, all employees understand the importance of handling personal data carefully and Act accordingly. Privacy considerations become *the way we do things* at every level, from product design to customer service to sales executives.

Such a culture means data protection principles are woven into daily work. Teams routinely ask whether collecting or using data is truly necessary, and they treat data as a sensitive asset. This shared attitude moves data protection from a narrow compliance task to a collective responsibility. When privacy is core to culture, complying with the law becomes more natural. For example, the DPDP Act requires that personal data be processed only for lawful, specified purposes with valid consent (or another legal basis), and that Data Principals receive clear notice of how their data is used. In a strong privacy culture, employees anticipate these requirements and build them into processes from the start, rather than reacting later.

Embedding a data protection culture takes time and effort, through consistent messaging, leadership support, training, and incentives, but the payoff is significant. Organizations with strong privacy cultures are more likely to follow policies instinctively, reducing the risk of breaches. They build trust internally (teams feel confident sharing data responsibly) and externally (customers see the company as ethical and reliable). In short, culture transforms privacy from a liability into a competitive advantage.

Leadership accountability and tone at the top

Data protection culture begins with top executives who must maintain constant situational awareness, monitoring for emerging risks, near-misses, or actual breaches. The CEO, CISO, CIO, and board members must visibly champion privacy and security, demonstrating through their actions that safeguarding personal data is non-negotiable. When executives set the example, allocating resources, prioritizing risk assessments, and staying informed of threat intelligence, every level of the organization takes notice.

Under the DPDP Act, accountability is mandatory. The law makes the *Data Fiduciary* (the entity determining how data is processed) legally responsible for compliance, regardless of any contractual arrangements with vendors or processors. Leadership should therefore establish a robust governance framework, such as a privacy steering committee chaired by the CEO or another senior executive and including the CISO, CIO, legal counsel, and the **Data Protection Officer** (**DPO**) that meets regularly to review risk dashboards, incident reports, and remediation plans.

For Significant Data Fiduciaries, the Act requires appointing a DPO in India. This officer serves as the primary liaison for regulators and Data Principals and reports directly to top management. Even smaller organizations benefit from naming a privacy lead who has direct board access. Leaders must empower this individual to flag concerns immediately, whether it is a suspicious system alert, an attempted phishing incident, or a gap discovered during an audit, so that the executive team can respond swiftly.

Building and sustaining a privacy culture demands investment. Leaders must commit budget to security tools, training programs, system upgrades, and professional expertise. Cutting corners, such as postponing a critical vulnerability scan or bypassing secure design reviews, undermines trust and leaves the organization exposed. When a breach or policy violation does occur, executives must respond transparently and constructively: convene the incident response team, learn root causes, update controls, and communicate lessons learned across the company. A clear no-retaliation policy for reporting privacy concerns ensures that employees feel safe escalating issues without fear, further reinforcing strong situational awareness at the top.

In summary, effective leadership in data protection means more than setting policy; it requires CEOs, CISOs, CIOs, and board members to remain vigilant, informed, and ready to Act on any sign of risk, and not just DPO championing for this cause. Their visible commitment, ongoing oversight, and strict accountability form the bedrock of a resilient, trustworthy data protection culture.

Educating and empowering employees

Leadership can set direction, but every employee must live the culture, and in a large organization with divisional priorities, sales goals, and customer support, the privacy narrative is often lost. Ongoing *training and awareness* are essential so that each person understands their role in protecting data. Training should not be a one-off seminar, but a continuous, role-based program. New hires need onboarding that covers basic privacy and company policies. After that, regular refreshers (e.g., annual courses or workshops) reinforce the message as laws and threats evolve.

Training should be practical and relatable. Tailor content by role: for example, finance and HR teams learn about secure handling of employee data and access controls; marketing learns about obtaining valid consent and respecting "do not contact" preferences; IT / security staff learn the Act's technical safeguards (e.g. encryption, access logs) for IT division, customer support or call center staff learning how to verify identities before sharing account data. Explain DPDPA requirements in context: for instance, show how failing to follow authentication processes could trigger hefty penalties, while the correct use of encryption or secure file transfer can prevent breaches.

Awareness campaigns also help. Companies often use newsletters, posters, or brief bulletins to highlight privacy tips or recent incidents (e.g., *Remember: always lock your computer when stepping away* or *New DPDPA amendment approved – check updated consent forms*). Integrating privacy into everyday communications keeps it top of mind. Leaders and managers should lead by example: when executives visibly attend privacy training, provide guidance from the DPO, or mention privacy in team meetings, it underscores that data protection is a shared priority.

Training content under the DPDPA

An effective training program must first explain the *what* and *why* of data protection. In the Indian context, employees need to understand the essentials of the DPDP Act, 2023, and how it applies to their specific roles. The training should cover the following key topics:

- **Understanding personal data:** Employees must learn what qualifies as *personal data* under both the law and the organization's policies. Personal data includes any information with which an individual can be identified, whether provided directly (such as a name, email, or phone number) or indirectly through combined data points. Relevant business examples, such as customer purchase histories, device IDs, or location data linked to an individual, help establish that all such information requires careful handling.

- **Lawful and limited processing:** It is essential to explain the principles of data processing legality and minimization. Under the DPDP Act, personal data may only be processed for lawful purposes, with the explicit consent of the Data Principal or under other permitted grounds. Employees should understand that there must be a valid and documented reason for collecting or using personal data. This includes adhering to the principles of purpose limitation, using data only for the originally specified purpose, and data minimization, collecting only what is necessary. For example, a marketing team conducting a campaign should collect only the required data fields rather than an entire customer profile.

- **Consent and choice:** The Act sets clear standards for obtaining consent. Employees, particularly those involved in customer-facing roles or product design, must learn that consent must be free, informed, specific, unambiguous, and given clear affirmative action. Training should demonstrate how to present choices to users, for instance, through an app onboarding process that clearly explains why access to a user's contact list is needed. Additionally, it should stress that consent under the DPDP Act is revocable, meaning that if a customer withdraws their consent, the data can no longer be used for that purpose. Handling withdrawals and honoring customer preferences, such as opt-outs from marketing communications, should also be covered.

- **Individual rights under DPDPA:** Employees need to understand the rights granted to Data Principals, such as the right to access, correct, and erase personal data, the right to nominate, and the right to grievance redressal. Training should outline the internal procedures for verifying and processing such requests in a timely manner. For example, a customer support agent should know the steps required to verify a user's identity before routing a *right to erasure* request to the relevant team. It is important to emphasize any specific timelines or formats mandated by the DPDP Act for handling these requests.

- **Transparency and notice:** The DPDP Act requires that individuals receive clear notice about what personal data is being collected and for what purpose before or at the time of collection. Employees involved in drafting customer communications or managing forms and websites need to understand how to create clear, easily understandable privacy and consent notices. All staff should be aware that these notices create binding commitments. If a notice states that data will be used solely to service an account and not shared with third parties without further consent, then all relevant departments (such as marketing) must adhere to this promise. In addition, training should cover the process for communicating any changes in data usage to customers.

- **Data security basics:** Every employee must understand the practical measures to protect personal data in day-to-day operations. Training should translate the organization's IT security policies into actionable guidelines. Topics might include the use of strong passwords, multi-factor authentication, recognizing phishing attempts, secure internal data sharing (using approved encrypted channels), and proper disposal of documents. The DPDP Act requires companies to implement *reasonable security safeguards* to prevent personal data breaches. Concrete instructions, such as locking computer screens when away, avoiding the use of untrusted USB devices, and following secure document disposal practices, reinforce that security is everyone's responsibility.

- **Breach reporting and response:** Despite best efforts, personal data breaches or policy violations can occur. Employees must be taught to promptly recognize and report potential personal data breaches, such as sending an email with personal data to the wrong recipient, losing a laptop, or encountering a suspected malware infection. The training should outline the immediate steps for reporting incidents, typically notifying the IT/security team or the DPO, emphasizing that internal reporting must be quick and unhesitant. While the exact timeframe may be clarified by additional regulations (a window similar to 72 hours may be referenced), the underlying principle is that any suspected breach must be reported immediately. Scenario-based training (for example, addressing an accidentally exposed file on a public server) can help employees understand the proper channels for incident reporting.

- **Roles like the DPO and grievance redressal:** To ensure accountability, the organization should clearly define the role of the DPO or an equivalent privacy leader. Training must inform employees about the DPO's responsibilities as the central point of contact for data protection matters and grievance redressal. It should outline the correct procedures for escalating privacy complaints, for instance, what to do if a customer contacts the company with a data misuse complaint, and ensure that such issues are addressed in line with the prescribed timelines of the DPDP Act. Clarifying these internal roles helps prevent confusion and negligence when a privacy issue arises.

- **Cross-border data transfers:** If personal data is transferred outside India, for example, when using overseas cloud servers or collaborating with a foreign parent company, staff must be aware of the relevant restrictions. The DPDP Act generally permits cross-border transfers except for countries specifically restricted by the Indian government. Training should emphasize that international data transfers must comply with company guidelines (such as transferring data only to approved entities or jurisdictions) and be conducted with proper safeguards in place, like contractual agreements. A simple rule, such as *never export personal data without consulting the legal or privacy team,* can help ensure compliance. By covering these areas, the training program aligns employees with the specific requirements of the DPDP Act and the best practices for maintaining privacy and security. Real-world examples, such as anonymized case studies of breaches or success stories where vigilance prevented a potential incident, can help make these lessons tangible. The goal is to ensure that every employee understands how their daily actions impact individual privacy and the organization's overall compliance standing.

Making training engaging and practical

Information alone is not enough; how training is delivered is just as critical to building a lasting, privacy-aware culture. Adults learn best by doing and by seeing how the information is relevant to their own context. Therefore, privacy training should avoid being a dry legal lecture and instead use engaging, interactive methods that help employees internalize key concepts.

Some effective techniques and best practices for privacy awareness training include:

- **Interactive workshops:** Rather than solely relying on slides or documents, incorporate workshops where employees can discuss and ask questions. For example, have small groups analyze a hypothetical scenario: *You found a USB drive in the parking lot labeled 'confidential.' What do you do?* Each group can then share their ideas, while a facilitator guides the discussion toward the correct approach (e.g., never plug it in; report it to IT). Workshops encourage participation and transform training into an active experience.

- **Role-playing and simulations:** Set up simulations of privacy incidents or decision-making dilemmas. One popular approach is a simulated personal data breach exercise; for instance, send out a mock phishing email during the session to see who clicks it, then use it as a springboard to discuss phishing awareness. Alternatively, simulate the steps involved in handling a customer data request by having one employee Act as the customer and another as the company representative. These role-plays enable employees to practice responses in a safe environment, reinforcing the proper procedures in case a real incident occurs. Training experts agree that learning by doing greatly improves the retention of complex principles

- **Real-life case studies:** Leverage actual examples from industry or the company's history. Present brief stories of organizations that faced heavy fines or public outrage due to privacy mishaps, for example, a telecom company fined for a data leak or an e-commerce company that lost customers after misusing data. Discuss what went wrong and how a strong data protection culture could have prevented the issue. Conversely, share success stories where good privacy practices made a difference, such as a scenario where encryption thwarted a breach or where a quick response earned public praise. These stories make the importance of data protection more relatable.

- **Quizzes and knowledge checks:** Short quizzes and interactive polls during and after training reinforce key privacy concepts and ensure engagement through gamification. Friendly competitions, such as quizzes with small rewards for top scorers, can increase motivation and highlight areas needing further clarification. Given their access to customer data, it is essential to deliver targeted training and closely track compliance within marketing, sales, and customer support teams:

  o **Marketing and analytics teams**: Training should emphasize the necessity of obtaining explicit consent before conducting promotional activities or communications. Teams must understand constraints on data usage, including techniques like anonymization, when analyzing customer behavior data to protect individual privacy.

- **Customer support and sales teams**: Employees require detailed guidance on securely authenticating customer identities before sharing personal information. They must also be equipped to handle privacy inquiries and complaints respectfully, promptly, and securely, reinforcing the organization's commitment to data protection and customer trust.

By providing targeted training and ongoing tracking for these teams, organizations effectively safeguard personal information, maintain regulatory compliance under the DPDP Act, and strengthen customer relationships through demonstrated respect for privacy.

Embedding privacy in all organizational processes

To make privacy a living, day-to-day practice rather than a policy on paper, organizations must weave specific safeguards into every workflow and decision point:

- **Strengthening compliance through Privacy by Design principles:** The implementation of PbD and data protection by design transforms data protection into an integral part of every organizational process. These principles demand that privacy considerations be proactively built into every workflow, system, and decision-making process at the organizational level. The DPDP Act mandates that organizations adopt comprehensive technical and organizational measures to embed these principles into their operations.

- **Proactive risk management across departments:** Organizations must instill risk-awareness and privacy training tailored to individual departments, ensuring every team, from Marketing to IT, understands their role in safeguarding data. Regular risk audits and reviews allow organizations to identify vulnerabilities across all workflows, enabling preemptive action and fostering compliance

- **Default to minimal data collection and access:** Organizations should configure processes to automatically limit data collection, retention, and access to the minimum necessary for operational needs. For example, systems should enforce strict default settings, such as disabling non-essential data sharing and marketing communications, until explicitly required. Automated data deletion mechanisms aligned with organizational retention schedules further embed privacy at the process level.

- **Embedding privacy into workflow architecture:** To operationalize privacy principles, organizations should incorporate privacy-centric measures into workflow design:
  - **Design reviews**: Conduct systematic reviews during the development of processes and systems to ensure compliance with PbD, from consent mechanisms to pseudonymization practices.

- o **Role-based access**: Implement granular access controls that restrict personal data views to authorized personnel based on workflow requirements.

- **User-centric controls integrated into processes:** Privacy must be inherent in all user-facing organizational processes. This includes providing intuitive dashboards for Data Principals to view, correct, or delete their data, as well as designing consent forms and privacy notices that meet the accessibility and transparency standards of the DPDP Act.

- **End-to-end security integrated across operational layers:** Strong encryption and multi-factor authentication should be applied uniformly across organizational processes, ensuring data security from collection to retention. Segmenting networks and mandating secure VPN access for remote work further reinforces compliance at every operational level.

Practical strategies for operationalizing Privacy by Design

Organizations can solidify PbD at the process level through the following strategies:

- **Departmental privacy checklists**: Develop tailored checklists for each department, embedding privacy controls into daily workflows. Whether for marketing, HR, or finance, these checklists ensure data protection compliance is integrated into routine processes.

- **Data Protection Impact Assessments (DPIAs):** Conduct DPIAs for high-risk processing activities to proactively identify privacy risks and mitigate them at the operational stage.

- **Minimized data access**: Enforce the principle of least privilege across workflows, ensuring employees and systems access only the data essential to their duties.

- **Automated data deletion mechanisms**: Configure data systems to enforce retention schedules automatically, purging or anonymizing data once it is no longer needed.

- **Privacy validation testing:** Regularly test processes and systems for privacy controls, validating their effectiveness during QA and security testing phases.

By embedding privacy principles into organizational processes at every level, organizations do more than comply with the DPDP Act; they create a culture of proactive data protection that turns compliance into a competitive advantage.

Implementing data protection procedures and guidelines

In addition to high-level policies, detailed **standard operating procedures** (**SOPs**) and guidelines operationalize specific aspects of data protection. These "how-to" documents bring the principles of the DPDP Act into everyday practice:

- **Incident response plan:** Develop a documented procedure for handling personal data breaches and security incidents. This plan should outline step-by-step actions, define the roles of the incident response team (including IT, PR, legal, and management), and include communication templates for notifying authorities and Data Principals. Although not every employee may see the full plan, the relevant teams must rehearse it regularly. A robust incident response plan not only ensures swift compliance with the DPDP Act's breach notification requirements but also fosters a culture of responsible reporting.

- **Data classification and handling guidelines:** Establish clear categories for data (e.g., public, internal, confidential, highly sensitive) with corresponding handling rules. Personal data should be classified as confidential or highly sensitive, especially if it includes financial or health information. Guidelines should specify that data classified as confidential must not be emailed without encryption or uploaded to public cloud services without approval. They should also address physical handling, for example, that printed documents containing personal data must be stored securely and shredded when no longer needed. These rules assist employees in making daily decisions regarding data storage and sharing.

- **Consent collection procedure:** Standardize the process for obtaining valid consent in accordance with the DPDP Act's criteria (free, informed, unambiguous, and provided by clear affirmative action). Use templates or approved wording for all consent forms and require that any new initiative involving data processing obtain clearance from the DPO. Consistent, compliant consent practices build trust with Data Principals and reduce the risk of non-compliance.

- **Vendor management checklist:** When engaging third-party service providers (e.g., cloud hosts, SaaS providers, data analytics firms), employ a checklist or assessment form. This tool should verify the vendor's security certifications, ensure that a Data Processing Agreement is signed with appropriate data protection clauses, and confirm whether data transfers meet cross-border requirements. This process extends the data protection culture to external partners, demonstrating accountability and compliance with the DPDP Act.

- **Data principal request handling workflow:** Create a detailed workflow that expands on the policy's provisions for handling Data Principals' requests. Specify how requests for access, correction, deletion, or nomination are logged, tracked, and verified. Define internal service-level agreements (e.g., responding within 15 days), and include templates for responses. Typically, the DPO or privacy team should coordinate this process, ensuring that no request is overlooked and that responses are consistent and timely.

- **Data transfer and cross-border protocols:** Develop procedures to govern the transfer of personal data outside India. Require that any cross-border data transfer be preceded by a transfer assessment form detailing the data fields, destination country, purpose, and confirmation of adequate protection (or use of standard contractual clauses). Obtain approval from legal/DPO prior to transfer, thereby formalizing compliance with governmental restrictions and DPDP Act requirements.

- **Encryption and password policies:** Establish clear rules regarding encryption and password security, which are critical to preventing unauthorized access. Specify when encryption is required (e.g., for portable devices, databases, or emails containing personal data) and detail password requirements (minimum length, complexity, rotation, and multi-factor authentication). These measures support the DPDP Act's mandate for reasonable security safeguards and may mitigate the need for breach reporting if data remains encrypted and unreadable.

- **BYOD and remote work guidelines:** In today's flexible work environment, outline clear requirements for personal device usage and remote work. Policies should mandate that personal devices used for company purposes install mobile device management software, enable remote wiping, and use VPNs to access personal data. Additionally, remote work guidelines should instruct employees on safe practices when using public Wi-Fi and managing device security, ensuring continuous compliance with data protection standards.

- **Email and communication policy:** Provide guidelines on the appropriate use of email and other communication channels when handling personal data. For example, prohibit sending large sets of personal data via email unless encrypted, and caution employees against phishing by verifying unexpected requests. These rules, while overlapping with broader cybersecurity policies, are vital to preventing inadvertent data leaks.

All these procedures and guidelines should be living documents, developed in consultation with relevant departments to ensure practicality. They should be neither overly draconian nor out of touch; for instance, instead of prohibiting salespeople from storing any client data on laptops, a nuanced rule might allow temporary storage if data is encrypted and promptly uploaded to a central system.

Consistency in enforcement is essential. If a high-ranking executive violates the data policy, such as using an unauthorized cloud service, disciplinary action must be taken to reinforce that no one is exempt from compliance. The DPDP Act does not explicitly demand internal policies, but it implicitly requires organizations to maintain mechanisms that ensure compliance.

Regulated entities are expected to demonstrate accountability through documented policies and procedures.

Consider this example, where a new employee at an Indian healthcare startup receives the company's code of conduct and Data Protection Policy on day one. The policy clearly states that patient data is highly confidential, must be accessed only via secure health records systems, and should never be copied to personal devices or shared via unapproved messaging apps. It also specifies whom to contact if a breach or complaint is suspected. This clarity enables the employee to make informed decisions, such as accessing data via a secure VPN rather than downloading a spreadsheet for home use, thus ingraining privacy-conscious behavior from the outset.

In summary, well-documented supporting procedures and guidelines Act as the backbone of an effective data protection culture. They provide employees with clear instructions, ensure consistency in handling personal data, and help institutionalize privacy practices that align with the DPDP Act and its rules. With these systems in place, technology and process management have become powerful allies in protecting data at scale.

Role of DPO's communication with Data Principals

A robust data protection culture hinges on the pivotal role of the DPO, who acts as the primary liaison for grievances, breach notifications, and rights requests, ensuring transparent and trust-building communication with Data Principals. The following are the ways the DPO keeps Data Principals fully informed and protected:

- **Transparent notices and consent:** The DPO takes charge of crafting and maintaining plain-language privacy notices, consent forms, and terms of use. These documents clearly outline the Data Fiduciary's identity, processing purposes, data categories, retention periods, and mechanisms for exercising rights. By regularly updating these materials to reflect new uses of data, the DPO ensures clarity and transparency for Data Principals.

- **Proactive breach and risk communication:** In the event of a breach or significant risk, the DPO promptly communicates with affected individuals, detailing the nature of the incident, mitigation measures, and protective recommendations. This proactive approach not only fulfills Section 8(6) requirements but also exemplifies accountability and reinforces trust.

- **Grievance redressal and ongoing support:** The DPO plays a central role in managing grievance channels, including email, hotline, or portals. They oversee investigations, ensure regular status updates to Data Principals, and coordinate timely resolutions. By maintaining responsive communication, the DPO ensures concerns are systematically addressed, further solidifying trust.

- **Empowering rights requests:** The DPO facilitates user-friendly mechanisms for Data Principals to exercise their rights to access, correction, or erasure of data. They validate requests, ensure statutory timelines are met, and communicate outcomes with precision. Posthumous data-handling requests are also managed by the DPO, demonstrating their broad oversight and commitment to compliance.

- **Community engagement and education:** The DPO spearheads initiatives such as user forums, feedback surveys, and educational campaigns, encouraging dialogue and responsiveness. By fostering mutual responsibility, the DPO helps build a privacy-conscious community among Data Principals.

  By positioning the DPO as a visible, active point of contact and embedding transparent communication into every interaction, organizations not only meet DPDP Act obligations but also cultivate enduring confidence among their Data Principals.

- **Engaging employees and internal stakeholders:** The DPO's leadership is indispensable in embedding privacy practices across internal teams. Serving as the primary privacy advisor within the organization, the DPO guides policy interpretation, risk management, and department-specific processes, ensuring that privacy considerations are consistently integrated into all operations.

- **Proactive liaison and advisor:** The DPO actively collaborates with frontline teams, offering briefings on emerging risks, new breach scenarios, and regulatory updates. By participating in marketing kick-offs, HR policy reviews, and support-team huddles, the DPO ensures privacy considerations inform customer interactions at every level.

- **Tailored training and support:** As the central privacy advocate, the DPO leads tailored training programs for key departments. They work closely with marketing to validate consent mechanisms, partner with HR to design onboarding modules for secure data handling, and coach customer support teams on authentication protocols and complaint-handling scripts.

- **Cross-functional privacy champions:** The DPO appoints and mentors *privacy champions* across departments, empowering them to translate DPDP Act requirements into daily practices. These champions ensure that processes, such as anonymizing data in Finance or securing records in operations, remain aligned with privacy standards.

- **Feedback and continuous improvement:** The DPO facilitates regular forums for teams to discuss privacy concerns, share near-miss incidents, and recommend process enhancements. By ensuring prompt follow-up and recognizing contributions, the DPO fosters an environment of continuous improvement and vigilance.

Through their proactive guidance, cross-functional collaboration, and continuous engagement, the DPO transforms privacy into a living, self-sustaining culture that permeates every aspect of the organization.

Role played by finance when engaging with vendors

A robust data protection culture extends beyond in-house teams to every external division handling your personal information, including outsourced finance, IT support, HR/payroll, marketing agencies, customer service centers, and cloud or analytics providers. Under the DPDP Act, the Data Fiduciary remains fully accountable for personal data processed by any third-party. Finance teams can weave DPDPA compliant privacy controls into every vendor relationship by focusing on the following areas:

- **Vendor and partner governance:**

  o **Contractual safeguards:** Finance and outsourcing teams play a critical role in embedding DPDPA-compliant clauses in all agreements, mandating security controls, breach reporting, data deletion on contract termination, and audit rights. This includes contracts involving finance teams for **purchase orders (POs)** and invoices, IT support for system administration, HR/payroll for employee records, and marketing agencies for campaign data.

  o **Supplier code of conduct:** Finance and outsourced teams should adhere to rigorous privacy standards through regular training programs. Formal privacy training for external teams ensures the same level of care for organizational data as is maintained internally. Annual refresher certifications and consequences for non-compliance reinforce this commitment.

  o **Ongoing due diligence:** Finance divisions and outsourcing partners undergo periodic assessments led by the DPO. These evaluations verify adherence to access controls, encryption protocols, incident-response readiness, and data-handling practices, ensuring compliance across outsourced functions.

- **DPO as a primary liaison**: The DPO drives continuous engagement with compliance teams from external partners, including finance and outsourcing divisions. Joint reviews of privacy controls clarify obligations under the DPDP Act, and streamlined communication channels ensure prompt notification and remediation of breaches or near-misses. By centralizing these interactions through the DPO, you foster a unified privacy mindset across the entire organizational ecosystem.

- **Regulatory and industry collaboration**: Organizations are encouraged to proactively collaborate with the Data Protection Board of India and industry bodies. Sharing updates on regulatory changes with finance and outsourcing stakeholders, integrating their feedback into privacy programs, and actively participating in best-practice forums further strengthen compliance.

Through clear contracts, ongoing training, and empowered oversight, finance and outsourcing divisions, alongside HR, IT, marketing, and customer support, become essential partners in upholding the data protection culture. These teams safeguard personal data with the same vigilance as internal departments, ensuring a seamless and cohesive approach to privacy across all operations.

Conclusion

Ultimately, cultivating a data protection culture transforms legal obligations into everyday practices. As technology advances and regulations continue to evolve, organizations with a robust data protection culture remain committed to safeguarding personal data. Prioritizing proactive leadership, continuous employee training, PbD, clear and enforceable policies, strategic use of technological safeguards, and ongoing vigilance allows organizations to tightly align their operations with the requirements of the DPDP Act.

This cultural alignment does more than merely prevent penalties; it creates a foundation of trust. Customers and employees who witness consistent, responsible data handling are more willing to engage with an organization, thus providing it with a competitive advantage. In the DPDP Act era, viewing data protection as more than just compliance overhead is essential; it is a strategic asset that builds resilience, satisfies regulatory expectations, and reinforces customer loyalty. Organizations that embed privacy into their core operations and actively engage all stakeholders, internal and external, ultimately position themselves to successfully navigate a dynamic, data-driven landscape with confidence and integrity.

The next chapter looks at the business apps that matter most, CRM, finance, and HR, showing why they are ground zero for DPDPA risk and must anchor any data protection culture.

Join our Discord space

Join our Discord workspace for latest updates, offers, tech happenings around the world, new releases, and sessions with the authors:

https://discord.bpbonline.com

CHAPTER 12
Building Data Protection Across LOB Apps

Introduction

The **Digital Personal Data Protection (DPDP)** Act 2023, along with its Draft Rules (2025), significantly transforms India's data protection framework by introducing rigorous requirements for enterprises handling personal data. In previous chapters, we have examined the legislation, the roles and responsibilities of companies or data fiduciaries, and the expectations of users or Data Principals themselves. In today's cloud era, companies of all sizes frequently utilize SaaS services for functions such as finance, HR, and customer support. These business applications, including **customer relationship management (CRM)** systems, financial platforms, and **human resource (HR)** systems, store vast amounts of personal and sensitive data, rendering them central to regulatory compliance efforts.

Given the inherent complexities of modern application landscapes, which often encompass hybrid on-premises infrastructures, cloud environments, SaaS offerings, and legacy systems, ensuring DPDPA compliance is both crucial and challenging. This chapter explores best practices for structuring, configuring, and managing enterprise applications and security frameworks to comprehensively meet DPDPA requirements. It provides technical, regulatory, and business-oriented insights designed to help organizations safeguard data effectively while maintaining operational agility.

Structure

In this chapter, we will cover the following topics:

- Securing CRM, financial, and HR systems
- Protecting data in CRM, financial, and HR systems
- Best practices with Saas and ISV solutions
- Protecting Customer PII with Microsoft solutions

Objectives

Organizations today rely on a multitude of systems to run their business operations, spanning diverse domains such as Finance, HR, CRM, telecalling, and recruitment. These systems can include SaaS solutions, on-premises platforms, homegrown applications, and vendor-provided technologies. Ensuring that all these digital systems comply with India's DPDPA regulations is a complex and ongoing endeavor. The challenge lies in the dynamic nature of these systems as they continuously evolve, undergo upgrades, and adapt to changing business needs. Achieving compliance is not a one-time accomplishment but a continuous journey, requiring proactive measures, regular audits, and a commitment to integrating privacy and data protection at every stage of the system's lifecycle. This approach not only safeguards sensitive data but also fosters trust and resilience in an ever-changing regulatory and technological landscape.

Securing CRM, financial, and HR systems

CRM, financial, and HR platforms serve as the backbone of modern enterprises, aggregating customers' personal profiles, transaction histories, and employee records. Since these systems concentrate vast amounts of sensitive personal data, breaches can have an enormous financial and reputational impact. Under India's DPDP Act 2023, failure to safeguard such data can incur *hefty fines*. Breaches in these domains often lead to massive regulatory penalties and public fallout – triggering customer churn, lawsuits, and lost trust that can far exceed the immediate remediation costs. In short, compromises of CRM, finance, or HR systems not only disrupt billing, payroll, or customer support; they threaten the very continuity and credibility of the business.

DPDPA 2023 adds layers of compliance obligation on top of these risks. The law demands explicit, purpose-specific consent for each use of personal data, strict minimization of data collection and retention, and rapid breach notification to authorities and affected individuals. These requirements interplay with existing sector regulations: for example, financial data systems must already satisfy RBI and anti-money-laundering rules, and HR data often falls under labor and health privacy laws. Noncompliance can therefore mean cascading fines under multiple regimes. In practice, this means organizations must maintain detailed audit trails, dynamic consent logs, and encrypted storage, or face penalties in the hundreds of millions of rupees and mandatory public disclosures in the event of a breach.

Within this high-stakes context, each platform brings its own vulnerability profile. CRM systems (e.g., Dynamics 365 Sales, Salesforce, Zoho) hold comprehensive customer 360° views, contact details, purchase and interaction histories, and marketing opt-in preferences. Such rich PII makes CRM a prime target for identity theft and targeted phishing. Moreover, DPDPA mandates that every marketing communication be backed by up-to-date, revocable consent. Sending an unsolicited campaign not only enrages customers but also directly violates the law. For example, a recent case study involved a spear-phishing attack on a retailer's CRM: thousands (in fact, an undisclosed amount) of customer records (emails, addresses, purchase preferences) were exposed, triggering a government audit of the company's consent and security practices. This incident highlights why techniques like role-based access control, encryption of customer fields, and automated consent management (for instance, via Microsoft Purview or similar data-governance tools) are essential to limit damage and demonstrate compliance.

Financial systems (SAP, Oracle Financials, Dynamics 365 Finance, etc.) are equally high targets. They store invoices, bank account numbers, credit card data, and even integrated payroll registers. Attackers who breach these systems can manipulate payment workflows for fraud or money laundering. Compounding the threat, these systems operate under stringent retention laws, often requiring organizations to archive transactional records for 5–7 years or more. However, DPDPA's data-minimization principle forbids indefinite storage of personal details once their purpose lapses. In practice, this demands automated retention policies (e.g., via Azure Policy or Microsoft Purview) that balance legal archiving with timely purging of excess data. A real-world example shows the cost of neglect: when hackers compromised a manufacturer's ERP, confidential financial statements *and* employee banking details were stolen, prompting prolonged regulatory probes and fines. Proper defenses, such as field-level encryption on account numbers, tight **privileged access** (PIM) for financial admins, and continuous log monitoring (with SIEM tools like Azure Sentinel or Splunk), could have dramatically reduced the impact.

HR systems (Workday, Oracle HCM, Dynamics 365, etc.) are repositories of the most sensitive personal data, employee IDs, addresses, payroll, benefits, medical records, and performance reviews. Breaches here can immediately trigger employee lawsuits, morale collapse, and regulatory action, especially if health or biometric data is leaked. Under DPDPA, even employees are Data Principals: they can withdraw consent (for example, from wellness program data) or request deletion of records after they leave. Violations of these rights (or exposure of salary and health info) attract strict scrutiny. In one notable case, a healthcare company's HR breach leaked pay grades and medical information, causing *plummeting employee trust, threatened lawsuits, and a regulatory probe into potential DPDPA violations*. The lesson is clear: HR data requires vigilant safeguards, enforcing strict *least privilege* access (for instance via Azure AD conditional access and **Privileged Identity Management** (PIM)) and encrypting sensitive fields end-to-end, to prevent internal misuse or external theft.

Importantly, these risks multiply when systems interconnect. Modern enterprises often link CRM, finance, and HR under a single identity framework or ERP suite. This means a single compromised credential, especially a high-privilege Azure AD account, can "pivot" laterally across all modules. For example, attackers might piece together partial data from CRM (email, phone) and finance (billing address, purchase) to construct complete identity profiles. To counter this, organizations must adopt strict segmentation and least privilege policies. Identity and access management solutions (such as Azure AD Conditional Access or vendor-neutral IAM like Okta/Ping) enforce MFA and context-aware login rules. SIEM platforms (Azure Sentinel, Splunk, Elastic) aggregate and analyze logs across CRM, finance, and HR to spot anomalies early. PIM tools ensure that even administrators get access only on a just-in-time basis. Together, these controls curb the *domino effect* where one breach cascades into a full-blown enterprise disaster.

In summary, CRM, financial, and HR systems must be top security priorities because they store the highest concentration of regulated personal data. The DPDP Act's toughest obligations (dynamic consent, data minimization, breach reporting) converge on these platforms. Protecting them is not just about avoiding fines; it preserves customer and employee trust, shields the company from multiple compliance regimes, and ensures core operations are not derailed. By implementing modern identity, data-governance, and monitoring solutions (for example, Azure AD for identity, Microsoft Purview for data classification/retention, and Azure Sentinel for cross-domain threat detection), organizations can satisfy DPDPA requirements and build resilient infrastructure. In doing so, they uphold both legal compliance and the operational resilience needed in today's hyperconnected business environment.

Protecting data in CRM, financial, and HR systems

We have already discussed why it is critical to protect CRM, financial, and HR systems, given their concentration of sensitive personal data. Now, let us focus on how these systems can be effectively secured.

This concentration of data makes these platforms high-value targets for cybercriminals and internal threat actors alike. Attackers increasingly exploit these environments using ransomware, credential theft, or AI-powered reconnaissance. Meanwhile, the growing complexity of IT ecosystems, characterized by the use of unsanctioned SaaS tools, decentralized plugins, and shadow IT, creates further gaps in visibility and control.

Compounding these technical and operational risks is India's DPDP Act, 2023. The law introduces stringent legal mandates for any organization processing personal data, with specific expectations for consent management, data minimization, retention policies, and breach notifications. Non-compliance can lead to substantial financial penalties, operational disruptions, and personal liability for senior leadership.

This section unpacks how CRM, financial, and HR systems intersect with data protection regulations, the risks unique to each system, and how leading solutions, particularly those from Microsoft, can support organizations in meeting their legal and ethical obligations under the DPDPA regime. Before we protect these systems, let us also look at how the DPDPA, including consent management implications, impacts these systems and processes.

DPDPA's impact on enterprise applications

The DPDP Act establishes core principles for the lawful processing of personal data, many of which directly impact how enterprise applications must be configured and managed:

- **Consent management:** All personal data must be processed based on valid, informed, and purpose-specific consent. This consent must be revocable at any time, and organizations are obligated to stop processing upon withdrawal.

- **Purpose limitation and data minimization:** Applications must collect and use personal data strictly for the intended and disclosed purpose. Over-collection or retaining data longer than necessary can constitute a compliance breach.

- **Right to erasure:** Data principals (individuals) have the right to request deletion of their personal data. Applications must facilitate such requests and ensure downstream systems cease related processing.

- **Security safeguards:** Adequate technical and organizational measures are required to secure personal data, proportionate to its sensitivity. These include access controls, encryption, and monitoring systems.

- **Breach reporting:** In the event of a data breach, organizations must notify both the regulator and affected individuals within defined timelines, requiring applications to support swift detection and auditability.

In practical terms, these mandates require enterprises to re-architect their CRM, financial, and HR systems with Privacy by Design and default. This includes maintaining data inventories, applying encryption to sensitive fields, controlling access through roles, and enabling transparent logging and consent flows.

System-specific considerations

The system-specific considerations are as follows:

- **CRM systems:** CRM platforms, such as Microsoft Dynamics 365, Salesforce, and Zoho, store a unified view of customer information, including names, email addresses, behavioral data, and purchase histories. They often serve as the interface for marketing, sales, and service functions, and are thus rich in personal data and subject to frequent user access.

- o **Key risks:**

  - **Phishing and identity theft:** A compromised CRM record can enable widespread fraud or impersonation.

  - **Consent violations:** Untracked marketing outreach or profiling without valid opt-in consent can directly breach DPDPA obligations.

- o **Compliance strategies:**

  - Implement consent-tracking mechanisms with time-stamped logs linked to specific processing purposes.

  - Enforce data minimization by routinely purging outdated or irrelevant records.

  - Apply field-level encryption for PII both at rest and in transit.

  - Integrate CRM workflows with consent management systems and privacy dashboards to operationalize user rights.

- **Financial systems:** Financial platforms, ranging from SAP and Oracle Financials to QuickBooks and Microsoft Dynamics Finance, handle transactional data, billing information, tax IDs, and sometimes employee payroll data.

  - o **Key risks:**

    - **Fraud and laundering:** Exposure of account numbers or payment histories can be exploited for malicious financial activity.

    - **Non-compliance with retention laws:** Storing financial data beyond regulatory timelines could violate not only DPDPA but also financial laws.

  - o **Compliance strategies:**

    - Establish strong audit trails that track who accessed or altered financial data and when.

    - Use encryption for sensitive fields, including bank account and tax ID numbers.

    - Apply automated retention rules to archive or delete outdated financial records as permitted under law.

    - Implement segregation of duties to limit access, ensuring, for example, that HR personnel cannot access vendor payment data.

- **HR systems**: HR systems often manage deeply personal information such as identification details, health data, performance evaluations, and compensation. This makes them uniquely sensitive under any data protection framework.

- o **Key risks:**

  - **Insider misuse or leak:** Employees with broad access rights may inadvertently or maliciously leak sensitive records.

  - **Litigation exposure:** Mishandling of health or disciplinary records can lead to lawsuits and regulatory fines.

- o **Compliance strategies:**

  - Enforce least privilege *access*, ensuring HR staff have access only to what is necessary for their function.

  - Obtain explicit consent for any optional processing (e.g., wellness programs, surveys).

  - Configure automated data deletion workflows for ex-employee records, aligned with labor and retention laws.

  - Track and audit user activity, especially around sensitive modules like medical benefits or disciplinary records.

Different business systems handle personal data in unique ways. The DPDPA compliance program must address the specific risks and requirements of each class of application.

Key implementation challenges

Organizations managing compliance across multiple systems typically encounter six core challenges. These systems are often owned by companies and delivered either as **Independent Software Vendor (ISV)** solutions or **Software as a Service (SaaS)** platforms. This dynamic places the responsibility for addressing these challenges on both service providers and customers.

While providers must ensure their platforms offer adequate settings and configurations to meet DPDPA compliance requirements, the onus ultimately falls heavily on customers to assess, configure, and implement these measures correctly. It becomes even more complex when the necessary configurations are absent or insufficient. In such cases, customers must proactively communicate and escalate these issues with their service providers. If resolutions are not forthcoming, they may need to consider switching to alternative providers, a decision that demands thorough evaluation and effort.

Navigating these scenarios requires skilled personnel with expertise in compliance, system configuration, and risk assessment. Ensuring a compliant state is not a one-time task but an ongoing process that involves collaboration, vigilance, and a clear understanding of regulatory landscapes. Ultimately, both providers and customers must work in tandem to uphold personal data protection within these interconnected systems. Here are the six most common challenges that organizations must proactively address to keep their CRM, financial, and HR landscapes compliant and secure:

- **Data sprawl:** Personal data often resides in disconnected systems with inconsistent retention and security postures.

- **Consent and purpose tracking:** Legacy systems rarely support dynamic consent mechanisms, making compliance difficult to enforce at scale.

- **Access control complexity:** Overlapping roles across ERP platforms can create *privilege creep*, where users accumulate unnecessary rights.

- **Lack of centralized monitoring:** Without consolidated logging and analytics, detecting and responding to breaches becomes reactive and delayed.

- **Regulatory overlaps:** DPDPA intersects with other frameworks (e.g., RBI guidelines for finance, medical record standards for healthcare), requiring nuanced compliance strategies.

- **Human and third-party risk:** Employees, vendors, and contractors remain significant risk vectors if not subject to clear policies and technical controls.

Successfully navigating these challenges requires coordinated action between IT, security, legal, and compliance teams.

Integration with existing security measures

While every external system, whether SaaS or ISV, brings its own configurable controls, these must align and integrate seamlessly with the enterprise's existing implementations across identity management, SIEM, and governance layers. For instance, tools like Microsoft Purview, leveraging Purview SDK kits, can ensure that personal data protections are consistently applied across these layers, enabling unified compliance and security strategies. To translate these high-level security goals into day-to-day practice, organizations should focus on five technical pillars that knit external applications into the enterprise's broader defense-in-depth architecture:

- **Identity and access controls:** Use centralized IAM (e.g., Azure AD) to manage user identities across CRM, ERP, and HR apps. Implement **role-based access control (RBAC)** so that only necessary roles (sales reps, finance clerks, HR managers) can see relevant personal data. Enforce MFA and conditional access policies for all admin or data-access roles; *appropriate measures to control access* are part of *reasonable security safeguards.*

- **Data encryption and tokenization:** Apply encryption and masking as per Sec 8(5) of the DPDPA, read with Rule 6 of draft rules. For example, in a CRM database, encrypt sensitive columns (emails, SSNs) at rest. Azure Purview or SQL's transparent data encryption can automate classification and encryption. If using SaaS, ensure the provider offers encryption keys (e.g., **Bring Your Own Key (BYOK)**).

- **Monitoring and logging:** Implement comprehensive logging of data access. Tools like Microsoft Sentinel (or alternatives like Splunk) can ingest logs from CRM/ERP/HR systems and apply anomaly-detection rules. The draft rules emphasize *visibility on accessing personal data… through appropriate logs, monitoring, and review*. For instance, record every query or download of personal data and alert them to unusual patterns (e.g., a helpdesk employee downloading thousands of customer records at night).

- **Data governance:** Use data governance solutions (Microsoft Purview governance and equivalent) to classify data fields in each application. Tag data based on sensitivity (personal, financial, health) and apply policies automatically (e.g., DLP rules that block exporting salary data to personal email). Integration with **Security Information and Event Management (SIEM)** ensures that governance and security tools share context.

- **Incident response:** Align breach procedures across applications. If a compromised credential or vulnerability is detected (via Sentinel or Defender), have an automated workflow to isolate affected systems, revoke access, notify authorities/board, and plan remediation. DPDPA requires prompt breach notification, so test this end-to-end.

In summary, DPDPA compliance should not be bolted on; rather, it should harmonize with existing security frameworks. Enterprises can leverage Microsoft technologies (Azure AD for identity, Purview for classification, Defender and Sentinel for threat protection and monitoring) to build on their investments. At every layer, the goal is to *secure personal data through encryption, obfuscation or masking or the use of virtual tokens* and *monitor and review access for unauthorized use.*

Best practices with SaaS and ISV solutions

While bringing external SaaS or ISV services into your HR, finance, legal, and other business automation processes, it is essential to ensure that these integrations adhere to robust security and governance practices. These best practices offer a unified framework for safeguarding sensitive data and aligning operations with the DPDP law, strengthening both compliance and organizational resilience.

Secure configuration management follows these best practices:

- **Baseline hardening:** Adopt industry benchmarks (such as CIS Benchmarks or DISA STIGs) for operating systems and applications. Use tools like Azure Policy or AWS Config to continuously audit cloud resources against these baselines. For on-prem servers, configuration management tools (Chef, Puppet, Ansible) can enforce secure settings (e.g., disabling unused services, enforcing strong TLS).

- **Least privilege and network segmentation:** Configure systems so that services or users have only the permissions they need. For instance, the CRM database account should not have superuser rights. Segment networks (using Azure VNETs or VLANs) so that CRM, financial, and HR apps live in isolated zones; this limits lateral movement if one app is compromised.

- **Secure defaults:** Ensure new application deployments (even trial SaaS tools) have secure default settings. Require MFA for admin accounts from day one. When migrating legacy systems (ERP upgrades or on-prem to cloud), review the vendor's security guides. Microsoft's security baselines (for Windows, SQL, etc.) are good references.

- **Consistent environment provisioning:** Use Infrastructure-as-Code (Terraform, ARM templates) so that environments (dev, test, prod) are created uniformly. Embedding security rules (such as mandatory encryption-at-rest) into the code ensures compliance by design.

- **Vendor configuration and patching:** For off-the-shelf apps (e.g., SAP, Oracle, Salesforce, Workday HR), follow the vendor's security best practices. Keep these systems updated: subscribe to their security advisories and apply patches promptly. For custom apps, adopt a DevSecOps pipeline that includes static and dynamic code scanning (e.g., OWASP ZAP) before deployment.

- **Patch management process:** Establish a policy to test and deploy patches (OS, middleware, applications) in a timely manner. Critical and high-severity patches should be applied within defined windows. Use automated patch tools (Windows WSUS or Intune for Microsoft stacks; SUSE/RHEL Satellite for Linux). Cloud environments can leverage automated patching (e.g., Azure Update Management).

- **Legacy and third-party software:** Legacy ERP or on-prem systems may not have modern auto-updates. Maintain a strict inventory of these applications and use vulnerability scanners to find missing patches. For unsupported software, consider virtual patching (using IPS/WAF rules or isolation) until the system is upgraded.

- **Zero-day mitigation:** Deploy IDS/IPS solutions (e.g., Microsoft Defender Vulnerability Management, or open Suricata) to detect unusual exploit behavior for vulnerabilities not yet patched. For critical services like databases, consider immediate protective measures (such as limiting client connections) when patches cannot be installed quickly.

- **Testing and rollback:** Always test patches in a staging environment (especially for critical applications) before rolling out to production. Maintain backups so that if a patch causes instability, you can roll back safely. Document patch cycles and track patch compliance as part of audits.

Protecting customer PII with Microsoft solutions

Contoso Insurance, a leading provider of life and property insurance, faces significant challenges in safeguarding its customers' **personally identifiable information** (**PII**) against modern cyber threats. These threats primarily emerge from email-based attacks, risky downloads, and inadequate data governance. By leveraging Microsoft Defender for Office and the suite of Microsoft Purview products, Contoso Insurance has adopted a proactive approach to securing sensitive data.

Threats from email, phishing, and malware

Email remains the primary attack vector for cybercriminals seeking to compromise customer PII. Phishing schemes often impersonate trusted entities, deceiving employees into divulging sensitive information or granting unauthorized access to systems. Malware-laden email attachments, such as ransomware or spyware, pose additional risks, allowing attackers to steal or encrypt critical data.

Microsoft Defender for Office plays a pivotal role in mitigating these threats:

- **Advanced threat protection**: Scans incoming emails for malicious content, including links and attachments, preventing phishing attacks and malware infiltration.

- **Real-time alerts**: Notifies administrators of suspicious email activities, enabling prompt investigation and action.

- **Zero-day threat detection**: Identifies previously unknown vulnerabilities exploited through email-based attacks.

Risks from downloads

Unverified downloads, whether from websites or email attachments, are another pathway for cyber threats. Employees may inadvertently download files containing malicious payloads or compromised customer PII stored within Contoso Insurance's systems. Threats such as trojans and data exfiltration malware can exploit these vulnerabilities to extract sensitive customer data.

Microsoft Defender for Office and Endpoint solutions

To address these risks, Contoso Insurance utilizes Microsoft Defender for Office alongside Microsoft Defender for Endpoint:

- **Content filtering:** Blocks unsafe files from being downloaded or opened, reducing exposure to malicious software.

- **Sandboxing**: Isolates suspicious files for analysis before they are allowed into the network.

- **Endpoint monitoring**: Tracks device activity to detect unauthorized file executions linked to download-related attacks.

Safeguarding PII with Microsoft Purview

At the heart of Contoso Insurance's strategy is the protection of its customers' PII, names, addresses, financial information, and medical histories. The breach or theft of such data not only jeopardizes customer trust but also exposes the company to regulatory penalties under frameworks like India's DPDP Act.

Multiple Microsoft Purview products are integrated to ensure comprehensive data protection:

- **Microsoft Purview Information Protection:**
  - **Sensitive data classification**: Automatically identifies and labels customer PII across databases and documents.
  - **Data loss prevention (DLP):** Monitors data usage and movement, preventing unauthorized sharing or transfer of sensitive information.

- **Microsoft Purview Compliance Manager:**
  - **Comprehensive compliance tracking**: Seamlessly tracks adherence to privacy regulations like India's DPDP Act and other global standards.
  - **Third-party ISV integration:** Works effectively to monitor compliance for external systems such as third-party ISVs, including those integrated with Salesforce CRM systems.

- **Microsoft Purview SDK:**
  - **Enhanced customization**: Offers developers the ability to extend compliance features across both native and integrated environments, ensuring compliance across third-party systems.
  - **Real-time compliance updates:** Provides tools to help organizations continuously stay updated and adapt to evolving regulatory requirements.

Salesforce CRM integration

Contoso Insurance's Salesforce CRM system plays an integral role in managing customer-related data. Integration with Microsoft Purview ensures that sensitive data accessed or stored within Salesforce conforms to strict compliance standards. Purview Compliance Manager tracks and audits all data interactions within Salesforce, highlighting areas of concern and enforcing rules to prevent unauthorized access. Additionally, Salesforce's integration with Microsoft Purview Information Protection aids in securing data transfers and preventing unauthorized data leakage, complementing Contoso's holistic approach to compliance.

By deploying Microsoft Defender for Office and Defender for Endpoint to mitigate email and download-based threats, alongside Microsoft Purview solutions for comprehensive data governance, Contoso Insurance has fortified its defenses against the loss or theft of customer

PII. The integration of Salesforce CRM and third-party ISV systems, enhanced by Purview Compliance Manager and Purview SDK, further strengthens the company's capacity to maintain compliance with data protection regulations. This integrated approach ensures not only adherence to regulatory frameworks but also reinforces customer trust in the security of their personal information.

Conclusion

Protecting personal data in enterprise applications is both a technical challenge and a business imperative under India's DPDPA framework. By designing application architectures with integrated security and privacy controls, from Azure AD identity to Purview data classification, from Defender monitoring to Sentinel analytics, organizations can satisfy DPDPA's *reasonable security safeguards* while enabling innovation. Structured approaches (policy-as-code, automated workflows) help enterprises meet DPDPA's retention and breach requirements, such as erasing old data after periods defined in the third Schedule or notifying principals before erasure. The complexity of modern environments (SaaS, legacy, multi-cloud) demands a holistic strategy that includes vendor-neutral tools where appropriate. Real-world use cases illustrate this approach: telecom operators, for instance, leverage AI-driven anomaly detection to monitor customer data streams and billing records, while healthcare providers explore decentralized identity and zero-knowledge proofs to authenticate patients without centralized data repositories. By combining these best practices with continuous monitoring and compliance audits, IT leaders and legal teams can ensure that CRM, financial, and HR systems not only support business goals but also fully comply with the DPDP Act's requirements.

Join our Discord space

Join our Discord workspace for latest updates, offers, tech happenings around the world, new releases, and sessions with the authors:

https://discord.bpbonline.com

CHAPTER 13
Conclusion and The Road Ahead

Introduction

As India takes a significant leap forward with the **Digital Personal Data Protection (DPDP)** Act, 2023, the landscape of compliance is being redefined. No longer will compliance be viewed as an annual audit ritual or a reactive legal requirement. Instead, it will become an ongoing, intelligent, and embedded function across both digital and physical layers of the enterprise. This transformation is driven by AI, automation, and a growing need for operational transparency.

Structure

The chapter covers the following topics:

- Rise of autonomous compliance
- Industry transformation and Compliance-as-a-Service
- Final thoughts

Rise of autonomous compliance

The future of compliance lies in its autonomy. With the proliferation of AI agents and machine learning technologies, organizations can transition from manual, checklist-driven assessments to systems capable of continuous monitoring and enforcement. These agents will not only audit system logs and configuration settings but also interpret physical inputs such as CCTV footage, entry badge logs, and workstation usage to ensure that sensitive data environments are physically secure and access policies are followed.

Take, for example, Contoso Bank, a leading financial institution implementing the DPDP Act. Rather than waiting for quarterly audit cycles, Contoso deploys AI-based compliance agents that perform daily reviews of user access patterns, unusual data downloads, or failure to follow consent protocols. These agents are programmed to flag anomalies, simulate regulatory checks, and communicate autonomously with other agents (A2A). For example, a Consent validator agent could request additional context from a data lineage tracker agent before escalating to human review.

Role of AI agents and agent-to-agent interactions

In this new ecosystem, specialized AI agents will handle various aspects of compliance through autonomous collaboration:

- **Consent validator agents**: Continuously check if customer interactions align with recorded consent terms.

- **Data lineage tracker agents**: Monitor the flow of personal data from collection to deletion, providing audit-ready trails.

- **Evidence auditor agents**: Auto-verify that each privacy control or safeguard has proper, timestamped evidence.

- **Policy compliance agents:** Cross-check system configurations and employee behaviors against DPDP-mandated norms.

These agents can communicate with each other (A2A communication), autonomously resolving compliance queries or validating each other's findings before escalating to human approvers. For example, if a policy compliance agent detects a deviation, it may request lineage validation before creating an alert. This model enables distributed intelligence and a self-correcting compliance layer.

Human oversight in a machine-driven world

Despite the power of AI, human judgment remains irreplaceable. Compliance officers, risk managers, and privacy teams will serve as interpreters and ethical gatekeepers. They will perform the following tasks:

- Validate AI-generated findings and resolve edge cases.

- Handle exceptions, policy escalations, and user complaints.

- Define governance thresholds and acceptable risk levels.

For example, if an AI agent flags a breach due to excessive file access, it is the human team that evaluates whether it was a malicious Act or a business-critical operation. Humans also play a key role in training and tuning these agents, providing context to avoid false positives.

Future role of the DPO

The **Data Protection Officer (DPO)** of the future will evolve into a strategic orchestrator of intelligent systems and governance frameworks. Rather than conducting periodic manual checks, the DPO will oversee a network of AI agents operating autonomously across systems. Their role will include calibrating risk thresholds, managing the ethics of automated decision-making, handling escalations from agent networks, and engaging directly with regulatory bodies. DPOs will also Act as the organizational conscience, ensuring that automated compliance does not override individual rights or ethical considerations.

Dynamic ingestion of regulatory updates

One of the most powerful shifts in the compliance model will be dynamic regulatory ingestion. As the Government of India or sectoral regulators update rules, AI-based compliance agents will automatically parse legal texts, identify relevant changes, and update enterprise controls accordingly. Risk scores will be recalculated in real-time, and dashboards will inform teams of action items, automating a process that currently takes weeks of legal and IT coordination.

For instance, if the Data Protection Board of India releases a new rule mandating shorter breach notification timelines, the system will immediately identify affected workflows and recommend updated alerting policies or escalation paths.

Real-time data visibility for individuals

A central tenet of the DPDP Act is empowering the Data Principal. In the near future, when a user makes a **Data Subject Request (DSR)**, they will not just receive a download of their data; they will get a live, interactive lineage view. This view will show where their data was collected, how it was processed, who accessed it, what decisions were influenced by it, and where it currently resides.

Consider an individual logging into a telecom provider's portal and seeing:

- That their call metadata was used to generate network usage insights.
- That their location data was accessed by an internal analytics team.
- That no third-party sharing has occurred in the past 90 days.

Such transparency will not only drive trust but also become a key compliance differentiator in the market.

Industry transformation and Compliance-as-a-Service

Just as the early days of cybersecurity centered on basic tools like firewalls and antivirus before evolving into modern **Security Operations Centers** (**SOCs**), the compliance SOC market is now in its infancy, steadily integrating and maturing alongside the broader SOC industry.

Creation of the SOC industry

The SOC industry emerged as a response to the growing complexity of cyber threats and the need for real-time monitoring and defense mechanisms. Initially, organizations relied on reactive approaches that addressed issues after they occurred. However, the rapid digitization of industries and the increasing sophistication of cyberattacks necessitated a shift to proactive measures. The SOC industry was born out of this urgency, combining cutting-edge technologies with human expertise to identify, analyze, and mitigate threats on a continuous basis.

Early SOC implementations were limited to large enterprises with significant budgets, but as technologies like artificial intelligence and cloud computing matured, the barriers to entry lowered. Today, SOCs are accessible to businesses of all sizes, acting as the nerve center of cybersecurity operations. They are instrumental not only in defending against external threats but also in ensuring compliance with evolving regulatory standards.

Compliance, from periodic to continuous monitoring

Traditionally, compliance was viewed as a periodic exercise conducted at specific intervals, often leading to last-minute scrambling to meet audit requirements. Compliance was treated as an isolated checkbox rather than an integrated aspect of daily operations. This *point-in-time compliance* approach proved insufficient in a world where regulatory landscapes are constantly shifting, and data flows are increasingly dynamic.

The advent of continuous compliance has revolutionized this model. Instead of reactive, sporadic assessments, organizations now employ tools and processes that ensure compliance in real-time.

Continuous compliance leverages intelligent systems that monitor, analyze, and report on regulatory adherence without interruption. This paradigm shift minimizes risks, enhances efficiency, and builds stakeholder trust, all while reducing the burden of manual audits. In addition, evidence supporting compliance will increasingly be authenticated, geo-tagged, and service-verified by automated systems, rather than relying solely on PDFs and images manually shared by humans, as is common today. This advancement ensures greater integrity, traceability, and reliability of compliance documentation, further strengthening trust and auditability in real-time.

Compliance-as-a-Service

As compliance becomes more complex, organizations are turning to **Compliance-as-a-Service (CaaS)** offerings to navigate these challenges. These modular, AI-powered platforms provide tailored solutions that address industry-specific needs. CaaS encapsulates the principles of continuous compliance and packages them as a service, allowing businesses to manage regulatory requirements at scale with minimal overhead.

Banks, healthcare providers, and e-commerce platforms are among the sectors adopting CaaS. For instance, at Contoso Bank, AI-based tools monitor **personally identifiable information (PII)** across core banking and **customer relationship management (CRM)** systems, ensuring alignment with regulations such as RBI and DPDP standards. These platforms integrate seamlessly with tools like Microsoft Priva and Azure Purview, offering unified dashboards, automated policy enforcement, and actionable insights.

Agents driving compliance transformation

Central to this transformation are compliance agents, specialized tools, and professionals who Act as the catalysts for change. These agents are powered by sophisticated algorithms and machine learning, enabling them to detect non-compliance, recommend corrective actions, and ensure adherence across multiple regulatory frameworks. In essence, they are the backbone of modern compliance infrastructure.

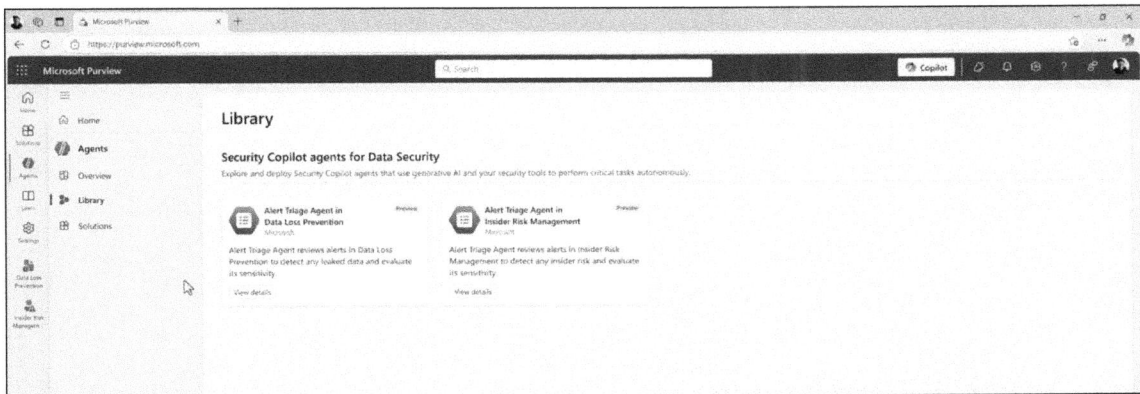

Figure 13.1: Agentic Compliance future

Agents also play a critical role in bridging gaps between technology and human expertise. By automating routine tasks, they free up compliance professionals to focus on strategic initiatives and complex problem-solving. They embody the principle of *compliance as a continuous journey*, guiding organizations through the intricacies of regulatory landscapes with precision and foresight.

Final thoughts

The SOC industry and CaaS are reshaping the way organizations approach security and regulatory adherence. The shift from point-in-time compliance to continuous compliance, wrapped into service models led by agents, marks a significant milestone in operational transformation. As industries evolve, so too does their approach to compliance, intelligent, automated, and deeply integrated into daily operations. The DPDP Act, paired with advancing technologies like AI and machine reasoning, is setting the foundation for a future where compliance is not a constraint but a competitive advantage.

As the ecosystem matures, we foresee a collaborative model where agents handle the bulk of enforcement, with **agent-to-agent communication** (**A2A communication**) ensuring coordinated oversight, and humans providing governance, ethical reasoning, and final decision-making. Compliance teams will evolve into governance architects, privacy designers, and strategic advisors. With this shift, India's vision for Digital India and Viksit Bharat will be underpinned by resilient, responsive, and ethical data governance.

The future is already unfolding, and it is one where compliance works in real-time, powered by intelligence, and guided by trust.

Join our Discord space

Join our Discord workspace for latest updates, offers, tech happenings around the world, new releases, and sessions with the authors:

https://discord.bpbonline.com

Index

www.ingramcontent.com/pod-product-compliance
Lightning Source LLC
Chambersburg PA
CBHW061801210326
41599CB00034B/6839